READINGS IN
PHYSICAL DISTRIBUTION
MANAGEMENT

Readings in PHYSICAL DISTRIBUTION MANAGEMENT

The Logistics of Marketing

Edited by

Donald J. Bowersox
Michigan State University

Bernard J. La Londe
Ohio State University

Edward W. Smykay
Michigan State University

The Macmillan Company
Collier-Macmillan Limited, London

First Printing

Library of Congress catalog card number: 75-76588

THE MACMILLAN COMPANY
COLLIER-MACMILLAN CANADA, LTD., TORONTO, ONTARIO

PRINTED IN THE UNITED STATES OF AMERICA

Acknowledgments

The authors wish to express their sincere appreciation to the following associations, journals, periodicals, and individuals who generously granted permission to reprint their work in this text.

American Marketing Association
Journal of Marketing
Donald J. Bowersox, "Physical Distribution Development, Current Status, and Potential," January 1969, pp. 63-70; James L. Heskett, "A Missing Link in Physical Distribution System Design," October 1966, pp. 37-41; Wendell M. Stewart, "Physical Distribution: Key to Improved Volume and Profits," January 1965, pp. 65-70.
Journal of Marketing Research
Louis P. Bucklin, "Postponement, Speculation, and the Structure of Distribution Channels," February 1965, Vol. 2, pp. 26-31.
Proceedings
Donald J. Bowersox, "Changing Channels in the Physical Distribution of Finished Goods," *Marketing and Economic Development,* September 1965, pp. 711-721; Alfred A. Kuehn, "Logistics of Physical Facilities in Distribution," *Marketing and Economic Development,* September 1965, pp. 688-695; Bert C. McCammon, Jr., "Alternative Explanations of Institutional Change and Channel Evolution," *Toward Scientific Marketing,* December 1963, pp. 477-490; Louis W. Stern, "Channel Control and Inter-organization

Management," *Marketing and Economic Development,* September 1965, pp. 655-665.

Business Horizons

Raymond LeKashman and John F. Stolle, "The Total Cost Approach to Distribution," Winter 1965, pp. 33-46.

Business Management

Marvin Flaks, "Total Cost Approach to Physical Distribution," August 1963, Vol. 24, pp. 55-61.

MSU Business Topics (Reprinted by permission of the publisher, the Bureau of Business and Economic Research, Division of Research, Graduate School of Business Administration, Michigan State University.)

Robert E. Weigand, "The Management of Physical Distribution: A Dilemma," Summer 1962, pp. 67-72.

Distribution Manager (Distribution Age)

Wallace I. Little, "Why Not Truly Integrated PD Management?" November 1967, pp. 31-36; William B. Saunders, "Designing a Distribution System," January 1965, pp. 32-36.

Handling and Shipping

Ronald H. Ballou, "Quantitative Methods—What They Are and How You Can Use Them," December 1967, pp. 39-43; F. R. Denham, "Making the Physical Distribution Concept Pay Off," October 1967, pp. 54-59; Aaron J. Gellman, "The Most Influential Factor in Distribution Economics," November 1967, pp. 62-65; Burr W. Hupp, "Inventory Policy Is a Top Management Responsibility," August 1967, pp. 47-49; B. F. Rowan, "Linear Programming: A Straight Line to Distribution Efficiency," November 1965, pp. 56-60.

Harvard Business Review (The following three articles are copyrighted © 1960, 1960, and 1967, respectively, by the President and Fellows of Harvard College; all rights reserved.)

John Magee, "The Logistics of Distribution," July-August 1960, pp. 89-101; Harvey N. Shycon and Richard B. Maffei, "Simulation—Tool for Better Distribution," November-December 1960, pp. 65-75; John F. Stolle, "How to Manage Physical Distribution," July-August 1967, pp. 93-100.

Houston Business Review

Edward W. Smykay, "Physical Distribution, Military Logistics, and Marketing Management," Winter 1964-1965, pp. 1-10.

Richard D. Irwin, Inc.

Elwood S. Buffa, *Production-Inventory Systems: Planning and Control* (Homewood, Ill., 1968), p. 75; E. J. McCarthy, *Basic Marketing: A Managerial Approach, 3rd ed.* (Homewood, Ill., 1964), p. 17.

Macmillan Company

Paul T. Cherington, *The Elements of Marketing* (New York, 1928), p. 96.

Management Services

Bertram A. Colbert, "Pathway to Profit: The Management Information System," September-October 1967, pp. 15-24; Hak Chong Lee, "The Organizational Impact of Computers," May-June 1967, pp. 39-43; Ronald J. Lewis, "Strengthening Control of Physical Distribution Costs," January-February 1968, pp. 37-46; L. Gayle Rayburn, "Setting Standards for Distribution Costs," March-April 1967, pp. 42-52.

McGraw-Hill Book Company

Ralph F. Breyer, *The Marketing Institution* (New York, 1934), p. 142.

Modern Materials Handling

Ruddell Reed, Jr., "What to Watch Out For in Planning Systems," August 1967, pp. 40-45.

National Council of Physical Distribution Management
   Peter F. Drucker, "Physical Distribution: The Frontier of Modern Management," Speech reprint.
Ronald Press Company
   Theodore N. Beckman, *Wholesaling* (New York, 1926), p. 112.
Stanford Research Institute
   Robert L. Johnson, "'Interface,' Computerized Management Information Systems and Corporate Management," Speech reprint, March 1967.
Transportation and Distribution Management
   Donald J. Bowersox, "Emerging Patterns of Physical Distribution Organization," May 1968, pp. 53-59; Harry J. Bruce, "Management Intuition Plus Mathematics and Logic Equals Effective Distribution," July 1968, pp. 20-27; H. G. Miller, "Accounting for Physical Distribution," December 1961, pp. 6-11.
Transportation Research Forum
   James L. Heskett, "Costing and Coordinating External and Internal Logistics Activities," Speech, October 1964.

For Carol, Barbara, and Ann

PHYSICAL DISTRIBUTION DEFINED:

A term employed in manufacturing and commerce to describe the broad range of activities concerned with efficient movement of finished products from the end of the production line to the consumer and in some cases includes the movement of raw materials from the source of supply to the beginning of the production line. These activities include freight transportation, warehousing, material handling, protective packaging, inventory control, plant and warehouse site selection, order processing, market forecasting, and customer service.

–THE NATIONAL COUNCIL OF
PHYSICAL DISTRIBUTION MANAGEMENT

PHYSICAL DISTRIBUTION MANAGEMENT DEFINED:

Physical distribution management is defined as that responsibility to design and administer systems to control raw material and finished goods flow.

–PHYSICAL DISTRIBUTION MANAGEMENT
Donald J. Bowersox, Edward W. Smykay, and
Bernard J. La Londe (The Macmillan Company,
1968, p. 5)

Preface

During the past two decades the field of physical distribution management has almost literally exploded onto the American business scene. From a relatively obscure understanding of potential cost reductions available from integrated control of physical distribution functions, we have come rapidly to a recognition and utilization of the total cost concept and systems technology. As one would expect, we find understanding of this emerging discipline and the expansion of theoretical and practical contributions moving at a rapid pace. It is from this dynamic nature of the field of physical distribution management that the authors perceive the need for the present book.

Readings in Physical Distribution Management consists of a collection of articles which depict the past, present, and apparent future direction of the physical distribution concept. As a group of individual contributions, the articles have been selected to supplement and expand text treatments of physical distribution. The individual articles are keyed to major texts currently available.

Special attention is directed to the marketing implications of physical distribution. Many teachers prefer to develop classroom treatment of physical distribution beyond typical coverage of the marketing text. The selection of articles provides ample supplement in the areas of marketing and distribution channels.

In terms of a general overview, the readings have been grouped into three parts. Part One, "Physical Distribution and the Market Environment," contains selections concerned with the business and competitive structure within which a firm plans, designs, and implements a physical distribution system. Part Two, "System Design," presents a wide coverage of various aspects of developing a physical distribution operation. Special attention is directed to the role of quantitative methods in system design. Part Three is devoted to the subjects of organization, administration, and control.

The contributions, in total, present a balance between those developed by practitioners and academicians. A brief review of the authors of the thirty-six articles as well as the sources of original publication will provide the reader with a good perspective on the vast impact of integrated physical distribution.

The editors wish to acknowledge the assistance of the National Council of Physical Distribution Management by dedication of this collection to the principles and objectives of NCPDM and its many members as well as the individual authors of the articles. These scholars and businessmen are the doers who are making integrated physical distribution a reality. The authors also wish to acknowledge the able assistance of Lloyd Mitchell during manuscript preparation and Miss Kay Gillett for her most able typing and editorial assistance.

D. J. B.
B. J. LaL.
E. W. S.

Contents

PART TWO. System Design

PART THREE. Organization, Administration, and Control

READINGS IN
PHYSICAL DISTRIBUTION
MANAGEMENT

Part One

PHYSICAL DISTRIBUTION AND THE MARKET ENVIRONMENT

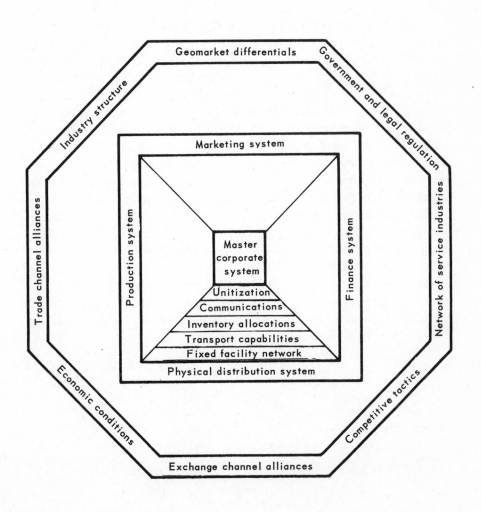

Editors' Introduction

Physical distribution activities of a firm must be viewed within the scope of total marketing effort. This viewpoint is essential because the battle for corporate survival is fought in the marketplace, not in the plant or the warehouse. Therefore, an overall market orientation must guide planning and implementation of physical distribution programs. This viewpoint, widely accepted as the marketing concept, does not mean that physical distribution is a function of marketing nor that it should be administered within the marketing organization. Rather, a market-oriented position is advocated because effective and efficient physical distribution constitutes an integral part of a firm's competitive offering.

What constitutes a firm's physical distribution system at any given point in time will depend significantly upon that firm's market goals and the competitive structure of the market. However, the relationship that the firm enjoys with wholesalers, retailers, or manufacturers, whichever are applicable, will have a great deal to do with the range of alternatives available in system design. In addition, the firm must design and implement an action system within an imperfect structure of geomarket differentials. From this complex network of interacting forces, the firm must shape that system most capable of meeting customer service goals at the lowest total cost and then implement that system. The shaping, implementing, and administering of the distribution system is the job of physical distribution management. The articles in Part One were selected to explore the challenge of physical distribution from a number of different vantage points. The objective of Part One is to develop insight into the process and environment in which the firm mobilizes, organizes, and allocates resources to establish and achieve physical distribution objectives. As such, these contributions provide the basic perspective for the remaining articles.

I

Physical Distribution: The Frontier of Modern Management

PETER F. DRUCKER
New York University

Around 85 per cent of gasoline sales in Japan are made in the two major metropolitan areas—the one around Tokyo and the other around Osaka. A certain company has its two big refineries in these two areas and the bulk of its production travels no more than twenty miles. But in Japan, wholesalers or trading companies are used. The company's gasoline is therefore sold to a national trading company, which in turn sells it to a regional one, which in turn sells it to a local one, which in turn sells it to the retailer. That may make sense. But the gasoline is actually handled accordingly. It is pumped into a truck at the refinery and taken about two blocks to the tank farm of the national trading company and put into tanks there. Then it is pumped out again and put into another truck and taken another two blocks to the regional trading company, and so on. It is loaded and unloaded eight times—when two would do. Obviously, it could be shipped directly from the refinery to the retailer, no matter where the papers go or how the markups are distributed.

The point is not that all this loading and unloading is expensive and time consuming. The point is that an exceedingly capable management did not know about it and could not have known about it unless, for some reason, the executives had felt like going out with the trucks. The trading companies are at least autonomous, if not independent businesses, so that this pouring of gasoline into tanks, and then pumping it back out of tanks, and then pouring it back into tanks a total of eight times does not show up in anyone's books. The cost is hidden in five places—each of them an independent business. The greatest limitation of the accounting model is the fact that it defines what it measures by

3

legal terms and not by an economic definition; it measures what is within the legal confines of the corporate picture but not what is within the economic structure. Therefore, accounting figures will never show such a situation and cannot show it. The other reason that this Japanese situation is perfectly normal is that nobody is responsible for physical distribution. The refinery manager is concerned with yields and is highly technical in his point of view. The marketing people are concerned with getting new dealers and with promotion and pricing. No one, but no one, is concerned with the physical distribution of the gasoline. In business, whatever is left to itself does not manage itself; it deteriorates. Things left to themselves slowly float down to the lowest possible point they can reach.

Many situations come up which are similar to the one in Japan. There is no one business in which the bulk of physical distribution costs actually lie. They are always distributed over several independent businesses—even in very highly integrated industries. Therefore, one does not, by using conventional data, see what the costs cover. Then too, no one is responsible because physical distribution is not within a function nor part of any one function.

Physical distribution is simply another way of saying "the whole process of business." You can look at a business, particularly a manufacturing business, as a physical flow—the flow of materials. Here, there, and yonder, the flow is interrupted. When something is done to the materials—cut this or shape that, handle it, put it down and pick it up, store it, and so on—these turbulences interrupt the flow, which extends, for example, all the way from the iron ore to the galvanized garbage can. Because the flow runs through all functions and all stages, it is not being managed. It does not fit into the traditional structure of a functional organization.

Physical distribution is therefore the one big area in which something can still be done about costs.

Physical distribution is a cost area and purely a cost area. All one can do, by physically moving material, is to harm it—one can spoil it and break it and scratch it and soil it. One cannot endow it with new economic characteristics. Physical movement is therefore purely a cost center, yet it is never looked at as a whole. Usually there is no idea how big a cost area it is. The one cost element that managements have traditionally seen, freight of finished products, goes in many cases up to 10 per cent of what the customer pays. And yet, it is a fairly small cost. The actual costs of physical distribution of materials all the way along the economic process may be 30 per cent or 50 per cent of the total cost. Even though the total costs are unknown, they are certainly the largest single item in the cost structure.

Costs have been studied for a hundred years in the manufacturing areas. It probably could be imagined that one hundred years ago the physical distribution costs were as much as they are today. But the total share in the cost was much less than it is today, simply because so much of the manufacturing and other costs have been whittled down. As a result, physical distribution has become the largest single cost element. It varies for economic processes and industries, but it is very large.

At the same time, physical distribution is the most exciting area. One can make fantastic gains as one starts on a very low base and can therefore really make a difference. And within the last few years people have gained both the perception and the tools to do the job. They have gained the perception to see systems which essentially people did not have 30 years ago, or 20 years ago. Now the physical distribution of materials can be seen as one of the dimensions of a business from the mine to the ultimate consumer. This perception is truly new. In fact, the first man in American history who had a concept of the management of physical distribution could not make any one understand, and this was just about 40 years ago. That man was Henry Ford, who, when building River Rouge, very clearly had a concept of physical distribution all the way from the rubber plantation to the automobile customer, the whole thing managed and synchronized and brought together. Ford's concept never got off the ground because no one could understand what he was talking about.

But even if someone had seen it then, Ford could not have had the tools because this is the one area where tools—whether they are called systems analysis, operations research, or something else—are truly decisive. In this area, quantification is comparatively simple, since the concern here is with physical phenomena, which has an economic dimension, and not with economic phenomena, which may or may not have a physical dimension. Physical phenomena can be organized and measured, and in this area the new tools are as effective as they are because the switch from piecemeal handling of details— some freight management here, some warehouse management there—to a systems approach has very great impact.

This is, therefore, the area in which great advances should take place. They are needed because costs are very high and because it is to be expected that there will be a continuing pressure on costs and profits. A highly competitive period is to be anticipated. The question is, therefore, what costs can be cut? Physical distribution is the only area in which there is still a great deal of room for improvement. In a well-managed plant, it is not really possible to cut costs of the machine work substantially. The problem with sales expenses is not that they are too high, but that salesmen are not productive enough. When it comes to costs, physical distribution is about the only area in which efforts really pay off. A 10 per cent improvement in physical distribution costs is probably worth a 40 per cent improvement in true manufacturing costs. Usually the costs of actually changing physical characteristics of a material (that is, the true manufacturing costs) are not much higher than 10 per cent of the price the customer pays, whereas physical distribution runs to 40 to 50 per cent. And yet, the industrial engineers tend to be far more concerned about the machine work than with shipping costs.

It is not enough to do what a good many other people in this field are doing—that is, to start at the loading ramp. The largest single physical distribution cost happens to exist under the roof of the manufacturing plant. In a typical manufacturing plant the manager says: "There's nothing in the shipping room that would interest you." Yet the shipping room is where the labor costs are, and in our economy, these costs are high. Even so, the shipping room typically is poorly managed. The manufacturing manager is a technical man and is interested in engineering considerations rather than in the area of physical distribution. Neither is the marketing man interested in the shipping room and the plant warehouse. These are under the plant roof, but it is very difficult to establish the costs in these areas because they are in the "miscellaneous manufacturing overhead."

Unless one starts with the management of physical distribution in the shipping room, if not with the finishing room, one cannot manage physical distribution at all. At best, one can only improve things slightly.

The best way to start out, even if the start is severely limited, is with a rough model of the entire physical flow, beginning with what flows into the business and continuing right through the plant and on to the ultimate consumer. Pay no attention to legal title, because economics pays no attention to legal title. It is totally irrelevant whether title passes when the goods leave the loading dock or whether title passes when the ultimate consumer has paid the last installment.

It is equally irrelevant that the costs of physical distribution in one place are incurred for moving materials and supplies and in another stage for moving finished goods. Both are costs of physical distribution. The only truly adequate way of examining individual stages is to see the whole, so that one knows which the really important areas are and what the impact of doing something in the shipping room might be on the rest of the system. For example, in making and selling typewriters, it may make very little sense to run through the plant those parts that are purchased on the outside and sold for replacement. It might be better to run them around the plant straight to the service department. (The only people who seem to practice this is Sears, Roebuck and Company. They have done so since 1919.) These are elementary matters. But, unless one traces the entire physical flow, one does not see them.

If this is too demanding, at least make certain that the whole economic process can be seen from the stage where goods are physically finished—that is, where they come off the machines—to where they are purchased by the consumer. Otherwise one cannot be sure that the main costs are where he sees them, since they may be beyond his immediate four walls. Incidentally, it is not necessarily true that it takes longer to get things changed in the wholesaler's or distributor's system than in the manufacturing company. It takes just about as much time and hard work to make changes in both cases. Physical distribution can be drastically altered even where there is no apparent direct control, limited only by anti-trust laws.

Techniques will not be discussed, because the basic problems are not technical. The crucial thing is to make sure that the work is done as one of the major dimensions of a business, for the physical flow is certainly a major dimension of any manufacturing business. One may therefore come up with business decisions and not with technical answers. The following difficult questions will arise: What customer service is given to whom, and on what and where? And does it make any sense to try to give the same service to all customers anywhere on everything?

These basic problems in financial management may occur. For example, to what extent should financial charges be traded off against operating economies? Very real problems of financial structure may arise. Often more capital investment will be needed to achieve major operating economies, so that the capital structure is affected. Buying problems may come up. Because physical distribution is an important dimension of the entire business, all of the basic business decisions somehow will enter into it.

One should not do what the technical man always tries to do, which is to avoid these decisions in order to find the technically good answer. These decisions involve a certain amount of risk and are usually not very easy to make. One of the functions of the good analyst is to bring to light the unresolved decisions in a business and make sure that management has a chance to think them through. Anything that obscures the fact that these are difficult, risky decisions only does harm in the long run. Thus there is no call for the technical man to take business risks. For technical studies, relatively unimportant questions need to be asked: "And what risks have you decided the company should take?" There are always some risks, and yet they are almost never mentioned in the presentation, which tends to consist of axiomatic statements and mathematical formulas. Yet in the long run—even in the short run—these risks are quite obviously not going to remain submerged. It is better to have them out and risk having one's elegant solution postponed for a year than to gloss over them, have the solution put in, and then have it thrown out entirely later because of the risk-taking decision that had been ignored. In other words, although this is an area of technical work, the decisions are very largely business decisions and should be treated as such.

In this area, perhaps more than in any other, the line between the business risk that makes sense and the costs saving is a very blurred one. Sometimes a fairly small step-up in risk produces very large savings; sometimes a very small hedging against risk destroys all the savings. This is delicately poised, and therefore this risk-taking decision has to be brought out and fought through or else the benefit of the work decreases.

Those who want tools and techniques are probably not satisfied with this approach. Although tools and techniques are very important, also of importance is the means by which they are acquired. People generally know where to go to get the tools and what kind of techniques apply to what kind of a problem or situation. But, unless the entire flow is kept in perspective, people are likely to doctor symptoms. Shifting costs from one place to another is likely without really having lasting results.

It is also known that a company's costs alone are not relevant. Total cost is the only important concept because the ultimate customer is concerned only with this. Therefore, if the total cost structure is not kept in perspective, one would not be likely to know where the real costs are. It is usually advisable to change first the basic attitude of management, and then the techniques. The object is to create understanding on the part of management that physical distribution exists and matters. Management must understand that the costs vary in the traditional reports and figures because they do not occur in any one function but, instead, cut across all. A management committee is needed to change situations in which no one is responsible for physical distribution, for this is complex and very expensive and therefore somebody must be responsible for it.

Where physical distribution is placed within the structure of the business is not important. It probably does not belong in manufacturing, but whether it is put into marketing, into purchasing, or whether it is set up as a separate function is not important. What really matters is to have a first-rate man in charge, because this is hard work in which results do not occur immediately. One has to be able to move from the general system to a specific problem. Traditional managerial concepts which are usually taken for granted must be utilized.

A very elementary example: It is traditionally assumed that a district sales office, the warehouse, and the district administration go together naturally. It is taken for granted that if there are sixty district offices, then there are sixty warehouses and sixty offices for the paperwork. Today, it is known that this is not an invariable rule. There might be sixty sales offices but only eight warehouses servicing them and only one office where all the paper is handled. Therefore, someone who is able to look at the whole system but who is also diligent enough to study the individual warehouse is needed. Someone who is concerned with physical distribution as a specific area of responsibility is needed.

There are quite a few possible models of a business, such as the accounting model, for example. A model that sees the whole business in terms of customer satisfaction is possible. This is what is meant by the "total marketing approach." A business can be imagined as a flow of information, ideas, and decisions. These are all powerful concepts. But so far they are only concepts. The only model of a business that can so far be truly designed—the only operational system, in other words—is that of the business of physical distribution, as a flow of materials. And because the new tools are particularly adept at handling such physical phenomena, tremendous results can be achieved as soon as the studying, analyzing, and reshaping of this system takes place.

Physical distribution is thus today's frontier in business. It is the one area where managerial results of great magnitude can be achieved. And it is still largely unexplored territory.

2

Early Development of Physical Distribution Thought

BERNARD J. LA LONDE
Ohio State University

LESLIE M. DAWSON
Northeastern University

The task of storing and physically moving goods has existed since economic activity rose above the levels of subsistence and simple communal living. Recognition of the task is not new; however, the physical distribution concept is expressed today in terms far different from those generally characteristic of the early marketing literature. This article focuses upon a selected sampling of the marketing literature published prior to 1940, in an effort to trace the early evolution of thought concerning the physical distribution activity of the firm.

An Environmental Perspective

The changing view of the nature and importance of physical distribution is partly a response to environmental change. Physical distribution is a problem-solving activity of business management. The basic "problem" involved in the physical distribution task is creation of time and place utility. However, the nature and scope of the problem has changed dramatically with the evolution of the U.S. economy from an agriculturally based economy to an industralized, urban economy.

What might be called "the old problem" relates to an economy such as that which existed in the United States throughout most of the nineteenth century. The American economy of that era was agriculturally based, and consequently, was subject to seasonal production peaks. Manufacturing activity was heavily

9

concentrated along the Eastern seaboard. Imports were an important source of finished products, and the great import-export centers were concentrated in the Eastern port cities. Much of the nation's trading activity involved the movement of agricultural surpluses from the Midwest and South to the East in exchange for manufactured goods. As long as manufacturers remained relatively small, wholesalers dominated trade channels. Wholesale centers developed first in the important port and river cities to be accessible to water transport, and later in the key rail centers. In an environment of limited transporation technology and with the necessity of moving a large bulk of perishable goods, transportation and storage were viewed as the primary elements of the physical distribution task.

What might be called "the new problem" came with the emergence of a mass production economy in America beginning with the end of the nineteenth century. The Industrial Revolution, an increasing urban labor supply, and a growing awareness of the possibilities and advantages of scale economies contributed to the rapid growth in size of industrial firms. A rapidly expanding railroad network linked local markets with regional and national markets and further contributed to potential scale economies in manufacturing. Large producers began to assume greater control over the distribution of their products. Efforts to differentiate products and to expand markets were facilitated by rapid advances in communication and transportation technology. Proliferation of brands, styles, and sizes of products kept pace with the growing affluence and discretionary buying power of the urban consumer. Such conditions created new strains on the physical distribution system.

Large producers covering large regional or national markets faced logistical problems far more complex than mere outward transportation of finished goods to consumers. New methods of more rapid transportation and technological advances in storage and preservation changed the movement and storage function into an element of managerial strategy. Coordination of physical distribution with market demand and cost efficiency in the physical movement of goods became key aspects of the firm's struggle to remain competitive.

The transition from the old problem to the new was evolutionary in nature; in fact, it is still occurring. The marketing literature of the early 1900's reflects a primary focus on the transportation and storage elements of the physical distribution task. The early "principles" texts of the 1920's generally covered the physical distribution area in a section or chapter on transportation. Gradually, however, as the task of distributing an increasing amount of differentiated products to regional and national markets grew, greater recognition was given to the deeper strategic implications of physical distribution activities.

Some Early Views

Arch W. Shaw

Early in this century, Arch W. Shaw set out in search of a body of generalities, truths, and principles which he believed to be the preconditions for the shaping of a science of business. Much of his notable work, *An Approach to Business Problems*, focused upon the businessman's situation in the market place.[1] At this early date (1916), Shaw made a clear statement of the conceptual division of marketing into two halves, demand creation and physical supply. Many of Shaw's comments revealed his perception of the strategic possibilities inherent in the physical supply function. For example:

> The relations between the activities of demand creation and physical supply, in fact, illustrate again the persistence of the two principles of interdependence and balance. Failure to coordinate any one of these activities with its group-fellows and also with those in the other group, or undue emphasis or outlay put upon any one of these activities, is certain to upset the equilibrium of forces which means efficient distribution. ... The physical distribution of the goods is a problem distinct from the creation of demand, though it is one which must be considered at every step in any solution arrived at. ... Not a few costly failures in distribution campaigns have been due to such a lack of coordination between demand creation and physical supply. ... Instead of being a subsequent problem, this question of supply must be met and answered before the work of distribution begins.[2]

Paul Cherington

Paul Cherington, one of the pioneer contributors to marketing "principles" thought of the 1920's, made some notable contributions to physical distribution thought in *The Elements of Marketing* published in 1920.[3] Cherington identified four maladjustments of a mass production economy: (1) quantity produced and consumed; (2) quality (grades); (3) time between production and consumption; (4) place of production and consumption. Cherington then identified the four marketing activities intended to rectify the maladjustments: (1) assembling and disbursing; (2) grading and classifying; (3) storage; (4) transportation and moving. Most of the author's specific physical distribution discussion was contained in a chapter entitled "The Transporting Function." Little appeared in the chapter in the nature of detailed descriptions of railroad facilities and practices, rate structures, and similar descriptive data which gave corresponding chapters in other corresponding texts a "traffic manager" flavor. Cherington made the following distinction between the commercial and the physical transfer functions:

> The commercial function of correcting the maladjustment between the place of consumption and the place of production should not be confused with the phenomena concerned with the mechanical tasks involved in the physical transfer of goods from place to place. ... The transportation

---

[1] Arch W. Shaw, *An Approach to Business Problems* (Cambridge, Mass.: Harvard University Press, 1916).

[2] *Ibid.*, pp. 101-110.

[3] Paul T. Cherington, *The Elements of Marketing* (New York: The Macmillan Company, 1920).

industry lies outside of, although it is wholly indispensable to, the mechanism for the commercial distribution of merchandise. What is here under consideration is in short the commercial, as distinct from the physical, movement of merchandise.[4]

Cherington's analytical approach is illustrated by his population-distribution map of Iowa (Figure 1), upon which he suggested a producer might superimpose a network of plants and warehouses for optimum distributive efficiency.

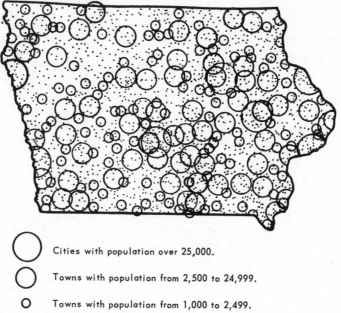

⃝ Cities with population over 25,000.

◯ Towns with population from 2,500 to 24,999.

○ Towns with population from 1,000 to 2,499.

Source: Paul T. Cherington, *The Elements of Marketing* (New York: Macmillan Company, 1920), p. 96.

Figure 1. Population-Distribution Map of Iowa.

Fred E. Clark

Fred E. Clark wrote *Principles of Marketing*[5] in 1922, a text similar to Cherington's functional approach to marketing. Clark too saw the exchange functions as one part of marketing, and the physical supply functions—consisting of transportation and storage—as the other. He was one of the first to speak of the principle of concentration and dispersion in the movement of goods. Clark included a chapter entitled "Physical Distribution," but it was far more transportation oriented than the corresponding chapter in Cherington's *Elements*. As the following passage suggests, Clark's main focus was upon the role

[4]*Ibid.*, p. 91.

[5]Fred E. Clark, *Principles of Marketing* (New York: The Macmillan Company, 1922).

of transportation rates as a factor affecting market delineation and competitive success:

> Other things being equal, the seller who has the lowest transportation costs on the materials, equipment and supplies which he uses and on the shipment of his product to market can sell at the lowest price, makes the greatest net profit, and, if his supply is great enough, may even control the market.[6]

Clark organized an important part of the then unstructured marketing literature into his "readings" book of 1924, which was almost completely revised in 1933.[7] Both volumes contained whole sections devoted to "Physical Supply," but the selection of articles tended toward the technical problems of distribution rather than the broader strategic implications of distribution activities.

Theodore N. Beckman

Wholesaling,[8] written by Theodore N. Beckman in 1926, was the earliest comprehensive treatment of the wholesale level in the marketing channel. It offers a good example of the "traffic management: conception of the physical distribution function." Beckman visualized "three more or less distinct phases of traffic management: receiving, shipping, and local deliveries."[9] The traffic manager would specialize, according to Beckman, in tariffs, rates, and regulations applying to common carriers, but would not necessarily directly manage the receiving or shipping departments. The author provided an organization chart (Figure 2) which reveals his conception of the loci of physical distribution activities in the "modern" wholesaling operation.

Toward a More Integrated View of the Physical Distribution Task

A Cost Awareness

In 1927, Ralph Borsodi wrote a book addressed to the problem of rising distribution costs.[10] Borsodi was disturbed by the fact that "in 50 years between 1870 and 1920 the cost of distributing necessities and luxuries has nearly trebled, while production costs have gone down by one-fifth. . .what we are saving in production we are losing in distribution."[11] It was Borsodi's contention that:

---

[6]*Ibid.,* p. 305.
[7]Fred E. Clark, *Readings in Marketing* (New York: The Macmillan Company, 1924), 2d ed., 1933.
[8]Theodore N. Beckman, *Wholesaling* (New York: The Ronald Press Company, 1926).
[9]*Ibid.,* p. 491.
[10]Ralph Borsodi, *The Distribution Age* (New York: D. Appleton & Company, 1929).
[11]*Ibid.,* p. 3.

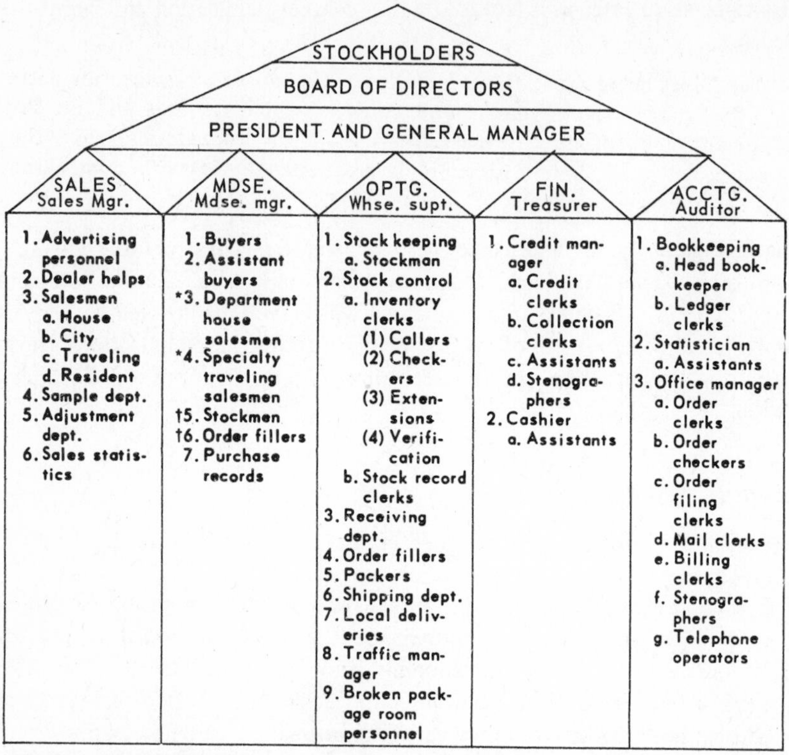

STOCKHOLDERS

BOARD OF DIRECTORS

PRESIDENT AND GENERAL MANAGER

SALES Sales Mgr.	MDSE. Mdse. mgr.	OPTG. Whse. supt.	FIN. Treasurer	ACCTG. Auditor

1. Advertising personnel
2. Dealer helps
3. Salesmen
  a. House
  b. City
  c. Traveling
  d. Resident
4. Sample dept.
5. Adjustment dept.
6. Sales statistics
	1. Buyers
	2. Assistant buyers
	*3. Department house salesmen
	*4. Specialty traveling salesmen
	†5. Stockmen
	†6. Order fillers
	7. Purchase records
		1. Stock keeping
		  a. Stockman
		2. Stock control
		  a. Inventory clerks
		    (1) Callers
		    (2) Checkers
		    (3) Extensions
		    (4) Verification
		  b. Stock record clerks
		3. Receiving dept.
		4. Order fillers
		5. Packers
		6. Shipping dept.
		7. Local deliveries
		8. Traffic manager
		9. Broken package room personnel
			1. Credit manager
			  a. Credit clerks
			  b. Collection clerks
			  c. Assistants
			  d. Stenographers
			2. Cashier
			  a. Assistants
				1. Bookkeeping
				  a. Head bookkeeper
				  b. Ledger clerks
				2. Statistician
				  a. Assistants
				3. Office manager
				  a. Order clerks
				  b. Order checkers
				  c. Order filing clerks
				  d. Mail clerks
				  e. Billing clerks
				  f. Stenographers
				  g. Telephone operators

*Peculiar to dry goods and similar trades.
†This arrangement obtains principally when receiving and stockkeeping are decentralized.

Source: Theodore N. Beckman, *Wholesaling* (New York: Ronald Press Company, 1926), p. 112.

Figure 2. Principal Divisions of a Wholesale Organization.

(1) Distribution costs in this country, both for physical distribution and for marketing, have risen out of proportion to production cost; (2) high freight rates and cross-hauling and unnecessary transportation are principally responsible for the rise in the cost of physical distribution. . . . (3) manufacturers engaged in mass production and mass selling have been the active factors in the development of extravagant marketing and unnecessary transportation—that they are responsible for the breaking down of that skillful and skeptical buying by retailers and consumers which tends to raise standards and to lower costs.[12]

Borsodi had an interesting pyramid, or multiplier, theory which he claimed pointed up the impact of physical distribution expenses upon consumer prices. He sought to demonstrate how each dollar spent in a channel on distribution activities would be "marked up" before reaching the consumer as part of the retail price:

[12]*Ibid.*, p. 9-10.

In 1913, the cost of transporting one dollar's worth of cornflakes from the farm to the elevator was 2.9 cents. By 1921, the cost of transportation had increased to 5.9 cents. The cost of transportation at this early step in the distribution of cornflakes increased three cents in eight years. As this increase in the cost of transportation was pyramided by each of the factors subsequently involved in the distribution of the cornflakes, it was passed on to the consumer not at the original three cents but at an increasing progression, varying with the margins upon which the various factors involved operate their businesses, until it amounted to over eleven cents. . . . It will be seen that the increase of three cents in the transportation cost at the very beginning of the process of distribution, after four mark-ups, actually resulted in the consumer paying over eleven cents when buying cornflakes—nearly four times the amount of the increase.[13]

Borsodi laid the blame at the producer's door for bringing all of this about, if not deliberately, then unmindfully. He charged the manufacturers with fighting with one another for national markets with utter disregard for the effect of this upon consumer prices, and with pointlessly invading territories far away from those in which they could market most efficiently and economically.

As an economy matures, there appears to be a general tendency for distribution costs as a per cent of the consumers' dollar to increase. This is due to the increased costs of serving larger geographical markets, wider and deeper inventory assortments and emphasis upon consumer convenience. On the other hand, unit costs of production in a mass production automated industrial environment as a per cent of the consumers' dollar frequently decline due to the economies inherent in large scale production. Borsodi overgeneralized on this phenomenon, and to him, it represented waste in distribution. Borsodi's major contribution would seem to be his recognition of the significance of physical distribution costs in an expanding market.

Some of the basic questions raised by this author were more forcefully stated and analyzed some ten years later in the Twentieth Century Fund Study entitled *Does Distribution Cost Too Much?*[14]

New Directions

Some of the periodical literature of the late twenties indicated an increased recognition of the role of physical distribution in marketing planning. A good example is an article by Richard Webster, entitled "Careless Physical Distribution: A Monkey-Wrench in Sales Machinery," which appeared in the July 6, 1929, issue of *Sales Management*. Webster stressed the importance of physical distribution activities to the sales and profit success of the firm. He complained that all too often such activities were relegated to "factory minds" which failed

---

[13]*Ibid.*, p. 69.
[14]Paul W. Stewart and J. Frederic Dewhurst, *Does Distribution Cost Too Much?* (New York: The Twentieth Century Fund, 1939).

to perceive the strategic gains which could be made by effective physical distribution. Webster pointed out that existing cost accounting procedures were inadequate with respect to physical distribution, inasmuch as they often failed to pinpoint the real costs involved in terms of excessive inventories and customer dissatisfaction. The author, in this early version of a "physical distribution concept," recommended that such activities be represented at the top organizational level of the enterprise.[15]

Another perceptive article,[16] written by Richard Waterman, appeared in the May, 1931, issue of *Nation's Business*. Waterman emphasized the importance of physical distribution management even in the small or medium size firm. He described a multifunctional role for "modern" traffic administration. In addition to the more conventional functions of rate management, contact with transport agencies, and in-plant physical handling, Waterman provided a picture of the strategic side of the task which sounds strikingly similar to contemporary descriptions of the physical distribution manager's role:

> Administrative functions include cooperation with all departments within the organization in such things as locating plants, warehouses and branches; keeping executives informed of changes in freight rates and service; determining the proper size of purchase and sales orders from a transportation standpoint; designing containers and selecting proper packing materials; and also cooperating with local, state, and national organizations in such matters as filing complaints and intervening in rate cases, testifying before carrier rate committees. . . .Traffic and transportation activities not only facilitate manufacturing but are an integral part of it. . . .A competent traffic manager is entitled to rank with any other department head and be a member of the firm's executive committee.[17]

Toward an Integrated Concept

Marketing texts appearing in the late 1920's and early 1930's began to assume more of a managerial orientation. Commensurate with this; attempts were made to better integrate the physical distribution function in the total complex of the firm's marketing activities.

Paul Converse in *Selling Policies*, published in 1927, discussed physical distribution with a positive managerial strategy orientation:

> The seller who can make the quickest delivery has a decided advantage, as the buyer can buy in smaller quantities, carry smaller stocks, and thus use less capital with a minimum danger of losing business due to goods being

[15]Richard Webster, "Careless Physical Distribution: A Monkey-Wrench in Sales Machinery," *Sales Management*, XIX (July 6, 1929), 21.

[16]Richard Waterman, "Who Needs Traffic Management," *Nation's Business*, XIX, May, 1931, 51.

[17]*Ibid.*, pp. 51-52.

"out of stock." . . .This is not necessarily the most economical method of marketing goods, but the point we are making is that these manufacturers choose this method of securing business under highly competitive conditions.[18]

Converse dealt with the competitive strategy implications of the locating of manufacturing plants, assembly plants, and warehouses. Emphasizing the importance of customer satisfaction, and the competitive dangers of stockouts, the author discussed the wisdom of reserve stocks and strategically located regional stocks.

Of particular significance in Breyer's work is his integration of the physical distribution function into a total marketing system. Of perhaps equal importance is his treatment of the physical distribution function from a time (temporal) and space (spatial) perspective.

Ralph Breyer, in his 1934 book, *The Marketing Institution,* sought to show "how the unified, synthesized marketing institution is affected by and operates under various market attributes or conditions."[19] Breyer discussed physical distribution within the context of "The Marketing Institution and the Space Element." The author followed a concentration-dispersion theory and used the concept of "eye photographs" to abstract particular movement patterns from the total complex of the physical movement of goods. For example, Breyer presented an "eye photograph" of the flow of goods from a producer of machinery and hardware to consumers (Figure 3).

Summary and Conclusions

The concept of the scope and nature of the physical distribution activity changed radically during the first four decades of the twentieth century. In the early twentieth century management tended to equate physical distribution with transportation and, to a more limited extent, with storage. The physical distribution task was considered a static rather than a dynamic task as much or more a part of production than an aspect of marketing. In the later part of this period there was a growing recognition of the vast potential for cost efficiency in physical distribution management and of the potentially significant role of physical distribution activities in competitive marketing strategy.

The changing perspective of the physical distribution function can be attributed in large part to environmental change. Transportation and storage were the key physical distribution activities of an agriculturally based American economy, and they were also vital imperatives for young mass producers seeking to link separate markets in order to create a large scale regional and national market. Ultimately, however, the sheer size of the nation's transportation bill (and the urgency of the Depression) forced a deeper consideration of the

[18] Paul D. Converse, *Selling Policies* (Englewood Cliffs, N. J.: Prentice-Hall, Inc., 1927).

[19] Ralph F. Beyer, *The Marketing Institution* (McGraw-Hill Book Company, 1934).

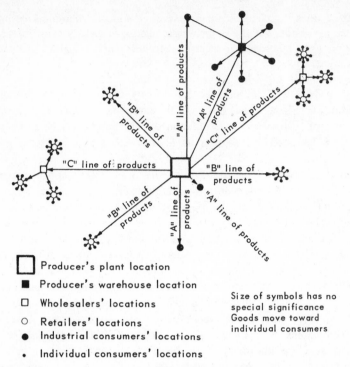

Producer's plant location

■ Producer's warehouse location

□ Wholesalers' locations

○ Retailers' locations

● Industrial consumers' locations

.   Individual consumers' locations

Size of symbols has no
special significance
Goods move toward
individual consumers

Source: Ralph F. Breyer, *The Marketing Institution* (New York: McGraw-Hill Book Company, 1934), p. 142.

Figure 3. A Geographic Pattern of the Flow of Goods from One Producer of Various Lines of Products (Machinery and Hardware) to Numerous Consumers.

potentials for cost efficiency in the movement of goods. A growing emphasis on customer satisfaction combined with a focus on cost efficiency compelled a new view of physical distribution. Gradually, a perspective emerged which recognized the broad scope of the physical transfer of goods in a trade channel, of intrafirm and interfirm relationships in the movement of materials and goods through time and space; and of competitive marketing strategy potentials within the physical distribution area. As environmental and technological change continues today, so does management's concept of physical distribution change—as witnessed by the impact of computer technology upon current physical distribution thought.

3

The Logistics of Distribution

JOHN MAGEE
Arthur D. Little, Inc.

American business is awakening to a new, exciting opportunity to improve service and reduce costs—better management of the flow of goods from plant to user. Capitalizing on this opportunity means:

●Thinking of the physical distribution process as a *system* in which, just as in a good hi-fi system, all the components and functions must be properly balanced.
●Taking a fresh look at the responsibilities, capabilities, and organizational positions of executives in traffic, warehouse management, inventory control, and other functions which make up the over-all system.
●Re-examining the company's physical plant and distribution procedures in the light of technical advances in such areas as transportation, data processing, and materials handling.

In this article I shall first examine the pressing need for improved management of companies' distribution systems. Then I shall outline some of the most promising ways by which progress in "industrial logistics" can be achieved, with special attention to the implications of technological advances for policy, the problems of getting started with a new look at a company's system, and the steps that should be taken in making a good distribution study.

Stubborn Pressures

The need for progress in distribution is a product of not one but several trends—trends in costs, in product-line policy, and in the market place. More often than not, the challenge posed is to the system as a whole, not just to the particular part or function where trouble is most obvious.

19

Rising Costs

For years, businessmen and economists have looked with mixed feelings on the increase in distribution costs in our economy. Over the past half century, tremendous strides have been made in reducing the costs of production, but these feats have not been duplicated in other areas. If the over-all efficiency of companies is to continue to improve, management must turn its attention increasingly to holding distribution costs in line. Physical distribution costs in particular, estimated by some to represent the third largest component in the total cost of business operation, are a logical center for management attention.

The problems of cutting these costs pose certain new and interesting questions for business. Whereas in many production operations it has been possible in the past to substitute a machine for human labor and to cut the cost of one operation without seriously disturbing the rest of the production system, this is hardly the case in efforts to cut physical distribution costs. Indiscriminate cost reduction in any one of the individual cost elements, such as inventory maintenance, warehousing, transportation, or clerical activities, can have a disastrous effect on the efficiency of the system as a whole. To illustrate this point:

●Suppose we cut inventories. Certainly a reduction in inventories will save capital investment and the costs of supplying capital, and it may save some expenses in storage, taxes, and insurance. On the other hand, an indiscriminate reduction in inventory levels may seriously impair the reliability of delivery service to customers and the availability of products in the field. An inventory reduction which saves money but destroys competitive position is hardly a contribution to a more effective distribution system.

●We can cut transportation costs, perhaps, by changing to methods showing lower cost per ton-mile, or by shipping in larger quantities and taking advantage of volume carload or truckload rates. But if lower transportation costs are achieved at the expense of slower or less frequent movement of goods, we face the risk of: (a) cutting the flexibility and responsiveness of the distribution system to changes in customer requirements; (b) requiring greater field inventories to maintain service; (c) creating greater investment requirements and obsolescence risks.

Similarly, blanket refusal to allow cost increases in any one part can wipe out opportunities to make the system as a whole more efficient. For instance:

New Methods of high-speed data communications and processing may in fact increase the clerical costs of operating the distribution system. On the other hand, they may cut down delays in feeding information back to govern production operations and to control lags in getting material moving into the distribution system in response to customer demand. Thus, they may actually cut *total* distribution system costs because of their impact on improved production and inventory control.

It takes a careful analysis of the total physical distribution system to know whether net costs will be increased or decreased by efforts to cut the cost of any one component.

Proliferating Product Lines

Physical distribution systems in recent years have been put under tremendous pressure induced by changes in product-line characteristics. Until recently, for example, products like typewriters, light bulbs, appliances, and plumbing fixtures were largely utilitarian, with differences in product characteristics rather closely related to function. A typewriter manufacturer did not have to worry about matching typewriter color to office décor or type style to company "image." Light bulbs used to be white and sometimes clear, and they varied by wattage. Now, however, typewriters come in pastels and two-tones. Light bulbs are sold not only to provide light but atmosphere, with a corresponding increase in the number of products that have to be shipped, stocked, and controlled. Appliances and plumbing fixtures are available to customers not only in the classical antiseptic white, but in a wide range of color and style combinations. In short, style and individuality have become strong competitive weapons.

In an almost unending list of products in the consumer field, variations in color, packaging, and other features have imposed heavy burdens on the distribution system. In the marketing of industrial goods, variations in grade, color, and size have had a similar impact. In paper manufacture, for example, the wide variety of package sizes required for consumer products has led carton manufacturers to demand correspondingly wide ranges of kraft board roll widths from paper manufacturers, and these demands have created difficult problems of scheduling, inventory control, and distribution.

The growth and change in product-line characteristics in both consumer and industrial products have meant that manufacturing plants have had more items to make, and the distribution system has had more items to handle and stock. More items mean lower volume per item and correspondingly higher unit handling inventory and storage costs. Take, for example, just the impact on inventory requirements of substituting three items for one:

Suppose we have substituted items B, C, and D for an old item A. If sales among these items are broken down 60% to B, 30% to C, and 10% to D, with no over-all increase in sales compared to the volume on the old item A, then Exhibit 1 shows what is likely to happen to field inventory requirements—an increase of more than 60%. (This figure is based on characteristic relationships between inventory and sales in companies with which I am familiar. In general, the larger the sales, the lower inventory can be relative to sales. Thus, product D with 10% of sales needs a much higher proportion of inventory than product B, with 60% of the sales.)

At a carrying cost of 20% a year, this increase represents a handsome expense for maintaining competitive position.

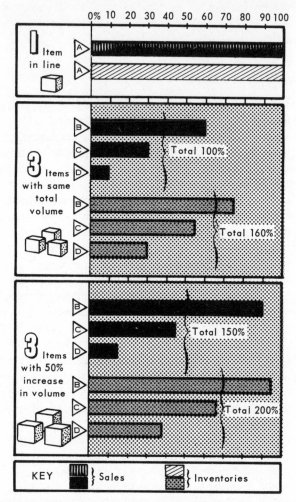

Exhibit 1. What Happens to Inventories When the Product Line Is Broadened?

Let us be optimistic, however, and assume that items B, C, and D do more than yield the same total volume; let us assume that total volume increases by 50%. Even so, the inventory requirements would double, and inventory cost per unit sold would increase over 30%—a substantial source of pressure on the distribution system.

These figures illustrate the impact of small-volume items on the cost of operating the distribution system. Yet diversity of product sales is characteristic in American businesses, whether selling in consumer or industrial markets. Exhibit 2 shows the typical relationship between the number of items sold and the proportion of sales they account for. The figures are based on the records of a large number of firms in the consumer and industrial products fields. The

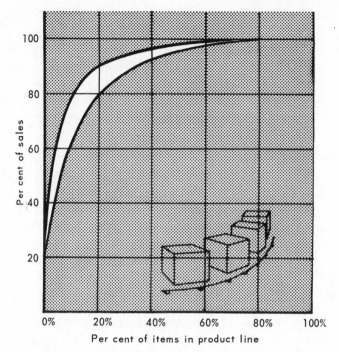

Exhibit 2. What Fraction of Total Sales Is Accounted for By What Fraction of Total Items in the Product Line?

exhibit reveals that while 10%–20% of total items sold characteristically yield 80% of the sales, half of the items in the line account for less than 4% of the sales. It is the bottom half of the product line that imposes a great deal of the difficulty, expense, and investment on the distribution system.

Alternative Courses

Increased cost, selling, and product-line pressures suggest that management should take a hard look at alternative distribution patterns, as a means of cutting logistics costs without a major sacrifice in service. Here are a few of the possibilities:

•The company can carry central stocks of low-selling items only. To get the right balance of transportation costs, handling costs, and service, it may be necessary to stock these items at one central point and ship them against individual customer orders as the latter arise, perhaps by expedited service or air freight.

•For many items in the line, a good compromise may be to carry some low- or middle-volume items in only a few large regional warehouses, as a compromise between the excessive storage costs incurred from broad-scale stocking and the transportation and service penalties incurred by attempting to meet demand from manufacturing points alone.

●Warehouse points can be consolidated. With improvements in transportation and in mechanical material- and data-handling methods, large opportunities exist in many businesses for cutting down on the number of field warehouse points. With increased volume through the individual warehouses, carrying a broader product line at the local points begins to make greater economic sense.

Sales-Generating Capacity

The first and most basic job of the distribution system is to get customers, to turn interest and orders into sales. As business has grown more competitive and the public has become harder to please, management has focused increasing attention on the *quality* of its logistical operations. What can be done to make products more readily available for purchase in local markets? What improvements can be made in backing up product merchandising and advertising programs with adequate deliveries and service? Obviously, questions like these are affected by cost considerations, but as marketing objectives they deserve individual attention.

In analyzing the capacity of a distribution system to produce sales, executives will do well to examine three key characteristics:

1. *Location*—It has been estimated, for example, that from 5 distribution points a company can reach 33% of the U.S. consumer market within a day; while from 25 warehouse locations, 80% can be reached in one day.

2. *Inventories*—Judging from my own and associates' experience, approximately 80% more inventory is needed in a typical business to fill 95% of the customers' orders out of stock than to fill only 80%.

3. *Responsiveness*—The ability of a system to transmit needs back to the supplying plant and get material needed into the field determines how quickly the business can shift with changes in customer preferences to meet demand with minimum investment and cost.

Revolution in Technology

The pressures on distribution methods have led to exciting new technological advances for getting goods to the user at lower cost to the company—with less labor and materials expended and less capital tied up in inventories and facilities. When these advances are introduced in proper balance, the distribution process can better meet the needs of the consumer. Major technological changes are now taking place in transportation, information handling, and material handling. Let us examine each of them in turn.

Costs vs. Transport Time

Transportation thinking has been dominated too long by preoccupation with the direct traffic bill. Too much attention has been paid to transport cost per ton-mile and not enough to the contribution transportation makes to the effectiveness of the distribution system as a whole.

Railroad rate structures are to an outsider an eye-opening illustration of what can happen when a transportation system is put under the cost-per-ton-mile pressure for too long. Rail rate structures, despite frequent attempts to introduce some rationale, have degenerated into an unbelievable hodgepodge of unrealistic and uneconomic rate compromises as the roads have succumbed to the pressure of giving each shipper the lowest cost per ton-mile, often at the expense of service. While improvements in equipment, such as the introduction of the diesel locomotive, have led to greater efficiency on the track, in some cases at least the longer trains and increased classification problems that have resulted have meant little or no net increase in over-all distribution efficiency. The gap between traffic and marketing thinking is painfully evident in many companies' distribution methods; little has been done to relate transportation methods and service to the objectives of the distribution system in support of marketing efforts.

Transportation costs are important indeed, but they are only part of the story. For example, think of the value of materials in transit:

●Data collected on sample shipments in various parts of the country indicate that material may spend one to two weeks in transit and that the capital value of assets tied up in the transportation system may, depending on the pressure for capital, add as much as 1% to the economic cost of the goods.

●Service, or reliability of the transport system, is also important. Goods must get to the user promptly and reliably, to permit him to operate systematically with low inventories.

●The direct and indirect costs of damage in transport are another large item in the traffic bill that at times gets overlooked in the pressure for low cost per ton-mile.

Clearly, transport time is one of the key determinants of the efficiency of the distribution system. Its impact is not vivid or dramatic, and executives do not always appreciate what a difference it makes, but in a great many companies it is a significant factor in financing. To take a simple illustration:

Suppose that in a company doing an annual business of $100 million, time in transit is reduced from 14 days to 2. Time between reorders is 14 days, communication and processing time is 4 days, and field stocks average $12.5 million. In such a situation the reduction in transit time might well lead to a reduction in distribution inventory investment of $6 million, made up of: (1) a reduction of $3.3 million in transit, i.e., 12 days' sales; (2) a reduction of $2.7 million in inventories required to protect customer service resulting from a faster, more flexible distribution system response.

Speeding up Service

Changes in transportation leading to improved opportunities in distribution have been truly revolutionary since World War II. Major superhighway systems have been built, truck speeds have increased substantially and so have trailer capacities. The growth in the use of trucking for industrial distribution is now well known. The stimulus from subsidies is only part of the story; trucks have been able to compete at characteristically higher ton-mile costs because they have offered speed, reliability, and flexibility to shippers

Without doubt, railroads are responding to this challenge. A recent survey showed that almost all Class I railroads are offering some form of piggyback or expedited motor-carrier service. At least some railroads are showing new merchandising awareness in concentrating on customer service. Whether the industry will be able, in the face of inherent limitations, to reverse the decline in its share of manufacturers' freight business is still an open question.

Air freight represents a challenge to both rail and over-the-road haulers. Today most industry executives still tend to view air freight as a luxury, as a service available for "orchids and emergencies." However, the trend in air freight rates has been sharply downward in recent years. With new planes coming into service, even further reductions can be projected—down to 8 cents to 12 cents a ton-mile from present-day rates of approximately 22 cents. Much depends on the success of efforts to develop aircraft equipped for freight handling and for flexible operation under a wide range of conditions (for example, modest runway lengths), and to build up the ground service needed to match air-handling speeds so as to avoid the danger faced by the railroads—the collapse of service as a result of concentration on mass, low-cost, terminal-to-terminal movement.

Impact of New Methods

What is the significance of the ferment in transportation methods? For one thing, improvement in local truck service opens up opportunities to serve wide-flung markets through fewer and larger distribution points. With larger distribution centers, the chance that mechanized material handling and storage systems will pay off is enhanced, and inventory requirements are reduced through consolidation.

To suggest the size of the opportunity, one analysis with which I am familiar showed that cutting the number of field distribution points for a national product line from 50 to 25 would increase total transport costs 7% but cut inventories 20% and cut *total* physical distribution costs 8% (the latter representing roughly a 1% cut in the total cost of delivered product). This was accomplished at the cost of serving a few small markets—about 5% of the total—with second-day instead of first-day delivery.

Rapid truck or air service increases the feasibility of relying on shipments from a few central points to back up service. Here are two ways in which this can be employed:

1. The many low-volume items in the typical product line, the items on which local storage and handling costs outweigh the penalty costs of expedited shipment, can be held centrally and moved to the market where they are needed, as needed. For example, the bottom 50% of the product line, which as Exhibit 2 shows often accounts for only 4% of sales, may require 25% or more of the warehousing costs and inventory capital charges. Turnover of the stocks of these items is often only one eighth that of the high-volume half of the line. In a *relatively* high number of cases, special shipments could be made at a cost well below that of storing the items at local distribution centers.

2. If there are substantial reserve stocks designed to protect customer service located in the field, it is possible to pare them down in the knowledge that additional supplies can be moved in promptly to meet sudden customer demands.

In a typical distribution system a large share of the inventory—as much as 90%—is carried to protect delivery service to customers in the face of fluctuating demand and system delays. This safety stock is most likely to be used at the end of the reorder cycle, when stocks hit their low point before new receipts. Exhibit 3 illustrates a common situation, with safety stocks being partly

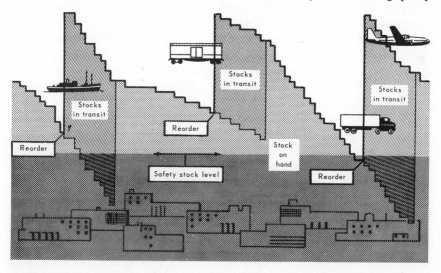

Exhibit 3. What Is the Characteristic Inventory Pattern of Stocks On Hand in the Typical Company?

depleted at intervals just before a new shipment arrives. During the period of the first reorder, demand has been heavy. In many reorder cycles, however, stocks will not be touched at all; this is the case before the second reorder in the illustration (middle of the chart) comes in. Note that inventory in transit represents a fairly significant proportion of the whole.

How much of safety stocks is actually used depends on the reorder system and level of service maintained. Typically, the last 10% may be needed only once or twice a year—a turnover rate roughly one sixth the average; and the last 30% may be needed only two to four times a year. Warehouses and inventory carrying charges on this portion of inventory, then, may easily run to 10%–20% of the sales they make possible.

There is an opportunity in many companies for management to cut material held in the field and back up customer service though regularized high-speed delivery service. This possibility will deserve increasing attention from management as the costs of high-speed transport, communication, and data processing drop.

Information Processing

Revolutionary data-processing methods were noisily battering at established business methods some six or seven years ago, but the impact was more in noise generated than in accomplishment. Now that a lot of the superficial excitement has died away, however, a broad and solid structure of accomplishment in modern data-processing techniques is quietly being built.

For one thing, computers seem to have become much more broadly accepted than was anticipated. When the earliest internally programed machines were announced, computer manufacturers' optimistic estimates were in the dozens. Today the number of machines installed or in the process of installation is in the thousands. In support of computing or processing facilities, great improvements are taking place in communications systems, especially systems designed to feed into or out of computers. In distribution management, fast, reliable communication is equally as important as fast, reliable processing.

The *use* being made of modern information-processing equipment in distribution is just as significant as its broad market acceptance. For instance, machines are being used to maintain local inventory balances, forecast near-term demand, employ forecasts and inventory balances as inputs in calculating item orders, prepare tentative purchase orders, allocate item balances among stock points, and draw up production schedules and work force requirements. These are not mere compiling and accounting functions, nor is it fair to call them "decision making." In these functions, the machine systems are interpreting rules or procedures to work out the decisions implicit in them in light of the facts of the situation. In other words, the equipment is doing what we would like intelligent clerks to do: diligently following policy and weighing costs to arrive at day-to-day actions.

The forecasting function in particular deserves special attention. I refer not to the longer term economic forecasts, annual business forecasts, or even shorter term (e.g., quarterly) business predictions, but to short-term forecasts of sales, item by item, over the replenishment lead time. These forecasts are made implicitly or explicitly in every inventory control system. In most companies they are left up to the individual stock clerk or inventory controller to make as best he can, usually with little or no training or guides. Management will spend hundreds of hours of industrial engineering time simplifying or improving a job method here and there to take a few pennies out of labor cost. Yet the stock clerk making inventory control forecasts may, through his control over product distribution and assets tied up in inventories, be costing his company many pennies indeed.

Many people still argue that one cannot forecast routinely because intuition and background knowledge count too heavily. They fail to recognize that objective procedures for short-term prediction of item sales have the same merits as, say, routing and tooling lists in a shop. Experience leaves little doubt that great gains can be made by substituting powerful systematic methods for casual or unrecognized ones.[1]

Changes in Material Handling

Mechanization is slowly spreading from the making of things to their handling in distribution. For instance:

One company in the clothing industry has installed a new data-processing system first to handle sales orders and then inventory control and production-scheduling systems. At the same time, it has been developing a bin-and-conveyer system which will permit economical mechanization of order-filling activities. The goal toward which both of these efforts are directed is a unified system in which the customer order not only serves as an input in automatic order handling but will also, after suitable internal mechanical processing, activate the warehouse system to select and consolidate the customer's order. This customer order data will also be processed internally for inventory management and production planning purposes.

How will such changes in warehousing and materials handling influence the planning of distribution systems? The effects will take at least three forms:

1. *Integration of systems for (a) material storage and transport and (b) information handling.* This development should create opportunities for significant "automation" of the distribution function and for reduction of manual drudgery. Ultimate full-scale mechanization of materials handling will not only require redesign of warehouse and transport facilities, but will have an impact on design of products and packages as well.

---

[1] See Robert G. Brown, "Less Risk in Inventory Estimates," *Harvard Business Review*, July–August 1959, p. 104.

2. *Pressure to reduce the number of distribution points or warehouses.* Mechanized warehouses cost money. One way to improve the efficiency of capital utilization is of course to increase throughput.

3. *Pressure to concentrate ownership of warehousing facilities.* Mechanization takes capital. This factor will be another force behind the tendency for manufacture, distribution, and maintenance service to become integrated under one ownership roof.

Getting Started

Some managers view the opportunities presented by changes in distribution technology with about the same air with which a bear views a porcupine: the possibilities look interesting, but where can you start to get your teeth in?

Improvements in distribution efficiency cost money. Higher speed, more flexible transport generally costs more per ton-mile. Mechanized warehousing systems or materials-handling systems are not cheap. The cost of working out, installing, and testing new information-processing systems may make direct clerical cost savings look like a rather thin return on investment. In fact, direct payoffs from distribution changes (e.g., modified transport methods leading to a direct cut in transport costs) may often be small or nonexistent. The payoffs, often handsome ones, are likely to be indirect, coming about from "tradeoffs" such as paying a higher transport bill to save material investment, putting in warehouse investment to cut over-all shipping costs, and so on.

Because tradeoffs so often are involved, it is not always easy for management to get an aggressive, functionally operated group of people to think *through* the problems. It is not easy for men in production, sales, warehousing, traffic, merchandising, and accounting to grasp other functions' needs or express their own needs in terms which make the advantages of tradeoff and balance clear. Many times the distribution *system* has been run too long as a collection of more or less independent *functions*. Any changes, any tradeoffs to get the system into better, more economical balance, any modifications to take advantage in the whole system of new technical developments—these are bound to be disruptive and to some extent resisted.

The difficulties in facing up to a searching look at the distribution system are not confined to the individual functions concerned. Some of the toughest questions arise at the general management level. For example:

●What degree of sales service is the system to provide? How far will the firm go to meet customers' service desires?

●What standards are to be used to judge investment in facilities and inventory so that it can be weighed against any cost savings that are made possible?

●What policy will the company take toward ownership and operation of the distribution, transport, warehousing, and information-processing facilities? Will the company operate its own facilities, lease them, contract for services, or rely on independent businesses to perform some or all of the necessary distribution system functions?

●What is the company's policy toward employment stabilization? To what extent is the company prepared to pay higher distribution costs to absorb demand variations and to level employment?

Approach to the Issues

Grappling with all of these problems is like untangling a tangled skein of yarn. Each decision has an impact on other choices and for this reason is hard to pin down. The distribution problem is a system problem, and it must be looked at as such. If it is examined in total and if the experience and methods available for studying it are used, the issues just mentioned can be resolved in an orderly, mutually compatible way.

In my experience, three key conditions have, when present, made for a sound distribution system study and an effective implementation program:

1. Recognition by company management that improving distribution means examining the full physical distribution system.

2. Use of quantitative systems analysis or operations research methods to show clearly the nature of tradeoffs and the relation between system operation and company policies.

3. Cooperative work by men knowledgeable in sales and marketing, transportation, materials handling, materials control, and information handling.

In the following sections we shall see the need for these conditions asserting itself again and again as we go through the steps of making a good distribution study.

Making the Study

How should a distribution system study be made? What principal steps should be taken? As far as I know, there is no formula for the approach. The relative emphasis put on different phases of the study can vary, as can also the degree of detail; the order of analysis can be changed; and so on. But there are important steps to take at some point in any study, and I shall discuss them in logical order.

1. *Data on the company's markets should be organized in a helpful way.*

The distribution system study starts with a study of customers. This does not need to be a field interview program; to a large extent what is required is the organization of market facts which are available. Occasionally, a moderate amount of skilled field interview work may be desirable to obtain customers' estimates of service requirements and their comparison of the company with its competition.

A great deal of useful information can be obtained by analysis of sales data. Here are some of the key questions of interest:

•Are we servicing several fundamentally different markets through different distribution channels? Are these markets located differently? Do they buy in different patterns, in different quantities, and with different service and stock availability requirements?

•How are our sales distributed among customers? We have found that the top 10% of a company's customers characteristically account for from 60% to 80% or even more of its business.

•Do the same customers tend to buy our high-volume items as well as slow-moving items? The answer to this question has an important bearing on how the slow-moving items, for which distribution and sales service costs are often relatively high, should be handled. Few companies seem to have really examined this problem, though strong opinions on it exist in most.

2. *Statistical analyses of product characteristics should be made, with special attention to the nature of sales fluctuations.*

Sometimes the facts about products can be established fairly readily. An example is the susceptibility of items in the line to spoilage or damage. The degree to which sales volume is concentrated among a few fast-moving items (as illustrated in Exhibit 2) can often be ascertained rather quickly, too. But data of this kind do not tell us nearly enough.

Statistical analysis is needed to establish certain key sales characteristics of the product line, all related to the *variability* of item sales. The significance of variability must be emphasized. Business managers are used to thinking in terms of averages or average rates, but the answers to many important questions affecting distribution system design depend on the characteristics of short-term sales variations about the average.

Most items exhibit unexpected day-to-day variations in sales about the average or expected level. In some cases the fluctuations are extremely wide and short-term in character; in other cases they are quite steady and predictable. The statistical characteristics of these variations determine in a very significant way how a distribution system will work and how it should be designed to operate economically.

3. *In analyzing sales variations, special attention should be paid to size, time, area, and volatility.*

Executives interested in the practical implications of short-term sales variations might focus on the following questions:

•How big are the ups and downs? The magnitude of sales variations *over the replenishment lead time* will determine how large the inventory of an item must be to maintain a desired level of delivery service. The amount of an item on hand at a field point or on order must always equal the maximum reasonable demand over the lead time. Thus, the bigger the sales fluctuations, the more inventory of an item must be carried in the distribution system—at local warehouses, at the factory—to provide a given level of delivery service.

●Are the variations correlated from one time period to the next? If one day's sales are above or below average, are the chances considerably better than 50-50 that the next day's sales will be above or below average, too? If sales are highly correlated from one week to the next, or from one month to the next, this means that the range of accumulated variation over the replenishment lead time increases nearly in proportion to the lead time itself. Doubling the warehouse lead time would nearly double the range of sales variations and the inventory requirements, while cutting the lead time in half would cut inventory requirements nearly in proportion. If sales are *not* correlated from one period to the next, chance variations tend to offset to some degree; doubling the lead time would increase inventory requirements only 40%—50%, while cutting it in half would cut inventories 30% or so.

High correlation in sales puts a premium on cutting lead times to make the distribution system react faster, perhaps through more expensive but higher speed transport, communications, and sales-information processing. By contrast, lower correlation means it may be more economical to let lead times lengthen and save expense in information handling and transport at the cost of somewhat higher inventories. Exhibit 4 illustrates all this graphically for a hypothetical firm: The dotted line represents transport, handling, and data-processing costs, tending to fall as a longer lead time permits less frequent reordering and slower, less expensive methods of shipment. The solid lines represent unit inventory costs, increasing nearly in proportion to lead time in the case of high sales correlation and at a slower rate in the case of low correlation. The higher the correlation, the further the point of minimum total cost is shifted toward the left—that is toward a shorter lead time—even in the face of higher transport, handling, and processing costs.

●Are sales variations correlated between areas or markets? Is an unexpected increase in an item's sales in, say, the Pittsburgh area likely to coincide with an increase in Cleveland, or are variations unrelated from one market to another? Some causes of expected sales variations may affect a wide geographic region (e.g., weather, rumors); others may be related entirely to local conditions (e.g., individual customers' plans).

The degree of cross-correlation in chance sales variations occurring in different markets has a significant influence on warehouse location decisions. For example, if the cross-correlation is low, so that chance variations in sales in one market tend to offset those in another, there is a potentially substantial economy in consolidating warehouses, in having fewer distribution points to serve the same total market. But if the cross-correlation is high, little would be saved to offset possibly greater transportation costs.

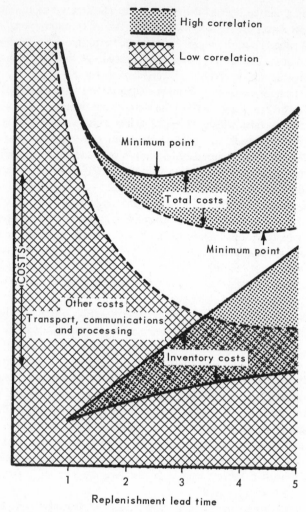

Exhibit 4. Impact of Sales Correlation on Lead Time Cost.

•How do sales variations compare among items? Are sales of high-volume items relatively more stable than sales of low-volume items? Generally (but not always), one finds evidence that the higher the sales volume of an item, the more stable will be sales, relatively speaking. Differences in the sales volatility of products influence distribution system choices. The more changeable the sales of an item, other things being equal, the better the chances that centralized stocking in regional distribution centers or plants will be advantageous.

4. *Inventory functions should be examined and related to other company needs.*

Characteristically inventories are made up of: (a) stock in transit; (b) supplies arising from periodic shipments; (c) reserves carried to protect service in the face of unusual demand (safety stock). In some businesses, inventories are also carried to accommodate seasonal sales patterns and to permit a smoothed load to be put on manufacturing. These inventory functions and methods for analyzing have already been discussed in *Harvard Business Review*[2] and there is no need to outline them again here. Suffice it to say that one important job in a distribution study is to identify the functions actually served by inventories and to characterize the factors—e.g., transport times, reordering principles used, and service requirements—that are responsible for existing inventory levels and costs.

5. *The costs of warehouse storage and handling, traffic or freight, and clerical procedures should be determined.*

Many of these costs are difficult to obtain from normal company accounting records or engineering studies; direct unit costs often just are not maintained in these records. However, statistical analyses of operating cost records can often serve quite adequately.

Warehouse costs are as good an illustration as any of the approach I have in mind. Included here are:

a. *The costs of holding inventory*—These are generally related to the average or maximum inventory level in a distribution center and include space rent (including maintenance and janitor services, heat, and so on) and inventory costs (taxes, obsolescence and spoilage, and especially the cost of capital tied up in inventory). In our experience, careful study of the storage bill typically yields costs of 20%–35% per year on the capital value of the inventory, depending on the financial resources and policies of the company.

b. *The costs of handling*—These include the costs of physically moving material into and out of storage or through terminal marshaling areas.

What is wanted here are cost factors which can be used to calculate the warehousing and handling costs under different system plans. These factors usually take the form of:

● A fixed charge per warehouse per year X number of warehouses (the fixed charge is generally $5,000–$10,000 per warehouse per year, depending on the character of space).

● Warehousing cost per year per unit in inventory X average inventory in the system.

● Handling cost per year per unit through the warehouse.

[2] See John F. Magee, "Guides to Inventory Policy: Part I, Functions and Lot Size," January–February 1956, p. 49; "Part II. Problems of Uncertainty," March–April 1956, p. 103; "Part III. Anticipating Future Needs," May–June 1956, p. 57; and Robert G. Brown, *op. cit.* See also John F. Magee, *Production Planning and Inventory* (New York, McGraw-Hill Book Company, Inc., 1958) and Robert G. Brown, *Statistical Forecasting for Inventory Control* (New York, McGraw-Hill Book Company, Inc., 1959).

These cost factors can be built up from an engineering study or derived from statistical analysis of existing cost data. They will, of course, differ for different types of facilities and operating methods. For example, a mechanized warehouse operation will of course have a quite different order of costs from a nonmechanized operation.

Clerical cost factors for alternate operating systems can be derived in similar fashion. Transport costs must also be collected, usually in the form of specimen rates collated with shipment volumes for alternate transport methods. Such possibilities as in-transit privileges, "marriage" of shipments, and forwarding schemes should be reviewed.

6. *Management should analyze alternative distribution plans on paper.*

The effect of alternative numbers of warehouses, changed locations, different transport methods, and different response times should be tested, using the methods of inventory analysis and programing techniques. Existing manufacturing capacities and locations may be used as a starting point. Alternatively—or as a second step in the analysis—the effect of changes in manufacturing facilities, in capacities, or in the product assigned to individual plants can be tested.

The first broad system studies are used to see where the biggest payoffs or traps may be. On paper, it is possible to make some arbitrary changes in lead times, warehouse locations, plant capacities, flexibility, and so on to see what the gross impact on distribution costs will be and thus whether detailed implementation studies are justified. It is important that the system study be based on current demand conditions, such as gross volume, product mix, and regional balance, as well as demand conditions projected roughly five to ten years ahead.

The facilities analysis is a step-by-step process. As the studies proceed, they will indicate potentially useful modifications in the distribution system. For example, a high concentration of sales among a few customers may indicate the need for special distribution plans, or the degree of concentration among products and the statistical characteristics of demand will suggest the need for regional stocking, changed warehouse numbers or locations, or similar alternatives. Again, an inventory study may indicate payoff possibilities in reducing lead times, in modifying service standards, or in introducing new, more flexible transport and handling methods.

Generally, as a result of broad analyses of facilities and operations, special studies will be indicated. Such studies as these may be in order:

•Detailed analysis of the information-processing methods and costs to (a) take advantage of advancing technology to improve forecasting and control and (b) cut replenishment lead times.

•Investigation of the costs of employment variations and manufacturing changes. Additional inventory—or changes in production technology—may be justified to minimize these costs. If so, however, the additions or changes should be clearly recognized; "manufacturing cost" is too often a lame excuse for careless, inefficient management of materials in distribution.

●Study of product redesign or regrouping, especially where the product line may have evolved without much thought having been given to logistics concepts.

●Analysis of special ordering procedures, stock locations, and transport methods for handling low-volume items.

Organization Plans

Distribution system management poses some puzzling organization problems to the typical, functionally organized firm. Distribution is not a sales function; it is not traffic management; it is not a manufacturing responsibility. It is an aspect of *all* of these functions. At the same time, the effectiveness of its managers will determine the conditions under which men in the individual functions must work.

Most companies prefer not to put all aspects of distribution management—sales order processing and analysis, field stock control, warehouses, traffic, production control—under one organizational unit, but to divide responsibility among several interested units. Such a division leads, however, to difficulty principally because of failure to (a) recognize the need for specific coordinated distribution systems planning, (b) specify planning and control responsibilities, and (c) set up performance measures consistent with over-all system efficiency and with assigned responsibilities.

In revising an organization to meet current needs and in keeping it up to date, executives should try to have five questions uppermost in their minds:

1. What are the necessary planning steps, policy decisions, and operating decisions to be made?
2. Who is the right person to make each of the decisions?
3. What information does he need, and how can he get it most expeditiously?
4. Does each person know how to recognize an emergency calling for nonroutine action? Does he know how to resolve it?
5. What performance measures reflect what is expected of each person in terms of the operation of the whole system?

Conclusion

To sum up, a number of pressures have piled up on today's distribution systems. As manufacturing efficiency has increased and product cost has come down, costs have grown. Physical distribution costs are a significant share of these.

Business in many fields is becoming increasingly competitive, with competition taking new forms, including availability of goods and reliability of delivery. Product changes are forcing new pressures on the distribution system—more items to carry, faster obsolescence, lower unit sales and inventory turnover. In particular, changes in merchandising practices, such as the introduction of style as a merchandising weapon, have significantly complicated the distribution problem. Pressures for improvement in logistics also include internal forces—for example, the need to stabilize production and insulate production levels from short-term fluctuations in sales.

In the face of these trends, a number of revolutionary changes have taken place. Substantial improvements have come about in essentially all forms of transportation methods. Tremendous strides forward have been made in information-handling methods, including schemes for assimilating and processing data dealing with product demand and with the need for replenishment. Materials-handling methods, ranging from mechanized stock keeping to extensions of the pallet concept to eliminate item-by-item handling, have been gaining acceptance. Finally, and perhaps as important as improvement in physical facilities and concepts, there has been progress in ways of looking at the logistics problem and at methods for analyzing distribution systems.

Long-Run Implications

So far, we have seen farsighted companies taking advantage of the changes I have described by redesigning their distribution systems to cut costs and increase the support given to sales programs. The next step is now beginning to be felt—the insinuation of distribution concepts into certain aspects of long-term planning and capital budgeting, especially the analysis of facility requirements, the location of distribution points, and the determination of financial requirements to support distribution.

Of course, we must avoid the trap of thinking that all management problems will be resolved in terms of efficient distribution. Nevertheless, the long-range impact of distribution-system thinking on production, on product design, and on manufacturing location may be substantial. Perhaps one of the most significant changes will be in concepts of organization, in the assignment of functions and responsibilities. Efficient physical distribution poses a challenge to business in integrating what is essentially a system approach with the functional approaches that hitherto have tended to govern business organization planning.

In the long run, at least two possible directions are open for making a wide variety of products available in local markets. On the one hand, manufacturers can move toward centralized manufacture, with the specialty or small-volume items being made in enough volume to permit reasonable manufacturing economy and then being moved rapidly, perhaps by air freight, to the local markets as needed. On the other hand, management can try to achieve diversity through superficial differences built into a few basic product lines. Low-cost mass transport methods, perhaps rail freight, can be used to move parts and components from centralized manufacturing points with heavy equipment into widespread local assembly or modification plants. At the local points, the final touches can be put on the product to meet customer demand.

One thing seems sure: the choice of distribution system each company makes will have a significant impact on product design, plant investment, and organization. Industrial logistics and trends in logistics technology will receive increasing attention from business, along with markets, capital resources, and product development, in the formulation of corporate plans for the decade ahead.

4

Making the Physical Distribution Concept Pay Off

F. R. DENHAM
Stevenson & Kellog, Ltd.

Unless a business is very unusual, moving goods from the plant to consumer costs almost as much as acquiring the materials and manufacturing the goods.

Typically, 25 to 50 cents of the consumers' dollar is spent in moving goods. Physical distribution represents the third largest cost component in meeting the demand for a company's products. If this cost could be reduced, profits could be higher, and consumers could get bargains. Yet it remains unmanaged.

Why is this? In most profit generating or cost incurring activities management has analyzed operations and implemented meaningful improvement programs. Costs have been reduced and profits increased. For example, studies of labor, maintenance, machine efficiency, layout, methods, and tool design have all contributed to lower manufacturing costs.

Physical distribution has not been subjected to comparable analysis nor have significant benefits been realized. Some of the reasons include:

- Difficulty in bridging organizational boundaries within the company.
- Difficulty in bridging legal and proprietary boundaries outside the company.
- Complex interactions between all stages of the distribution process.
- Difficulty of reconciling apparent conflicts between related organizational units.
- Lack of suitable measures of effectiveness.
- A shortage of suitable skills and background.
- Compartmentalized thinking by management.

It is true that some companies have begun to examine some aspects of the distribution problem. Typically:

Industrial engineers are improving warehousing operations such as receiving, picking, packing, and shipping.

Traffic managers are negotiating lower rates and agreed charges with carriers.

The better known techniques of inventory management—Economic Order Quantities (E.O.Q.) and Re-order Points (R.O.P.'s) have gained wide acceptance.

Production planners recognize their need to balance inventory costs and manufacturing costs.

Containerization, unit loads, and "swap bodies" have effectively reduced costs in many applications.

But often these improvements have been marginal—in comparison with the potential. This is so because management has concentrated on improving specific components of distribution instead of examining the overall system and the relationships between components. In fact, many piecemeal studies have actually led to an increase in total costs because apparently what appears to improve one phase of operations causes major cost increases in others.

There are many examples of the adverse effects of optimizing a subsidiary segment of a distribution system without regard to the effect on other portions of the system. The following four cases illustrate the problem.

1. *The right answer to the wrong question.* This company distributes a style item throughout Canada from a factory in Ontario. Distribution is through a series of company-owned warehouses in seven major centers. Service from the warehouses was poor. Stock-outs amounted to more than 35%, yet inventories were increasing.

These symptoms prompted management to install an inventory control system in each warehouse. The results were unsatisfactory. It was still impossible to achieve the desired service with acceptable inventory levels.

The company then asked a consultant the question—"How should inventories be controlled?" The consultant found he needed the answer to the question, "Why are inventories needed in the warehouses?" Using this as a tool, he was able to study the entire distribution system.

The outcome: The company changed to use of parcel post and air freight direct from plant to consumer. This change enabled them to close their warehouses, reduce inventories, provide better service, and increase profits.

2. *E.O.Q.'s are not necessarily the answer.* A company producing and distributing 6,000 different items to the construction industry faced a serious inventory problem. Management could not reconcile the conflicts arising from three aims: to give 24-hour freight to customers; to reduce freight costs; and to keep inventories within an acceptable level.

The manufactured products were stored in a warehouse beside the factory. From there they moved on demand to twenty company-owned branches and a greater number of jobbers.

The company's service policy was clear: shipment of goods within 24 hours. It applied equally to warehouse and to branches. Initially this policy led to a sharp increase in inventories. Later, under a reduce inventory drive, freight costs soared as branches placed too-frequent orders for small quantities. Finally, when a ceiling was placed on inventories and freight costs, customer service deteriorated.

To resolve these conflicts, a revised inventory control system was introduced in the branches. Balancing the costs of too much inventory against the costs of too frequent shipments, the system called for branches to purchase E.O.Q. lots from the factory. As might be expected, this resulted in lower overall costs in the branches. But E.O.Q. lots imposed a highly variable demand on the factory. These fluctuations could be absorbed only by lowering the service level, or increasing inventories.

In this case, the problem was aggravated because management tried to optimize one single part of the distribution system without studying the effects on other segments.

A subsequent simulation study of the overall system produced quick and economic operating rules. Service level increased from 87% to 93%; inventories were lowered from $4,900,000 to $2,900,000, and freight costs increased by only $45,000 per year.

3. *Freight reduction at any cost.* A large company produces its consumer goods in several plants in eastern Canada, including one in Toronto. They distribute nationally through branches in centers across the country, one of which is in Toronto.

Trucks were originally employed to transfer goods between the Toronto plant and branch warehouse, at a contract rate of 30c per cwt. As a result of inquiries and negotiation by the traffic manager, the railroad agreed to haul the goods for 25½c—a saving of 4½c per cwt.—equivalent to $4,150 per year.

However, the time taken to move goods by rail was about 3 days compared to less than 8 hours by truck. This difference required an increase of $112,500 in inventories—sufficient to cover the 3 days intransit. Valuing inventory at 15% meant an increase in inventory costs of $16,900 per year. Thus the reduction in freight rates led to an increase of $12,750 in total distribution costs. When this situation came to light some time later, management reverted to trucking.

4. *In favor of motherhood.* In this company, industrial engineering studies showed substantial material handling savings if goods were taken directly from the production line, loaded into railcars, and shipped to regional branches.

Prior to the study, the company had used the "Mother Warehouse" concept. Under this system, goods were taken from the production line and stored in the warehouse until needed in outlying regions.

Implementation of the recommendations did generate savings in the plant warehouse, but the savings were more than offset by poorer customer service and the corresponding need for higher inventories.

In all these cases, and many others like them, management failed to appreciate the need to study the entire physical distribution system before introducing changes.

This then is the *Physical Distribution Concept*—a set of physically related functions that must be looked at together to find out how each one of them must be operated in the best interests of the firm.

In the past, there was some excuse for non-management. Techniques suitable for studying entire systems were not available. Consequently the distribution process was fragmented; each manager was charged with improving his own operation. Similarly, the necessary analytical skills combined with knowledge of traffic, inventory, production, purchasing, and sales were not readily found. The result was a tendency to use a "gut feel" or "seat of the pants" approach to distribution problems.

These limitations no longer exist. Systems analysts, management scientist, and operations researchers have already shown that the techniques and skills are available. It now remains for business to recognize distribution as a major segment of industry, with its own policies, organization planning, and control activities.

These are management problems. Consequently, in looking for the pay-off, management must think in terms of objectives, planning, organization, and control.

Objectives. Many managers think of the objectives of distribution as: "Moving goods at least cost." This definition is too narrow. The approach to any corporate activity should be to maximize profit. In turn, this may lead to the following goals for the distribution function:

●Minimize stock-out.
●Solidify relations with customers.
●Increase delivery discounts.
●Improve market coverage.
●Free marketing people to create demand. Plus such cost reducing as reducing inventory levels and lowering freight and warehousing costs.

It is important that these objectives start with the customer, not with the end of the company's distribution facilities. This implies an understanding of where the customer buys, how much, how often, and what kind of service he expects for specific products in specific geographic markets.

Two considerations illustrate what the customer-oriented approach means. First, the consumer, not the company, pays for all costs incurred in moving goods to the customer. Consequently, any action which will reduce overall costs between plant and customer, regardless of whether they occur within the manufacturer's domain or at a later stage in the distribution channel, will enhance company profits and competitive position. For this reason the manufacturer should be vitally concerned about inventory levels and turnover at the wholesale and retail level. Slow moving stocks at these points represent a cost which must be absorbed by the consumers' dollar, leaving that much less for profits and dividends.

Second, what is the meaning of stock-out in a company branch warehouse if jobbers, who have come to expect stock-outs, carry two weeks stock?

The direct cost of a stock-out in terms of lost sales or a lost customer is probably low. But over the longer term, stock-outs cause the jobber to inflate his inventory; the increased cost of inventory to the jobber will affect his profit, then, in turn, his relationship with the manufacturer, and lead to pressure for greater discounts or other costly concessions.

Planning. For profitable distribution, planning must highlight the means and costs involved. It should be thought of in two stages: Determining cost performance parameters of present system; and determining cost/performance parameters of alternative systems.

The first stage is an essential prerequisite for the second. Only by using the existing system most effectively is there a meaningful basis of comparison and justification for additional investment and system changes.

The steps involved in carrying out these analyses should typically include:

1. Overall assessment of present operation:
   Demand pattern; frequency and size of orders, number of items per order.
   Variation in demand; deviations from forecast, trends, seasonality.
   Geographic distribution of demand.
   Service levels; by product group, customer class, geographic area.
   Important competitive aspects.
   Marketing objectives.
2. Identify current means and costs:
a. Transportation:
   Tonnages, by mode, between points.
   Costs, by mode, between points.
   Cost of f.o.b. policy.
b. Warehousing operations:
   Fluctuations in throughput.
   Incremental facility and equipment costs. Staffing requirements for various throughputs.
c. Inventory:
   Carrying costs.
   Service needs—by product group.
   Reordering and replenishment practices.
d. Communication system:
   Order processing procedures.
   Costs.
   Delays and time required.

Initially, distribution objectives are thought of as guidelines evolved jointly in discussions with marketing and manufacturing managers. The planning phase includes analyzing the costs of attaining these objectives in varying degrees and evaluating alternative policies.

Operations research techniques such as linear and dynamic programing have enabled management to develop the best distribution pattern under specified conditions. Using a computer to simulate operations under a wide range of operating conditions enables management to formulate policies and know in advance what the cost will be.

In other words, policies need no longer be arbitrary rules hopefully selected to guide the company towards maximum profits. Instead, policies can be tested before implementation so that management will know their economic implications.

For example, service and inventory levels are closely related and both have a marked effect on profitability. Higher inventories mean better service and, in turn, more sales. But, they also mean higher costs. Under these conditions how does management establish a realistic service policy? In the past, decisions have been arbitrary and frequently conflicting. Now, using the approach, shown in Figure 1, management can formulate policy rationally.

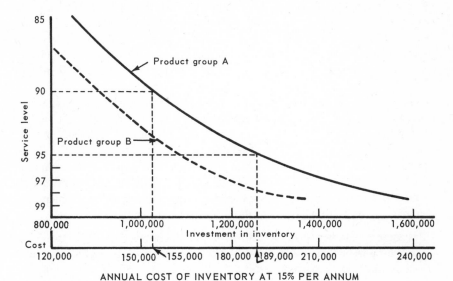

ANNUAL COST OF INVENTORY AT 15% PER ANNUM

Service and inventory levels are closely related and both affect profitability. Pre-testing by computer simulation enables management to determine the best policy without expensive trial-and-error.

Figure 1. Rational Policy-making—Service Level vs. Inventory Costs.

In this case, it is seen that the inventory level and cost to provide a service level of 90% for product group A is $1,034,000 and $155,000 respectively; while 95% will require inventories of $1,260,000. Thus management is faced with the question: Will an increase in service of 5% generate sufficient additional sales to offset the added inventory cost of $34,000? For another product a similar relationship but different values prevails.

Further simulation might show that if the error in the sales forecast could be reduced 30%, inventories could be reduced 15%. Also, if the lead time between issuing a replenishment order for more goods and receiving the goods were reduced by five days the same levels of inventory would support a service level of 95% instead of 90%.

As is now well known, though not so well used, these scientific methods enable management to make rational systematic decisions—so important if the distribution concept is to pay off.

This example should not imply that uniform policies will be applied to all products. Quite the contrary. By simulating the different demands for growth products and decaying products, management can rationally set high inventory levels for promising growth products and lower levels for decaying products, where lost sales are of less importance.

The second stage of planning is directed at longer-term system improvement. Using the model developed for current operating and policy decisions, management can establish factual economic answers to alternatives such as:

●What is the optimum number and location of distribution warehouses?

●What is the best number of plants and where should they be located?

●What is the best number and size of trucks, or railcars?

●What is the overall effect of better materials-handling methods which increase the capacity of existing warehouses, reduce unit costs of handling and storing goods, and reduce order cycle time by faster billing?

●What are the economic benefits of providing more timely information to operating managers? Reducing the replenishment lead time through the use of data-links and other high speed data transmission devices can materially reduce inventory levels for a given degree of service.

●What are the economic advantages of using public rather than company owned and operated warehouses? This alternative is frequently advantageous where throughput fluctuates, as in a seasonal commodity, or where shipments to customers can be consolidated with those of other users of the warehouse.

This second planning stage consists of developing a range of alternatives and subsequently evaluating each in terms of its effect on corporate profits.

Goal setting. An important result of the planning phase is the setting of balanced goals for all operating divisions within the distribution system. These goals should be so structured that they provide individual managers with the motivation necessary to harmonize their operations with the other system components.

For example, in one company, before the physical distribution study, a prime factor in evaluating the performance of the warehouse manager was the number of overtime hours worked. The manager soon realized this and took the obvious remedial action; he hired more men. Overtime declined, the warehouse operation apparently improved, but total costs increased.

A simulation study of the warehouse operation showed that there was a best-size crew for a given number and variation in orders. Above this number the cost of idle time more than offset the further reduction in overtime. Below this number overtime was excessive.

In another common situation, the manufacturing manager wanted long production runs. The distribution manager, in his efforts to reduce inventories, scheduled frequent changeovers. The result: Antagonism between manufacturing and distribution.

This problem was overcome by dividing responsibility for changeover costs. The manufacturing manager was held accountable only for the cost of changeovers compared with the standard cost. The distribution manager was accountable for the number of changeovers, compared with a standard number allowed for in planning.

Organization. A major reason for the slow acceptance of the physical distribution concept has been inter- and intra-company organizational barriers, and the related organizational goals. For example, although all company divisions are striving to increase profits, they place different interpretations on this objective:

●Traffic is judged on its ability to negotiate lower rates with carriers, even if this results in higher inventories.

●Production wants to minimize manufacturing costs. It can do so by scheduling long runs with few changeovers. Resulting excess inventories appear as a cost elsewhere.

●Purchasing wishes to minimize costs of materials, frequently causing excessive inventories and materials-handling costs.

●Sales desires the ultimate in service to customers, frequently demanding heavy inventories and small, expensive shipments to attain this goal.

These organizational problems must be overcome if physical distribution is to be managed effectively. Three alternative structures suggest themselves:

●A staff organization set up to study alternative systems, to initiate the necessary changes, to advise line management, and coordinate activities through effective goal setting.

●A line organization which has independent responsibility for the physical distribution functions embracing traffic, inventory management, production planning, warehousing, order processing, packaging, research, etc.

●A combination of the above, with separation of the operating and planning functions.

One type of organization development is shown in Figures 2 and 3. This is not intended in any way to be typical. It merely serves to illustrate how one large company approached the problem.

Prior to the change, three managers—purchasing, production planning, and distribution exercised authority over distribution. As frequently happens under such a structure, no one below the president was accountable for inventory levels, for service, or distribution costs.

Under the revised structure (Figure 3) the distribution manager has authority over and is accountable for all these functions. To insure that distribution is

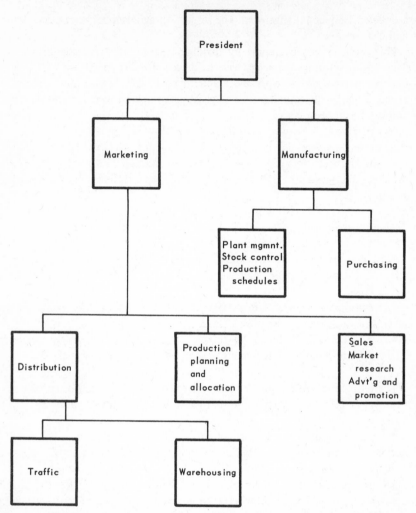

Figure 2. Organization Structure Before Recognition of Physical Distribution Function.

represented in major decisions, the distribution manager is at the same level as the managers of marketing and manufacturing.

Although no general rules can be laid down for developing the organization structure, the following questions will provide suitable guidelines:

●What planning and operating decisions are implied in the company's objectives?

●What information is necessary to make these decisions?

●Is this information available in meaningful form—accurately and promptly—to the person making the decision?

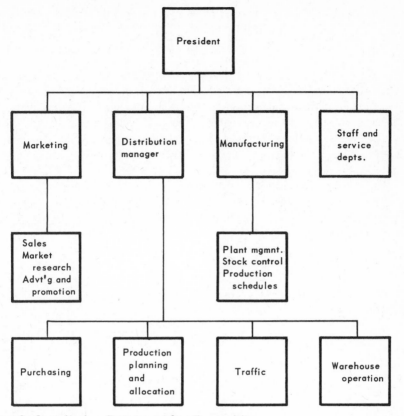

Figure 3. Organization Structure After Recognition.

●Can performance measures be developed which reflect the requirements of the position in relation to the objectives of the entire system?

Evaluation. Paralleling the organization structure must be a control system comparing performance with goals. This system is distinct from the communication system which triggers materials movement in response to demand at various points in the distribution system.

The control system must be designed to highlight emergencies and non-planned conditions calling for non-routine action. Typically it should report comparisons between:

●Actual service level and planned service levels for each product group in each geographic area.
●Actual errors in the demand forecast and the range of probable errors assumed in developing the system. Forecasts outside the range of acceptable accuracy indicate an "out of control" condition which will lead to excessive stockouts.

•Actual and planned costs in each leg of the system, including costs incurred in other sections of the organization as a result of decisions in the distribution function.

The elements of physical distribution management—transportation, inventory control, storage, packaging, and so on, are individually important, and do receive attention from management. But the essential principle of physical distribution management is to expand management's horizon and to encourage it to think of traffic, warehousing, inventories, and production planning as elements in a *system*, which only operates effectively when all elements are in tune with each other.

When the reader is called on to install standards in a warehouse, or set up an inventory control system, he should first ask—"Why do we have a warehouse, or stocks, at this location?" With such an approach, the physical distribution concept will pay off.

5

Physical Distribution, Military Logistics, and Marketing Management

EDWARD W. SMYKAY
Michigan State University

Among business costs perhaps the most neglected, until recently, has been that of physical distribution. The irony of this neglect is suggested by Table 1, which shows estimated physical distribution cost for the American economy in 1963.

Table 1. Estimated Cost of Physical Distribution—1963*

Cost Item	Total Dollars Billions of Dollars	Estimated Physical Distribution Cost Per Cent	Estimated Physical Distribution Cost Billions of Dollars
1. Transportation (freight only)	45	100	45
2. Packaging	20	50	10
3. Inventory	25	50	12.5
4. Handling	NA	–	–
5. Communications and order processing	NA	–	–
TOTALS			67.5

*Author's estimate.

Although man created distribution problems when he first developed crops in anticipation of future consumption, the birth of modern physical distribution management may be dated as recently as the start of World War II and the

51

advent of computer technology. Pertinent research, initially designed to fulfill military logistical requirements, quickly interested businessmen. Linear programming in solving problems with simultaneous multiple variables, and subsequently a repertoire of largely quantitative methods of the "operations research" type, evolved.

The development of model-building techniques especially concerned physical distribution management. Simulation permits a wide range of quantifiable considerations and operating circumstances involving production runs, inventories, transportation, etc. In effect, simulation provides the analytical techniques of an empirical science whereby optimum solutions are possible regardless of present operations.

However, budgetary constraints of military logisticians and of business administrators do not completely coincide. Whereas military budgets depend upon political appropriation, private-enterprise budgets are based upon markets and competition. Military budgets are implemented by sanctioned authority; private-enterprise budgets are founded upon sales revenue. Military logisticians may enjoy *ad hoc* budgetary increases; a businessman's budget is largely restricted by his satisfaction of customer requirements. Briefly stated, the success of military logistics is founded upon authoritarianism; the success of physical distribution in private enterprise depends upon market competition and customer good will.

Marketing Management and Physical Distribution

The marketing concept, a scientific expression of "the consumer is king," rose concurrently with modern computer technology, military logistics, and physical distribution management. Historically, so long as scarcity ruled the market, producers had been certain of satisfactory sales. But since the advent of a buyer's market, business that is primarily production-oriented has failed to maintain its relative position. Mainly because of the shift from an economy of relative scarcity to one of abundance, and because of an apparent absence of consumer loyalty, major emphasis in business concepts has moved from production to marketing.

The "four *p*'s" of marketing—*p*roduct, *p*rice, *p*romotion, and *p*hysical distribution—identify the major foundations of effective marketing practice. Application of the four *p*'s within the marketing concept implies tailoring and balancing to maximize impact in the market.

1. Product

Product design, founded upon customer satisfaction, leads to a widening of product lines through differentiation of consumer needs and wants. The Chevrolet Division of General Motors, for instance, may produce in one model year as many as 2,000,000 unique cars. The relationship of physical distribution to product design is associated with the impact of product differentiation on total distribution cost; consequently, an extensive widening of the line will increase distribution cost through excessive inventory requirements. Indeed a doubling of product line may more than double the inventory necessary to serve market demand. Historically, the era of "any color you want so long as it's black" reduced not only production costs but also distribution expense. In terms of product design, physical distribution principles can lead to achieving product diversity while maintaining inventories within manageable limits.

For example, magic numbers in the food business include 24 or 48 units of a product in a single-case lot. But the average retail grocery store moves 90 per cent of all items at the rate of one case or less per week. Thus the selection of case size influences product turnover. Combining several products in a single case, the quantities of which are adjusted to consumer-demand patterns, may substantially increase inventory turnover. Although not extremely common today, such practices apparently exist and are increasing.

2. Price

Pricing in today's market revolves around the continuing cost-price squeeze. And, factually, whereas virtually every important economic ratio shows an increasing trend, the level of business profit in the post war period has remained in splendid and virtually isolated stagnation. Following the 1948 postwar adjustments, after-tax profits of American business were about twenty billion dollars. Having hovered around that level since then, they stood in 1963 at 28 billion dollars. While prices increased somewhat, profit levels apparently could not be generally improved to keep pace with other economic sectors by means of across-the-board price increases.

Marketing management provides the framework within which a more sophisticated approach to selective pricing can improve profit positions and market shares. The extension of the price line to complement product line extensions is apparent in the automobile industry. In the past, pricing tended toward few classes in this industry. Today, however, many price options are available to meet market needs. Nowhere is the pressure toward more astute pricing more clearly evident than in the auto industry's response to foreign small-car competition.

Physical distribution relates to pricing on the cost side of the market equation. Through distribution cost reductions, greater variations in pricing are possible. Again in the auto industry, the tri-level car in the United States has permitted pricing adjustments through cost savings that measure in the hundreds of millions of dollars. If the average transport costs of a car were $300 before the tri-level car, and industry reports of 50 per cent reductions on transport cost are reasonably correct, then for Chevrolet alone these savings could be about $300,000,000. That large a saving permits quite substantial pricing variations without affecting profit adversely.

3. Promotion

As in the other three *p*'s, the marketing concept indicates use of precise tools to enhance maximum impact on tailored markets. In the din of advertising and promotion today, impact depends on selection and identification of markets, which then have specialized promotion and advertising programs aimed at them.

Physical distribution relates to timely promotion. In a national soap advertising campaign, sales may increase by 40 per cent above normal. Stocks must be strategically located in order to ensure product availability at the optimum moment during the campaign. Production runs must be carefully fitted to ensure logistical support to advertising expenditures.

Alternatively, promotion may be carefully timed in a sequence of markets. The advantage in this approach is its effect on leveling production runs with attendant economies. Again, careful scheduling of inventory locations and patterns must precede implementation of promotional plans.

4. Physical Distribution

The fourth and most recently introduced of the four *p*'s, physical distribution, provides the necessary support of markets by assuring the right quantity of goods placed at the right point at the right time. Thus, while marketing has its four *p*'s, physical distribution has its three *r*'s.

The two constraints of physical distribution are cost and service. Each of the three *r*'s contains these two elements. Thus, in terms of right quantity, service considerations dictate large supplies, but cost requires small quantities in the interest of reduced inventory costs. Right-point considerations, in terms of service, require numerous stock points located adjacent to customers. But cost constraints dictate reducing the number of points in the interest of reduced warehousing costs. Right time requires scheduling accomplished, for example, through the use of air freight. But transport costs dictate use of slower modes of transportation, such as rail and motor carrier.

Proper application of physical distribution principles, therefore, requires a constant balance between the needs of revenue-producing policies, as reflected in customer service requirements, and cost-reducing aspects which adversely affect service. In the interest of economic opportunities based on cost criteria, physical distribution points to larger shipment sizes, smaller inventory levels, and fewer stocking points. Service considerations point to smaller shipment sizes to fit customer orders, larger inventory levels, and many warehousing points.

Evidently the careful balancing of these diverse considerations depends on the particular marketing plan followed by a specific firm in a designated industry. Often two firms in the same industry follow what appear to be diametrically opposed physical distribution programs. While these differences may be partly explained by differences in managerial skills, it seems that the more dominant forces are marketing plans of the firms involved.

Market Analysis

In order to develop a sound physical distribution system, market analyses must be made. Of special interest to the physical distribution analyst are the geographic and product dimensions of the market. Present methods of reporting data satisfy the needs of political units outside the firm or management groups that have no special interest in a sophisticated geographic reporting system.

Accounting largely is centered in the production process and has few geographic considerations built into it. Selling, while broken down into territories, almost exclusively relates territorial considerations to sales balance by territories and salesmen. Production is the clearest nongeographically-oriented group.

Of additional interest to the physical distribution specialist is the measure of activity by product. It seems a natural law that a small percentage of a population accounts for a majority of a group by some selected criterion. The best known example of this phenomenon is that a relatively small percentage of the population accounts for a surprising large percentage of income produced. A small percentage of all the states accounts for a relatively large percentage of the population, and so on. The illustrations of this phenomenon apparently are endless.

Precisely the same phenomenon applies to economic activity by products. A rank array of sales volume by items universally shows that a small percentage of the items available for sales accounts for a large percentage of the revenues. This fact enables the physical distribution analyst to isolate much of his problem. For example, such a study may show that 20 per cent of the items account for 80 per cent of the sales volume. In that case, focusing attention on these items generally yields much higher rewards than indiscriminately planning an across-the-board attack. Invariably a firm which approaches its physical distribution problems from this perspective finds immediate and substantial rewards.

In the same way markets may also be arranged by size. This sorting provides useful information relative to such important problems as retail-store and distribution-center location.

Transportation

Transportation influences physical distribution decisions by its impact on transit stocks, transport costs, handling expense, and packaging cost.

Reduction in transit stocks via shorter transit periods may lead to rather surprising cost economy. For example, if average daily transit stocks are $1,000,000 and average transit time is ten days, then average transit inventories are $10,000,000. When one reduces transit time to five days via faster transportation, average transit stocks are only $5,000,000. This becomes a capital recovery item of $5,000,000 initially and also a permanent reduction in operating expense due to reduced inventory levels.

The major force which influences a decision in favor of shortened transit periods is value of the product. Generally the higher the unit value, the higher the inventory value and the greater its carrying cost.

Since reduced transit times are associated with higher transportation costs, the trade-offs involve changes in inventory levels against changes in transport expense. The value-of-service concept in transport pricing, therefore, is closely related to the effect of transit on inventory costs. Consequently much finer adjustments of transport rate determination are possible. Apparently this implies that for very low-valued products, transport costs dominate distribution decisions, whereas for very high-valued commodities, inventory considerations predominate.

The stages and incidental delays of handling affect a product's ultimate cost. Water transportation delay costs at terminal point may reach 50 per cent of the total transportation bill. Concerning motor carriers, the best estimate shows about 25 per cent of transport costs embedded in terminal-type operations. Recent studies have shown that reductions in handling cost and terminal expense affect demand for a specific form of transportation much more than does the actual rate.

A few recent examples demonstrate the point. Before the all-door boxcar was introduced, virtually no lumber moved by rail in the South. The main reason was that side-loading of boxcars virtually required loading by one stick at a time. Motor carriers, since they could be end-loaded, economized the handling expense of lumber. In fact, for this reason alone, rail rates had to show a 75 per cent advantage over motor carriers just to break even on shippers' total cost. Since lumber rates already rested at depressed levels, such rate reductions were impossible.

With the introduction of the all-door boxcar, handling costs dropped for rail shipments to such a degree that total costs favored rail over motor carrier. In fact, rail rates could have been raised somewhat with still an advantage to the shipper, based on his total cost. The important point here is that the transport purchase decision was made on the basis of handling-cost differential and not mere rate comparisons.

Packaging costs account for a surprising 20 billion dollars in the United States. While much packaging relates to marketing, advertising, and production, it also affects distribution decisions. Transport media have different characteristics which affect packaging requirements.

Just a few years ago it would have been safe to assert that protective packaging in transportation would show highest costs via rail shipment. This statement no longer contains its former validity. While rail shipments generally require more protective packaging than do other modes, as reflected by insurance rates, numerous exceptions must now be made. With the increase in damage-free cars, sliding sills, collapsible dunnage, etc., damage ratios for rail shipments have recently declined.

More sophisticated aspects of packaging relate to unitized loading. Loading 3,000 croquet sets by hand from a vehicle to a warehouse results in substantially greater costs than unloading the same quantity in 50 palletized and unitized loads. Package design engineers invest much time in package design to fit an integrated distribution and transportation system. As an example, choosing the least efficient package design in a palletized truck-rail movement can result in a 30 per cent loss of over-all efficiency in cube utilization. With transport rate structures increasingly moving to a cost-based system, such inefficiencies simply cannot be permitted.

Organization

Organization of the physical distribution function frequently requires a reassessment of present organizational charts. The diversity of elements affecting physical distribution creates difficulty in their proper managerial assignment.

Inventory control may fall to purchasing, manufacturing, or sales, each with equally valid grounds for such a structure. Transportation must be responsive to purchasing for inbound materials and sales for finished goods. Materials handling, like packaging, also crosses many functional lines.

In short, any attempt to consolidate all functions related to physical distribution requires such a broad definition of authority as to foreclose real potentials inherent in its application. The general organization pattern seems to follow the particular causal factors which demonstrate distribution requirements. This results in diverse organizational structures difficult to classify. In one company critical production processes require that distribution be subordinate to manufacturing. In another, high value of finished goods force a sales or marketing orientation. In a third, heavy transport expenses create a transportation orientation.

The organizational question clearly relates to the orientation of goals and objectives. Physical distribution management principles merely provide an outlook which permits more appropriate construction of corporate effort to reach predetermined goals. Of course, the most important of its influences requires orientation to the market place and, ultimately, the efficient satisfaction of consumer needs and wants.

6

Physical Distribution: Key to Improved Volume and Profits

WENDELL M. STEWART
A. T. Kearney & Company

Distribution is the sale and movement of goods to customers. The term "physical distribution" refers to that portion of the total distribution activity devoted to the addition of time and place utility to the form utility provided by manufacturing.

Physical distribution has been variously described as "The Economy's Dark Continent,"[1] and the last frontier of cost reduction in American business. "You can't cut prices, labor or material. The only fat left in this business is (physical) distribution."[2]

These typical comments highlight a condition which is receiving greatly increased management attention in today's highly competitive industrial marketing economy: the fact that improvements in distribution technology have not kept pace with improvements in manufacturing efficiency and marketing effectiveness.

What Is Physical Distribution?

In essence, physical distribution is the "science" of business logistics whereby the proper amount of the right kind of product is made available at the place where demand for it exists at the time it exists. Viewed in this light, physical

[1] Peter Drucker, "The Economy's Dark Continent," *Fortune*, Vol. 65 (April 1962), pp. 103, 265, 266, 268 and 270.
[2] John R. Staley, "Nineteen Ways to Save Time and Money in Distribution," *Business Management*, Vol. 26 (September 1964), pp. 43–46, 72, 74, and 76–78.

distribution is the key link between manufacturing and demand creation. As such, it has a profound effect on the success of both activities, and consequently on the basic profitability of the enterprise.

Physical distribution is a system of interrelated activity "cogs," all centered around the key "inventory management" cog. The individual cogs comprising a typical system are shown in Figure 1.

Responsibility for individual activity cogs has traditionally been allocated to various company departments—as shown in Figure 2—with the result that the final responsibility for integrating these activities into an economical flow of goods to customers has rested with the chief executive officer, or someone in a general management position.

The present trends toward unification of these activities under a single manager of distribution is nothing more than recognition of the need for specialized management of an increasingly important and costly corporate responsibility—that of developing satisfied customers.

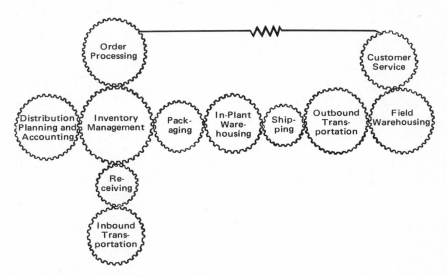

Figure 1. Activity "Cogs" in a Distribution System.

How Much Does Physical Distribution Cost?

In the United States the storage and movement of products from plants to markets is estimated to cost between $50 and $75 billion annually, with some estimates running as high as $100 billion when inventory carrying and order processing costs are included.

An analysis of physical distribution costs in various industries indicates that these costs range from a low of approximately 10% of sales in the machinery

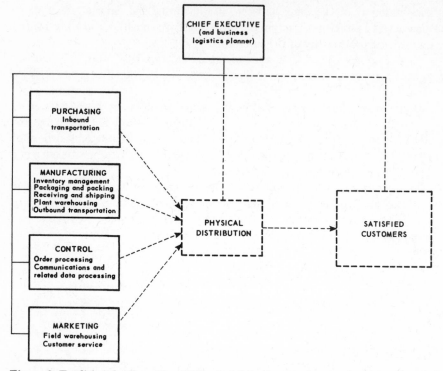

Figure 2. Traditional Allocation of Physical Distribution Functions.

Table 1. Physical Distribution Costs by Function*

Functional activity		% of sales
Administration		2.4
Transportation:		
Inbound	2.1	
Outbound	<u>4.3</u>	6.4
Receiving and shipping		1.7
Packaging		2.6
Warehousing:		
In-plant	2.1	
Field	<u>1.6</u>	3.7
Inventory carrying costs:		
Interest	2.2	
Taxes, insurance,		
obsolescence	<u>1.6</u>	3.8
Order processing		<u>1.2</u>
Total		<u>21.8%</u>

*Source: Same reference as footnote 4.

industry to a high of almost 30% in the food industry.[3] Another study shows that the all-industry average amounted to 21.8% of sales, spread between the individual distribution activities as shown in Table 1.

Attention on Physical Distribution

A number of other reasons appear to be behind the focusing of increased management attention on physical distribution.

1.   The Trend Toward a Short-order Economy

Inventory-carrying costs, which now amount to between 18 and 24% of the value of the goods, have stimulated managements in all kinds of businesses to improve their control over inventories. At the same time rapid advances in computer capabilities have facilitated this effort.

The result is a general trend toward the more frequent ordering of smaller quantities, with increased demands for customer service on each order, in order to improve inventory utilization. More frequent ordering by customers forces manufacturers to handle a greater number of orders to achieve the same volume of business.

More orders, each moving more rapidly through the distribution system, have caused many manufacturers to realize that their present systems cannot efficiently produce the levels of service now required of them.

2.   The Rapid Expansion in SKU's

In addition to more frequent ordering of smaller quantities, customers are demanding a continually increasing variety of models, styles, colors, packages, and price variations in the goods they buy.

This increase in product variation means more stock keeping units (SKU's) in inventory, with correspondingly less movement in each.[4] This condition tends to move geometrically in a multiple-warehouse situation to create obsolescence and stock availability problems, as well as imbalance in inventories.

3.   The Revolution in Marketing

Beginning with the discount house there has been a modern-day revolution in the marketing of consumer goods, which has carried over into the distribution of industrial goods. Pressure for lower prices has forced the development of new, more direct, and more efficient channels of distribution.

[3] Richard E. Snyder, "Physical Distribution Costs," *Distribution Age,* Vol. 62 (December 1963), pp. 35–42.

[4] A study in 1962 of industrial distribution costs and trends in the distribution practices of 270 American corporations, conducted by A. T. Kearney & Company for the American Trucking Associations, Inc., Washington, D. C.

This represents a major force behind the trend in many industries away from traditional methods of physical distribution. The need for individual companies to make a complete review of their distribution systems has never been greater.

4. Limits on Pricing Flexibility

Significant limitations now exist on basing-point and zone-pricing systems, and on delivery discount structures.

Price differentials and discounts must now be cost-justified more completely than ever before. This is forcing many companies to determine, perhaps for the first time, their actual distribution costs on individual product groups moving to individual markets and classes of trade, rather than to rely on broad national cost averages.

5. Physical Distribution As a Tool of Competitive Marketing Strategy

Competitive strategies were at one time centered largely around product features and prices. This list has now been expanded to include physical distribution. Many companies are creating strong competitive advantages for themselves by out-performing their competition on customer service and product availability.

Moreover, by helping to lower the customer's inbound freight, receiving, and inventory costs, an even stronger advantage can be gained. The realization that a highly responsive, reliable physical distribution system can facilitate marketing efforts and actually help to generate additional sales volume is spreading rapidly.

How Can Physical Distribution Generate Sales?

There are a number of ways in which a properly designed physical distribution system can help to generate additional sales volume. The following are some of the more obvious:

1. Minimize out-of-stock occurrences. By minimizing out-of-stock occurrences through more accurate inventory placement and control, sales lost due to being out of stock will be minimized. This has the double advantage of increasing both actual sales volume and the level of customer satisfaction.

2. Reduce customer inventory requirements. A responsive distribution system can mean shortened customer order cycles, and, consequently, reduced customer inventories. To the extent that one company can develop a more responsive distribution system than its competitors, it will be possible for customers of that company to obtain an economic advantage by doing business with it.

3. Solidify supplier-customer relationships. A soundly conceived distribution system can help to solidify and perpetuate a supplier's relationships with its customers. This can be accomplished through integration of the supplier's delivery facilities with customers' receiving facilities, consignment of stocks to customers, and other devices of a similar nature.

4. Increase delivery discounts. The development of more efficient physical distribution procedures frequently produces sufficient cost savings to enable the sharing of part of these savings with customers in the form of increased delivery discounts.

5. Enable expanded market coverage. More efficient distribution operations frequently permit a company to compete more profitably and more effectively in distant markets, or in markets that previously were marginal. In this way the company is enabled to expand its distribution, which leads in turn to increased sales volume.

6. Allow greater concentration on demand creation. The development of a well-organized physical distribution activity in which a separate administrative group is established to plan and operate the distribution system can free up marketing and sales personnel—to allow them to concentrate more attention on their basic responsibility, demand creation. In many companies this has led to an expansion in the number of sales offices and a decrease in the number of warehouses, with a consequent reduction in total distribution costs.

How Can Distribution Costs Be Reduced?

The development of a productive approach toward distribution cost reduction requires an understanding of:

1. The nature of the individual cost elements normally associated with distribution.

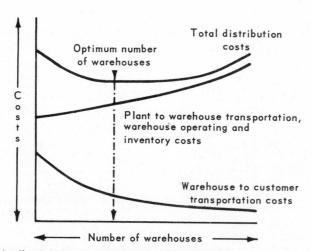

Figure 3. Distribution Costs vs. Number of Warehouses.

2. The manner in which these costs vary when changes occur—for example, in the number of warehouses or in the level of customer service to be produced by the system.

A knowledge of cost-variation characteristics provide a frame of reference within which a representative range of alternate distribution plans may be selected for evaluation for cost-reduction opportunities.

Figure 3 presents a simplified example of the manner in which transportation, warehousing, and inventory carrying costs vary as the number of warehouses is increased.

Note that the bottom line, representing warehouse-to-customer transportation costs, declines as the number of warehouses increases and the average distance from warehouse to customer is reduced. At the same time, however, plant-to-warehouse transportation costs, warehousing costs, and inventory costs, as shown by the middle line, go up as the number of warehouses increases.

The increase in plant-to-warehouse costs is due to the fact that smaller shipments to a greater number of points cost more than transporting the same volume in large shipments to a relatively few points.

Warehousing and inventory-carrying costs go up primarily because of duplications in overhead, and the reduced inventory utilization which results from the increased number of warehouse locations.

The important thing to note is that, up to a point, the cumulative effect of both cost lines is a reduction in the top or total cost line. However, as the larger cost elements continue to increase, a point is reached where they more than offset the diminishing warehouse-to-customer transportation costs, with the net result that total costs go up.

Directly below the low point on the total cost curve is the optimum number of warehouses at which total physical distribution costs are minimized.

Distribution costs must be identified in considerable detail in order to be of use in efforts to reduce costs. For example, transportation costs might be classified in terms of the activity for which they were incurred, such as:

Inbound from suppliers	Interwarehouse
Interplant	Plant to customer
Local cartage	Warehouse to customer
Plant to warehouse	Customer pickup allowances
Freight absorption	

These individual "building blocks" might then be further subdivided into:

- Fixed and variable costs
- The amount of each applicable to each origin-destination combination
- The amount of each applicable to each basic product group

Typical Opportunities for Cost Reduction

Once present distribution costs are known, it is possible to begin looking for improvements in the existing system. Savings in distribution can come from any one or more of the following typical opportunities for cost reduction:

1. Simplification of the system. Physical distribution is primarily the movement and storage of goods. Therefore, the more streamlined the system can be made, the lower will be its cost of operation. A good example of simplification would be the elimination of a field warehouse, supplying customers in the market direct from the plant. Result—one complete field-handling eliminated from the system.

2. Reduction in inventories. Frequently it is possible to reduce inventories by consolidating inventories at fewer locations, centralizing slow-moving items, or shortening the replenishment cycle for field warehouses. Reduced inventories not only cut down on carrying costs but free up capital for other uses in the business.

3. Improvements in packaging. All too often, packaging designers and even product designers fail to recognize the practical limitations placed on design by physical distribution. Smaller, more dense, uniform package sizes permit greater efficiency in transportation and warehousing.

4. More efficient methods and procedures. Not only is it important to eliminate cost through simplification of the distribution system, but it is also important to assure attainment of maximum efficiency from whatever system is being used. This refers to the selection and use of the most efficient:

- Materials-handling procedures and equipment
- Warehouse layout and space utilization
- Warehousing and shipping methods
- Order processing procedures
- Usage of alternate modes of transportation and types of transportation equipment

5. Use of technological innovations. In recent years an increasing number of technological improvements affecting the distribution area have been forthcoming. These include such developments as containerization, high-speed computers and communications equipment, air freight, new and more automatic materials-handling equipment, new types of trailer equipment suitable for both over-the-road and local delivery service, integral trains, motor carrier distribution tariffs, and so-called cube rates. Frequently it is possible to reduce distribution costs through the use of one or more of these innovations.

6. Revised channels of distribution. Of course, it is possible that the basic reason for high distribution costs may be found in the channels of distribution being used. Certain channels are inherently higher cost than others. Depending on the company's volume, its sales objectives and policies, and the nature of its markets, it may be possible to lower distribution costs appreciably by revising the channels of distribution being used—assuming that this can be accomplished without imparing marketing effectiveness. The marketing aspects of the problem are so closely related to the purely physical aspects as to be inseparable.

The mere fact that something has been done in a certain way for 10 or 15 years is all the more reason to give it a thoroughly objective look in an effort to find a better, less expensive way of doing it. Typical results of major cost reduction studies range from 3, 4, or 5% up to as much as 25%.

Procedure for Studying Physical Distribution Operations

Once management becomes aware of the need to improve distribution, a decision must be made as to how this can best be accomplished.

Experience would indicate that there is no substitute for a complete, balanced review of the entire distribution activity. Anything less than this will produce only limited cost reduction.

For example, it makes little sense to concentrate on improving the efficiency of a warehouse when economic or service justification for the warehouse itself is lacking. The complete review will take time; but it provides a background of basic understanding that cannot be obtained any other way. Such a review involves four steps:

Step 1—Developing proper perspective. In order to develop perspective, it is helpful to:

●Analyze present distribution patterns and demand requirements, by quantifying customer ordering habits such as the frequency and size of order, number of line items per order, the relative volume of demand by item and so on.

●Review the nature of demand, that is, the degree and duration of sales fluctuations, volume growth trends and product mix trends.

●Analyze the geographic concentration of sales and study the present concentration versus anticipated future concentrations.

●Review competitive distribution programs.

●Evaluate the company's distribution image with key customers.

●Determine the company's present customer service levels by:

—product group

—geographic area

—class of trade or channel of distribution

●Review marketing plans, policies, and objectives as these have a bearing on distribution operations.

●Develop a clear understanding of key distribution problems and their causes.

Step 2—Delineate present distribution methods, costs, and volumes. This is done for the purpose of establishing a basis of comparison for alternate plans. Information should be developed on the following where applicable:

a. With respect to *transportation* it is helpful to know:
- operating costs by mode, product group, and geographic location. These need to be stated in unit costs if linear programing is to be used to develop the optimum distribution plan.
- tonnage volume by mode, product group, and geographic location
- relative usage of various modes—rail versus truck versus forwarder, and the economic or service justification for each
- relative expense of owning or leasing a private fleet
- the cost of the company's f.o.b. policy

b. *Concerning warehousing, receiving, and shipping,* it is necessary to determine:
- operating costs, both in-plant and in the field, for all private and public warehousing done by the company
- facility and equipment costs—owned versus leased
- through-put volumes at each location, to determine relative efficiency
- manning requirements at each location
- methods and procedures, including possibilities for increased automation or more mechanical handling (short of full automation)
- utilization of present company-operated facilities
- clerical work volume, cost, and productivity
- economic service areas of existing locations

c. In connection with *inventory*, determine:
- average month-end unit levels
- turnover rates by location
- average value (investment)
- carrying costs

d. With respect to *order processing, communications* and *related data-processing activities,* determine:
- systems requirements and work load
- present costs
- capacity of present system (machine utilization)
- feasibility of practical alternatives
- need for compatibility with other company data processing procedures

e. With respect to *packaging,* look at:
- filling and container costs
- repackaging costs
- ICC packing requirements
- possibilities for standardization
- changing customer needs

In the process of reviewing present methods, costs, and productivity, it is quite possible that a number of short-range improvements can be found that can be put into effect almost immediately.

Step 3—Develop a representative range of alternative methods and plans.

Knowing present costs and customer distribution requirements, it is possible to begin developing a representative range of alternative distribution methods and plans.

Start by attempting to simplify the system. Since it costs money to handle the product, which handlings—if any— can be eleiminated? Is more direct shipment to customers possible? Can the present channels of distribution be simplified? What would happen if the present order cycle were shortened? Is it necessary to make all warehouses "full line"? Is it economically feasible to consign stocks to customers and let them handle warehousing? Can the use of premium transportation enable more-than-offsetting cost reductions in field-warehousing and inventories? Are fluctuations in demand gradual enough and sufficiently predictable to enable further centralization of inventory? Is the present distribution system keyed to handling the troublesome exceptions or the easy-to-handle, run-of-the-mill type orders?

Next, look at possibilities for utilizing the more recent technological innovations.

Can standard containers or specially designed bulk packs be used to unitize loads and thereby reduce piece handling? Can the product be stored and transported in such a way that it can be unloaded directly into the customer's processing operations—thus reducing packaging, handling, and delivery costs?

Opportunities should also be sought for improvements in packaging and product design, to permit better utilization of the available cubic capacity of warehouses and transportation equipment. Perhaps bulk packaging of certain items can save money.

Step 4—Evaluate alternatives and select the optimum plan.

Once alternative plans have been selected for evaluation, their operating and facility costs and the levels of customer service they are capable of producing need to be projected.

To accomplish this requires the development for each alternative of specific information about operating costs, transportation rates and schedules, and the subsequent simulation of the operation of each alternative under a representative range of operating conditions. From this it will be possible to select the best alternative and to prepare a practical plan of implementation.

Various mathematical techniques, such as linear and non-linear programing, are also available to facilitate the process of evaluation. The continuing use of mathematical models in distribution planning is a rapidly developing science.

A word of caution! Changes in distribution must be palatable to the company's customers. Changes which provide cost benefits only to the company without corresponding benefits to customers may be more difficult to implement than those that offer incentives to customers to accept the change.

7

Distribution Logistics: The Forgotten Marketing Tool

DONALD J. BOWERSOX
Michigan State University

Not so many years ago, a few lonely voices extolled the virtues of integrated physical distribution management. Today, physical distribution represents one vital new force in business management—a new force destined for greater attention during the coming decade of exacting competition and increased operating costs.

In a technical sense, physical distribution is defined as that management responsibility to *design* and *administer* system to control raw material and finished goods flow. In a practical sense, physical distribution is concerned with directing the desired assortment of products to the right place, in marketable conditions, in a manner timely to sales or processing requirements. Physical distribution then engages the management of product flow. In the livestock and meat industry such physical distribution flow originates with the initial transport of livestock and ends when a particular cut or assortment of meat is sold for consumption.

Between origin—livestock—and destination—final sale—a great deal happens in physical distribution that costs a great deal of money. If the meat industry is similar to most other industries—the products are handled, rehandled, and then handled some more—often times mishandled. They are tossed, hung, cut, stripped, boxed, stored, transported, retransported, then transported again and generally put to the most severe tests of endurance. Perhaps one of the greatest marvels of mass distribution is the fact that products do arrive at retail locations in saleable condition at prices buyers are able to afford. A marvel of greater magnitude is the way in which most firms go about the physical distribution management process. Responsibility for product flow is more often than not diffused and hidden among and between corporate departments without any central philosophy of operation, without any consistent statement of distribution policy. This diffusion of responsibility results in duplication, waste, and often to the wonderment of top management, out and out hindrance of anticipated operational results.

The Physical Distribution Concept simply states that all management functions related to product flow must be totally integrated as a single control system. Application of systems technology to physical flow is based upon some basic principles.

1. It is the performance of the total system which is singularly important.

2. Expenditures on individual activities such as packaging material handling, transportation, warehousing, and inventory control are of importance only as they relate to total cost and performance of the integrated system. This is widely known as the total cost concept.

3. There exists between individual activity centers a functional relationship which may stimulate or hinder integrated performance. This is known as system tradeoff.

4. Individual activity centers linked together as an integrated system can produce greater end results than attainable by a series of individual efforts. Such superior performance may be reflected in lower total physical distribution cost and/or improved customer service.

In summary, the Physical Distribution Concept advocates that it makes little difference if a firm spends more or less for any given activity—boxed primal cuts, for example—as long as integrated corporate objectives are accomplished at the lowest total cost.

Physical distribution costs a great deal. Depending upon industry and firm, total dollar expenditure may range between 5 and 50 per cent of gross sales. The total cost of physical distribution as a per cent of sales in the meat industry probably ranges from a low of 5 or 6 per cent in fresh meats to a high of near 20 per cent for some canned and processed meats. However, percentages are misleading since a small per cent cost on a heavy volume of production amounts to millions of dollars of total expenditure.

In the economy in general, many experts now estimate aggregate annual expenditure to be as great as $150 billion, or over 20 per cent of gross national product. When one considers that the most recent estimate of our National Inter-City Freight Expenditure is $62.6 billion, it is easy to see why physical distribution represents much more than transportation. It is of little wonder that physical distribution has been referred to as the last commerical frontier for cost reduction. The opportunities are great because so little has been done to date.

However, integrated physical distribution is much more than a way to cut costs. Perhaps, the greatest benefit to be gained is one of improved marketing support. Little of any importance occurs in a firm until a sale is made. Thus, physical distribution will always be a cost center and not a profit center. In many cases firms have selected to spend *more* dollars than previously spent to develop an exacting support system for marketing activities. It would appear to me that the meat industry—offering relatively standardized products, faced with shrinkage and processing of a perishable commodity—would find the marketing benefits of integrated physical distribution most tempting.

Similar to most basic concepts, the doctrines of physical distribution management as outlined here are relatively simple. In fact, development and implementation are often obscured by the realization that all activities grouped in physical distribution have always constituted a significant part and cost of business operations. It is a basic fact that all firms who survive have always needed to complete the physical distribution process. Many a skeptic has discarded the entire notion with the rationalization, "Change ain't always progress." Since the days of the Yankee peddler, managers have fully realized and accepted the adage, "You can't do business from an empty wagon." However, only the dynamic interfaces of global competition have clearly focused the real message this adage contains. The yardstick of *how* to replenish the wagon may well mean the difference between long-range survival or failure.

The newness of physical distribution is primarily one of management orientation. A fresh approach is needed for a traditional problem. The question is not one of should we do or not do the physical distribution task. Rather the question is how *effective* will the performance be in terms of total cost outlay, market penetration, and return on invested capital.

In the final analysis the job of implementing the Physical Distribution Concept is one of balancing and coordination. The balancing job is difficult because most business managers are trained, organized, and evaluated on the basis of traditional management functions. Under traditional concepts managers are motivated to independent action by the simple fact that they are allocated resources by independent budgets and they are measured by traditional accounting. A major top management reorientation is required to develop cross-departmental controls and performance measurement. Without top management awareness, the activities of a given department may be falsely condemned or praised without full measurement of total system impact. Without top management awareness and motivation little of a truly integrated effort will materialize.

Physical distribution creates a new requirement for interdepartmental compromise. Under traditional practice it would be a rare and broadminded manufacturing executive that could envision an increase in transportation expenditure (accountable to manufacturing) in order to decrease inventories (accountable to finance) and improve customer service (accountable to marketing). Not only would the benefits of resources allocated to manufacturing go to other departments, the actual dollar expenditures would be committed to transportation, a secondary effort of the manufacturing department. I repeat, without top management awareness and motivation, little of a truly integrated effort will materialize. Thus, the inevitable question arises: Is reorganization necessary to achieve benefits of integrated physical distribution?

In the early days, it was assumed that a firm must establish a so-called Distribution Department. Confusion stems from the fact that many firms have no formal department and still manage to do an excellent job. Others have Vice Presidents of Physical Distribution and do an inferior job. What seems to have happened somewhere along the line is confusion between organization structure and philosophy of operation. Regardless of planned organization, unless management at all executive levels recognizes the over-all potential of integrated physical distribution, not much will happen to improve the situation. Thus, philosophy of operation must exist or reorganization is premature.

Evidence seems persuasive that most firms will find it desirable in the future to establish a formal physical distribution organization. It also seems logical that such organizations will be centralized in scope and will rely heavily upon computers and high-speed data transmission to track multinational operations. In fact, the distribution department will probably emerge as one of the four main units of corporate organization aligned on an equal footing with marketing, manufacturing, and finance. It may well be that the future will see widespread development of a new corporate position known as the distribution controller. Similar to the financial controller, the distribution controller will become the corporate-wide coordinator for physical distribution systems.

Such dramatic changes are now taking place in an increasing number of firms. Each firm must appraise its own potential gain. However, in making such an appraisal, top management must fully appreciate the true value of a highly integrated physical distribution system. Unlike a price adjustment or an advertising campaign, physical distribution capabilities are not easily duplicated by competitors. Such capabilities represent a combination of men, facilities, and systems which become a proprietary asset of the firm. These capabilities pay off in the market place and are not readily duplicated by competitors.

Thus, it seems time for appraisal of current practices in this oldest area of commercial activity. Perhaps appraisal on the part of top management is already long overdue. It is common knowledge that analysts from the financial community now look to how aggressively firms have come to grips with traditional physical distribution practices as one measure of corporate vitality.

The following six questions provide some interesting departure points for initial self-appraisal. The answers should go a long way toward helping to determine the degree of ferment currently at work.

1. Has the question of physical distribution reorganization been a major subject of concern at a policy level?

2. Have steps been taken to develop total cost measurement of physical distribution flow?

3. Does a clearly stated policy concerning physical distribution performance exist?

4. Have any modifications in traditional methods of marketing or processing been proposed to achieve physical distribution economies or improved service?

5. Have members of your organization been active in continuing education as the techniques of integrated physical distribution have been maturing?

6. Does current planning for automated data processing extend to day-to-day operations and control of all facilities as an integrated network?

Once the concept of physical distribution is defined, then change is important as evidenced in the following quote:

> Experience teaches that men are so much governed by what they are accustomed to see and practice, that the simplest and most obvious improvements in the most ordinary occupations are adopted with hesitation, reluctance, and by slow graduations.

The speaker was Alexander Hamilton, the date was December 5, 1791. Unfortunately, implementation of integrated physical distribution systems does not represent an ordinary change, nor can aggressive firms afford themselves the luxury of adapting changing technology in slow graduations. Physical distribution will be around for a long time to come because it deals with the tangible aspects of business—material, time, and space. The degree to which a specific firm capitalizes upon this potential is limited only by desire, resourcefulness, and imagination. Alert management will prevent rather than solve their inevitable physical distribution problem of tomorrow.

8

Costing and Coordinating External and Internal Logistics Activities

JAMES L. HESKETT

Harvard University

A recent study of the 22-county area comprising the Metropolitan New York Region found that there were over 1,400 separate governments in the area.[1] Each had the capacity to raise and spend money and to provide services. Findings of the study implied that rather than aiding in the government of the area, many of these local governments actually hindered effective government for the area as a whole. The study group found that the external relationships between governments were much more vital to the long-run development of the area than the internal relationships within them. Coordination of the efforts of those governments with overlapping and somewhat artificial jurisdictions was suggested as a step toward more effective overall government for the area.

There is a strong lesson for business management in the findings of the New York study group. For what greater parallel to the governmental pattern exists than that of the loose federation of related firms engaged in making goods and distributing them from original producers to ultimate consumers? Each firm, acting in its own immediate best interests, may be impeding the efficient functioning of the entire process by which the goods in which it deals are created and distributed.

While perhaps giving lip service to the environment in which a firm operates, for years the individual firm has been implicitly regarded as the most appropriate business entity for purposes of problem definition and analysis. Although this may have been a good point of view with which to approach a firm's internal

---

[1] Raymond Vernon, *Metropolis 1958* (Cambridge: Harvard University Press, 1960), pp. 166–189.

operations, it is certainly not appropriate for the analysis and administration of the distribution process, particularly that portion of it that involves logistics. The nature of logistics does and will require that all firms interrelated in a channel of distribution be regarded as a superorganization greatly in need of decision coordination and control.

Essential to the functioning of the superorganization in a channel of distribution is the supplier of equipment, supplies, and services to the channel. For the latter, represented in large measure by transportation carriers, the concept of the superorganization has fundamental importance. The overall point of view with which operating problems, including those of logistics, will have to be viewed for ultimate advances is illustrated by Figure 1. Several important points in this illustration that are worth noting and keeping in mind throughout this discussion are:

1. There is a much greater number of external management relationships, shown as dotted lines, than internal relationships, pictured by means of solid lines.

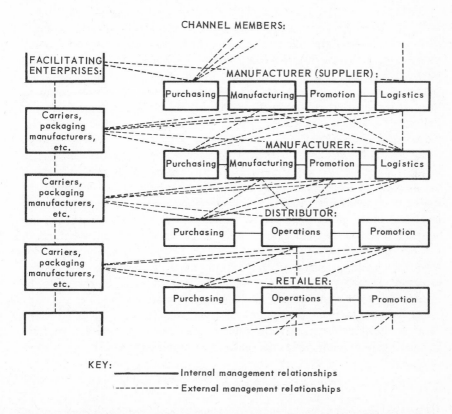

Figure 1. Organization Relationships in a Portion of a Channel of Distribution.

2. The necessity often arises for one producing or distributing firm's organization to work through another in dealing with a third.

3. In contrast to the second point, suppliers, carriers, and other facilitating organizations largely have direct relationships with all firms in a channel of distribution.

If the channel of distribution shown in Figure 1 was multiplied by tens of thousands, the managerial anatomy of our distribution system would be reasonably represented. Within the context of the anatomy, this presentation proposes to: (1) Define internal and external management, particularly for logistics; (2) point out the possibilities for either real or illusory logistics cost savings in channels of distribution; and (3) enumerate the possible opportunities for, and responsibilities of, transportation firms in an environment characterized by this point of view.

Internal and External Logistics Management

The terms internal and external logistics management can be defined in both a positive and negative manner. Internal logistics management deals with problems in which a single organization or business entity has complete control over a problem—for example, the shipment, receipt, and carriage of a material being physically relocated from a company-owned plant to a company-owned warehouse in company-owned and operated transportation equipment. External logistics management is concerned with problems outside the direct control of individuals in a single organization, problems requiring the coordinated efforts of individuals in several firms.

Notice that the difference between internal and external logistics management lies in the *degree of control* over a situation which can be exercised by the management of a single firm involved in a given problem. It does not lie in the *nature* of the activities managed. Transportation, warehousing and materials handling, order processing, inventory control, and supply scheduling are activities that might be managed either in an internal or external context. Further, the difference between these managerial contexts has nothing to do with the techniques employed to overcome respective problems in each. For example, the well-worn technique, total cost analysis, could be applied to the investigation of both internal and external logistics problems.

Clearly, external management problems predominate in our economy today. There are no firms sufficiently integrated in their operations that they need not become involved in externally oriented logistics problems.

The Emergence of Dominant Firms

There is growing recognition of the fact that our competitive system is made up not so much of competing firms but of competing groups of firms organized by channels. Thus, producers, processors, wholesalers, retailers, and suppliers of equipment and services such as freight carriage are deeply involved in assuring the successful distribution of one soapflake brand as opposed to another. Producers, who probably have the greatest stake in the successful distribution of most products, are coming to realize that diseconomies or disruptions of operations at any stage in a distribution channel can affect the total landed cost of the product for the ultimate consumer and the dependability with which that product is made available to him. It is but a short step from landed cost to price, and cost-price relationships influence the volume of sales and the profit or loss for every firm involved in the distribution process.

It is little wonder that dominant firms, called "channel captains" by some, have arisen in channels of distribution. Dominant firms invariably are deeply concerned with the successful distribution of one or more products. Whatever their major role in a distribution channel, they are characterized by the willingness to take more than their share of the responsibility for the success of the overall manufacturing and distribution process. How many shipper-customers are you familiar with, for example, that assume responsibility for freight claims arising out of their dealings with both suppliers and customers whether or not they are legally bound to do so by the terms of purchase and sale under which they do business? It is in the overall best interest of the dominant firm, because by helping suppliers and customers with problems they are less able to cope with, it often increases its volume and profit. Whether the issue at stake involves a supplier and the dominant firm, a customer and the dominant firm, or even two institutions neither of which is a dominant firm in the channel, the dominant firm is concerned. This being the case, it is easy to see that most of the problems confronting a dominant firm's logistics organization are external in nature. Out of the solutions to these problems there is a much greater tendency for firms to settle for illusory rather than real cost savings.

Real and Illusory Cost Savings

The total costs of a number of enterprises involved in the manufacture and distribution of a product will determine the ability of that product to compete in the marketplace. Competition between channels of distribution rather than between individual firms best describes the competitive situation in the creation and distribution of goods in our economy today. This being the case, it is important that the real nature of changes in costs resulting from a logistics system adjustment be determined. A hypothetical and greatly simplified example will serve to illustrate this point.

An Example Situation

A manufacturer of livestock feeds offers distributors a one per cent seasonal discount on feed purchased and shipped in July and August rather than

September and October. An additional element of the proposal is seasonal dating in the billing; that is, the orders are shipped two months earlier than in previous years but are billed at the same date as before, September 30 or October 31, respectively. This is a rather common "package" of trade terms.

From Figure 2 it can be seen that the value of a 100-pound bag of feed in the manufacturer's warehouse is $4.00, based on raw material, manufacturing, and internal handling costs. The regular price of each bag of feed to a distributor-customer is $5.00, less one per cent, delivered to his door and including a 40¢ transportation charge to the manufacturer. Because of relative efficiencies of warehousing practices and facility sizes, the manufacturer's cost to carry inventory approximates 10 per cent of the average annual inventory whereas the distributor's cost amounts to 15 per cent. These inventory carrying costs do not include cost of capital; it does not apply here because of the unchanged billing and payment dates. Further, the example assumes that the distributor will not necessarily sell more feed sooner by having the product in his hands two months earlier than would otherwise be the case.

The results of this proposed change in trade terms are rather definite, based upon the most important costs of both manufacturer and distributor undergoing change, shown in Figure 2. From the standpoint of the manufacturer only, his inventory carrying charges resulting from insurance, warehousing expenses, taxes, and damage or obsolescence would be reduced by more than the cost to him of the one per cent price discount or the cost of capital invested in a transportation bill which could not be recovered until the regular billing date of October 31. If this manufacturer performed a so-called total cost logistics analysis of the impact of the proposed price discount on his company's operations only, he would probably conclude that it would be beneficial, resulting in a net saving of 1¢ per bag of feed. This type of total cost analysis typifies those performed in perhaps the majority of industrial and commercial logistics organizations today.

In terms of the channel of distribution as a whole, however, it is quite clear that the saving described above would be illusory, not real. For the distributor taking advantage of the seasonal discount and dating arrangement would incur more inventory carrying charges than he would save in discounts. One might ask why any distributor would take advantage of this offer. He would, and many do today, because of a lack of knowledge of his inventory carrying charges as opposed to the readily apparent fact of the price discount.

If the total cost analysis performed by our manufacturer's logistics department were more extensive, it would take into account external costs arising from distributors' increased inventory carrying activities as well as costs internal to the organization. An analysis of this type would provide the basis for several alternative courses of action:

1. The one per cent discount could be offered in hopes that the customer-distributor would not recognize the penalties incurred in taking advantage of it.

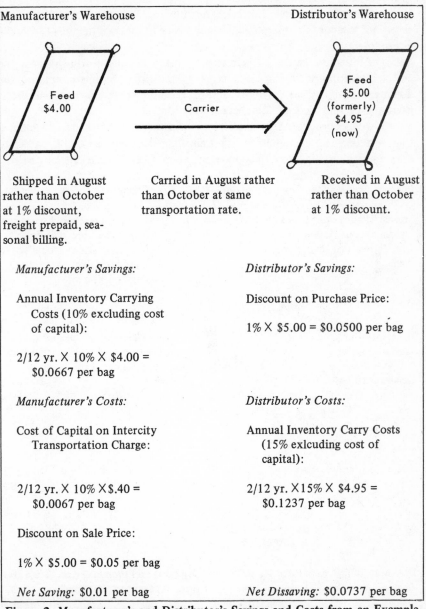

Figure 2. **Manufacturer's and Distributor's Savings and Costs from an Example of Seasonal Pricing and Billing of Goods to Update Shipment.**

It should be pointed out that this is not an uncommon result of such analyses today. Penalties to the channel have been overlooked by an executive in a dominant firm where a given action would improve the cost performance of his firm's logistics organization at the expense of another's. From the standpoint of the customer-distributor in this case, the visible gains in the form of a one per cent price discount are more tangible and easier to measure than the less visible diseconomies.

2. The discount could be increased to make it truly worthwhile for the customer-distributor to take advantage of the offer. In this alternative the dominant firm would have to absorb penalties both to its own profit performance and that of the channel as a whole.

3. The discount could be increased and some attempt made to obtain a transportation rate reduction to offset apparent diseconomies to the parties to the transaction. This course of action is very familiar to the carrier executive.

Illusory Channel Cost Savings per Bag		*Real Channel Cost Savings per Bag*	
Terms: 1% discount to distributor with seasonal billing; no transportation cost saving or rate change.		Terms: 3% discount to distributor with seasonal billing; 10¢ per bag transportation rate reduction and attendant saving for seasonal movement.	
Manufacturer's Savings (and Costs):			
Inventory Carrying Costs	$ 0.0667	Inventory Carrying Costs	$ 0.0667
Cost of Capital on		Transportation	0.1000
Transportation	(0.0067)	Cost of Capital on	
Discount to Distributor	(0.0500)	Transportation	(0.0050)
	$ 0.0100	Discount to Distributor	(0.1500)
Net			$ 0.0117
Carrier's Savings (and Costs):			
Not Considered, if Any		Operating Savings	$ 0.1100
		Rate Reduction	(0.1000)
Net			$ 0.0100
Distributor's Savings (and Costs):			
Discount on Purchase Price	$ 0.0500	Discount on Purchase Price	$ 0.1500
Annual Inventory Carrying		Annual Inventory Carrying	
Costs	(0.1237)	Costs	(0.1213)
Net	(0.0737)		$ 0.0287
Total for Channel	($0.0637)		$ 0.0504

Figure 3. A Comparison of Alternative Situations Resulting in Real and Illusory Channel Cost Savings for the Example Shown in Figure 2

Implications for the Carrier

The total cost analysis is still not complete. The third major party to this external sales-logistics problem has not been mentioned. What of the carrier? No information has been presented regarding the benefits and cost to this party.

Under current carrier pricing practices, there would be no difference in the revenue received for the shipment of a bag of feed in August as opposed to October. However, there could be a sizeable difference in costs associated with the movement if August represented a slack business period and October a peak business period for the carrier in question. If the cost saving to the carrier caused by advanced shipments would amount to more than $0.0637 per bag, then the proposed action would represent a real saving to the channel as a whole. Of course, this assumes that in the long run, cost savings would be reflected both in carrier rates and product prices. Unless this would be the case, incentives necessary to influence managerial behavior in external management situations would be drained off in the form of abnormal profits to one or more parties to the logistics operation, thereby discouraging implementation of the system offering the potential for real savings.

If carrier cost savings of more than $0.0637 would result from the proposed action, a strong argument could be made for a seasonal carrier price reduction (disregarding current-day regulatory restrictions). For in the broadest view of the channel as a whole, transportation savings would have to more than offset dissavings resulting from the transfer of goods from a more efficient to a less efficient storage location if real economies were to result from the proposed action.

This is illustrated in Figure 3. Here it is seen that economic incentives must be present for every party to a logistics system change in addition to all parties as a whole. A 3 per cent discount to the distributor accompanied by a carrier rate reduction of 10¢ per bag would not only result in real economies for the channel of distribution, but would also provide the necessary incentives to all parties to implement the system change. Where carrier costs could be reduced by more than 10¢ per bag by such action, overall carrier volume would be maintained or increased with greater profit.

Current Shortcomings of External Logistics Management

Although there is a tendency for the dominant firm in a channel to assume responsibility for day-to-day activities of freight claim processing and settlement, carrier negotiation, and preparation of necessary documentation, this attitude and practice has not extended over into the analysis and implementation of external logistics systems to any degree. There are several possible reasons for this:

1. Information is harder to gather from organizations that are not captive to a dominant firm.

2. An analyst in a dominant firm's logistics organization may not wish to risk the charge of interference in another firm's operation, particularly since we have seen that the success of a channel of distribution depends in large degree on the ability to instill and maintain a cooperative spirit among all firms in a channel.

3. Coordination of logistics activities, even after an analysis is accomplished, is difficult to achieve.

It should be noticed that legal constraints have not been mentioned as a major deterrent to such analyses. Remember, the topic concerns cooperation and coordination between noncompeting firms.

The Role of the Carrier in Helping Overcome these Shortcomings

There are two major ways of overcoming the barriers described above. One is to vertically integrate the operations of a channel to the extent that they largely become internal to the management of a single firm. Another is to employ the services of a third party in accomplishing necessary analyses and implementation of logistics systems. This third party should not only be objective in such analyses, but should also have a vested interest in the success of the operation of the channel as a whole. The carrier is the most predominant and pervasive third party in most external logistics situations. Because vertical integration is a rather drastic and not always satisfactory solution to the problems described here, it is reasonable to assume that a growing number of major firms assuming the roles of dominant firms in their respective distribution channels will turn to carriers or other facilitating enterprises for assistance in dealing with these problems. Such assistance will take three forms: (1) study initiation; (2) information collection; and (3) implementation of results.

Study Initiation. Day-to-day contact with channel logistics problems often offers an opportunity for the carrier to detect correctable flaws or potential problems earlier than other parties to logistics problems. There is a growing number of instances in which carrier marketing organizations, especially those embattled in the competitive milieu of the eastern part of the country, have done just this.

Information Gathering. The relationship maintained by the carrier with all firms in many different channels provides a good vehicle for information gathering. From Figure 1 it is apparent that the dominant firm's logistics management deals largely with suppliers and customers. Even this relationship is likely to be indirect, carried on through purchasing agents, expediters, or sales representatives. As is usually the case, these means of gathering information are limited to the liaison's ability, willingness, and interest in dealing with a subject area secondary to his major mission. Where logistics management representatives attempt to collect information for total cost channel analyses direct from various institutions in the channel, they often encounter guarded cooperation at best and downright refusal at worst from their counterparts in other firms.

To a limited extent carriers have involved themselves in information gathering, especially railroad and airline organizations. This service becomes particularly important, however, when the relationship of the dominant firm and the system under consideration is broad in scope. This will be typical of the freight unitization schemes of the future which will attempt new ways of moving freight in large and small units of volume between channel institutions of various sizes by methods compatible with the materials handling systems of most or all participating firms. The forerunner to this problem is that involving the compatibility of pallet systems for freight shippers, carriers, receivers, or even receivers from receivers.

Implementation of Results. System control requires follow-up and a constant feed-back of operating results. Adjustments in original plans often result from control efforts. Once again, perhaps the greatest potential source of information feed-back to the dominant firm in charge, so to speak, of a system change is the carrier organization. This is particularly true for those information-supplying firms in a channel who are not contacted directly by members of the dominant firm's organization during the normal course of business.

The degree to which a carrier can initiate studies, gather information, and implement study results depends on a number of factors other than the capability of the carrier itself. The end objective must be realistic and selfish, not altruistic. However, in many types of situations the two attitudes may not be in conflict. What is good for a channel ought to be good for all firms associated with the channel in the long run. Further, because the dominant firm often controls the largest volume of freight shipments either directly or indirectly, the question of divided customer loyalties may be solved for the carrier in favor of the dominant firm.

A carrier intermediary will have to be prudent in applying the attitudes expressed in this paper. A number of shipper-customers are not ready for them; some never will be. Attitudes or points of view change slowly. The trend discussed here will be slow. However, short- and long-run competitive pressures make it inevitable.

Summary

In summary, external management problems will continue to make up the fabric of the American economy. Because of the difficulty of coordinating the actions of independently operated enterprises, the tendency is to shy away from external problems, perhaps even more so in management theory than in managerial practice. But the very success of one channel of distribution as opposed to another depends largely on the manner in which external management problems, many of them involving matters of logistics, are detected and solved. If channel logistics system changes are based on illusory rather than real total cost savings, not only competitive disadvantages but long-run disorder will result in the distribution of the goods involved.

It is axiomatic that the success of individual carriers and methods of transportation depends on the relative performance of competing goods and channels of distribution. With this in mind, it is little wonder that carriers of the future will find themselves involved in even more complex management problems than they have in the past. Opportunities for creative carrier planning and action will abound; penalties for the absence of such planning and action may be severe.

9

Channel Control and Inter-organization Management

LOUIS W. STERN
Ohio State University

Definition of Channel Control

Channel control is used here to signify the ability of one member of a marketing channel for a given product (or brand) to stipulate marketing policies to other channel members. For example, in a simple channel where a buyer interacts directly with a seller, the party gaining control in the bargaining process either through the use of sheer economic power, political or legal means, superior knowledge, more subtle promotional aids or other methods, obtains a major advantage in all aspects of their relationship. When marketing policies may be stipulated by any one party, this may have a marked influence on the efficiencies of both. Their goals may not be totally compatible; therefore, by complying with the dictates of buyers, for example, sellers may frequently be forced to alter their methods of operation in a manner that is not often profitable for them.

The exercise of channel control can, of course, vary widely. At one extreme are situations of channel tyranny in which one channel member insists on compliance to policies and practices from other members that he believes are in his best interests but which may not be in theirs. At the other extreme are situations of benevolent channel leadership in which the most powerful member is able to manage the channel so that over-all channel performance can be increased.[1] In the former case, the application of current management theories

[1] Bruce Mallen describes various channel relationships as approaching either autocracy, democracy, or anarchy in "Conflict and Cooperation in Marketing Channels," *Reflections on Progress in Marketing,* L. George Smith, editor (Chicago: American Marketing Association, 1965), pp. 65–85.

85

and tools to intra-firm problems often fosters narrow, self-oriented goal definitions and may result in decisions which impair the performance of other firms within the channel, thereby diminishing the performance of the entire system.[2] In the latter case, benevolence may be identified with enlightened long-run considerations on the part of the most powerful channel member.

Two Examples of Channel Control

Buyers or sellers rarely achieve complete control over the marketing activities of their channel opposites. One group or member may, however, exercise the balance of channel power. This latter factor provides the means by which the "victors" in the vertical conflict are able to stipulate marketing policies to the vanquished. It is also likely that the extent of control achieved by a channel member may vary with the type of vertical conflict involved. For example, the seller may establish the price discount schedule for various quantities, but the buyer still determines (within the constraints of the seller's policy) the quantity actually purchased, which may or may not be the most profitable from the standpoint of the seller. In addition, there may also be an ephemeral quality to channel control. The following two examples serve to illustrate the emergence and/or existence of control at opposite ends of the channel of distribution.

Example 1: The Automobile Industry

Concerning the distribution of automobiles. Ridgeway has made the following observations: (1) An automobile manufacturer is in a strategic position to try to bring order and uniformity to the marketing channel for his products, because he occupies a centralized position within it. (2) "Manufacturers seek to control the activities and operation of the dealers individually and collectively." (The term "control" refers to "the ability of the manufacturer to have the dealer operate for the benefit of the system." (3) The manufacturer with his suppliers and/or dealers comprise a system and "this system is in competition with similar systems in the economy. In order for the system to operate effectively as an integrated whole, there must be some administration of the system as a whole, not merely administration of the separate organizations within that system."[3]

If, as Ridgeway appears to suggest, the marketing channels for automobiles can be "controlled" by manufacturers so that the final result of their inter-organizational management is desirable from the standpoint of all parties involved, then such a situation would approximate that of benevolent channel

---

[2]For a further discussion of similar reasoning, see Thomas L. Berg, "Designing the Distribution System," *The Social Responsibilities of Marketing,* William D. Stevens, editor (Chicago: American Marketing Association, 1962), pp. 481–490.

[3]Valentine P. Ridgeway, "Administration of Manufacturer-Dealer Systems," *Explorations in Retailing,* (Stanley C. Hollander, editor), Bureau of Business and Economic Research, Michigan State University, 1959, pp. 250 and 256.

leadership. There is, unfortunately, no tangible evidence that this optimum situation has been reached. In fact, there is some historical evidence that indicates that automobile manufacturers have exercised despotic control within the channel to achieve their short-run objectives.

In the years immediately following World War II, dealers were able to increase sales yearly. During this period, manufacturers became intensely interested in achieving even higher rates of growth than the dealers were supplying. As a result, dealers were placed under tight franchise agreements and were assigned sales quotas that were designed to permit the manufacturers to realize maximum operating economies as well as to increase their over-all growth rates. Dealers were forced to pay for shipments on delivery and then were expected to sell all the cars shipped by the plants. Dealers were also held to pricing and servicing standards set by the factory and were assessed part of the national advertising costs. If a dealer disagreed with these policy stipulations, he was disenfranchised. The manufacturers maintained this form of control until the middle 1950's, when the market for new automobiles slumped drastically. At that time, the dealers found it impossible to sell all of the automobiles being shipped and began to revolt against the inequities imposed by the manufacturers.[4]

It is not certain whether or not the remedial measures taken by the manufacturers as a result of the "revolt" have eradicated the form of control existing during the decade after World War II. Ridgeway's conclusions cited previously apparently refer to an idealized situation that would, no doubt, be satisfactory to all channel members. It is unlikely, however, that the form of control has changed so radically in the past ten years to bring the industry full circle from channel tyranny to benevolent channel leadership.

Example 2: The Wood Household Furniture Industry[5]

The wood household furniture industry (including both manufacturers and retailers in the term "industry") is bilaterally competitive. In other words, the industry is characterized by low degrees of market concentration on both the manufacturing and retailing levels in the channel of distribution. Channel control in the hands of either retailers or manufacturers should be non-existent or, at best, weak, because according to economic theory, the operation of open market forces should dictate the basic modes of doing business and thus should militate against the establishment of control in any one level of the channel. But control does, in actuality, exist in the wood household furniture industry; it resides at the retail level because furniture retailers have gained the greatest influence over the final sale of the products of the industry.

[4]The dealer revolt was well publicized. A description of it can be found in the following issues of *Business Week:* February 4, 1956 (p. 29); March 3, 1956 (p. 104); March 23, 1957 (p. 65); February 2, 1957 (p. 25); and April 6, 1957 (p. 173).

[5]A more detailed description of channel control in this industry is found in an unpublished manuscript by the author entitled, "Bilateral Competition and Channel Control."

The fact of this control is illustrated in retailers' buying methods. Many of the manufacturers' marketing practices have been stipulated by, administrated by, and/or enacted to placate furniture retailers, even though some of these policies and practices work to the detriment of manufacturers. For example, the furniture market system, under which manufacturers' exhibits are held periodically in major manufacturing and retailing centers, provides buyers with the opportunity to play off one manufacturer against another in the space of a few minutes within the same building. Manufacturers do complete a considerable volume of sales during the markets, but they have continually deplored their adverse bargaining positions and have sought ways to eliminate the markets for this and other reasons. Buyer insistence, however, has been a causal factor in influencing the manufacturers' policies with regard to market attendance and continuation.

Other examples of retail buying methods that often work to the disadvantage of manufacturers are (1) the emphasis on sold-order buying whereby retailers carry minimum inventories, thereby forcing manufacturers to maintain large inventories and to ship in uneconomical lot sizes, (2) demands for exclusives, and (3) the desire for cumulative (as opposed to non-cumulative) quantity discounts. In addition, furniture retailers look askance at and have effectively forestalled manufacturers' attempts to establish strong brand identity, especially where manufacturers may have wide distribution in the retailers' particular locales. The reason for this is that retailers know that consumers will shop for furniture and, if brand identity is established, will compare price from store to store on the same advertised pieces. The retailers also fear that if consumers become highly confident in their choices prior to entering a store, a furniture salesman's selling latitude will be limited. "Switching" by sales personnel from low margin to high margin items within the store is a jealously guarded and accepted retail practice.

In sum, the retailers' buying methods mentioned above indicate that, in the wood household furniture industry, retailers appear to have gained control over the channel in the sense that they have been able to stipulate many of the important marketing policies within the channel.[6]

Contributions of Economic Theory

In cases of vertical conflict, the locus of channel control is frequently related to the types of markets in which both sellers and buyers compete. In an excellent discussion, Heflebower has described the bargaining relationships between supplying and distributing industries when these industries compete in

[6] Preliminary investigations indicate that situations of channel control may be found within specific segments of the food industry. For documented examples of channel control in a variety of industries, see Valentine P. Ridgeway, *op. cit.; The Policies of Distribution* (Cambridge, Mass.: Harvard University Press, 1955); Ralph Cassady, Jr. and Wylie L. Jones, *The Changing Competitive Structure in the Wholesale Grocery Trade* (Berkeley and Los Angeles: University of California Press, 1949); and Bruce Mallen, *op. cit.*

markets characterized as oligopolistic and competitive.[6] Despite some of Heflebower's negative conclusions regarding the appropriateness of bilateral oligopoly theory for explaining the emergence of channel power among mass distributors, it is possible to attempt to make some modifications of his findings in order to show their applicability to the concept of channel control.[7]

Buyers or sellers operating in oligopolistic markets can frequently gain channel control when dealing with sellers or buyers operating in more competitive markets. One theoretical reason to explain the emergence of channel control in these situations is that oligopolists have, to some extent, stabilized competition among themselves. They interact under the constraints of a rather well-defined oligopolistic rationale while actors in a theoretically more competitive environment cannot rely on such a rationale to maintain some semblance of market stability. The latter have, almost by definition, less information about competitors' current and possible market activities and less available expertise. There is, therefore, little uniformity of action among competitors, and even if there were an opportunity for more competitive commonality, deviants would always be willing and ready to spoil the tranquility of the market. Another theoretical reason, among others, that might explain the emergence of channel control is the ability of oligopolists to utilize relatively large profits, gained through joint maximization, in developing strong consumer loyalties to their products or brands.

In addition, the theory of countervailing power can be extended to a theory of reaction to control. When a group of sellers, for example, "enjoys a measure of monopoly power and is reaping a measure of monopoly return as a result," and when that power can be exploited by large buyers,[9] the process of such exploitation is a factor signifying a shift in control. For example, through an increased emphasis on private labels, retailers have found an opportunity to share the gains of manufacturers' market and channel power, especially with regard to physically undifferentiated (or highly similar) items within a given product category. Retailers have used private labels as impressive bargaining levers in their negotiations with manufacturers. The implied threat by retailers to "push" their private labels at the expense of manufacturers' brands through the manipulation of shelf space, prices, and promotion has created the need for new and more retailer-oriented (oftentimes stipulated) marketing policies on the part of manufacturers in order to forestall possible disastrous consequences for their own brands. In many cases, manufacturers have been too slow in developing these policies, and retailers have, therefore, placed even more emphasis on

[7] See Richard B. Heflebower "Mass Distribution: A Phase of Bilateral Oligopoly or of Competition?" *Explorations in Retailing, op. cit.,* pp. 193-204. The situation whereby "competitive-like suppliers" sell to "competitive-like distributive trades" is mentioned but not discussed by Heflebower.

[8] *Ibid,* pp. 201-203.

[9] See John K. Galbraith, *American Capitalism* (Boston: Houghton Mifflin Company 1956), pp. 111-112.

private labels.[10] As retail markets have become more concentrated, the locus of control has begun to shift away from manufacturers, and the private label phenomenon has been an important vehicle influencing the shift.[11]

In sum, if, in a number of industries, control and, concomitantly, the balance of bargaining power are centralized in one organization within a system of inter-related organizations, e.g., a marketing channel, the application of existing economic theory should provide a means by which the location of control can be determined. On the other hand, a weakness in economic theory is that it too often concentrates on price manipulation as the main determinant in bargaining situations. A lasting contribution of marketing studies to economic theory has been the discovery that, in most situations, price manipulation is only one element in the mix of competitive methods available to firms and that even if price is stabilized, control can be established and maintained through the manipulation of other elements. Further, implicit in economic literature is the sometimes unstated bias against central channel control, born out of a distrust for the powerful business firm.

Inter-organization Management: The Needs and the Obstacles

It was suggested earlier that, in situations approximating channel tyranny as opposed to benevolent channel leadership, the results may work to the benefit of the controlling party and possibly to the detriment of other members of the channel of distribution. For example, Balderston has delineated problems that may arise because of intra-organizational conflict, and his remarks can be easily related to marketing channels viewed as organizations or systems. He has written that

> Conflicts often arise between groups of functionally specialized executives, e.g., between physical distribution executives and merchandising men. For display and other promotional reasons, the merchants may favor large retail units and the holding of correspondingly large inventories at the retail level, whereas physical distribution men will point to the economies of holding stocks in intermediate warehouses and of restocking retail units according to notions of efficient physical commodity flow. Similar conflicts may arise over the broadening of "captive" manufacturing facilities, and many other issues. Fundamentally, these difficulties arise in power struggles over priorities, criteria of performance, and assignments of responsibility.[12]

In this regard, various members of the channel react in like manner to the executives Balderston describes. They have vested interests and attempt to

[10] Additional thoughts relating to the effects of increased private label activity may be found in a manuscript by the author entitled "The New World of Private Brands" to be published by the *California Management Review.*

[11] See Richard B. Heflebower, *op. cit.*

[12] F. E. Balderston, "Discussion," *Explorations in Retailing, op. cit.,* p. 206.

enhance these interests through the adoption of narrow, self-oriented goal definitions. In a system in which members are inflexible or where there is no leader to direct channel activities, the outcome may be chaotic, or at best, inefficient.

> Many of the phenomena of inter-group conflict are almost indistinguishable from the phenomena that we might consider under [conflict within organizations]...[13]

> The distinction between units in a production-distribution process that are "in" the organization and those that are "out" of the organization typically follows the legal definition of a particular firm. We find it fruitful to use a more functional criterion that includes both the suppliers and the distributors of the manufacturing core of the organization (or its analogue where the core of the organization is not manufacturing)...[14]

The need to view the channel as an organization of an interrelated group of firms rather than as a loose and oftentimes temporary amalgamation of competing parties has been urged by Balderston, Ridgeway, Berg, Alderson, March, Simon, Mallen, and others.

For example, Berg has emphasized that

> Connections with suppliers, networks of financial intermediaries, and trade channels are examples of external organizations. Although they may not appear on company charts or in manuals, these should be regarded as logical extensions to the internal organization of the firm. Internal and external organizations are similar in that both deal with economic functions performed by interdependent human agents requiring motivation and coordination through communication. Both involve continuous personal relationships, routinized tasks, and stable expectations of reciprocal performance.[15]

In practice, the beginning point in organizing a channel or in forming a coalition among channel members would be to locate a potential channel leader through an economic and sociological analysis of the existing power structure within the channel. The next step would be to convince this channel member to adopt a managerial philosophy that would permit the channel, through his leadership, to achieve effective over-all performance. A recent study by McKinsey and Company is certainly an example of an effort to bring this important message to the food industry.[16]

[13] James G. March and Herbert A. Simon, *Organizations* (New York, John Wiley and Sons, Inc., 1958), p. 131 (parenthesis supplied).

[14] *Ibid*, p. 89.

[15] Thomas L. Berg, *op. cit.*, p. 482.

[16] McKinsey & Company, Inc., *Opportunities to Improve Relations Between Chains and Manufacturers*, (Washington, D. C.: National Association of Food Chains, October 1962) and *The Economics of Food Distributors*, (New York: General Foods Corporation, October 1963).

There is, however, the necessity of obtaining a leader who would be capable of formulating and directing the adoption of a set of inter-organization policies and practices. If the channel is to be managed as an organization, it must be characterized by explicit goals, an elaborate system of explicit rules and regulations, and a formal status structure with clearly marked lines of communication and authority.[17] The task of manipulating such an organization will, no doubt, be complex. As Talcott Parsons has written,

> The integrative problem within an organization most directly concerns the human agents. This point can be generalized to inter-organizational integration. The central problem concerns the institutionalized norms which can effectively bind the actions of individuals in their commitments to organizations. An important feature of all complex societies is that the normal individual is involved in a multiplicity of roles. From one point of view these roles constitute membership in or commitments to collectivities, of which in turn organizations are one principal type. The focus of the integrative problem on a trans-organizational level, then, is the problem of the determination of the loyalties of participant persons. . . . Clearly this allocation of loyalties, not within the organization but within the society between collectivities, is intimately connected with values.[18]

Parsons also suggests that,

> The management of the organization must, to some degree, take or be ready to take measures to counteract the centrifugal pull, to keep employment turnover at least down to tolerable levels, and. . .to bring the performances of subunits. . .more closely into line with the requirements of the organization than would otherwise be the case. These measures can take any one or a combination of three fundamental forms: (1) coercion—in that penalties for noncooperation are set, (2) inducement—in that rewards for valued performance are instituted, and (3) "therapy"—in that by a complex and judicious combination of measures the motivational obstacles to satisfactory cooperation are dealt with on a level which "goes behind" the overt ostensible reasons for the difficulty by the persons involved.[19]

The Need for Redirection Through Research

Although there may be some agreement among certain writers that coordination of the activities in marketing channels through inter-organizational management is desirable, especially after they have noted the negative effects of

[17]Peter W. Blau and W. Richard Scott, *Formal Organizations* (San Francisco: Chandler Publishing Company, 1962), p. 14.

[18]Talcott Parsons, *Structure and Process in Modern Societies* (Glencoe, Ill.: The Free Press, 1960), pp. 36-37.

[19]*Ibid*, pp. 33-35.

vertical conflict,[20] such coordination demands a major redirection of individual organization efforts and objectives. To date, little research has been completed that tests the applicability of intra-organization management principles to the "management" of inter-organization coalitions, that indicates the means by which coordination might be achieved, or that estimates the probable results of such coordination, once accomplished. To this end, J. L. Heskett and the author have formulated a set of tentative hypotheses to be used as a basis for research. These hypotheses are presented below. In large part, they represent a summary and conclusion to this paper. It is hoped, however, that they will evoke constructive criticism from others who have an interest in the subject matter.

1. Power (in the form of inter-organizational control) gravitates to one organization within a system of inter-related organizations. The emergence of a leader within such a system is not only likely, but inevitable.

2. Power structures within inter-firm organizations more commonly than not permit the formulation and pursuit of a set of inter-organization policies and practices.

3. The performance of an inter-organization coalition depends, to a significant extent, on the acceptance of broad long-run considerations by the coalition member with which the greatest power rests.

4. The use of current management theories and modern decision tools which contribute to rational[21] intra-firm management decisions: (a) fosters narrow, self-oriented goal definitions, and (b) often results in decisions which impair the performance of individual firms within a group of inter-related firms, thereby diminishing the performance of the entire system.

5. In a system characterized by vertically linked activities (such as a channel of distribution), a set of positive or negative incentives can be established on a systematic basis by the inter-organization leader to encourage the development of coordinated behavior among its members.

6. The means now exist to expand management theory and restate decision tools, where necessary, to allow a conscious pursuit of long-run effective over-all performance for a group of inter-related firms.

Channel control is, in a great sense, a central concept underlying the above hypotheses. But the most significant premise is that inter-organization management, once accomplished, can achieve effective channel performance and a more efficient allocation of resources among channel members.

---

[20]For example, see John A. Jamison, *The California Fresh Deciduous Fruit Industry: Structure, Organization and Practices,* Giannini Foundation of Agricultural Economics Report No. 275, April 1964, pp. 95-96.

[21] "Rational" is used here to denote that which seeks to maximize, optimize, or satisfy.

10

Changing Channels in the Physical Distribution of Finished Goods

DONALD J. BOWERSOX
Michigan State University

Today, retailers sell wholesale, wholesalers sell retail, hardwares sell soft goods, department stores sell food, food stores sell appliances, they all sell toys, and discount stores sell everything. Channel jumping is not limited to retailing. Finished goods often move to the same retailer from wholesalers, distributors, jobbers, assemblers, and producers. In some cases, goods by-pass the retailer altogether moving directly to consumers. In short, traditional classifications of middlemen, trade channels, and goods have lost considerable validity.

The cost pressures of scrambled marketing have forced a careful review of physical distribution practices. While "you can't do business from an empty wagon," the yardstick of how you replenish the wagon may mean the difference between profit or loss.[1] Physical distribution is recognized as the management responsibility to design and administer systems for controlling raw material and finished inventory replenishment.[2] Case studies of firms who have improved physical distribution efficiency are widely publicized in business and trade journals.[3] This spurt of attention to physical flow has resulted from sheer

[1] Adopted from feature article "Distribution—Growth Pattern for Tomorrow," *Annual Report of Dun and Bradstreet, Inc., 1964.*

[2] For expansion see: Donald J. Bowersox, "The Role of the Marketing Executive in Physical Distribution," in George L. Baker (ed.), *Effective Marketing Coordination, Proceedings American Marketing Association* (Chicago: American Marketing Association, 1961), pp. 393–399.

[3] For examples see: H. J. Bullen "New Competitive Selling Weapon—Physical Distribution Management," *Sales Management,* May 1965. pp. 41–52; "The Next Place for Paring Costs," *Business Week,* May 1, 1965. pp. 132–136; Joel F. Olesky, "Distribution Comes of

magnitude of expenditure and the relatively untapped opportunities for cost reduction.

Many corporate costs of replenishment are hidden between traditional departments of an enterprise and not necessarily under the control of any given department. In addition, the actions of any single department may reduce that department's share of expenditure and at the same time increase total corporate cost of physical distribution.[4] It takes a major revision in management philosophy to achieve interdepartmental control over physical distribution costs.

Little consideration has been given to the problems of coordinating or controlling physical distribution beyond the legal boundaries of individual firms.[5] Most physical distribution flow proceeds from production to consumption through a variety of specialized enterprise units linked together as a distribution channel. Each of these independent units may perform an excellent individual job of physical distribution while simultaneously the channel as a group suffers from expensive duplication.

The entire notion of loosely aligned middlemen seems to condemn distribution channels as being inherently endowed with duplication, waste, and inefficiency. The social justification for intermediaries has always appeared in doubt leading to the general belief that one road to increasing marketing efficiency depended on elimination of middlemen. Despite this condemnation, specialized middlemen have survived and increased in importance.[6]

The intentions of this paper are limited to some observations concerning the problems of channel-wide physical distribution. One promising way to increase marketing efficiency is to improve physical movement between intermediaries. Advantages in operations result when physical flow is separated from other flows in the distribution process. Thus, a scheme for channel classification is presented. The functions necessary to complete physical exchange represent cost centers in the channel. Therefore, the second task is to examine exchange functions. Next, attention is focused upon the total channel distribution

---

Age," *Dun's Review,* January 1965. pp. 36–38; and John R. Staley, "Nineteen Ways to Save Time and Money in Distribution," *Business Management,* September 1964. pp. 42–46.

[4]Physical distribution applications of the total cost concept are explained in: Howard T. Lewis, James W. Culliton, and Jack D. Steel, *The Role of Air Freight in Physical Distribution* (Boston: Division of Research Graduate School of Business Administration, Harvard University, 1956), and Edward W. Smykay, Donald J. Bowersox, and Frank H. Mossman, *Physical Distribution Management* (New York: The Macmillan Company, 1961), Chapter IV.

[5]Two notable exceptions are: J. L. Heskett, "Costing and Coordinating External and Internal Logistics Activities." Unpublished paper before joint seminar of The Railway Systems and Management Association and The Transportation Research Forum, Chicago, October 6, 1964; and Frank H. Mossman and Newton Morton, *Logistics of Distribution Systems* (Boston: Allyn and Bacon, Inc., 1965), Part I.

[6]Reavis Cox, *Distribution in a High-Level Economy* (Englewood Cliffs, N.J.: Prentice-Hall, Inc., 1965), p. 51.

network. Finally, the objectives of the channel as a single system of action are examined.

Channel Classification

Several classifications develop the idea of flow separation within the basic distribution channel. Two such classifications have been utilized to develop the framework presented here. The Vaile, Grether, and Cox treatment directly engaged separation of eight flows which occur in the channel.[7] Breyer's recent grouping of channel members as trading and non-trading entities offers an approach to separation.[8]

The present approach singles out two flows. In order to accomplish satisfactory marketing, a flow of transaction creating efforts and a flow of physical fulfillment efforts must exist. These two flows—physical fulfillment and transaction creating—are considered primary. All other flows in the distribution channel are considered secondary.

J. R. Commons differentiated elements of a bargaining transaction with the process of physical exchange.[9] The bargaining transaction was viewed as containing three steps: (1) negotiation—reaching a satisfactory agreement; (2) contract—establishment of obligations; and (3) administration—performance of obligations. Exchange, in contrast, was viewed as the mechanical and labor process of physical delivery.[10]

Separation of exchange fulfillment and transaction creation is based upon the simple notion a product may arrive physically; however, not arrive economically or legally. Factors increasing or decreasing the cost of physical flow have no respect for ownership boundaries. Conversely, advertising, credit, personal selling, and other transaction creating efforts of marketing have little influence upon the economics of physical flow. The responsiveness of each primary flow to specialization is unique to the circumstances surrounding that flow. In any given marketing situation primary flows may best be accomplished by different middlemen. The most effective network for achieving profitable transactions may not be the most efficient arrangement of exchange intermediaries. Based upon specialization in primary flow, the distribution channel is classified as containing transaction channels and exchange channels.

The transaction channel consists of a grouping of intermediaries who engage in the establishment of trading. The goal of the transaction channel is to negotiate,

[7]Roland Vaile, E. T. Grether, and Reavis Cox, *Marketing in the American Economy* (New York: The Ronald Press Co., 1952), p. 113.

[8]Ralph F. Breyer, "Some Observations on Structural Formation and the Growth of Marketing Channels," in Reavis Cox, Wroe Alderson, Stanley J. Shapiro, Editors, *Theory in Marketing* (Homewood, Ill.: Richard D. Irwin, Inc., 1964), pp. 163–175.

[9]John R. Commons, *The Economics of Collective Action* (New York: The Macmillan Co., 1950), p. 53.

[10]*Ibid., p. 45.*

contract, and administer trading on a continuing basis. Thus, the full force of creative marketing action exists within the transaction channel. Participants in transaction channel activities are marketing specialists.

The exchange channel contains a network of intermediaries engaged in the functions of physical movement. Participants in the exchange channel are physical distribution specialists. Their concern is one of solving problems of time and space at a total expenditure consistent to trading specifications.

This classification differs from Professors Breyer's to the extent that his trading and nontrading channels may each engage in exchange. The difference in current classification and that of Vaile, Grether, and Cox is one of emphasis between primary and secondary flows.

The tendency toward separation is easily observed in business practice. The best example is the factory branch office which carries no inventory. The office exists for the sole purpose of transaction creation. The physical exchange between seller and buyer may move in a variety of combinations of transport and storage depending upon value, size of shipment, bulk, weight, perishability; plus, time and location requirements. There is no economic justification for locating warehouses with each branch office. The network of branch offices is best selected to provide maximum transaction impact. The selection of exchange intermediaries is designed to achieve physical distribution economies. Examples of firms enjoying such separation benefits are Pillsbury, Heinz, Johnson and Johnson, and the E. F. MacDonald Company.

A second example of separation is found in retailing. It is now common for retailers to limit stocks to display models. Sales are negotiated based on a commitment to deliver at a particular time and place, a specified model and color. Although the transaction is initiated at a retail store, physical exchange may consist of direct shipment to the consumer's home from retailer's, distributor's, or factory warehouse. Such warehouses may be geographically located many miles from the point of transaction. Examples of this form of separation are J. L. Hudson, Macy's, and Polk Brothers.

A final example of separation comes from the rapidly growing mail order industry. An order placed at a local catalog desk may be shipped from a distant factory direct to the buyer's home. Although the flow pattern described is only one of many observable arrangements in mail order, all such systems are designed to create separation and thereby specialization.

Separation of transaction and exchange increases the structural opportunities available for development of specialized channels. This does not mean separate legal enterprises are necessary to enjoy benefits of specialization. The degree of enterprise separation depends upon the necessity of specialization, economies of scale, available resources, and managerial capabilities. When a single enterprise engages both primary flows, specialization of management is required.

Transactions are never complete until physical exchange is fully administered. Depending upon the category of goods—convenience, shopping, or speciality— the exchange process may start in anticipation of, simultaneous with, or after actual negotiation is initiated. The final exchange act occurs in accord with specifications established during the negotiation phase of the transaction. Such exchange specifications relate to time, location, or terms of transfer. Given any set of specifications, minimizations of exchange expense is essential to achieve a mutually satisfactory transaction.

Contributions of efficient exchange are not limited to cost reduction. By achieving time and place utility, exchange can enhance transaction capabilities.[11] The ability to promise and provide dependable delivery of a proper assortment serves as a stimulant to agreement. Actual performance according to specifications creates a tendency toward continued transaction and the benefits of routinization. Thus, although present concern is with exchange mechanics, exchange capabilities may greatly enhance or dilute transaction potential.

Channel Functions of Exchange

Exchange goals are more readily stated than accomplished. Exchange exists to create an assortment of finished goods and to present such assortment at the proper location at the correct time.

Exchange flow in a channel is analogous to the workings of a ratchet wrench. Physical movement is designed for economies of one-way movement toward terminal user locations with scheduled stops occurring at a minimum of predetermined points. The frequency of such stops is determined in part by specifications with respect to time, place, and assortment, and in part by alternate structures available for achieving desired results. Thus, the exchange channel is subject to scrutiny by two measures: (1) capability in time, place, and assortment closure; and (2) evaluation of total cost expenditure between alternate structures capable of achieving closure. The fact that exchange is concerned with physical properties makes quantification, experimentation, measurement, and evaluation more readily achieved than in the more complicated systems of transaction.

Several functions must be performed in the exchange process. Five such functions are singled out and discussed independent of performance point in a channel: (1) adjustment; (2) transfer; (3) storage; (4) handling; and (5) communication.

The function of adjustment has received considerable treatment in marketing.[12] Adjustment is the aspect of exchange concerned with creating an

---

[11]For two discussions of the impact of physical distribution on sales see: Wendell M. Stewart, "Physical Distribution: Key to Improved Volume and Profits," *Journal of Marketing,* January 1965, pp. 67–68, and Thomas A. Staudt and Donald A. Taylor, *A Managerial Introduction to Marketing* (Englewood Cliffs, N.J.; Prentice-Hall, Inc., 1965), p. 222.

[12]This concept has long standing in marketing literature. Two early treatments are found in: Percival White, *Scientific Marketing Management* (New York: Harper & Row, 1927), and Fred E. Clark, *Readings in Marketing* (New York: The Macmillan Co., 1924). For

assortment of finished goods. At some point in the exchange process goods must be concentrated, sorted, and dispersed to another level in the channel. Concentration refers to the collection of large lots of a single good or large groupings of several goods earmarked for final sale in an assortment. Sorting is the process of reducing large groupings into custom offerings. Dispersement consists of placing the custom assortments in the anticipated time and place perspective. The economies of specialization and the inherent risks of adjustment are two main justifications for the existence of middlemen.

The function of transfer constitutes the mechanics of collection and dispersement. A single good or an assortment of goods must be physically transported to achieve temporal and spatial value. The cost of transfer may be the greatest of all functions of exchange. Each transfer in the exchange process is a singularly conclusive act with associated costs. As such, the margin for error is narrow and the related penalties are great. It is not surprising to find specialized transfer intermediaries who engage in the mechanics of movement. Such specialists, in the form of motor, rail, water, and air carriers, engage in the specialization of movement accepting only performance risks. The risks of timing and directing the strategy of transfer remain with other intermediaries in the exchange channel.

Storage occurs because a great deal of concentration, sorting, and dispersement is in anticipation of future transaction. Given conditions of uncertainty in demand and supply, the exchange process must develop certain hedges in order to satisfy future transaction requirements. The risks in storage may be the greatest of all exchange functions since a certain depreciative factor occurs when inventories stand idle. A continuous exchange flow from processing through adjustment and on to consumption would be the least risky for all channel members. However, in a buyer's market continuous movement seldom exists. The exchange channel must be structured to postpone functions as long as possible without endangering transaction capabilities.

Handling may be the least risky of exchange functions. The expenses associated with handling are significant. Once a lot or an assortment of goods reaches a stopping point, shuffling begins. Cartons are moved in, placed, moved about, moved about some more, and hopefully finally moved out. The costs of handling are like the costs of transfer. Each handling has a separate and unique cost. Consequently, the fewer the total handlings, the lower the total cost. The economic justification for container and unitized loads stems from this basic fact.

Communication is a two-way function in the exchange process. In one direction messages relay the stimulus for exchange action. In the other direction communications monitor progress toward desired end results. From stimulant to feedback, the direct costs of communication are overshadowed by the

refinement and expansion, see among others: Wroe Alderson, *Marketing Behavior and Executive Action* (Homewood, Ill.: Richard D. Irwin, Inc., 1957), Chapter VII.

implications of faulty message content. Since a great deal of exchange is initiated in anticipation, communication of overly optimistic potential may stimulate an exchange channel into a fever of ultimately useless work. Recent analysis of communications between channel members suggests such anticipation has a tendency to increase in amplification as it proceeds between consecutive intermediaries in an exchange network.[13]

In summary, successful exchange requires channel members to perform the functions of adjustment, transfer, storage, handling, and communication. Only through coordination of all functions are transaction specifications satisfied. Peter Drucker recently concluded that physical distribution contributes little if anything to the physical characteristics of a good product. It does, however, create the attributes of time and place—it brings the product to the customer.[14] Such attributes continue to be accomplished most efficiently through networks of intermediaries.

The Exchange Network

Since a number of functions must be performed in the exchange process, each with related risks, it is not surprising that a number of individual enterprise units combine to create a channel or network. These enterprises are specialists in one or more exchange functions. To various degrees each channel member enjoys rewards or suffers losses based upon the overall success of the channel. The intermediary serves in the capacity of specialist. His existence spreads the risk of a given endeavor.

Risk in an exchange network is not equally spread among all participants. A motor carrier performing one transfer function in a channel has relatively little risk with respect to ultimate transaction. A retailer has some risk related to the sale of a single product which he hedges by offering a wide assortment. In contrast, a processor or manufacturer of a few products may risk his survival on the capabilities of a movement channel.

This disproportionate spread of risk among channel members is of central importance in the exchange process. Some channel members have deeper vested interest in the ultimate accomplishment of successful exchange than other members. Therefore, they are forced to take more active interest and responsibility in channel destiny. Without guidance, a great many of the costs of exchange occur between channel members and legally outside the boundaries and traditional concerns of any single enterprise. Such costs must be controlled if the channel is to realize maximum exchange capabilities. However, control in an exchange channel is difficult to obtain since the only alternatives to ownership are persuasion or coercion.

[13] See Jay W. Forrester, *Industrial Dynamics* (Cambridge, Mass.: The M.I.T. Press, 1961), p. 62.

[14] Peter Drucker, "The Economy's Dark Continent," *Fortune*, April 1962, p. 103.

Ownership, of course, consists of vertical integration of two or more consecutive links in the exchange channel by a single enterprise. The ultimate of vertical integration in an exchange channel would be a producer shipping via private transportation through his own storage points to factory sales outlets, who in turn handled the physical transfer to the consumer. The exact extent of vertical integration during the past two decades is difficult to appraise. There is increasing justification for concluding that perhaps the transaction channel has undergone more dramatic vertical integration than the movement channel. The most radical shift in types of intermediaries has been in the transfer channel between so-called agents and factory sales offices.[15] It likewise appears that merchant wholesalers have increased at the very time when vertical integration by large retailers and manufacturers was supposed to have eliminated their basis of economic justification.[16] The potential economies of vertical integration in exchange may not be offset by corresponding loss of innovative specialization and risk spreading.

The tactics of persuasion and coercion appear to offer the most practical methods for controlling exchange channel activities. Within the exchange channel, this basic need for common action under leadership guidance has been referred to as super-organization management.[17] Although all firms have a desire to cooperate, individual profit orientation and legal boundaries seem to instill elements of conflict. In addition, there exists a degree of conflict over which member will assume financial responsibility for performing the more risky exchange functions. The analysis of motivation of conflict and cooperation in both trading and exchange channels is currently receiving substantial attention in the literature.[18] A review of such work is beyond the intentions of this paper. The essential point is that the ultimate survival of a channel may depend upon creative leadership.

A great deal of future improvement in marketing efficiency depends upon substantial increase in managerial concern with channel group objectives as opposed to preoccupation with the firm as an individual channel member.

Objectives of Exchange Channels

As a competitive group, an exchange channel desires to complete the necessary functions of exchange in accordance with some well-defined objectives. The

---

[15] Cox, *op. cit.*, p. 55.

[16] *Ibid.*, p. 56.

[17] Heskett, *op. cit.*, p. 2.

[18] For example see: J. C. Palamountain, Jr., *The Politics of Distribution*. (Cambridge, Mass.: Harvard University Press, 1955); Valentine Ridgeway, "Administration of Manufacturer-Dealer Systems," *Administrative Science Quarterly*, March 1957, pp. 464–483; Bruce Malle, "Conflict and Cooperation in Marketing Channels," in L. George Smith (ed.), *Reflections on Progress in Marketing, Proceedings American Marketing Association*, (Chicago: American Marketing Association, 1964), pp. 65–85; and Bert C.

objectives are singled out as: (1) minimum possible transfers; (2) maximum postponement in adjustment; and (3) minimum massed reserves.[19]

The objectives of minimum possible engagements encourage the least amount of transfer, handling, adjustment, and storage possible. Although important to the total process, the costs of duplication in such functions rapidly accumulate. Thus, the fewer nodal points physical products flow through, the more inherently efficient the channel.

The objective of maximum postponement in adjustment encourages the holding of homogeneous concentrated lots as long as possible in the exchange process. Since a great deal of exchange activity is in anticipation of future transaction, the longer a concentration is maintained, the greater the ability to adjust custom assortments in various volumes. The ideal approach is to concentrate lots based upon transaction anticipation with postponement of sorting and dispersement until a firm commitment is at hand. The longer an exchange channel can postpone final adjustment, the more flexible the total exchange process. Remolding a previously established assortment adds ancillary costs to the total process.

The objective of minimum massed reserves may appear to stand in contrast with the objective of postponement. However, why hold homogeneous lots at consecutive levels in an exchange channel? For a long time it was fashionable to mass finished inventory at various levels of the channel in anticipation of transaction. In practice, there appears to have been extensive pressure on the part of trading groups for inventory support in each market as a prerequisite to successful transaction. The tendency is now toward the staging of a central supply as far geographically separated from the market as economically feasible. The rapid expansion of product offerings in all trade channels has created serious risks in holding reserves for each specialized market. Given conditions of erratic demand, the lowest total cost movement expenditure may well be expensive fast physical transport as late in the transaction process as technologically possible. Inventories in the total exchange channel must be minimized without diluting transaction support capabilities. Only if such minimization is achieved are the benefits of innovation encouraged and the forces of rigidity eliminated.

The objectives outlined above are channel-wide considerations. Their accomplishment embodies an understanding on the part of all enterprise members concerning the degree of interdependence necessary for efficient exchange. Lack of united effort to achieve these objectives leads to increased costs as members duplicate functions of exchange.

MaCammon, Jr., "Alternative Explanations of Institutional Change and Channel Evolution," in Stephen A. Greyser (ed), *Toward Scientific Marketing, Proceedings American Marketing Association*, (Chicago: American Marketing Association, 1963), pp. 477–490.

[19] A great deal of this section is based upon Alderson, *op. cit.*.

Conclusion

It has been suggested that issues of channel analysis are clarified by separation of transaction and exchange flows. Whereas some enterprises engage in both transaction and exchange, the functions and objectives of exchange favor specialized intermediaries.

Within the legal and managerial boundaries of a given firm, significant advancements have been made in reducing the cost and improving the effectiveness of physical distribution. Many of these advancements have resulted from a willingness to discard outdated ideas concerning internal cost measurement and physical flow management. At best, these desirable advancements improve the short-range efficiency for individual firms. Developments in exchange must expand to boundaries of the movement channel. Only when firms linked together for joint economic gain acknowledge the existence of duplicated and ancillary functions of exchange will the waste in movement be eliminated.

The exchange process is physical in nature representing something we know how to manipulate, mold, and perfect at today's level of knowledge. Perhaps the ultimate efficiency of exchange is more directly related to channel structure than trading as a result of superior quantification potential. Because so little attention has been devoted to exchange on a channel grouping basis, the prospects for improved marketing efficiency are encouraging.

In the case of highly branded or differentiated products, innovation for efficiency may result from manufacturers. Retailers, having substantial market acceptance, may initiate such action. Finally, in cases of wide assortments accumulated from small processers and distributed to small retailers, the wholesaler may provide the impetus for increasing exchange efficiency. The consumer cares very little about who receives the proceeds from a purchase. He does care about the total amount of such proceeds.

11

Postponement, Speculation, and the Structure of Distribution Channels

LOUIS P. BUCKLIN
University of California

The Concept of Substitutability

Underlying the logic of the principle to be developed is the hypothesis that economic interaction among basic marketing functions, and between these functions and production, provides much of the force that shapes the structure of the distribution channel. These interactions occur because of the capability of the various functions to be used as substitutes for each other within certain broad limitations. This capability is comparable to the opportunities available to the entrepreneur to use varying ratios of land, labor, and capital in the production of his firm's output. The substitutability of marketing functions may occur both within the firm and among the various institutions of the channel, e.g., producers, middlemen, and consumers. This substitutability permits the work load of one function to be shrunk and shifted to another without affecting the output of the channel. These functional relationships may also be seen to be at the root of the "total cost" concept employed in the growing literature of the management of the physical distribution system.[1]

A familiar example of one type of substitution that may appear in the channel is the use of inventories to reduce the costs of production stemming from cyclical demand. Without the inventory, production could only occur during the

---

[1] Stanley H. Brewer and James Rosenweig, "Rhochematics," *California Management Review*, 3 (Spring 1961), 52–71; and, Edward W. Smykay, Donald J. Bowersox, and Frank J. Mossman, *Physical Distribution Management* (New York: The Macmillan Company, 1961), Chapter IV.

104

time of consumption. Use of the inventory permits production to be spread over a longer period of time. If some institution of the channel senses that the costs of creating a seasonal inventory would be less than the savings accruing from a constant rate of production, it would seek to create such a stock and retain the resulting profits. The consequence of this action is the formation of a new and alternate channel for the product.

The momentum of change, however, is not halted at this point. Unless there is protection against the full brunt of competitive forces, the institutions remaining in the original, and now high-cost channel, will either be driven out of business or forced to convert to the new system as well. With continued competitive pressure the excess profits, initially earned by the institutions which innovated the new channel, will eventually be eliminated and total channel costs will fall.

In essense, the concept of substitutability states that under competitive conditions institutions of the channel will interchange the work load among functions, not to minimize the cost of some individual function, but the total costs of the channel. It provides, thereby, a basis for the study of distribution channels. By understanding the various types of interactions among the marketing functions and production that could occur, one may determine the type of distribution structure that should appear to minimize the total channel costs including those of the consumer. The principle of postponement-speculation, to be developed below, evaluates the conditions under which one type of substitution may occur.

Postponement

In 1950, Wroe Alderson proposed a concept which uniquely related certain aspects of uncertainty and risk to time. He labelled this concept the "principle of postponement," and argued that it could be used to reduce various marketing costs.[2] Risk and uncertainty costs were tied to the differentiation of goods. Differentiation could occur in the product itself and/or the geographical dispersion of inventories. Alderson held that "the most general method which can be applied in promoting the efficiency of a marketing system is the postponement of differentiation. . .postpone changes in form and identity to the latest possible point in the marketing flow; postpone change in inventory location to the latest possible point in time."[3] Savings in costs related to uncertainty would be achieved "by moving the differentiation nearer to the time of purchase," where demand, presumably, would be more predictable. Savings in the physical movement of the goods could be achieved by sorting products in "large lots," and "in relatively undifferentiated states."

---

[2]Wroe Alderson, "Marketing Efficiency and the Principle of Postponement," *Cost and Profit Outlook*, 3 (September 1950).
[3]Wroe Alderson, *Marketing Behavior and Executive Action*, (Homewood, Ill.: Richard D. Irwin, 1957), p. 424.

Despite its potential importance, the principle has received relatively little attention since it was first published. Reavis Cox and Charles Goodman[4] have made some use of the concept in their study of channels for house building materials. The Vaile, Grether, and Cox marketing text[5] also makes mention of it. As far as can be determined, this is the totality of its further development.

As a result, the principle still constitutes only a somewhat loose, and possibly misleading, guide to the study of the distribution channel structure. The major defect is a failure to specify the character of the limits which prevent it from being applied. The principle, which states that changes in form and inventory location are to be delayed to the latest possible moment, must also explain why in many channels these changes appear at the earliest. As it stands, the principle of postponement requires modification if it is to be applied effectively to the study of channels.

Postponement and the Shifting of Risk

If one views postponement from the point of view of the distribution channel as a whole, it may be seen as a device for individual institutions to shift the risk of owning goods to another. The manufacturer who postpones by refusing to produce except to order is shifting the risk forward to the buyer. The middleman postpones by either refusing to buy except from a seller who provides next day delivery (backward postponement), or by purchasing only when he has made a sale (forward postponement). The consumer postpones by buying from those retail facilities which permit him to take immediate possession directly from the store shelf. Further, where the consumer first contacts a number of stores before buying, the shopping process itself may be seen as a process of postponement—a process which advertising seeks to eliminate.

From this perspective it becomes obvious that every institution in the channel, including the consumer, cannot postpone to the latest possible moment. The channel, in its totality, cannot avoid ownership responsibilities. Some institution, or group of institutions, must continually bear this uncertainty from the time the goods start through production until they are consumed.

Since most manufacturers do produce for stock, and the ownership of intermediate inventories by middlemen is characteristic of a large proportion of channels, it is clear that the principle of postponement can reach its limit very quickly. As a result, it provides no rationale for the forces which create these inventories. Hence, postponement is really only half a principle. It must have a converse, a converse equally significant to channel structure.

[4] Reavis Cox and Charles S. Goodman, "Marketing of Housebuilding Materials," *The Journal of Marketing*, 21 (July 1956), 55–56.

[5] Roland S. Vaile, Ewald T. Grether, and Reavis Cox, *Marketing in the American Economy* (New York: Ronald Press Company, 1952), pp. 149–150.

Speculation

This converse may be labelled the principle of speculation. It represents a shift of risk to the institution, rather than away from it. The principle of speculation holds that changes in form, and the movement of goods to forward inventories, should be made at the earliest possible time in the marketing flow in order to reduce the costs of the marketing system.

As in the case of postponement, application of the principle of speculation can lead to the reduction of various types of costs. By changing form at the earliest point one makes possible the use of plants with large-scale economies. Speculation permits goods to be ordered in large quantities rather than in small frequent orders. This reduces the costs of sorting and transportation. Speculation limits the loss of consumer good will due to stock outs. Finally, it permits the reduction of uncertainty in a variety of ways.

This last point has already been well developed in the literature. It received early and effective treatment from Frank H. Knight.[6] He held that speculators, by shifting uncertainty to themselves, used the principle of grouping, as insurance, to transform it into the more manageable form of a relatively predictable risk. Further, through better knowledge of the risks to be handled, and more informed opinion as to the course of future events, risk could be further reduced.

The Combined Principle

From the point of view of the distribution channel, the creation of inventories for holding goods before they are sold is the physical activity which shifts risk and uncertainty. Such inventories serve to move risk away from those institutions which supply, or are supplied by, the inventory. Such inventories, however, will not be created in the channel if the increased costs attending their operation outweigh potential savings in risk. Risk costs, according to the substitutability hypothesis, cannot be minimized if other costs increase beyond the savings in risk.

This discussion shows the principle of speculation to be the limit to the principle of postponement, and vice versa. Together they form a basis for determining whether speculative inventories, those that hold goods prior to their sale, will appear in distribution channels subject to competitive conditions. Operationally, postponement may be measured by the notion of delivery time. Delivery time is the number of days (or hours) elapsing between the placing of an order and the physical receipt of the goods by the buyer.[7] For the seller, postponement increases, and costs decline, as delivery time lengthens. For the

[6]Frank H. Knight, *Risk, Uncertainty and Profit* (Boston: Houghton-Mifflin Company, 1921), pp. 238–239, 255–258.
[7]Smykay et al., *op. cit.*, p. 93.

buyer, postponement increases, and costs decline, as delivery time shortens. The combined principle of postponement-speculation may be stated as follows: A speculative inventory will appear at each point in a distribution channel whenever its costs are less than the net savings to both buyer and seller from postponement.

Operation of the Principle

The following hypothetical example illustrates how the postponement-speculation principle can be applied to the study of distribution channels. The specific problem to be considered is whether an inventory, located between the manufacturer and the consumer, will appear in the channel. This inventory may be managed by the manufacturer, a consumer cooperative or an independent middleman.

Assume that trade for some commodity occurs between a set of manufacturers and a set of customers, both sets being large enough to insure active price competition. The manufacturers are located close to each other in a city some significant distance from the community in which the customers are situated. All of the customers buy in quantities sufficiently large to eliminate the possibility of savings from sorting. Manufacturing and consumption are not affected by seasonal variations. Assume, further, that production costs will not be affected by the presence of such an intermediate inventory.

To determine whether the intermediate inventory will appear, one must first ascertain the shape of the various relevant cost functions with respect to time. In any empirical evaluation of channel structure this is likely to be the most difficult part of the task. For present purposes, however, it will be sufficient to generalize about their character.

The costs incurred by the relevant functions are divided into two broad categories. The first includes those costs originating from activities associated with the potential inventory, such as handling, storage, interest, uncertainty, and costs of selling and buying if the inventory is operated by a middleman. It also includes those costs emanating from transportation, whether the transportation is direct from producer to consumer or routed through the inventory. All of these costs will, in turn, be affected by the particular location of the inventory between the producer and the consumer. In the present instance, it is assumed that the inventory will be located in the consumer city.

In general, this first category includes all the relevant costs incurred by the producer and intermediary, if any. These are aggregated on Figure 1. In this diagram, the ordinate represents the average cost for moving one unit of the commodity from the producer to the consumer. The abscissa measures the time in days for delivery of an order to the consumer after it has been placed. The curve DB measures the cost of using the speculative inventory to supply the consumer for the various possible delivery times. Curve AD' shows the cost of supplying the consumer direct without use of such an inventory. DD' is the

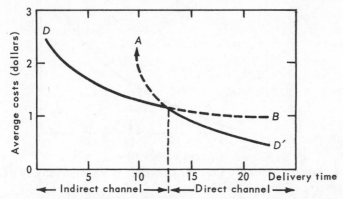

Figure 1. Average Cost of Distributing One Unit of a Commodity to a Customer with Respect to Delivery Time in Days.

minimum average cost achievable by either direct or indirect distribution of the commodity.

The diagram shows that DD' declines as the delivery time is allowed to increase.[8] With very short delivery times the intermediate inventory is absolutely necessary because only in this way can goods be rushed quickly to the consumer. Further, when virtually immediate delivery is required, the safety stock of the inventory must be kept high in order to prevent temporary stockouts from delaying shipment. Also, delivery trucks must always be available for short notice. These factors create high costs.

As the delivery time to be allowed increases, it becomes possible to reduce the safety stocks, increase the turnover and reduce the size of the facilities and interest cost. Further increases permit continued savings. Eventually, a point will be reached, I in Figure 1, where the delivery time will be sufficiently long to make it cheaper to ship goods directly from the factory to the consumer than to move them indirectly through the inventory. This creates the discontinuity at I as the costs of maintaining the inventory and the handling of goods are eliminated.

In part, the steepness of the slope of DD' will be affected by the uncertainties of holding the inventory. Where prices fluctuate rapidly, or goods are subject to obsolescence, these costs will be high. The extension of delivery time, in permitting the intermediate inventory to be reduced in size, and eventually eliminated, should bring significant relief.

The second category of costs involves those emanating from the relevant marketing functions performed by the customer. Essentially, these costs will be those of bearing the risk and costs of operating any inventory on the customer's

[8]John F. Magee, "The Logistics of Distribution," *Harvard Business Review*, 38 (July-August 1960), 97–99.

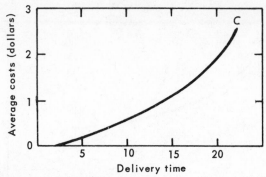

Figure 2. Average Inventory Cost for One Unit of a Commodity to a Customer with Respect to Delivery Time in Days.

premises. These costs are shown as C on Figure 2 with the ordinate and abscissa labelled as in Figure 1.

The shape of C is one that increases with delivery time. The longer the delivery time allowed by the customer, the greater the safety stock he will have to carry. Such stock is necessary to protect against failures in transport and unpredictable surges in requirements. Hence, his costs will increase. The greater the uncertainty cost of inventory holding, the steeper will the slope of this function be.

Determination of the character of the distribution channel is made from the joint consideration of these two cost categories, C and DD'. Whether an intermediate inventory will appear in the channel depends upon the relationship of the costs for operating the two sets of functions and how their sum may be

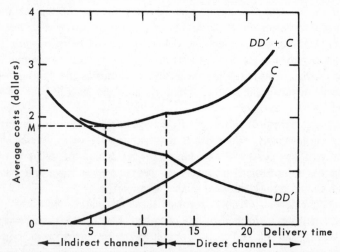

Figure 3. Total of Average Distributing and Customer Inventory Costs with Respect to Delivery Time in Days.

minimized. Functions $DD' + C$ on Figure 3 represent the sum of functions DD' and C. The diagram reveals, in this instance, that costs of postponement are minimized by use of a speculative inventory as the minimal cost point, M, falls to the left of I. If, however, the risk costs to the customer had been less, or the general cost of holding inventories at the customer's home (or plant site, as the case may be) had been lower, then C would be farther to the right. M would also shift to the right. With a sufficient reduction in consumer cost, M would appear to the right of the discontinuity, indicating that direct shipment in the channel would be the means to minimize postponement cost.

Significance of the Principle

As developed, the principle of postponement-speculation provides a basis for expecting inventories to be present in channels because of production and distribution time requirements. In particular, it treats the role of speculative inventories in the channel. The concept, as a consequence, extends beyond the physical flow of the goods themselves to the flow of their title. Speculative inventories create the opportunity for new institutions to hold title in the channel. Without such inventories, there may be little economic justification for a title-holding intermediary to enter the channel. The economic need to have such an inventory in the physical flow opens the door to a middleman to show whether he is capable of reducing the risk cost of that inventory below the level attainable by either the producer or some consumer cooperative.

The presence of an inventory in the channel for either collecting, sorting, or dispersing does not create the same type of opportunity for a title-taking intermediary to appear in the channel. Such inventories are not speculative in character. They do not need to hold uncommitted stocks of goods available for general sale in order to fulfill their purpose. For example, the REA Express, the parcel post system, freight forwarders, and even the Greyhound Bus Corporation's freight system sort a substantial volume of goods through many nonspeculative type inventories each day. Milk producers establish handling depots where bottled milk is transferred from large, long-distance vehicles to city delivery trucks. Catalogue sellers discharge full truck shipments upon the post offices of distant cities where customers reside. None of these inventories involves the risk of unsold goods. None of these inventories provides the basis for the emergence of a title-holding middleman.

From this perspective, the principle of postponement-speculation may be regarded as a concept which broadens the channel analyst's understanding of the intimate relationship between title and physical flows. The intertwining of the roles of ownership and the holding of speculative stocks provide a fundamental rationale for the position of the merchant middleman. The principle of postponement-speculation, as a consequence, can be employed to provide at least part of the explanation for the number of ownership stages in the channel.

This, of course, is one of the basic questions toward which traditional distribution analysis is directed.[9]

In this light, for example, the principle may be of use in explaining the emergence of an "orthodox channel of distribution." This concept, developed by Shaw,[10] was used to characterize the nature of the distribution channel through which a large proportion of products traveled, to wit: the manufacturer-wholesaler-retailer route. That such a concept should emerge to characterize products, whose sorting needs are different because of diverse physical characteristics and market reach, is of extreme interest. Similarities among channels for different products imply that forces, which may not vary significantly among many types of goods, should be sought as explanatory variables of channel structure. Since many groups of consumer goods generate similar temporal types of risk, the principle of postponement-speculation may provide a major explanation for this phenomenon.

Testing the Principle

The principle of postponement-speculation will not be easy to test for a number of reasons. First of all, it is normative. It is derived from assumptions of profit maximization and predictions are based upon what firms should do. Second, it approximates the real world only when the channel environment is sufficiently competitive to produce a variety of price-product-delivery time offers. Finally, it cannot predict the necessary time delays that occur in the channel for new facilities to be built or old ones abandoned.

Despite these problems, a number of hypotheses may be generated from the model and subjected to evaluation by surveys of existing channels. These surveys would locate any intermediate, speculative inventory in the channel and measure the time elapsing between the placing of an order by, and its delivery to, the customer. Use of industrial or commodity channels would undoubtedly be the best initial subjects for the surveys. The confounding effects of collecting, sorting, and dispersing in consumer channels will make the impact of the principle of postponement-speculation more difficult to isolate.

Six hypotheses which could be tested in this manner follow:

1. The shorter the delivery time, the greater the probability the channel will include an intermediate, speculative inventory.

2. The shorter the delivery time, the closer any speculative stock will be to the consumer.

3. The shorter the distance between a customer and a speculative stock, the greater the probability of a second such inventory in the channel.

[9] William R. Davidson, "Channels of Distribution—One Aspect of Marketing Strategy," *Business Horizons*, February 1961, pp. 85–86.

[10] Arch W. Shaw, "Some Problems in Market Distribution," *The Quarterly Journal of Economics* (August 1912), p. 37.

4. Products which are heavy, bulky, and inexpensive are likely to flow through channels with more intermediate, speculative inventories than products with the opposite characteristics.

5. Products which consumers find expensive to store on their premises, but whose use is both urgent and difficult to forecast, have a greater probability of passing through an intermediate, speculative inventory than products with the opposite characteristics.

6. The greater the inelasticity of consumer and/or producer cost with respect to changes in delivery time, the greater the stability of the most efficient channel type over time.

All of these hypotheses are subject to the *ceteris paribus* limitation. Tests, as a result, should include only those channels operating under reasonably similar economic conditions. This is particularly important with respect to the distance between the producer and the consumer. Variations in this factor will affect the cost of providing any given delivery time. Channels which traverse longer distances, in other words, are likely to require more speculative inventories than those which move goods less extensively.

The *ceteris paribus* limitation also contains an important implication beyond that of the problems of testing. Consideration of this limitation provides the rationale for the presence of several different types of channels supplying the same type of product to a given group of customers. Producers, for example, provisioning some market from a distance, may be forced to use channels distinct from their competitors located adjacent to the customers. This diversity of channels may also be produced by imperfections in competition as well as variations in the urgency of demand among consumers in the market. Those who can easily tolerate delays in delivery are likely to use a different channel from those patronized by customers with dissimilar personalities or capabilities.

Implications of the Principle

The principle of postponement-speculation, in addition to providing a basis for developing hypotheses for empirical testing, makes it possible to do some *a priori* generalizing concerning the type of channel structure changes one may expect to see in the future. Any force, or set of forces, which affects the types of costs discussed may be sufficient to move the balance from speculation to postponement, or vice versa.

One type of change, already occurring and which may be expected to spread in the future, rests upon the relationship between the cost of transportation and speed. Rapidly evolving methods of using air transport economically and efficiently are serving to narrow the spread between the cost of high-speed transportation and low-speed transportation. This has the effect of reducing the relative advantage of speculation over postponement. Hence, intermediate inventories will tend to disappear and be replaced by distribution channels which have a direct flow.

The increasing proliferation of brands, styles, colors, and price lines is another type of force which will affect the balance. This proliferation increases the risk of inventory holding throughout the entire channel, but particularly at those points closest to the consumer. Retailers will attempt to minimize this risk by reducing the safety stock level of their inventories and relying more upon speedy delivery from their suppliers. The role of the merchant wholesaler, or the chain store warehouse, will become increasingly important in this channel. Indeed, there will probably be increasing efforts on the part of retailers to carry only sample stocks in those items where it is not absolutely necessary for customers to take immediate delivery. General Electric, for example, is experimenting with wholesaler-to-consumer delivery of large appliances. Drugstores, where the role of the pharmacist appears to be slowly changing from one of compounding prescriptions to inventorying branded specialties, will become further dependent upon ultra-fast delivery from wholesalers.

Those stores, such as discount houses, which are successfully able to resist the pressure toward carrying wide assortments of competing brands are likely to utilize channels of distribution which differ significantly from their full-line competitors. Large bulk purchases from single manufacturers can be economically delivered directly to the discount house's retail facilities. Where warehouses are used in discount house channels they can serve stores spread out over a far greater geographical area than would be normally served by a wholesaler. Such stores are also apt to find their market segments not only in middle income range families, but also among those consumers who tend to be heavily presold by manufacturer advertising, or who simply are less finicky about the specific type of item they buy.

A final possible trend may spring from consumers who find that their own shopping costs represent too great an expenditure of effort with respect to the value received from postponement. As a result, such consumers are likely to turn more and more to catalogue and telephone shopping. Improved quality control procedures by manufacturers and better means of description in catalogues could hasten this movement. The acceptance of Sears telephone order services in large cities testifies that many individuals are prone to feel this way. If the movement were to become significantly enlarged, it could have a drastic effect upon the existing structure of distribution.

Summary

The study of distribution channels, and why they take various forms, is one of the most neglected areas of marketing today. Part of the neglect may be due to the absence of effective tools for analysis. The principle of postponement-speculation is offered in the hope that it may prove useful in this regard and stimulate work in the area.

The principle directly treats the role of time in distribution and, indirectly, the role of distance as it affects time. The starting point for the development of the constructs of the principle may be found in the work of Alderson and [others].[11] Postponement is measured by the change of delivery time in the shipping of a product. Increasing the delivery time decreases postponement costs for the seller, increases them for the buyer and vice versa. Justification and support for the relationships suggested between the costs of marketing functions and delivery time may be found in the recent literature of physical distribution.

The principle reveals the effect upon channel structure of the interaction between the risk of owning a product and the physical functions employed to move the product through time. It holds that, in a competitive environment, the costs of these functions be minimized over the entire channel, not by individual function. The minimum cost and type of channel are determined by balancing the costs of alternative delivery times against the cost of using an intermediate, speculative inventory. The appearance of such an inventory in the channel occurs whenever its additional costs are more than offset by net savings in postponement to the buyer and seller.

[11] Alderson, "Marketing Efficiency and the Principles of Postponement," *op. cit.*; Brewer and Rosenweig, *op. cit.*; and Magee, *op. cit.*

12

Alternative Explanations of Institutional Change and Channel Evolution

BERT C. McCAMMON, JR.

Indiana University

Marketing channels and institutions must adapt continuously to their environment in order to avoid "economic obsolescence." Most of the required adaptations are tactical in nature. Channel alignments, for example, can usually be maintained over an extended period of time by effecting a series of minor, though necessary, revisions in marketing practices. Individual firms, under normal conditions, can also maintain their competitive position without significantly altering prevailing policies and procedures. Thus, institutional change in marketing tends to be a process in which firms and channels maneuver for short-run advantage and in which they adapt almost imperceptibly to environmental disturbances.

Periodically, however, a firm's or channel's existence is threatened by a *major* change in marketing practices. The sudden appearance of new products, new methods of distribution, new types of competitors, and new sales approaches, may imperil existing institutional relationships. These abrupt departures from the *status quo* can disrupt prevailing patterns of competition, alter cost-price relationships, and "enforce a distinctive process of adaptation"[1] on the part of threatened organizations.

Schumpeter earlier, Barnet and Levitt later, argue that this type of competition, usually called innovative competition, is a prerequisite for economic growth.[2] Despite general acceptance of this position, very little is

[1] Joseph Schumpeter, *Business Cycles*, McGraw-Hill Book Company, New York, 1939, p. 10.

[2] Joseph Schumpeter, *Capitalism, Socialism, and Democracy*, Harper and Brothers, New York, 1947; Edward M. Barnet, *Innovate or Perish*, Graduate School of Business, Columbia

116

known about the innovative process in marketing. More specifically, we lack a body of theory that explains how new marketing practices are originated and diffused throughout the structure of distribution.

The emergence and acceptance of new practices is a complex process which has been analyzed extensively in the agricultural sector of our economy,[3] and in the medical profession.[4] For example:

> The farmers participating in the diffusion process are relatively easy to identify. Beal and Rogers have classified such participants as innovators (the developers or initial accepters of new ideas), early adopters, majority adopters, and laggards. "Indirect" participants, who occupy important positions in the communications network, are classified as key communicators, influentials, and skeptics. Each of these decision makers has a distinctive socio-economic profile and a differentiated mode of behavior. Researchers, by analyzing interaction patterns, can predict the rate at which a new farm practice will be accepted, and they can forecast the probable impact of this innovation on non-adopters.[5]

Unfortunately, comparable analysis has not been undertaken in retailing or wholesaling. The distinguishing characteristics of innovators, early adopters, and other participants in the diffusion process have not been identified, nor have the factors which inhibit or encourage change been isolated. Consequently, the explanation and prediction of institutional change in marketing tends to be a tenuous intellectual exercise.

The diffusion process in marketing is more complex than it is in agriculture because the counter strategies of non-adopters have to be considered as well as the spread of the innovation itself. The phenomenon of transient and selective adoption has to be recognized too. Individual firms may emulate an innovator in the short-run while devising long-run strategies, or alternatively these firms may adopt new practices on a limited or modified basis. Conventional department stores, for example, have recently emulated the discounter by opening self-service branches. This may be an interim strategy in the sense that the branches may change over time so that they eventually bear little resemblance to the original innovation. With respect to selective adoption of new practices, many supermarkets prepack meat but not produce, and numerous department stores operate self-service drug and toy departments while merchandising other lines on a full-service basis. Consequently, it appears that a complex model is needed to analyze the emergence and diffusion of new practices in the marketing structure.

University, New York, 1954; Theodore Levitt, *Innovation in Marketing,* McGraw-Hill Book Company, New York, 1962.

[3] See for example, E. M. Rogers and G. M. Beal, *Reference Group Influence in the Adoption of Agricultural Technology,* Iowa State University, Ames, 1958.

[4] See for example, J. Coleman, E. Katz, and H. Menzel, "The Diffusion of an Innovation among Physicians," *Sociometry,* December 1957, pp. 253-270.

[5] S. C. Dodd, "Diffusion is Predictable: Testing Probability Models for Laws of Interaction," *American Sociological Review,* August 1955, pp. 392-401.

The purposes of this paper are (1) to explore the barriers to change in the marketing structure, (2) to evaluate the sources of innovation within the structure, and (3) to suggest some hypotheses about the factors which determine the rate at which new practices are accepted.

Barriers to Change Within the Marketing Structure

Conventional economic analysis provides a useful frame of reference for explaining institutional change. The firm, in economic theory, attempts to maximize its profits and thus accepts technological improvements as soon as they appear. Innovations under these circumstances are absorbed quickly and the diffusion process is completed in a relative short period of time. Shifts in channel alignments are also susceptible to economic analysis. Client firms utilize intermediaries because the latter can perform specific functions (in a given location) at a lower cost per unit than can the former. Intermediaries, in this context, are sources of external economies to their clientele. Such economies are possible because intermediaries, by aggregating user requirements, can perform the designated function(s) at an optimum scale, or alternatively, intermediaries, by aggregating user requirements, can more fully utilize existing (though non-optimum) facilities.[6]

As output expands or as *technology changes*, the client firms reach a point at which they can perform the delegated functions at an optimum scale. When this point is reached, functions tend to be reabsorbed, and the channel becomes more completely integrated. This process of reintegration is not necessarily frictionless. The intermediary attempts to avoid being "integrated out" of the channel by changing his method of operation so that it more closely conforms to the client's requirements. Manufacturer's agents in the electronics field, for example, have retained their principals by carrying inventory, and building supply wholesalers continue to sell to large developers by offering goods on a cash and carry basis.

Economic analysis of institutional change can be and has been carried much further.[7] This type of analysis, however modified, inevitably assumes that the firm's behavior is determined by cost/revenue considerations, and thus it leaves unanswered some or all of the following questions:

[6] The latter source of economies is often called the "blending principle."

[7] See, for example, R. H. Coase, "The Nature of the Firm," *Economica,* New Series, Volume IV, 1937, pp. 386-405; George J. Stigler, "The Division of Labor Is Limited by the Extent of the Market," *The Journal of Political Economy,* June 1951, pp. 185-193; R. Artle and S. Berglund, "A Note on Manufacturers' Choice of Distribution Channel," *Management Science,* July 1959 pp. 460-471; Edward H. Bowman, "Scale of Operations: An Empirical Study," *Operations Research,* May-June 1958, pp. 320-328; Louis B. Bucklin, "The Economic Structure of Channels of Distribution," *Marketing: A Maturing Discipline,* (Martin L. Bell, Editor), American Marketing Association, 1960, pp. 379-385; and F. E. Balderston, "Theories of Marketing Structure and Channels," *Proceedings, Conference of Marketing Teachers from Far Western States,* University of California, Berkeley, 1958, pp. 134-145.

•Why is change resisted by marketing institutions even though it appears to offer economic advantages?

•Why do "uneconomic channels of distribution" persist over extended periods of time?

•Why do some firms accept change rapidly, while others lag in their adaptation or refuse to change at all?

Answers to these and related questions depend upon an analysis of sociological and psychological barriers to change, some of which are discussed below.

Reseller Solidarity[8]

Resellers in many lines of trade often function as a highly cohesive group, bargaining with suppliers and adjusting to their environment collectively as well as individually. Resellers "organized" on this basis must maintain internal harmony and a workable consensus. Consequently, they tend to support traditional trade practices and long established institutional relationships.

Several factors are apparently conducive to group action. Resellers tend to act as a unit when the firms involved are relatively homogeneous. Each of the entrepreneurs in this situation tends to be confronted by similar problems and has comparable expectations. Thus he identifies with other members of the trade and is willing to work cooperatively with them.

Resellers also tend to engage in collective action when the entrepreneurs have common backgrounds. The owner-managers of drugstores, for example, are often "highly organized" because most of them are pharmacists and are often alumni of the same universities. Business conditions affect reseller solidarity too. There is likely to be more group action during periods of adverse business conditions than during periods of prosperity. Finally, the degree of reseller solidarity that prevails is conditioned by the intensity and complexity of competition. A line of trade, confronted by unusually aggressive competition from outside sources, is more likely to engage in group action than would be the case if this threat did not exist.

The presence of a strong professional or trade association tends to reinforce conservative group behavior. Retail druggists, as an illustration, support long established professional associations which defend existing trade practices. Carpet retailers, on the other hand, are not represented by a trade association, and for this reason, as well as others, their industry is characterized by unstable retail prices and by constantly changing institutional arrangements.

To summarize, the presence of group solidarity within the structure of marketing tends to inhibit the rate at which innovation is accepted and thus slows down the diffusion process.

[8]The discussion in this section is based on the analyses contained in J. C. Palamountain, Jr., *The Politics of Distribution*, Harvard University Press, Cambridge, Massachusetts, 1955, and in E. T. Grether, "Solidarity in the Distribution Trades," *Law and Contemporary Problems*, June 1937, pp. 376-391.

Entrepreneurial Values

The entrepreneur's reaction to a change is conditioned by his value hierarchy. Large resellers, as a group, are growth oriented and their decisions are based upon economic criteria. Innovations that promote growth are regarded as being desirable, and technological alternatives are evaluated on the basis of "profitability" analysis.[9] Consequently, the large reseller, given sufficient time to adjust, tends to be responsive to innovation and will either accept it or otherwise react to it on the basis of cost-revenue relationships.

Small resellers often have a markedly different set of values. Wittreich, on the basis of his research, argues that small retailers tend to have relatively static expectations.[10] That is, they are interested in reaching and *maintaining* a given scale of operation, and reject opportunities for growth beyond this point. Such retailers tend to view their demand curve as being relatively fixed. Thus, they are inclined to resist innovation because it presumably cannot improve their position and could conceivably disrupt a reasonably attractive *status quo*.

Vidich and Bensman, in their study of life in a small community, reach essentially the same conclusions about the small merchant's behavior.[11] Furthermore, they argue that small retailers are extremely reluctant to invest additional funds in their businesses, almost irrespective of the profits involved. Instead they prefer "secure" investment outlets such as real estate and securities. The small retailers studied by Vidich and Bensman also believed that they had suffered a decline in status during the past three decades, and they resisted any institutional arrangements that would further depress their relative position within the community. This latter condition may partially explain why voluntary and cooperative groups have not been more successful. Retailers participating in these programs sacrifice some of their autonomy, and the loss of this autonomy may be perceived as a loss of status. Wroe Alderson, in another context, has argued that a behavior system will survive as long as it fulfills the status expectations of its participants.[12] Since the small retailer's status is a function of "being in business for himself," the desire to maintain independence may partially explain both the rejection of contractual integration and the persistence of "uneconomic channels."

To summarize, recent research indicates that the small retailer (and presumably other small businessmen) will resist innovation, because they "value" stability more highly than growth.[13] They will also resist innovations that

[9] See Bert C. McCammon, Jr. and Donald H. Granbois, *Profit Contribution: A Criterion for Display Decisions*, Point-of-Purchase Advertising Institute, Inc., New York, 1963.

[10] Warren J. Wittreich, "Misunderstanding the Retailer," *Harvard Business Review*, May-June 1962, pp. 147-159.

[11] Arthur J. Vidich and Joseph Bensman, *Small Town in Mass Society*, Doubleday and Company, Inc., Garden City, New York 1960, pp. 73 and 91-93.

[12] Wroe Alderson, "Survival and Adjustment in Behavior Systems," *Theory in Marketing* (Edited by Reavis Cox and Wroe Alderson), Richard D. Irwin, Inc., Homewood, Illinois, 1950, p. 80.

[13] For additional confirmation of this hypothesis, see Louis Kriesberg, "The Retail Furrier, Concepts of Security and Success," *American Journal of Sociology*, March 1952.

require a substantial investment of funds or that result in a perceived loss of status.

Organizational Rigidity

A well established firm is an historical entity with deeply entrenched patterns of behavior. The members of the organization may resist change because it violates group norms, creates uncertainty, and results in loss of status. Customers may also resent change and threaten to withdraw their patronage. Furthermore the firm has "sunk" costs in training programs, in office systems, and in equipment which it prefers to recover before instituting major revisions in its procedures. Consequently most firms absorb innovation gradually, or react to innovative competition through a series of incremental adjustments.[14] Because of these factors, the diffusion of an innovation through an industry and the distinctive pattern of adaptation it enforces takes considerable time.

The firm's reaction to change is also a function of the extent to which the innovator has penetrated the firm's core market. Most firms appeal to a specific group of customers who are uniquely loyal. These customers may patronize the firm for a variety of reasons, but the attraction is such that their patronage is virtually assured. As long as this core market remains intact, the firm can usually maintain sufficient sales to continue operations until it matures strategies to counteract the innovator.[15] If the core market is infringed, however, the firm must either emulate the innovator or develop immediate counter strategies.

To summarize, a firm, because of organizational rigidities, prefers to respond incrementally to innovation. It will gradually imitate the innovating firm or develop counter strategies over an extended period of time. If the innovator has penetrated the firm's core market, however, it must respond quickly to this challenge in order to ensure continued operation.

The Firm's Channel Position[16]

There is a dominant channel of distribution for most lines of merchandise. This channel, as compared with other institutional alignments, has the greatest prestige and often handles the bulk of the industry's output. Behavior within the channel is regulated by an occupational code which "controls" pricing policies, sales promotion practices, and other related activities. Deviation from the code's prescriptions are punished in a variety of ways, ranging from colleague ostracism to economic sanctions.

---

[14]For an interesting discussion of incremental adjustments to innovation, see Alton F. Doody, "Historical Patterns of Marketing Innovation," *Emerging Concepts in Marketing*, (William S. Decker, Editor), American Marketing Association, Chicago, 1962, pp. 245-253.

[15]Alderson, *op. cit.*, p. 81.

[16]The discussion in this section is based on the analysis that appears in Louis Kriesberg, "Occupational Controls Among Steel Distributors," *The American Journal of Sociology*, November 1955, pp. 203-212.

Individual firms can be classified in terms of their relationship to the dominant channel of distribution and in terms of their adherence to the occupational code. The *insiders* are members of the dominant channel. They have continuous access to preferred sources of supply, and their relatively high status in the trade is a by-product of channel membership. The insiders, as a group, prescribe the contents of the occupational code and enforce it. They are desirous of the respect of their colleagues, and recognize the interdependency of the firms in the system. In short, the insider has made an emotional and financial commitment to the dominant channel and is interested in perpetuating it.

The *strivers* are firms located outside the dominant channel who want to become a part of the system. These firms have discontinuous access to preferred resources, and during periods of short supply, they may be "short ordered" or not shipped at all. The striver, since he wants to become a member of the system, is responsive to the occupational code and will not engage in deviate behavior under normal economic conditions. Thus he utilizes the same marketing practices as the insider.

The *complementors* are not part of the dominant channel, nor do they desire to obtain membership. As their title suggests, these firms complement the activities undertaken by members of the dominant channel. That is, the complementors perform functions that are not normally performed by other channel members, or serve customers whose patronage is normally not solicited, or handle qualities of merchandise the dominant channel doesn't carry. Thus the complementors are marginally affiliated with the dominant channel and want to see it survive. Their expectations are of a long-run nature and they respect the occupational code.

The *transients* also occupy a position outside the dominant channel and do not seek membership in it. Many transients are mobile entrepreneurs who move from one line of trade to another; other transients are firms that owe their allegiance elsewhere, i.e., they consider themselves to be members of a channel other than the one in question. Therefore they utilize the latter channel's product as an "in and out" item or as a loss leader, since it is not their market "that is being spoiled" by such activity. All of the transients have short-run expectations and the occupational code is not an effective constraint.

Classification of firms into these four categories explains some of the competitive patterns which have emerged in the ready-to-wear field, in the toy industry, and in the TBA market. Transient firms, in all of these merchandise lines, have disrupted the *status quo* by engaging in deviate competitive behavior. Significantly, none of the four types of firms described above are likely to introduce major marketing innovations. The insiders and the strivers are primarily interested in maintaining existing institutional arrangements. The complementors also have a vested interest in the *status quo*, and the transients are not sufficiently dependent on the product line to develop an entirely new method of distribution. Thus the above analysis suggests that a firm completely outside the system will introduce basic innovations, and historically this has often been the case. Consequently, a fifth category for *outside innovators* is required to explain major structural realignments.

Market Segmentation

As market segments emerge and/or as they are recognized by entrepreneurs, firms that formerly competed directly with each other begin to compete in a more marginal sense. That is, former rivals begin to appeal to different types of customers, and as a result the tactics adopted by one firm may have a negligible potential impact on other firms. Competition, under these circumstances, becomes more fragmented, and the compulsion to accept or react to innovation declines—a condition that slows down the diffusion process.

The discount supermarket, for example, has not increased in importance as rapidly as many of its proponents initially believed, and the bantam supermarket has experienced much the same fate. It appears that these innovative methods of operation appeal to a limited number of market segments, and conventional supermarkets, appealing to other market segments, have not been compelled to react to these new forms of competition.

Sources of Innovative Activity

The Channel Administrator

An individual firm usually controls a given marketing channel in the sense that it directs the allocation of resources for all channel members. Manufacturers, farm marketing cooperatives, voluntary groups, and chain store buying offices are illustrations of organizations that direct the activities of other channel members. These decision makers do not set goals for the other firms in the channel, but they do decide what kind of firms shall be combined to form the distribution network for the systems they organize.[17]

The channel administrator often is an innovator, particularly when a new product is being marketed. Manufacturers of new fabricated materials, for example, often have to develop unique institutional arrangements to distribute their products,[18] and the Singer Sewing Machine Company pioneered the use of a franchise agency system and installment credit when it began to market sewing machines during the 1850's.[19] Furthermore channel administrators can be quite

[17] For a more complete discussion of the channel administrator concept, see George Fisk, "The General Systems Approach to the Study of Marketing," *The Social Responsibilities of Marketing* (Edited by William D. Stevens), American Marketing Association, Chicago, 1961, pp. 207-211.

[18] See E. Raymond Gorey, *The Development of Markets for New Materials*, Division of Research, Graduate School of Business Administration, Harvard University, Boston, 1956.

[19] Andrew B. Jack, "The Channels of Distribution for an Innovation: The Sewing-Machine Industry in America, 1860-1865," *Explorations in Entrepreneurial History*, February 1957, pp. 113-141.

responsive to *procedural* innovations. During the last decade, channel administrators have taken the initiative in developing new physical distribution
techniques, and they have accepted rather rapidly such innovations as
merchandise management accounting, PERT cost analysis, stockless purchasing
arrangements, and value analysis.

Channel administrators, however, tend to be well established firms, and thus
they are subject to the organizational constraints described above. More
specifically, they tend to resist an innovation that involves a major restructuring
of the firm's relationship with its customers, since they have the most to lose by
such restructuring and the least to gain.

Large firms can overcome their tendency to maintain the *status quo* by
underwriting *elite* activities. The elite members of an organization engage in
projects that have problematic, long-run payouts rather than certain, short-run
yields. The ratio of professional personnel to high status administrators is a
rough measure of the use of elite personnel within an organization. The higher
the proportion of professional personnel to proprietors, managers, and officials,
the more likely is the existence of staff departments preserving long-run interests
against the pressure of immediate problems. Stinchcombe, and Hill and Harbison
have analyzed the relationship between innovation and the proportion of elite
personnel employed.[20] Their findings indicate that innovating industries employ
proportionately more professionals than do non-innovating industries.

Furthermore, within a given industry, the firms with proportionately more
professionals innovate more rapidly than those with fewer. Significantly,
wholesaling and retailing are classified as "stagnant" industries, and the payrolls
of these types of firms contain significantly fewer professional employees per
hundred administrators than is the case in "progressive" industries. Admittedly,
the definitions of "progressiveness" and "stagnation" can be somewhat
arbitrary, as can the definition of a "professional" employee. Consequently, the
data just cited should be regarded as being suggestive rather than definitive, but
the suggestion is unambiguous—retailers and wholesalers could effect economies
and develop more productive institutional arrangements if they engaged in
additional research and underwrote more elite activities.

The "Outsider"

Institutional innovation, particularly in retailing, has historically occurred
outside of the established power structure. The retail innovator, in fact, has
tended to resemble Eric Hoffer's *The True Believer*.[21] J. C. Penney, Richard
Sears, King Cullen, and others were discontented "outsiders" who believed that

---

[20] Arthur L. Stinchcombe, "The Sociology of Organization and the Theory of the Firm."
The Pacific Sociological Review, Fall 1960, pp. 75-82. Samuel E. Hill and Frederick
Harbison, *Manpower and Innovation in American Industry*, Princeton University Press,
1959, pp. 16-27.

[21] Eric Hoffer. *The True Believer*, New American Library, New York, 1951, pp. 13-20.

they had discovered a technique of irresistible power. They had an extravagant conception of the potentialities of the future, minimized the problems of managing a large enterprise, and promulgated their merchandising doctrines with an almost evangelical fervor. The premise that the institutional innovator is likely to come from outside the established power structure is also inherent in the wheel of retailing concept which is the most comprehensive theory of innovation yet developed in marketing.[22] Silk and Stern, in their recent study, also conclude that the marketing innovator has traditionally been an "outsider," but they additionally argue that recent innovators have tended to be much more deliberate in their choice processes and much more methodical in their analyses than were their predecessors of several decades ago.[23] In any case, if we accept the assumption that significant innovation tends to occur outside the existing system, then it is important from a social point of view to create a marketing environment in which entry is relatively easy.

Analyzing Institutional Change

There is a tendency in marketing to refine analysis beyond the point of maximum usefulness, and this is particularly true when the phenomena under investigation are relatively complex. Quite obviously, many of the changes that have occurred in the structure of distribution during the past 50 years can be explained in terms of a relatively simple challenge and response model. The emergence and rapid growth of voluntary and cooperative groups in the food field is a logical response to the expansion of corporate vertical integration, and the rise of the cash and carry wholesaler in the building supply industry is a natural response to the growing importance of the large developer. Thus, if the marketplace is viewed as an arena in which firms constantly search for differential advantage and/or react to it, much of what appears to be rather complex behavior can be reduced to fairly simple terms.

Hypotheses

Systems theorists and sociologists have selectively investigated the diffusion of new ideas and practices. The hypotheses that have emerged from this research serve as useful points of origin for subsequent exploration in marketing. More specifically, *marketing analysts should consider the following hypotheses when attempting to explain institutional change:*

1. The rate of diffusion depends upon the innovation itself. Innovations that involve a substantial capital investment, a major restructuring of the firm's

---

[22] For a careful analysis of the wheel of retailing concept, see Stanley C. Hollander, "The Wheel of Retailing," *Journal of Marketing*, July 1960, pp. 37-42.

[23] Alvin J. Silk and Louis William Stern, "The Changing Nature of Innovation in Marketing: A Study of Selected Business Leaders. 1852-1958." *Business History Review*, Fall 1963, pp. 182-199.

relationship with its customers, and a sizable number of internal realignments are more likely to be accepted slowly than those that involve relatively minor intra- or inter-firm changes.

2. The innovator is likely to be an "outsider" in the sense that he occupies a marginal role in a given line of trade and is on the outskirts of the prevailing sociometric network. Such individuals are interested in innovation because they have the most to gain and the least to lose by disrupting the *status quo*.

3. A firm will respond incrementally to innovation unless its core market is threatened. If the latter is the case, the response to innovation will proceed swiftly. That is, the firm will parry the innovator's thrust by developing a counter strategy or it will emulate the innovator on a partial or total basis.

4. The higher the entrepreneur's aspirations, the more likely he is to initiate or accept innovation. Alternatively, the lower the entrepreneur's aspirations, the less likely he is to accept innovation, particularly when such acceptance conflicts with his other values.

5. The acceptance of innovation is not always permanent. A firm may emulate an innovator as a part of a transitional strategy. When the firm develops an ultimate strategy, the emulating features of its behavior will be discarded.

6. Innovation will be accepted most rapidly when it can be fitted into existing decision-making habits. Innovations which involve an understanding of alien relationships or which involve new conceptual approaches, tend to be resisted. Many small retailers, for example, have difficulty in accepting the supermarket concept, because it involves a fairly sophisticated understanding of cost-volume relationships.

7. Influentials and innovators are not always the same firms. Institutional innovators, since they tend to be "outsiders," have relatively little influence among their entrepreneurial colleagues. Other firms, occupying central positions in a given line of trade, possess considerable influence, and an innovation will not be adopted widely until these influential firms accept it.

8. Greater energy is required to transmit an innovation from one channel to another than is required to transmit it within a channel. The diffusion of innovation therefore tends to be confined to a given line of trade, before it is adopted by another. The supermarket, as an illustration, became dominant in the food field, before this method of operation was employed by ready-to-wear retailers.

The above hypotheses represent only a small sampling of those developed in other fields. They deserve careful consideration by researchers interested in explaining and predicting institutional change in marketing.

Part Two

SYSTEM DESIGN

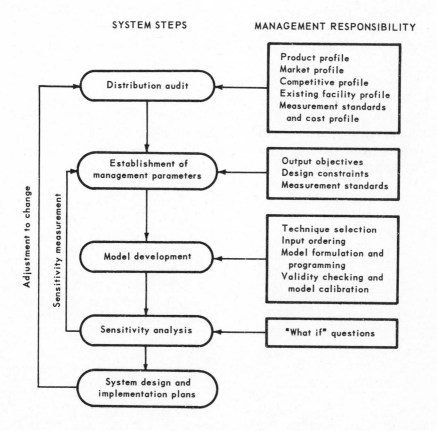

SYSTEM STEPS   MANAGEMENT RESPONSIBILITY

Distribution audit

Product profile
Market profile
Competitive profile
Existing facility profile
Measurement standards
and cost profile

Establishment of
management parameters

Output objectives
Design constraints
Measurement standards

Model development

Technique selection
Input ordering
Model formulation and
programming
Validity checking and
model calibration

Sensitivity analysis

"What if" questions

System design and
implementation plans

Adjustment to change

Sensitivity measurement

Editors' Introduction

The substance of physical distribution management rests in the design of operating systems. The system design becomes the major limiting factor to the degree of efficiency and effectiveness a firm can enjoy in physical distribution operations. A wide variety of different potential designs exist for each firm. Among the array of potential designs is one which will most consistently achieve that firm's customer service goals at the lowest total cost expenditure. The objective of physical distribution system design is to determine the best possible arrangement of logistical facilities and components for the firm.

The design of physical distribution systems requires a research procedure plus a detailed understanding of the interrelation of system components. The arrangement of components is measured on the basis of total cost in terms of alternative levels of performance. Therefore, it is necessary to understand the relationship of individual functional area costs. Finally, evaluation of alternative system designs can be greatly enhanced by the use of various quantitative techniques.

The articles selected for Part Two cover the wide range of subjects included in system design. Proceeding from the question of design procedures, the articles include discussions of various critical components, total cost analysis, and conclude with a selection of contributions dealing with quantitative applications to physical distribution problems.

13

Designing a
Distribution System

WILLIAM B. SAUNDERS
W. B. Saunders and Company

A physical distribution system embraces all of the physical handling required between the point of production and the point of consumption of a given material or product. It has been estimated that this phase of our economic activity accounts for the expenditure of $90 billion. This is about 15% of the total value of our national product. In some industries, distribution costs absorb something like 35 cents out of every sales dollar. It is no wonder, then, that distribution is considered one of the last frontiers for industrial management.

Transportation is only one element in this picture. In many industries, transportation is a very small and, indeed, a minor part of distribution costs. In tomorrow's scientific management era, transportation will be effective in selling itself if it recognizes that it is but one element in a total distribution system.

Transportation will, therefore, be most effective when it understands the needs of each industry for its particular kind of transport service as a part of its total distribution program. This is the key to future sales efforts on the part of transportation companies, and, in my opinion, it is the key to the future activities of the industrial traffic man. He will be a distribution manager, who will fit all the various handling· functions together to produce an optimum distribution system as a whole.

What Is It For?

The objective of a distribution system is, as in every other part of the business, directed toward producing maximum system efficiency. This is a matter of output per unit of input. We want to get the most output for every expenditure of labor and material.

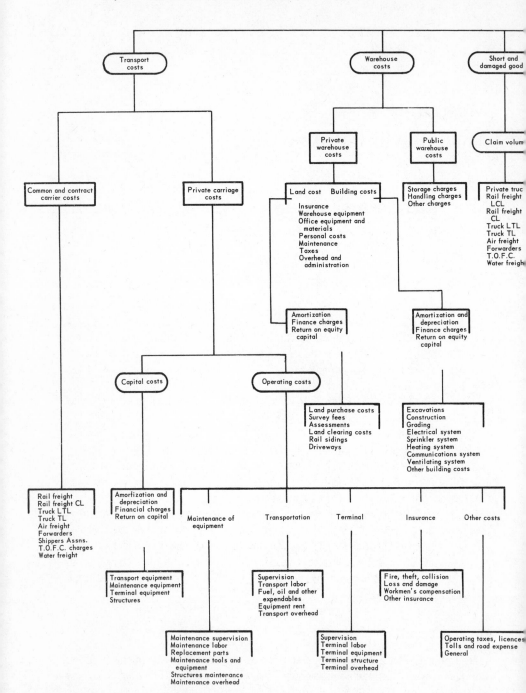

Chart 1. The Areas of Physical Distribution.

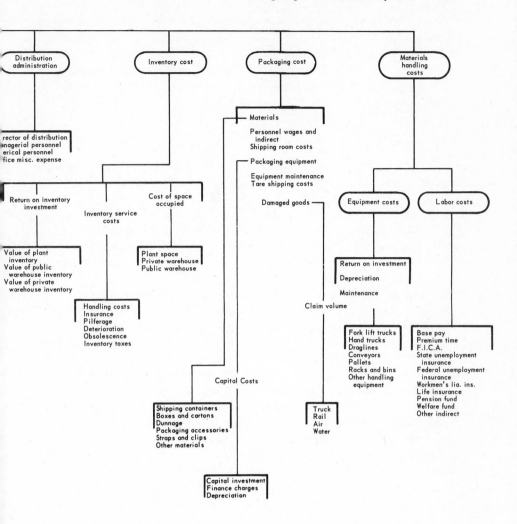

Distribution administration

rector of distribution
anagerial personnel
erical personnel
ffice misc. expense

Return on inventory
investment

Value of plant
inventory
Value of public
warehouse inventory
Value of private
warehouse inventory

Inventory cost

Inventory service
costs

Handling costs
Insurance
Pilferage
Deterioration
Obsolescence
Inventory taxes

Cost of space
occupied

Plant space
Private warehouse
Public warehouse

Packaging cost

Materials

Personnel wages and
indirect
Shipping room costs

Packaging equipment

Equipment maintenance
Tare shipping costs

Damaged goods

Claim volume

Capital Costs

Shipping containers
Boxes and cartons
Dunnage
Packaging accessories
Straps and clips
Other materials

Truck
Rail
Air
Water

Capital investment
Finance charges
Depreciation

Materials
handling
costs

Equipment costs

Return on investment

Depreciation

Maintenance

Fork lift trucks
Hand trucks
Draglines
Conveyors
Pallets
Racks and bins
Other handling
equipment

Labor costs

Base pay
Premium time
F.I.C.A.
State unemployment
insurance
Federal unemployment
insurance
Workmen's lia. ins.
Life insurance
Pension fund
Welfare fund
Other indirect

In physical distribution, the system output is a level of customer service represented by a certain composite of the following factors: product availability, order cycle time, stockout percentages, delivery frequency, delivery reliability, and so forth. Balancing the *cost input* against the *service output* determines the efficiency of the system. This provides the fundamental challenge of distribution system design.

How to Get There?

Now that we have agreed on what it is and what its purpose is, the question is—how to get there? How can you achieve the objectives of a distribution system?

I believe the first principle to bear in mind is that you have to start where you are. Most organizations have some built-in "practical" limitations. For example, the functions described in Chart 2 may now be the responsibilities of a number of different department heads. Each may have a primary interest other than its particular elements in the distribution system.

To deal with these complexities intelligently, a well-organized program of analysis is required. Chart 2 shows schematically the guidelines for such a program. The first step is the distribution audit.

In essence, this means making a traffic analysis to determine what shipments are made from where to where, in what frequency, under what conditions, by what modes, with what degree of reliability, etc. This requires cooperation of the marketing and sales departments, and it tells us what is now moving, what the customer requirements are, and how they are being met.

Another part of the distribution audit is to develop present costs of distribution. Referring to Chart 2, this involves adding up the pieces of distribution costs, being certain they are all included. The sum of all the costs now incurred is the total input required to produce the present service output.

When this step is completed, one can readily see the relative importance of the cost elements and determine where possible economies should be sought. The important question to ask may be, "How can the present standard of service be achieved with a lesser total cost?"

But another and perhaps more important question for some companies is, "How can I design a distribution system to meet a better standard of service at no greater cost than I am now incurring, or perhaps at even a lesser total cost?"

Before considering any changes in the system, however, it is important to establish with the marketing department just what future marketing plans and marketing strategy may be required. It may become critically important to know something about how competitors are approaching their distribution systems and what standards of "efficiency" must be met.

This is essential if a proper level of customer service is to be built into the program. This step, which in essence establishes the objectives of the distribution

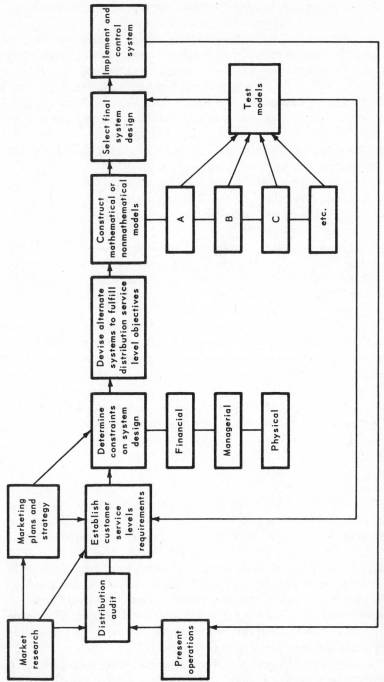

Chart 2. Guidelines for Distribution and Supply Systems Design.

system, is perhaps the most important in the whole process of systems design. It determines the requirements which the system must fulfill.

A miscalculation of customer service requirements can greatly increase costs without corresponding benefits. If a slight improvement in service would attract a 20% increase in volume, and a major increase in service would attract only a 25% increase in volume, the extra cost of the major service increase may not be worth the gain of an additional 5% in sales volume. This is a classic form of business problem—equating the marginal costs of a decision with the marginal revenue to be derived.

Having determined the objectives and constraints of the system, the next step is to devise alternate systems.

It soon becomes apparent that this requires some pretty extensive calculations. There are tremendous numbers of possible interrelationships. For example, we may know that the total transportaiton cost is $10 million for a particular company. How can we lower this?

Perhaps the present system involves the handling of a great many small shipments from factory to consumer. Transportation cost could be greatly reduced if volume shipments were made to a warehouse, then were distributed from the warehouses in small quantities to ultimate consumers over relatively short hauls.

Yet it is equally obvious that such a change, while reducing transportation costs, would add a new dimension—materials handling and warehousing costs. Whether it is a desirable change depends on the *aggregate costs* in comparison with the *aggregate benefit* to be derived from the alternative system.

Likewise, a new type of packaging might reduce loss and damage expense. But it may also require more cubic content per freight car. It would therefore result in lesser load of product per unit of shipping space, hence a higher freight charge per unit of product.

Using Test Models

At this point, models should be constructed to test the various alternative systems design, typically using modern mathematical-statistical techniques. Each alternative system model must be costed in terms of its specific dollar costs as well as its flexibility and responsiveness to market changes.

Each system can then be compared in terms of total cost per unit of output—that is, unit of customer service value. After the test models have been evaluated, the company and its advisors can select the final systems design.

To implement this decision, a full action program is needed—a complete blueprint of just how the new plan works. Chart 2 shows a most important management phenomenon—the concept of "feedback."

In other words, once the control system has been designed and approved, it must include some procedure to insure that the system really works. This means that some periodic or continuing costing process must be established so that there can be a review of the effectiveness of the plan.

Some industry people shy away from this sort of program because they fear becoming involved with the computer. I want to say a word about this in order to keep this matter in proper perspective. The computer aspect of this program can be greatly exaggerated.

The computer is really an idiot child that has been trained to do high speed arithmetic. It should be treated like one. We teach the computer certain specific things and the computer will do them—and only them.

Thus, the real trick is to know what to teach the computer. The consolation for all of us is that the decision on what to tell the computer is based very largely on fundamental economic issues. The only reason that the traffic man or the marketing man or the production man cannot tell the computer what to do all by himself is that he may not see all the pieces which must be plugged in if total costs are to be properly developed.

How to Value Inventory?

For example, how can inventory be valued? Unfortunately, there is no simple formula for this problem. The cost of capital for most companies is determined by the return which could be earned if the capital were put to some other use. If money is tied up in inventory, could it have been used for a productive research and development program? Could it have been used for reducing production costs by installing new machinery and equipment or redesigning the plant?

If we ask the questions in these terms, it may very well be that the cost of inventory is a varying factor depending on the stage of development in which the company finds itself. Thus, valuing inventory requires a certain amount of forecasting. Considering how capital can be used over the next five years may be the most important single element affecting the decision on what kind of distribution system should be established.

How to Value Service

The problem of inventory valuation is but one of the many issues involved in designing a distribution system which require turning to fundamental economic principles. Another example is the problem of how to value service. Railroad rate makers for many years talked about setting rates on the basis of the value of the service. This really meant applying some judgment to determine how high a rate could go, without causing the traffic to dry up!

Today, we need more scientific approaches to this matter of determining how much business can be generated by an improved service standard. As an economist, I call it simply a matter of evaluating the elasticity of demand for the product under varying circumstances.

Thus, the critical issues in designing a distribution system involve matters of economic theory, as applied to the specific circumstances of individual companies. This is not an automatic process. A computer cannot do it without being told what values must be built into the calculations.

The only thing the computer does is to make many more comparisons than would otherwise be economically feasible in determining the optimum distribution mix. But it is the *conceptual understanding* of the distribution system which actually determines the best design—not the *mathematics*.

Distribution systems design, then, is still a human science. As such it is somewhat imprecise, but it should not be left to guesswork—the costs are too high. By means of impartial, objective, and detailed analysis of all the many facets of distribution, this "last frontier of industrial management" can be pushed back to the mutual benefit of the producer, the carrier and the consumer.

14

A Missing Link in Physical
Distribution System Design

JAMES L. HESKETT

Harvard University

Undue, misplaced emphasis on spatial matters in physical distribution has prevented effective measurement of physical distribution activity and the development of truly valid system planning methods. There is evidence of both a macro- and micro-economic nature to support this view.

Macro-economic Symptoms

Economists and economic geographers have placed major emphasis on spatial (distance-oriented) measures of business.

The early studies by von Thünen[1] related to land use were landmarks in two senses of the word. Not only did they mark the beginning but also the direction of the work in economic geography for decades to follow. There was little reason for von Thünen to be concerned with other than spatial matters in his work. The areas near the city-state which he described by concentric rings emanating from the city center were relatively small and regularly described; and because of regular topography and limited traffic they were accessible to the city center in an inverse relation to their distance from it. He observed few irregularities in the pattern of agriculture resulting from the displacement of lower income crops by higher income crops on land of increasing value.

Assuming that perishability of agricultural products was of limited relevance, or only substantiated the spatial framework of von Thünen's theory by varying directly with crop value, temporal time-oriented considerations justifiably were given no emphasis in the theory.

---

[1] Johann Heinrich von Thünen, *Der Isolirte Staat in Beziehung auf Landwirthschaft und Nationalökonomie* (Berlin: Schumacher-Zarchlin, 1875).

Pursuing our landmarks further, we come to the work of Weber.[2] His relatively rich models of industrial location considered as variables: (1) the nature of raw material components and finished products, that is, whether they were localized or ubiquitous, weight-losing or pure; (2) the relative location of a two-dimensional plane of raw material sources and finished-product markets; and (3) the magnitude of labor (production) costs at all possible locations.

He assumed that both transportation costs and transit times were linear in relation to distance. If transportation "rates" of Weber's day and in his country were comparable to ours today, we know that the first part of his assumption is true, *if* we confine ourselves to a single method of transportation and disregard fixed costs.

Again, given the regular topography of his models and the limited transport alternatives of his day, it is understandable that he would assume time equated to distance to the extent that temporal aspects of the problem remained unmentioned. This assumption was to continue unduly to influence students of the subject for some time.

Among Weber's successors, various economists[3] with their linear market models, and also economic geographers of the location-theory school, neglected even to pay lip service to the model irregularities introduced by varying degrees of accessibility measured in units of time. The work of the latter group exhibits the lengths to which researchers have gone to eliminate inconstancies of time in formulating theory. For example, Lösch presumably did not choose the state of Iowa by accident as the area for much of his research in this country.[4] It provided him with a somewhat homogeneous economy, laced regularly with transport arteries, and sufficiently compact and landlocked to rule out most alternative modes of transportation. Only in the work of Dean is there an effort to consider effects of irregular topography and the impact of transportation technology in locations.[5]

Of the regional scientists placing major emphasis on techniques of input-output analysis, a great deal of empirical work has been done by Isard.[6] But his

[2] Alfred Weber, *Über den Standort der Industrien* (Tübingen: Mohr, 1909), translated by Carl J. Friedrich as *Alfred Weber's Theory of the Location of Industries* (Chicago: University of Chicago Press, 1929).

[3] For example, Harold Hotelling, "Stability in Competition," *Economic Journal*, Vol. 39 (March 1929), pp. 41-57; F. Zeuthen, "Theoretical Remarks on Price Policy: Hotelling's Case with Variations," *Quarterly Journal of Economics*, Vol. 47 (February 1933), pp. 231-253; and Edward H. Chamberlin, *The Theory of Monopolistic Competition* (Cambridge: Harvard University Press, 3rd edition, 1938), Appendix C.

[4] August Lösch, *Die Raumliche Ordnung der Wirtschaft* (Jena: Gustav Fischer Verlag, 1940), translated from the 2nd revised edition of 1944 by William H. Woglom with the assistance of Wolfgang F. Stolper, *The Economics of Location* (New Haven: Yale University Press, 1954).

[5] William H. Dean, Jr., *The Theory of the Geographic Location of Economic Activities, Selections from the Doctoral Dissertation* (Ann Arbor: Edwards Brothers, Inc., 1938).

[6] Walter Isard, Eugene W. Schooler, and Thomas Vietoriez, *Industrial Complex Analysis and Regional Development* (New York and Cambridge: John Wiley & Sons, Inc., and the Technology Press of the Massachusetts Institute of Technology, 1959), especially pp. 96-97.

most extensive published study did not have to deal with temporal aspects of the supply and distribution problem in determining what would be produced and where it would be stored. Those items in the petroleum-product family studied in which interregional (international) transportation was a factor were relatively homogeneous. One method of transportation, by water, was feasible. Inventory costs, while a variable, probably were not sufficiently important to influence the results of the analysis very much.

The concept of accessibility employed by graph theorists suggests the opportunity for the eventual use of *time rather than distance* in its computation. However, major studies of this type thus far have been concerned with the impact of alternative network investments on cumulative nodal accessibility for transportation networks containing only one mode of transport.[7] At such time as they are developed to the point where transportation systems describing modes with widely varying characteristics are superimposed upon one another, a consideration will be necessary of cumulative times rather than distances in measuring the degree of accessibility inherent in various systems and system combinations.

Only urban geographers appear to have placed some emphasis on temporal aspects of distribution on a somewhat macro-economic level.[8] This is natural, because the subject commodity of their location studies invariably has been people. And commuters or shoppers tend to measure distance in minutes, not miles. Their location decisions and consequently the "face" of the community, are altered by the factor of time.

By no means is this a complete list of examples; but each of the works mentioned has in some measure confused the issues related to system design at the micro-economic level.

Micro-economics of Space and Time

The micro-economics of physical distribution systems concern two major cost categories: transportation and industry.

The former are incurred in the connecting links on a distribution network. The latter are experienced primarily at system nodes, but also while goods are in transit. Costs of freight transportation approximated $60 billion and of inventory carrying $30 billion in the United States in 1964.

These major cost areas have spawned a number of models which can be grouped into related categories. Transportation costs, in combination with volumes of goods in movement, typically have provided the heart of location

---

[7]For representative works, see William L. Garrison, "Connectivity of the Interstate Highway System," in *Papers and Proceedings* (Philadelphia: Regional Science Association, 1960), pp. 122-137; and Karel Kansky, *Structure of Transportation Networks*, Department of Geography Research Paper No. 84 (Chicago: University of Chicago, 1963).

[8]For example, Lowdon Wingo, Jr., *Transportation and Urban Land* (Washington: Resources for the Future, Inc., 1961), especially pp. 43-62; and David L. Huff, "Defining and Estimating a Trading Area," *Journal of Marketing*, Vol. 28 (July 1964), pp. 34-38.

models regardless of whether the model has employed a linear-programing, center of gravity, or other approach. On the other hand, inventory models have been directly concerned with inventory costs. Accordingly, it can be said that:

1. Location models have been *spatially oriented* to date, while inventory models have and will always be *temporally oriented*.
2. A physical distribution system can be described completely for analytical purposes *only in terms of its inventories*, but not in terms only of its transportation elements.

If an integrated, accurate method of analyzing and controlling physical distribution systems is to be developed, time instead of space will be the relevant unifying dimension to be used.

Orientation of Location and Inventory Models

To date, the most popular approaches to location problems have been spatially oriented. The center-of-gravity method has been one of minimizing ton-miles accumulated between supply and demand points on a system. Where varying rates have applied to the ton-miles involved, a weighted ton-mile measure has been used. Nevertheless, with the exception of Bowersox's use of transit time between a grocery warehouse and retail outlets in an urban setting,[9] the object of center-of-gravity models has been to minimize distance rather than time.

Linear programing models for location invariably have employed transportation costs between potential system nodes.[10] To the extent that transportation costs are assumed to be linear in relation to distance, this is a spatial measure. Finally, in the most extensively used models, based on heuristic programing, distance is the factor employed to describe nodal relationships.[11]

In contrast, inventory models have no spatial orientation in the context of the definition given earlier. The relationship of a demand point to its supply point is stated in terms of time for all models allowing uncertainty. Of course, the relevant time is not transit time between inventory locations, but rather the order-cycle time required to complete the course of communications and order shipment, extending from the point of order to the supply point and back again to the point of delivery.

A major preoccupation with the time dimension is characteristic of propo-

---

[9] Donald J. Bowersox, "An Analytical Approach to Warehouse Location," *Handling & Shipping*, Vol. 11 (February 1962), pp. 17-20.

[10] For example, William J. Baumol and Philip Wolfe, "A Warehouse Location Problem," *Operations Research*, Vol. 6 (March-April 1958), pp. 252-263.

[11] Alfred A. Kuehn and Michael J. Hamburger, "A Heuristic Program for Locating Warehouses," *Management Science*, Vol. 9 (July 1963), pp. 643-666.

nents of both optimization models and simulation models for inventory management.[12]

In total, a physical distribution system can be described in terms of its inventories and their determinants. But this requires a description of inventories in transit as well as at nodal points on a network. Thus, a system of three plants, two distribution warehouses, and ten markets arranged as in Figure 1 can be conceived of as having over 100 inventory "cells" of all or some goods in a product line.

The figure shows only 45 of the more important cells. Momentarily, any one cell or even most cells may be empty. Over time, however, all eventually may

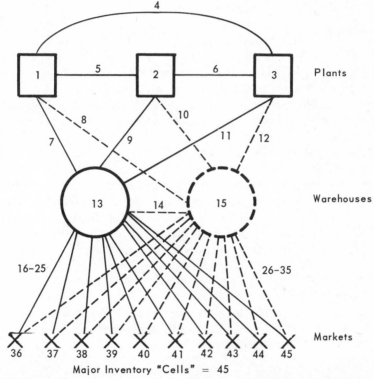

Figure 1. Designation of Inventory Cells in a System for Physically Distributing Goods from Three Plants Through Two Distribution Warehouses to Ten Markets.

[12] For examples of the former, see John F. Magee, *Production Planning and Inventory Control* (New York: McGraw-Hill Book Co., 1958), and Robert B. Fetter and Winston C. Dalleck, *Decision Models for Inventory Management* (Homewood, Illinois: Richard D. Irwin, Inc., 1961). An illustration of the latter is provided by Jay W. Forrester, *Industrial Dynamics* (Cambridge and New York: The M.I.T. Press and John Wiley & Sons, Inc., 1961), especially pp. 137-186.

contain something. The elimination of a warehouse in Figure 1 would eliminate not 1 but 15 inventories and probably affect many of the remaining 30.

Notice that the network in Figure 1 is dimensionless. Both distance and time are unsatisfactory dimensions for the graphic description of a physical distribution system. The shortcomings of distance as a measure have been discussed. Time as a determinant of inventory levels in various cells is a promising but confusing measure, for it takes on different meanings for inventories in transit, as opposed to those at nodal points.

The level of in-transit inventories is directly influenced, among other things, by transit times between a given set of nodes in a system. A different time period, that required for the completion of an order cycle, is relevant for a determination of the inventory levels at a nodal point.[13]

The first of these statements requires a re-evaluation of the assumption implicit in most location models—that in the location of one or more facilities on a network, a minimization of distance weighted by the freight volume to be moved between relevant existing nodes and the proposed nodes (least ton-mile points) will somehow lead to minimum transit times.

As has been pointed out above, where various transport methods can be employed to traverse a given distance, neither time nor cost necessarily bears a close relationship to distance.

On the other hand, the relevance of order-cycle times to nodal inventories requires an examination of the implicit assumption (stretched one step further) that distances between network nodes are somehow related to order-cycle times for goods ordered and shipped between them. The rationale for the assumption logically might be the direct relationships between distance and transit time on the one hand, and transit time and order-cycle time on the other.

However, time in transit represents roughly only 40% of the total order-cycle time.[14] Furthermore, in a sample of means of order-cycle times for two categories of products, carefully measured several years ago, the relationship between order-cycle times and distances for shipments moving from various manufacturers to a distribution warehouse was so low as to be almost meaningless. More specifically, the coefficients of determination were .11 and .16 for drug and candy products, respectively.[15]

---

[13] Donald J. Bowersox implies this in his article, "Total Information Systems in Logistics," in J. L. Heskett, Editor, *Business Logistics—Appraisal and Prospect* (Stanford: Stanford University Graduate School of Business, 1965), pp. 109-122.

[14] Evidence of this is presented in Richard A. Johnson and Donald D. Parker, "Optimizing Customer Delivery Service with Improved Distribution," *Business Review*, Vol. 21 (October 1961), pp. 38-46, at p. 44; and in Paul R. Stephenson, *Manufacturers' Physical Distribution Service Knowledge and Penalties: An Experimental Analysis,* unpublished Master's thesis deposited in the library of Ohio State University, 1963.

[15] Unpublished research by the author in collaboration with John Rider and Paul R. Stephenson.

One additional argument can be given for the lack of relevance of spatially oriented location models for the problem of physical distribution system design. Nearly all location models devised to date have had cost (weighted distance) minimization as their primary objective.[16] Unless demand is assumed constant regardless of a system design, cost minimization has little to do with profit maximization in a physical distribution system. In addition, the costs minimized in available spatial models often are not inclusive of all those incurred in physical-distribution activities.

In contrast, the time-oriented inventory model for conditions of uncertainty as a matter of course allows a consideration of order-cycle time and dependability as two of the determinants of demand. By facilitating the consideration of both demand (revenue) and costs, this type of model lends itself more readily than the spatially oriented model to planning with a profit-maximization objective.

Conclusions

Location and inventory models can be used as the basis both for planning and operational control of logistics system elements. Even where both types of models have been employed in the same company, however, their dimensional inconsistencies have prevented their integration.

Concentration on spatial relationships in physical supply and distribution, although the product of nearly a hundred years of effort in the formulation of macro-economic theory, has not yielded a valid comprehensive approach to the description and analysis of physical distribution systems.

Rather, such a system can be viewed most productively as a set of actual or potential inventory cells linked and partially determined by time—transit time for those inventory cells in network links, order cycle time for those cells at network nodes.

Time rather than distance will be the unifying dimension of an integrated model for helping plan and control a logistics system. This model—adapted to each company's special needs—will combine elements of a temporally oriented location model with an inventory model to produce information for planning purposes and a set of devices for the control of various elements of a company's logistics system.

[16]The one known exception is that reported in Frank H. Mossman and Newton Morton, *Logistics of Distribution Systems* (Boston: Allyn and Bacon, Inc., 1965), pp. 245-256, in which the effect of location on service and hence demand is explored in the context of a conventional location model.

15

What to Watch Out For in Planning Systems

RUDDELL REED, JR.
Purdue University

There has been a great deal of discussion, in recent years, about the systems approach to materials handling analysis. And up to a point, this is good. It is certainly true that you can't reduce costs effectively unless you give attention to the costs of the total system. You must look at the inter-dependencies between individual handling operations as well as at the operations themselves.

At the same time, however, a little realistic caution is needed when applying the latest methods of systems analysis. But first, let's look at some restrictions which must be recognized in materials handling problems.

1. There is presently no way to directly design the optimum plant system. You are restricted to designing alternatives of the systems, and then picking the best of the alternatives.

2. Increased automation does not, of itself, guarantee reduced costs. The first stages of automation may give substantial cost savings. But, as the level of automation increases, the rate of investment required will increase faster than the rate of savings. A point will be reached at which the marginal cost of adding the next level of automation will exceed the marginal savings. Or, the law of diminishing returns applies to automation.

3. The degree of equipment utilization has a significant effect on handling cost. Cost estimates based on an assumed fixed hours of use, per time period, will usually be wrong in proportion to the error between the actual use and the assumed use. This cost error may easily be enough to lead you to select a sub-optimum system. Statistical analysis of demand is desirable.

4. Minimum cost associated with equipment, and, in turn, minimum handling cost, will occur at something less than 100% equipment utilization. Or, put it this way: excessive loading of equipment increases cost. Too, there is an

144

optimum level of equipment maintenance for each level of utilization, and a deviation from it—high or low—increases the operating cost of the system.

5. You need detailed, accurate data to properly analyze handling requirements and associated costs. Your system design selection can be no better than the system-related cost data on which the decision is based.

6. The handling system is an integral part of the production system and, therefore, of the plant arrangement. Production planning and scheduling, the production process, production control and the plant arrangement design can be no more effective than the handling system which acts as the integrating link between successive stages or operations.

The key characteristic of the systems approach is that we work from the "big picture" toward the detail. There are those who propose that the starting point should be a theoretically ideal system. This means: eliminate the handling which adds cost but no product value. By "value" we mean the inherent quality of the item to the user for which he is willing to pay.

This approach is unrealistic.

The systems theorists next speak of an ultimate ideal system, a level below the theoretically ideal system. They say that the ultimate ideal system could be realized on a theoretical basis if you have ideal conditions and rigorous relationships between demands on the system and system components. Optimizing techniques under these work perfectly, since all system inter-relationships are perfectly defined. Given the criteria to be satisfied, the optimum system can be designed.

This, of course, assumes, first, that we have total information and, second, that the actions under total information can be defined in a rigorous manner. But total information is rarely, if ever, available. And if it *were* available, the rigorous definition of actions and inter-actions would rarely, if ever, be possible. From a practical viewpoint, therefore, we must concern ourselves with a technically workable system that is also feasible.

In the past, the planner looked at a single operation, or move, and considered how best to accomplish it. In effect, he then optimized its method. His eventual system was a combination of such optimum operations.

By contrast, the systems approach starts with the technically feasible system and then works down toward individual operations, forcing them to "give" to satisfy the overall system requirements. This approach is more likely to result in a near-optimum system design.

All this doesn't mean that we don't need detailed data relating to the operations. On the contrary, we need more data to measure the operation's effect on overall system effectiveness and cost. Further, to measure these effects, modern tools of analysis and design must be adapted to materials handling problems.

There is no magic formula for materials handling analysis. There are, however, some techniques which when combined with the analysis and design framework of the individual project will help to approach the optimum technically workable system.

Misunderstandings Regarding Costs

There are some strange misunderstandings in industry, regarding handling. Take, for example, costs. Seldom is the cost of handling alternatives related to the company's total cost curve. Too often, it is assumed that a lower handling cost means an automatic reduction in total company costs. But this is true only if the handling change does not raise costs in distribution, production, or some other phase of handling itself. Here are a few guides in cost analysis:

1. Strive for detailed cost data. This calls for working with accounting records, plus special cost gathering analysis on the part of the analyst.
2. Measure the effect of handling on the total costs of the firm. Comparisons for handling aspects alone may be dangerous.
3. Compare alternative systems on future unit costs and marginal costs, based on sales or product forecasts over the economic life of the equipment. Apply cash flow principles.
4. Adapt quantitative techniques, such as statistics and mini-max rules to decision making.
5. Summarize costs on alternative systems, rather than on alternative operations.
6. Ask for help in using recently developed techniques of analysis.

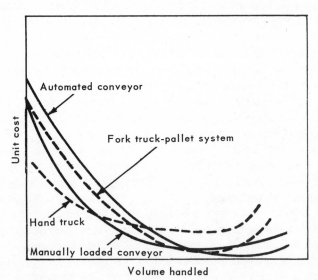

Figure 1. Mechanization Cuts Costs? Not Always. At Low-Use Level, Least Mechanized System Is Most Economical.

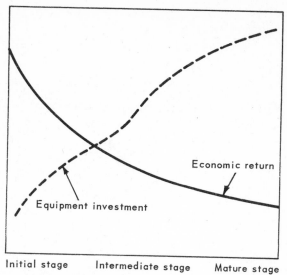

Economic return

Equipment investment

Initial stage   Intermediate stage   Mature stage

Figure 2. System Age Can Hurt When It Reaches the Point Where the Equipment Investment Exceeds the Savings.

Most handling costs—excepting ad valorem taxes, and insurance—tend to be variable and therefore marginal costs. They vary with equipment hours per year, operating costs per hour, and labor cost per operating hour. Because analyzing these costs as variables is usually complex, we assume a fixed or average rate per hour. This tends to disregard the effect a choice of method may have on the utilization of either men or equipment within the system. Yet the marginal costs which depend upon the level of utilization, not the average costs involved, should often dictate the proper choice.

In Figure 1, we see that a significant variation in cost may exist as volume handled changes.

The idea persists that increased mechanization reduces cost. Often this is not true. Look again at Figure 1. At low levels of demand, the least mechanized system is most economical. Figure 2 and Figure 3 show why this is true. Figure 2 shows that a point is reached at which cost exceeds savings, and Figure 3 indicates that this may occur in mechanization.

The cost curves in Figure 1 assume that labor can be assigned elsewhere when not needed for the operation. If not, each curve drops sharply toward the minimum marginal cost level. If labor has not been fully utilized, increasing production adds little to total cost.

Each curve rises rapidly after reaching the minimum point. Any system has an optimum operating level. Handling larger quantities depends on having an available buffer of material, thus an increased inventory investment. Increasing speed beyond optimum increases the chance of breakdown and resulting delay at the next or preceding operations. Another contributing factor, to increased cost

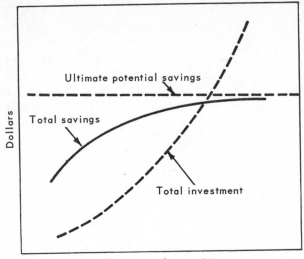

Figure 3. Law of Diminishing Returns Applies to Automation. You Save Only So Much, No Matter What You Spend.

at high output levels, is inadequate time for maintenance and therefore increased physical depreciation.

Developing cost curves for a total system is more difficult than developing curves for its elements, because the elements inter-act, continually affecting each other. But either way, total system or element, the lowest element's capacity limits system capacity. Keep in mind, in looking at costs for decision-making, that they must be the *total* cost to the company. Only in this way can you determine the system which will balance the lowest unit cost at present output and the lowest marginal cost at anticipated outputs, to provide lowest system-life costs.

Let's now take a quick look at some of the techniques which can be used for systems analysis and design. But keep in mind that, since we can only provide the technically feasible system and since handling is usually a relatively complex system, both quantitative and qualitative procedures may be necessary.

Further, because you may have to make simplifying assumptions to use certain quantitative techniques, their advantage may be in providing added knowledge for qualitative decisions, rather than as direct decision methods. In either case, we must get the important factual knowledge of handling flow: what-moves-where-when.

Getting Real Data

In the past, we prepared flow diagrams from operation sheet data. But too often, deviations from planned sequences occur. If we are to design for the problem, we must know what *does* happen, not what *should* happen. This requires sampling to find activity distributions within and between departments.

To summarize sample results, nothing better than the cross-reference chart has been developed. However, the total sample will provide relative frequency of moves along individual paths. It may be necessary to convert to volume-of-handling by studying the activity over a few move paths in detail for a significant period and then use relative frequencies to estimate the total moves along the other paths.

A handling method costing sheet can then be used to establish individual costs by different handling methods for each move path. Care must be used to be certain that handling method costs are accurate for the final system's utilization of men and equipment for each method. If utilization varies, cost varies, and another iteration of the system cost sheet is indicated.

The next most likely consideration is: for which operations do you select handling equipment first? The key is in the cross-reference sheet and a value curve. The value curve is no more than the cumulative distribution of the volume handling activities.

To develop the value curve: (1) list vertically the moves in the cross-reference chart from high to low volumes, and (2) draw a scaled bar graph for volume, for each activity, starting the bar of each succeeding move at the termination value of the preceding move.

The first move listed has the greatest value to the company since it involves the most activity. Therefore, optimize the handling method for this move first. Continue down the list in order, using any reserve capacity in earlier assigned equipment as feasible and economically justified, considering effects on and by the plant arrangement. Techniques of dynamic programming can be used to provide the minimum-cost handling system for the plant.

It should be recognized that the above is incomplete in the total analysis problem. Questions of alternative arrangements, storage requirements, maintenance policy and programs need to be considered before finalizing the system. When these problems arise, you may use analytical techniques including mathematical programming, decision models, queueing theory, simulation techniques and applied statistics to increase the total information available before making a final decision.

The chief caution to be emphasized here is that the technique used be tested to make sure it fits the quality of the data related to the problem. For example, don't use queueing formulas based on the assumption of an infinite queue if, in fact, you are establishing a significantly finite capacity for storage.

At present, no general analytical models exist for direct decision purposes in materials handling systems. The model assumptions, inherent in available models are too restrictive, in general, of the real world.

The interspersing of approximating models for individual phases of the problem may, however, significantly contribute to the knowledge of the planner, resulting in a much improved final design, arrived at by qualitative and "state of the art" techniques.

16

Accounting for Physical Distribution

H. G. MILLER
Diamond Crystal Salt Company

Physical distribution has emerged as an organizational and physical concept and, within a few years, has become a commonly accepted term in Traffic and Marketing circles. Definitions vary widely on what the term means and even on what the appropriate word should be. For the purposes of this article, I would like to use the definition, "Those functions involved in the physical movement of goods from the end of the manufacturer's production line into the buyer's point of use." The concept includes materials handling, packaging, storage and all transportation costs. It does not include selling or purchasing. It does cover both the inbound movement of raw materials and supplies and the outbound movement of products. This article will be directed primarily to physical distribution problems of basic industries selling to industrial markets rather than to the ultimate consumer. The basic concepts will apply to both industrial and consumer distribution, but the method of approach may differ.

The managerial functions and engineering skills involved in handling the various aspects of physical distribution have long been recognized by management and have been contributed to reduction of cost. The sudden interest in the new term covering the fields of materials handling, packaging, traffic, transportation, inventory control, terminaling and warehousing was stimulated by the recognition that these functions were closely interrelated. While divided managerially and geographically, they regulate a unified flow of cargo from production point to consumer and a counter flow from raw material supplier to the production plant. Even more important in the stimulation of top management interest in physical distribution was the recognition it represented the third largest area of cost of doing business. It was also recognized that regardless of where the function was performed geographically or who on the company organization chart controlled the decision, the functions were closely interrelated in their impact on total costs. These functions, which bridge the geographical and time gap between the production line and the customer, are more closely related to each other than to the traditional cost control centers of production and sales.

To fully benefit long range from treatment of all physical distribution operations as a unified system, the organization must be backed up by an accounting system that permits recognition, accumulation and control of these costs. Physical distribution must become an accounting concept as well as an organizational concept.

The creation of the physical distribution function as a management and accounting function will not automatically eliminate the gray areas between production and sales. Many decisions in the physical distribution area will have a direct bearing on both manufacturing and sales. The problem of inventory, discussed later, is an excellent example of the need for close coordination of the manufacturing, distribution and sales requirements to determine the most economic solution for the company.

In this article, I would like to review the major cost elements in the total cost approach to physical distribution and to note where these costs are normally found in the corporate accounts. I will illustrate how the traditional accounting methods fail to provide effective data for control. I will also note a few of the specific areas where the creation of an accounting entity for physical distribution may assist in the reduction of total costs and contribute to increased profits.

Total Physical Distribution Cost Analysis

Exhibit A is a summary of major physical distribution cost elements organized on the basis of where they occur in the movement of product from the end of the production line to the customer. I have also noted where you are likely to find these costs in traditional accounting records. No list of this type will cover all costs for all industries. The best method of determining these costs in specific studies is to actually follow the movement of product from the production point to customer and note and estimate the major costs which are incurred at each step. This method is particularly valuable when comparing the total cost of two alternate routes to supply a market.

The first area of costs are those which occur within the production plant and which are normally included in the cost of production. It has been customary to include in production cost, both single trip (i.e., expendable packages) and returnable containers (tank cars). Inclusion of tank car cost in a production account separates control over effective use of the equipment from the cost results. The number of tank cars required is a function of sales volume, location of the customers, carrier efficiency in moving equipment and most of all the average delays incurred in awaiting orders, storage at intermediate points and the delays in car unloading and release at the customer's plant. None of these

I. *Costs at Production Point*
   (Normally included in production cost by accounting.)
   A. Packaging
      1. Package cost
      2. Material handling and filling costs
   B. Storage and Handling Costs
      1. Labor and material handling equipment
      2. Space cost—rental or amortization, maintenance and taxes on facilities
   C. Financial Costs on Finished Goods Inventories
      1. Cost of working capital
      2. Taxes and insurance on inventories
      3. Loss from deterioration or obsolescence
   D. Administrative
      1. Order processing and inventory control
      2. Supervision of physical distribution functions
      3. Communications and travel

II. *Cost of Moving Materials to Customers*
    (Normally included in freight on sales or netted against gross sales.)
    A. Freight—From Plant to Terminal or Customer and from Terminal to Customer
       1. Freight payments or private carriage cost.
    B. Transportation Equipment Cost
       1. Net rental or ownership cost of transportation equipment furnished by shipper.
    C. Product Loss Not Recovered from Insurance or Carriers
    D. Miscellaneous Costs
       1. Insurance, demurrage, tolls and other charges.

III. *Cost of Outside Storage and Warehousing*
     (May be included in cost of goods sold, selling expense or distribution account.)
     A. Packaging Expense
     B. Storage and Handling Costs
     C. Financial Costs of Finished Goods Inventories (Same as Item 1C)
     D. Administrative
     E. Premium Freight Incurred as Result of Improper Location of Stocks

IV. *Customer's Costs*
    A. Transportation Cost Absorbed by Customer
    B. Storage and Handling Costs to Receive Material
    C. Financial Costs on Raw Materials Inventories (Same as Item 1C)
    D. Rental or Demurrage Charges on Carrier or Supplier Furnished Returnable Containers

Exhibit A. Physical Distribution Cost Categories—Industrial Marketing. Summary by Point of Occurrence.

variables are under the direct control of the production plant superintendent on whose accounts the resulting costs appear.

The second major area of physical distribution cost is the transportation of product from the production plant to terminal or direct to customer and the further movement from terminal to customer. It is important to consider freight to return empty containers and related charges such as demurrage and insurance.

The third major area of physical distribution costs are those incurred as a result of storage of products in the plant or at terminal or redistribution points outside of the production plants. Many of the cost elements of the storage and warehousing function are the same when incurred outside the plant as when they are incurred inside the plant, although the form of payment may be different. Too often, however, management tends to spotlight these costs when incurred outside the plant, while the same costs inside the plant gate are lost in production accounts.

One area of cost that often tends to be overlooked in distribution cost analysis is the financial cost of carrying inventories since, in most cases, no direct accounting charge is made for the cost of working capital. As noted, the same costs should be considered whether the inventory happens to be located inside the plant or outside.

The area of inventory control and establishment of inventory levels is one where there is divided responsibility between production, physical distribution and sales, and where careful analysis of the costs and benefits is essential to determine optimum levels.

For example, building an inventory may have several desirable results which must be weighed against the cost of maintaining the inventory:

1. It may permit more economic production runs and smooth out seasonal swings. In this case, the cost of maintaining inventory must be compared with the benefits of lower production cost by production management.

2. Larger inventories may permit more efficient movement of product to market. Savings in transportation cost must be weighed against the cost of maintaining the inventory by the distribution department.

3. Inventory in the market permits faster delivery of product and often makes smaller volume deliveries economically feasible. The availability of inventory at the right place may result in increased sales. This must be carefully weighed by the Sales Department.

While there is a tendency to charge field inventories to sales and plant inventories to production, the location of the inventory may have little relation to the economic function it performs. Most inventories serve more than one of the above functions. For effective control, it is essential that all relevant costs and economic advantages be considered. This is an excellent example of an area in which recognition of the total physical distribution function as an accounting entity for cost accumulation will give more complete cost data. But it is still essential to weigh the benefits to production, distribution and to sales to arrive at the optimum inventory level and location. Operations research techniques may have a valid application to better weigh the complex variables to reach an optimum profit decision. To complete the bridge of total physical distribution costs, I have noted those which are incurred by the customer. While this cost area fits nicely into our concept of smooth flow of product from the end of the supplier's production line to the start of the customer's process, there are obviously severe limitations to the ability of the supplier to control costs in this area. However, to ignore the customer's costs and to fail to recognize the impact of your actions on the customer can result in the highest distribution cost of all—"lost sales."

In summary, one approach to detailed analysis of total physical distribution cost is to follow the physical flow of product from the end of the production line to the consumer. While the product may cross several lines of departmental responsibility, including the point of exchange from supplier's to customer's cost, the major costs tend to fall into five categories: materials handling, package cost, storage cost (space cost), financial cost of maintaining inventory and transportation cost. Recognition of the essential continuity and close interrelation of these functions can assist in the accumulation of more meaningful cost data and more effective control of the supplier's cost. It also provides a basis for objective analysis of the effect of changes in these functions on customer's costs and the resulting impact on total sales.

How Physical Distribution Costs Are Handled in Standard Accounting Practice

It is difficult to generalize on the best or most common accounting methods for handling distribution costs. Perhaps an example of a problem we encountered in distribution of industrial chemicals may help illustrate the underlying problem.

A packaged product had been distributed by rail direct to a distant market. We determined by total cost analysis that a considerable reduction in physical distribution cost could be achieved by bulk barge movement of the product to a terminal centrally located in the market for packaging and distribution by truck and rail.

Using the method of cost analysis outlined in Exhibit A, the two routes resulted in the cost summarized in Table 1. The costs used are hypothetical, and I have simplified the presentation to focus attention on its impact on total cost and the accounting records.

In the illustration in Table 1, total physical distribution cost is reduced by $.0065 per pound or by $130,000 per year on the anticipated volume. All of the saving resulted from a reduction in transportation cost by $1.10 hundredweight which reduction was partially offset by increased terminal cost, extra handling, administrative cost and the higher financial cost of maintaining the higher inventories required by water movement. No change occurred in the customer's cost as he continued to receive product in the same manner.

Table 1. Comparison of Direct Rail and Barge Rail Delivery

	Cost Per Cwt.	
	Rail Direct	*Barge Rail*
Production Plant Cost		
Packaging	$1.00	$ .00
Storage and handling	.30	.10
Financial costs inventory	.10	.25
Administrative	.15	.05
Subtotal	$1.55	$ .40
Transportation Cost		
To customer	1.60	.20
To terminal	—	.30
Subtotal	$1.60	$ .50
Terminal Expense		
Packaging	.00	$1.00
Storage and handling	.00	.30
Financial costs inventory	.00	.15
Administrative	.00	.15
Subtotal	.00	$1.60
Total cost per cwt.	$3.15	$2.50
Total cost 20,000,000#/Year	$630,000	$500,000

In Table 2, I have summarized the effect of the change in distribution method on the various accounts involved. Where freight is netted against gross sales and is not shown as an expense item on the Profit and Loss Statement, the effect on the accounts is rather curious.

Plant production cost apparently decreases and the plant superintendent appears to be a hero if management looks at average cost only and doesn't recognize that the total reduction resulted from transfer of packaging to someone else's account.

The second major effect on the accounts is an apparent increase in net sales dollars as a result of the reduction in freight which is deducted from gross sales to get net sales. The accounting practice in some industries of treating freight as a reduction of sales dollars rather than a cost item on the profit and loss statement, has hidden this area from the attention of top management.

Outside warehousing and storage cost is substantially increased. Much of this cost was transferred directly from the production account when packaging was transferred from the plant to the terminal. However, if you were a marketing manager and charged with the cost of all out of plant stocks, you would be faced with explanation of a major increase in your costs while the

Table 2. Change in Accounts Resulting from Change in Distribution Method

	Cost Per Cwt.	
	Direct Rail	*Barge Rail*
Production Costs (Plant)		
All costs except physical distribution	$10.00	$10.00
Physical distribution	1.55	.40
Total production cost	$11.55	$10.40
Accounting effect—Apparent reduction in plant production cost.		
Transportation Cost		
Gross sales price	$15.00	$15.00
Net freight cost	1.60	.50
Net sales	$13.40	$14.50
Accounting effect—Net sales dollars increased.		
Warehousing and Storage (Field)	$ .00	$ 1.60
Accounting effect—Field warehousing cost substantially increased.		

offsetting reductions are occurring in areas outside of your cost responsibility.

This illustrates several problem areas in the accumulation of physical distribution costs by the accounting department in a manner that facilitates effective control by management. The following are a few of the major ones:

A. Freight, the Lost Cost

The illustration clearly indicates the problems in cost control which result when expenses of manufacturing and selling are increased to reduce freight if freight is netted against sales and does not appear on the accounting reports. Even where freight is treated as an expense, it may be difficult to relate specific changes in distribution methods to cost results unless a breakdown by product is available from accounting.

B. Loss of Meaning Through Averaging

Another limitation of accounting figures in distribution cost analysis is the presentation of these costs as averages which may represent a wide range of costs. For example, on a product sold at a uniform delivered price throughout the United States, the average freight cost is $.01 per pound and normal gross profit is $.03 per pound. Further analysis indicates actual freight ranges from

$.002 to $.045 per pound. While overall marketing is profitable, there are certain areas which are marginal or unprofitable markets. The vast number of transactions involved in physical distribution makes it necessary to use some arbitrary averages or indices to allocate costs.

C. *Separation of Supervisor's Responsibility for Cost-Causing Decisions and Actual Cost Allocation on Accounting Records*

We have noted that the product in physical distribution crosses many lines of management responsibility. Often the control of decisions affecting distribution cost is separated from the accounting responsibility for the resulting cost. Too often this separation of decision and cost result makes it difficult to determine the actual cost of the decision and results in a lack of effective control. This can easily result in programs which relocate costs rather than reduce them. Four specific examples may illustrate the popular corporate pastime of *relocating* rather than reducing costs.

1. A new flexible, reuseable container is advocated by the production plant because it reduces packaging and plant handling cost. However, the turnaround time on the container is much slower than anticipated and return freight costs are high. These combine to offset much of the saving in production and packaging cost.

2. Jumbo tank cars have received favorable rate attention by the railroads, but no adjustment has been made in mileage allowance to compensate for the higher rental cost. Much of the rate reduction is offset by increased equipment cost for the supplier. On products sold freight equalized or f.o.b. production plant the saving passed on to the customer may be substantially greater than the total reduction in distribution cost.

3. A distribution study indicates a substantial saving in shipping a customer 40,000 pound cars direct from the plant rather than truckloads from a nearby terminal. The shift is made, but within six months the account is lost to a nearby producer who offers better service

4. Marketing psychology changes package dimensions to increase attractiveness of the package. The change in size results in a 5 per cent increase in cube and changes the product's freight classification, substantially increasing freight cost.

Advantage of Assignment of Physical Distribution Costs to Common Accounts

While there are limits to the degree which the accounting department can adapt their financial and cost accounting systems to permit more effective control of these vital cost areas, some modifications may pay big dividends. The degree of detail which can be afforded and the control centers which are significant will differ with each company but the following guides may be applied generally:

1. Where freight is absorbed by the manufacturer, an accumulation of freight cost by product is important.

2. Accumulate costs in the accounts charged to the management groups making the decisions which can materially affect them.

3. Because many of the costs in the physical distribution area are closely interrelated, the grouping of all these costs in related accounts can materially aid in effective control.

One key point where the grouping of physical distribution costs in a group of related accounts can pay big dividends is in the application of this data in the pricing structure.

Physical Distribution Costs and Pricing

Physical distribution management should determine the total cost differences which are a result of different methods of distribution or types of package and order size. As outlined in Heckert's basic work in this field, *Analysis and Control of Distribution Cost,* these cost differentials should be carefully analyzed periodically to determine that price differentials represent actual cost differentials. It is through the establishment of proper price differentials that a supplier's costs are reflected in the customer's choice of distribution channels, packages and minimums. Industry tends to lag in reflecting changes in distribution methods and increases in physical distribution cost in these price differentials based upon minimums, package and shipping method. For example, many volume prices are based on 20,000 pound truckload minimums while the effective minimum for traffic and rate purposes has increased to 30,000 or 40,000 pounds.

The customer will buy that combination of package and minimum which is most economical to him. Therefore, unless the supplier places realistic differentials between the alternate methods of supply he offers, he will be subsidizing inefficient methods of shipment.

It must be recognized, however, that a company's ability to set these price differentials is limited by competitive practice in the industry. Mass distribution of commodities requires competitive participation in mass markets. Obviously, it would be difficult to maintain a price differential between packages or based on minimums significantly different from those offered by competition if you wish to remain competitive in the market. A supplier cannot ignore the fourth area of physical distribution cost listed in Exhibit A. The customer will base his decision to purchase on evaluation of cost from his side of the bridge. To sell, the supplier must be competitive as measured by the customer's total cost.

The past five years have seen tremendous changes in the philosophy of rate making, and many innovations in transportation and packaging equipment have occurred. In our industry, jumbo tank cars, compartment tank trucks, rubber tanks and containers are a few of these innovations. Too often only a partial evaluation is made of the impact of these new methods on total physical distribution cost and reflected in the vital area of pricing. The division of responsibility for the elements of physical distribution cost and the loss of these cost details in most accounting systems has contributed to general management myopia in this critical area.

Summary

The concept of physical distribution involves viewing the closely related functions of materials handling, packaging, warehousing, inventory control and transportation as a management and total cost entity which has a significant bearing on production cost and marketing effectiveness. The concept does not eliminate the need for creative action in each of these areas; in fact, all cost reductions must be made by reducing these basic cost elements. Effective physical distribution cost control can permit more effective action in each of these areas by eliminating programs which reallocate rather than reduce cost. It can also provide marketing management with more effective tools for establishing price differentials based on package, method of shipment and order size.

17

Setting Standards for Distribution Costs

L. GAYLE RAYBURN
Memphis State University

Standard costs are widely accepted in industry as a means of controlling production costs. This technique is much less commonly used in the distribution area, however, despite the steadily growing importance of distribution as a factor in total costs.

Some of the reluctance to apply standard costing to distribution undoubtedly stems from a feeling on the part of management that distribution costs are too variable and too difficult to measure. It is true that it is more difficult to set standards for distribution costs than for production costs—some compromises must be made—but it is far from impossible, as this article demonstrates.

Definitions

Before reviewing the basic procedures for determining distribution cost standards, it is desirable to define these terms. Standard costs, as used in this article, are predetermined costs set as scientifically as possible with the aim of attaining a certain goal of performance. Distribution costs are defined as all costs incurred other than those related to the production of products or the acquisition of goods to be sold. The inclusion of not only what are commonly known as selling and delivery costs but also of portions of administrative and financial management expense—particularly the expenses of the credit and collection department—would appear to be entirely justified. Thus, the distribution cost analyst is interested in the expenses that follow the gross profit figure in the income and expense statement.

160

Basic Steps

For proper control of distribution costs, these costs must be collected and recorded, they must be analyzed on some acceptable basis, and they must be controlled and interpreted through the use of predetermined standards. The approach advocated in this paper for the control and analysis of distribution costs involves the following basic steps:

1. Determine by what particular segment of the market the costs are to be accumulated: by territories, products, salesmen, methods of distribution, or any combination of these business segments.

2. Determine the functions to be costed, and accumulate costs by functions within the business segment. Break broad functions down into cost centers in which operations are reasonably homogeneous and under a single responsibility.

3. Determine the factors of variability for measuring the cost centers within the function. The factor of variability should reflect the principal activity in each center.

4. Establish standards for each of the functional factors of variability on the basis of past experience and industrial engineering studies or judgment. Translate standards into budgeted costs.

5. Compare standards with actual performance, and analyze cost variances by source and cause.

Manner of Application

Analysis by manner of application relates effort and cost to results obtained. The application of distribution costs varies with the nature of the analysis sought. In production cost accounting, overhead rates are usually applied only to the products; in distribution cost accounting, costs may be applied not only to products but also to sales territories, salesmen, method of distribution, and other business segments. Various business segments may be used for distribution analysis; business concerns should select the ones that will give their operations proper direction. The choice will depend on the specific nature of the business and the distribution cost problems involved.

Natural Expense Classification

A proper system of accounts for recording distribution cost is essential. The criteria used for choosing expense classifications are very important. These criteria should not permit the use of large miscellaneous classifications that contain many different expense elements; the items in each account should be homogeneous. On the other hand, no classification should be so small and so insignificant that the dollar savings will not justify the bookkeeping cost.

Analytical efforts will be considerably impeded if distribution costs cannot be properly accumulated through the account classification.[1]

Regardless of differences in the kinds of costs needed for managerial decisions, most companies keep their books of account so as to express distribution costs by nature or object of expenditure. This natural expense basis is often called the primary expense classification since it is usually made a part of the ledger accounts. Such traditional classifications of expenses as salaries, rent, and supplies describe the kind of service the company obtained for the expenditures. The natural expense classifications appropriate for a firm depend entirely upon the nature of the enterprise's activity. The number of accounts depends on the extent and detail of the information desired by management.

The natural expense classification serves a broad area since these expenses represent both production and distribution activities; consequently, this classification has little value in itself in determining the cost of various distribution functions. This type of analysis can be used only to tell the cost of the distribution function as a whole; the cost of performing specific operations is not known. Furthermore, this classification in itself has little or no use in determining the cost applicable to certain territories or product lines. If a business has no interest in the efficiency of particular distribution operations or no major decisions to make, analysis by natural expense classification may be adequate. However, since there are few if any business concerns in which these conditions prevail, additional analysis is needed.[2]

Functionalization

Since the natural expense classification does not relate groups of costs to people or provide a useful means for analyzing functional efficiency, natural expense accounts should be allocated to distribution functions. The distribution functions to be costed must be determined so that costs can be accumulated by functions within the business segment chosen. Functionalization of distribution activities permits consideration of cost responsibility since the responsibilities of individuals in a business organization generally follow the specific lines of a function. The expenses included in a functional group should always not only be closely related but also should vary according to the same factor of measurement.

Major Functional Classifications

There are many ways of describing the functions that comprise the distribution task and many ways of organizing distribution costs. Each company

[1]Hadley P. Schaefer, "The Distribution Cost Problem," *Accounting Review,* October 1958, p. 627.

[2]J. Brooks Heckert, "Back to Distribution Cost," *Journal of Accountancy,* June 1945, p. 456.

must prepare its own list of activities on the basis of a careful study of the exact work done. Since the selection of functions depends on the degree of cost control and cost responsibility desired, marketing executives and accountants should determine the functions jointly. The number of functions will vary from one company to another depending upon such factors as size, method of operation, and internal structure.

Since there are so many possible marketing procedures and practices in which concerns may engage, a representative functional classification of distribution costs would be difficult to establish. A study of the company organization can help in determining the grouping of functions. For the purpose of this article the entire distribution effort is divided into the following major functional classifications: warehousing and handling, transportation, credit and collection, direct selling, advertising and sales promotion, and general distribution activity.

Detailed Classifications

The approaches to functionalizing distribution costs vary, depending on the degree of functionalization and on whether the functionalization is integrated into the chart of accounts or is made independently off the books. The greater the degree of functionalization the greater the homogeneity of the distribution activities classified within categories. The expenses included in a functional group should not only be closely related but should also vary according to the same factor of measurement. For example, the function of advertising and sales promotion may require further breakdown into radio media, television media, direct mail, and other advertising media. The purpose of dividing major functions into small classifications of responsibility is to ensure that the work performed is of a homogeneous character. Generally, the more precise the functionalization the better, since a greater degree of control usually is obtained if the major distribution functions are broken down in detail.[3]

Use of Digit Codes

The chart of accounts can provide for accumulation of sales and distribution costs by control units through the use of digit codes. Digit codes can be incorporated for analysis both by functions and by manner of application, with charges coded at the source of the expenditure. In some cases the accounting classification can be set up on a functional basis with the major functions further subdivided by detailed functions. The incorporation of location or territorial codes into functional codes provides for the accumulation of major and detailed functional costs by territories. Product codes, customer codes, and salesmen codes can also be added to simplify additional analysis by manner of application.

---

[3]Harold E. Gannon, Jr., "Methods of Measuring and Controlling Distribution Costs," *NACA Bulletin*, Section 1, March 1955, p. 932.

If possible, the chart of accounts should be so designed that each function receives as many as possible of its charges directly, rather than through allocation; incorporation in the general ledger obviously facilitates periodic cost analysis and control. However, such refinements in the official account classification should not be carried beyond the point of feasibility.

Some natural expense items will have to be apportioned among several functional cost groups since they relate to more than one functional activity. Expenses directly allocable to a functional activity are prorated directly. Expenses not directly allocable to a functional activity must be prorated on equitable bases. The bases chosen should reflect as clearly as possible the benefits derived from the indirect costs by the various functions. The procedure is similar to the procedure in accounting for production cost in which the total of the burden is analyzed according to departments or other functional subdivisions of the production process.

Functional Factors of Variability

The factors that cause distribution costs to vary must be identified. Such a measure is known as the unit of variability; this measure is also known as the work or service unit. This unit will depend upon a number of considerations, such as the type of function, the product handled, and the sales territory used.[4]

The validity of the functional unit costs depends upon the reasonableness of the cost unit. If the work unit is not reasonable to begin with, the resulting functional unit standard cost will not be valid. Thus, care must be exercised in the selection of work units if the standards based upon the work units are to be meaningful and if the variances from standard are to be accepted in the measurement of performance. The work unit should be readily measurable, should produce results that are reasonably accurate, and should be economical in application. There should be a demonstrable relationship between the work unit and the distribution activity. The factor chosen must fluctuate concomitantly with the activity that is the source of the cost. Attention should also be focused on the objectives that management had in mind when the expenditures were authorized. The work unit selected for an operation must be a common denominator for all work done in that operation and should be fair and equitable.[5]

Order-getting Costs

There are some differences between standards as applied to production operations and as applied to distribution operations. Standards adaptable to production measure a direct relationship between effort and result. This

[4]Gordon Shillinglaw, *Cost Accounting—Analysis and Control*, Richard D. Irwin, Inc., Homewood, Illinois, 1961, pp. 398-399.

[5]The National Association of Accountants, *Analysis of Non-Manufacturing Costs for Managerial Decisions*, The National Association of Accountants, New York, 1951, p. 20.

relationship may not exist in some distribution costs, especially those concerned with order getting. In this analysis the two principal distribution functions, direct selling and advertising and sales promotion, are considered order-getting costs, those costs incurred in activities concerned with persuading the customer to buy. Direct selling differs from advertising and sales promotion in that the activities it includes represent primarily personal presentation of the service or product to the prospective buyer. Standard costs for order-getting activities are often based on units that measure effort expended rather than results obtained.

Order-filling Costs

Other distribution costs incurred for executing the sales order are designated as order-filling costs. Many order-filling activities relate to the physical handling of goods and to clerical operations. Order-getting activities include mainly nonrepetitive operations, while order-filling costs more often involve repetitive operations.[6]

Many executives believe that marketing functions vary so much between time periods and between companies that it is impossible to establish and use standard costs. However, close examination will reveal that many distribution activities are uniform and are susceptible to techniques for setting standards on a physical basis. The same basic techniques and methods used to determine production standards may be used in determining many distribution standards. Standards should be established for each of the functional factors of variability on the basis of past experience, industrial engineering studies, or judgment. The determination of a standard sales volume is the starting point in the establishment of standards for distribution costs. A standard functional unit cost should always be established for each distribution activity on the basis of a normal capacity.

Repetitive Operations

Distribution functions may be repetitive or nonrepetitive. A job audit or analysis should be prepared for every function. The object is to measure time apportionment among the tasks comprising the function. All the operations performed in each function should be listed as completely as possible on the job analysis. Once the jobs have been determined, each operation should be studied to determine if the procedures are repetitive and routine in nature and can be standardized.

For each distribution function in which there exists a fairly regular work routine, it is possible to study the routine (by means of time study and other

[6]The National Association of Accountants, *Cost Control for Marketing Operations,* Research Series Numbers 25, 26, 27, The National Association of Accountants, New York, 1954, pp. 31-61.

standard work measurement techniques) and record the time that each operation should require under normal existing conditions. Information can be obtained from the supervisor and the employees performing the operations and from previous time and motion study reports. However, overall averages of past performance should be avoided since they may contain unnecessary delays and thus may not reflect good performance.

The standard should be adjusted for nonproductive time lost through rest, interruption, fatigue, and other normal factors affecting production time in a normal working day. Before final acceptance the rate should be tested by a standards committee. A time standard can then be applied to each operation element and should reflect a fair performance expectancy for a worker of acceptable skill functioning at a reasonable pace. Once a standard time per operation has been determined, the standard number of operations that could be performed in any given time period can then be computed by dividing the total working time in that period by the standard time per operation. Standard time may then be converted into standard unit costs by applying the costs expected to prevail during the period for which standards are set.

Materials

An accountant familiar with standard costs should be in charge of the procedure for establishing standards for distribution materials. Year-to-date totals of material quantities should be studied and used as guides in setting the physical quantity of distribution materials needed. Work sampling can also be used in determining the standards for materials used in distribution. The engineering department may conduct tests under controlled conditions. A quantity of material can be put into the distribution process, and the results can be carefully analyzed. The accountant will also need assistance from distribution supervisors who are thoroughly familiar with the materials used in each distribution function. Together they should establish detailed information regarding the standard material components needed in each distribution function. This theoretical material quantity must include factors for scrap, shrinkage, and waste.

Warehousing and Handling

Warehousing and handling expenses are incurred from the time finished goods are received from the production process or from another concern until they are ready for shipment or delivery. The warehousing and handling operations performed are largely of a repetitive nature and lend themselves to standardization and cost control.

If all products are approximately the same size and weight, product units can be used for developing warehousing and handling standard costs. However, if the effort required to move and handle the various product lines differs because of

Work Units for Warehousing and Handling	
Function	*Work Units*
Receiving	Purchase invoice line
	Weight or number of shipping units
	Shipment
	Dollar of merchandise purchased
Pricing, Tagging, and Marking	Warehouse unit handled
	Invoice line
Sorting	Physical unit stored
	Dollar of average inventory
	Order
Assembling Stock for Shipment	Order
	Order line
	Item
	Shipment
	Sales transaction
Handling Returns	Return
Packing and Wrapping	Order
	Order line
	Physical unit shipped
	Shipment
Taking Physical Inventory	Warehouse unit
	Dollar of average inventory
Clerical Handling of Shipping Orders	Order
	Item
	Shipment
	Sales transaction
	Order line
Total Warehousing and Handling	Shipment
	Order line
	Item handled
	Physical unit of goods handled (product, weight, or weighted factor)

Exhibit 1.

disparity of size and weight among products, a table of unit equivalents for the products can be computed. For instance, the smallest item can be assigned a value of 1 unit, the next larger product 1¼ units, the next 1½ units, and so forth. This weighting factor compensates for the difference in packing and handling time resulting from the nature of the product. In order to determine the number of units put into stock, the actual number of product units can be multiplied by the proper unit equivalent.

Standard and actual unit costs can be developed using the most applicable of the units[7] listed in Exhibit 1.

Transportation

Transportation expenses as defined in this article begin at the point where the products are packaged ready for shipping and delivery, and consist of the shipping and delivery costs incurred in getting the products into customers' possession. Because the transportation function consists largely of physical operations, the techniques that are used in time studies of manufacturing operations can be employed. Typically, however, the operations whose times are studied are broader than the elements or motions observed in shops. For instance, the standard may be developed through day-long studies with the time study observer watching all operations and the time required to perform the operations the entire day.

Time standards expressed in minutes per day, per customer, per case, and per mile can be established for each detailed transportation expense. Since the times required for transportation functions will vary among companies and among markets, a review should be made of the methods employed, the characteristics of driving conditions, and other factors affecting time.

If the delivery trucks carry different types of products, different weightings representing relative space requirements in the hauling can be assigned to the products. Even though it costs more to ship larger containers, the smaller containers may have a certain minimum cost. The business concern should consider giving small containers a fixed minimum charge even when the weight factor is used in allocation. This technique is more useful than establishing standards for each shipment when the number of shipments is rather small and each shipment is fairly large.

In establishing standards for transportation costs, data should be compiled for like units of equipment. For example, the standard operating cost of a gasoline-operated truck is not the same as that of a diesel-operated truck. A set of functional unit costs should be computed for each class of automotive equipment. A separate set of functional unit standard costs should also be

[7]Many of the work units were developed from the following sources: J. K. Lasser Tax Institute, *J. K. Lasser's Standard Handbook for Accountants,* McGraw-Hill Book Company, Inc., New York, 1956, pp. 9-174 to 9-175, and J. Brooks Heckert and Robert B. Miner, *Distribution Costs,* second edition, The Ronald Press Company, New York, 1953, p. 247.

computed for line-haul equipment and pick-up and delivery equipment. City delivery trucks have a great deal of stopping, and trucks on long-distance hauls have a minimum of stopping. Mileage operated by each vehicle class should be recorded so that an actual expense per mile can be calculated and compared with the corresponding standard.

Transportation costs may be controlled by establishing standards and determining actual costs on such bases as cost per work unit[8] as is shown in Exhibit 2.

Work Units for Transportation	
Function	*Work Units*
Planning and Supervision	Sales dollar Route Customer served Ton-mile Unit shipped
Transportation Clerical Work Entries in Shipping Records	Shipment Delivery
Preparing Shipping Documents and Recording Shipment	Shipment Unit of product shipped Weighted unit of product shipped
Transportation Bills	Unit Audited Shipment
Handling Claims	Claim handled Shipment Entry
Loading and Unloading	Pounds loaded
Drivers' and Helpers' Wages	Truck hours of operation Truck miles Cubic foot space
Gasoline, Oil, Repair, and Maintenance	Mile Truck miles
Total Transportation	Dollar of shipments as delivered Unit of product shipped as delivered Weighted unit of product Unit of classes of product

Exhibit 2.

[8] Some of these work units were developed from the following sources: J. K. Lasser Tax Institute, *op. cit.*, p. 9-172; and Gordon Shillinglaw, *op. cit.*, p. 406.

Work Units for Credit and Collection	
Function	*Work Units*
Credit Investigation and Approval	Sales order Account sold Credit sales transaction
Credit Correspondence, Records, and Files	Letter Account sold Sales order Item
Preparing Invoices—Handling	Invoice
Preparing Invoices—Line Item	Order line Invoice line
Posting Charges to Accounts Receivable	Number of postings per hour Invoice Shipment
Posting Credits to Accounts Receivable	Number of postings per hour Remittance Account sold
Preparing Customers' Statements	Statment Account sold
Making Street Collections	Dollar collected Customer
Handling Window Collections	Collection
Total Credit and Collection	Sales order Credit sales transaction Account sold

Exhibit 3.

Credit and Collection

The credit and collection department has the general function of extending credit and subsequently collecting the money. Expenses are also incurred for credit services and for legal and other expenses pertaining to the collection of bad accounts. The nature of the functions and the work units applicable vary considerably with different types of business concerns.

Industrial engineering methods can be applied to establish standard times for these office operations. These standards may be set in detail, or broad standards can be based largely on past experience and expressed as the number of man-hours required to process a large number of orders rather than the number of minutes per line on an order.

The typing of each letter involves both uniform procedures, such as positioning the necessary paper and carbon in the machine, and variable factors, such as the length of the letter and the number of erasures made. Observations can be made to determine the standard variable rate per line in the body of the letter. Because letters vary considerably in form and content, different categories of letters should also be derived. If both electric and manual typewriters are used, a separate standard for each must be established for each type of letter. Work sampling can be used to set standards for transcribing materials consumed.

For the credit and collection functions the work units[9] could be those shown in Exhibit 3.

General Distribution Activities

There are certain general costs relating to distribution activities, such as accounting, office, and clerical expenses, that may or may not be significant in a particular company. Often these distribution costs are not of sufficient importance to be treated as a separate function. Distribution finance expenses are also included as a part of general distribution costs. The financial expenses as considering here include those costs incurred in obtaining capital and administering the financial program of the business.

Past experience and knowledge of the conditions within each enterprise should make possible the preparation of standards for many general distribution activities. Detailed studies of invoices and charges can often supply an adequate work unit for such joint costs as telephone, stationery, and supplies.

Units of measurement that can be applied to general distribution activities[10] are shown in Exhibit 4.

Nonrepetitive Operations

For some distribution functions, standards based on time and material studies are difficult to establish because there is such great variation in the details of the work. Or there may be special problems; for example, in some nonrepetitive distribution functions, such as advertising, the amount of expenditure affects the total sales volume. Businessmen usually have a definite plan underlying the

---

[9] Much of this information came from Heckert and Miner, *op. cit.*, pp. 258-259; and J. K. Lasser Tax Institute, *op. cit.*, pp. 9-175 to 9-176.

[10] Many of the operations and work units came from Heckert and Miner, *op. cit.*, p. 268.

performance of each nonrepetitive function; these plans can be modified to reflect general expansion or contraction of business activities. Standard costs can be estimated on such bases. In some cases standard functional unit costs for a distribution function can also be set by analyzing actual unit costs for a past period and eliminating any obvious excess costs from this actual unit cost.

Work Units for General Distribution Activities	
Function	*Work Units*
General Accounting including Auditing Fee, Salaries of General Bookkeepers, and Accounting Supplies	General ledger posting Customers' orders Invoice lines
Sales Analyses and Statistics	Order Invoice line
Financial Expense	Ratio of total distribution cost to sales Ratio of average distribution investment to sales Ratio of inventory turnover
Personnel Expense	Number of employees Number of persons employed, discharged, and reclassified
Filing and Maintaining Order and Letter Files	Order Letter Units filed
Mail Handling	Number of pieces in and out
Vouchering	Number of vouchers
Sales Auditing	Number of sales slips
Punching Cards	Number of cards
Tabulating	Number of cards run
Cashiering	Number of transactions
Fixed Administration and Market Research	Time spent

Exhibit 4

Direct Selling

Direct selling includes all expenses of obtaining orders by direct contact. This function does not include advertising and sales promotion but includes only those distribution costs that pertain directly to obtaining orders. Direct selling may be repetitive or nonrepetitive. Repetitive selling is well adapted to the establishment of cost standards; nonrepetitive selling, on the other hand, is difficult to standardize.

On the surface the setting of a standard time for each sales call may appear impossible since so many individual differences exist among salesmen and among sales situations. However, much progress has been made in standardizing sales techniques in product presentation and in the showing of photographs and samples. The prevailing practice in industry of using well developed sales training programs is evidence of this uniformity. Careful study and experimentation are necessary prerequisites to the determination of a standard time to be taken for each sales call.[11]

Since such conditions as the channels of distribution, terms of sale, and the products manufactured and sold will vary among companies, the work units chosen will also vary. The type of assistance that the salesman is to render each customer and the number of products the salesman is expected to sell to the customers must also be considered in establishing a standard for the number of calls a salesman is to make. Consideration must also be given to the type of sales call to be made; if some calls can be performed by telephone rather than on a personal contact basis, the standard number of calls can usually be increased substantially.

Direct selling expenses may be controlled individually or in total by reducing them to unit costs on such bases as cost per work unit[12] as shown in Exhibit 5.

Advertising and Sales Promotion

The major objectives of the advertising and sales promotion function are to create demand for the company's product and to establish and maintain consumer goodwill. Advertising and sales promoting activities range from the complex situation where all advertising is handled by the company with the company producing its own advertising and sales promotion materials to the simple situation where all advertising is handled by an outside firm. This function is probably one of the most difficult of all distribution efforts to measure in terms of cost standards. Accurate and immediate cost standards can be applied to some advertising and sales promotion, but for such expenditures as institutional advertising the cost measurement must be very general in nature

---

[11]Theodore Lang, Walter B. McFarland, and Michael Schiff, *Cost Accounting*, The Ronald Press Company, New York, 1953, p. 532.

[12]Many of the bases listed are from Heckert and Miner, *op. cit.*, pp. 219-221, and John G. Blocker and Keith Weltmer, *Cost Accounting*, third edition, McGraw-Hill Book Company, Inc., New York, 1954, p. 407.

Work Units for Direct Selling	
Function	*Work Units*
Salesmen's Salaries	Sales call
	Salesmen's hour
Commissions and Bonuses	Net sales dollar
	Product units sold
	Sales call
	Sales order
	Sales transaction
Subsistence	Days subsisted
Entertainment	Customer
General Sales Office Expense and Supervision Salaries	Salesmen
	Sales transaction
	Sales order
	Salesmen's hour
	Customer account
Salesmen's Traveling Expense	Miles traveled
	Days traveled
	Call
	Customer
	Sales order
Salesmen's Equipment	Sales call
Telephone Solicitation	Telephone call
	Order received
Salesmen's Training and Education	Number of salesmen
	Number of salesmen's calls
Routing and Scheduling of Salesmen	Number of salesmen
	Number of salesmen's calls
Making Quotations	Quotations made
Payroll Insurance and Taxes and Supplemental Labor Costs	Payroll dollars
Handling Sales Adjustments and Returns	Adjustments and returns handled
Total Direct Selling	Cost per unit of product sold
	Cost per sales transaction
	Cost per sales order
	Cost per customer served

Exhibit 5.

Work Units for Advertising and Sales Promotion	
Function	*Work Units*
Direct Media Costs	Sales transaction
Newspapers	Newspaper inches
	Gross or net sales (where this is chief medium used
Outdoor Billboards and Signs	Billboard and other outdoor sign units
Radio and Television	Minute of radio or television time
	Number of set owners
Letters, Circulars, Calendars, and Other Direct Mail	Gross or net direct mail sales
	Item mailed or distributed
	Inquiry received
Demonstrations	Demonstration
Technical and Professional Publications	Inquiry received
	Unit of space
Samples Distribution	Samples distributed
Directories, House Organs, and Theater Programs	Unit of space
	Inquiry received
Catalogs	Page or standard space unit
	Gross or net catalog sales when identifiable
Store and Window Displays	Day or window trimming and display
Advertising Allowances to Dealers	Unit of product cost
	Net sales
Dealers' Help	Pieces or units
	Customers
Entertainment of Visitors at Plant	Visitors
Advertising Administration (salaries, supplies, rent, miscellaneous administrative expenses)	Cost per dollar of net sales
	Cost per dollar of all direct advertising and sales promotional costs
Total Advertising and Sales Promotion	Sales transaction
	Prospect obtained
	Net sales
	Product unit sold

Exhibit 6.

and applied to periods of considerable length of time. Some of the standards used for advertising and sales promotion are quantity measurements only and do not reflect the quality of the output. Past experience is used extensively as a guide in budgeting advertising and sales promotion because companies often feel a need for continuity over a period of years in these projects.

Advertising Standards Possible

A complete study of the advertising program for the budget period should result in setting a standard advertising and sales promotion appropriation for each advertising medium and for each sales territory. Regardless of advertising methods used, the cost will generally bear varying ratios to the volume of sales. However, over a few years the average cost of advertising and sales promotion will show a fairly constant percentage ratio to sales. For this reason many companies develop standards for advertising and sales promotion as a percentage of net or gross sales.

However, a direct relationship between sales orders and costs often cannot be established. These activities are a cause rather than a result of sales; the volume of orders obtained may depend on the amount of money spent for these costs. An increase in advertising and sales promotion may increase sales volume, but sales may not increase at the same rate as the costs. Another reason for not using sales as the work unit on which to establish advertising and sales promotion standards is that there is usually an element of fixed costs in advertising and sales promotion costs. Many companies establish a minimum advertising amount as the cost of maintaining a minimum sales capacity.[13]

Advertising and sales promotional efforts and some bases for developing standard costs per unit[14] are shown in Exhibit 6.

Budget Preparation

After the individual distribution costs are classified on the bases of variation factors, a flexible budget should be prepared. A flexible budget shows the standards for each individual expense at all reasonable levels of distribution operation. It seems most reasonable to establish levels of distribution activity comparable to levels of production output.

Standards and budgets are closely related because standard costs serve as building blocks with which the budgets are constructed. Budgets attempt to set up a predetermined standard of operations for a period or project taken as a whole while standards are concerned with cost per unit. Thus, when standard

[13] The National Association of Accountants, *Cost Control for Marketing Operations*, Research Series Numbers 25, 26, 27, The National Association of Accountants, New York, 1954, p. 20.

[14] Many of the work units listed are from J. K. Lasser Tax Institute, *op. cit.*, p. 9-171, and Heckert and Miner, *op. cit.*, pp. 224-226.

costs are employed, the budget is largely a summary of standards for all items of revenue and expense.

In the Accounts

After the preliminary work has been done, the accounts needed for the system may be set up in the general ledger. Distribution standards may be incorporated in the ledger accounts by debiting the accounts for each function with the actual cost and crediting them with standard costs for the number of service units performed. Some accountants feel that executives will take standard costs and variances more seriously and be more responsive to cost reduction efforts if the standard costs and thus the variances are entered in the ledger accounts. The incorporation of distribution cost standards in the accounting system does provide an orderly and somewhat compulsory plan of cost analysis.

However, sometimes it is not practical to incorporate distribution standards in the accounting system. This also happens in certain aspects of production accounting, but it is more common in distribution costing because of the constantly fluctuating nature of distribution costs. However, the incorporation of distribution cost standards is not as important as the incorporation of production cost standards because distribution costs are not usually charged to inventory.[15]

The choice of the accounting method is not crucial as long as the actual distribution costs are subjected to proper measurements and control. It is fundamental to cost control that distribution cost standards be established. However, their use in connection with a standard cost accounting system is not essential. In some companies it may be more advisable to record actual costs in the accounts and compare these with budgets and statistical standards. For other organizations the actual reflection of distribution standards in the accounts may be preferable.

Variance Analysis

Actual costs are compared with standard costs, and the variance is analyzed for the purpose of identifying the factors that caused the difference between the standard and actual costs so that the inefficiencies can be eliminated. Each enterprise will have to decide what specific variance analysis it may want to use. Management has an excellent opportunity to determine the source and cause of the difference between actual and standard costs. However, the interpretation of variances may be difficult.

Management must establish criteria by which to determine whether a variance is significant enough to be investigated since management usually cannot

[15] E. W. Kelley, "Distribution Cost Analyses: 1952 Conference Proceedings," *NACA Bulletin*, Section 3, September 1952, p. 189.

investigate all variances. Disposal of distribution variances represents no difficult problem because variances arising in the accounts for distribution functions are generally treated as period costs at the end of a year.

Summary

While it must be admitted that it is difficult to establish standards for some distribution functions and that a greater tolerance must sometimes be allowed in the consideration of variances, much of the distribution activity is fully as measurable as production. Many of the same techniques used to establish production standards can be employed in selecting distribution cost standards. Other methods for selecting distribution cost standards can be used for those distribution activities that are nonrepetitive and are difficult to standardize. Those activities accomplished by human effort are usually capable of reasonably accurate measurement employing less scientific techniques.

Many people are under the impression that standard costs are always based on sound engineering studies and rigorous specifications. Although this approach is desirable, less scientific standards can provide a forceful and effective way of presenting information for the purpose of stimulating corrective action.

Standard costing in itself cannot be the complete answer to distribution cost problems. Intelligent leadership is needed to use this tool. However, standard cost does hold the promise of being able to provide management with better understanding of marketing data.

18

Inventory Policy Is a Top Management Responsibility

BURR W. HUPP

Drake, Sheahan, Sweeney and Hupp

Inventory means dollars. Dollars mean work.

But, just how hard do inventory dollars work?

Some companies are relatively successful with their inventories. Others are not. The typical *successful* company works its inventory dollars twice as hard as the *unsuccessful*. It achieves twice the sales for every $1 it has invested in inventories. (See Table 1.)

If the typical *unsuccessful* company did as well, it could double its sales with no increase in quantity of goods on hand. Or, with no change in sales, it could cut stock 50 percent.

Why the disparity? Companies face the same problems. They sell to the same customers, can hire the same type of people, have access to the same tools and techniques of successful inventory control.

One factor, however, is not the same—*management*. Not inventory management, but *top management*; the president or his alter ego the executive vice president or general manager.

The company president is the leader. The organization follows him. If he does not pay attention to inventories, no one else will.

Without a good policy, a company has either too little or too much inventory.

If inventory is too little, the company loses sales.

If it's too much, the company ties up its money, increases storage costs, risks product obsolescense, and loses its flexibility.

With too much inventory, a company holds stock too long, values go down but storage costs continue on and on. It becomes harder to introduce new items, to take advantage of lower purchasing prices, and to maintain a level rate of manufacture during slack seasons.

179

Table 1. Typical Successful Companies Make Their Inventory Dollars Work for Them

Types of business	Ratio of net sales to inventory (Net sales per $1.00 of inventory)		
	Successful company ratio	Unsuccessful company ratio	Number of companies
Retailing:			
Building materials	15.1	5.2	96
Department stores	7.3	3.9	202
Discount stores	7.5	4.4	180
Gasoline service stations	21.2	5.4	84
Groceries and meats	23.0	12.7	156
Tires, batteries & accessories	8.4	3.9	69
Variety stores	6.0	3.5	63
Women's specialty shops	9.4	4.8	208
Wholesaling:			
Chemicals & allied products	16.2	7.3	55
Drugs and sundries	10.2	5.6	110
Electrical parts, supplies	10.2	5.6	156
Electronics equipment	5.6	3.3	56
Household appliances	10.6	4.8	111
Machinery & equipment	10.9	5.0	211
Metals and minerals	11.4	4.1	68
Paper	9.7	5.5	157
Petroleum products	41.1	13.0	75

Source: *Dun's Review*

The president, when making company policy, should take into account all factors that have a bearing on the matter, and he should be aware of the consequences or results of his policy. Here are eight suggestions to company presidents on how to make inventory policy.

1. *Balance all your costs.* When inventories increase, you tie up more capital, fill more storage space, risk more obsolescence. So some costs go up. But larger inventories save on manufacturing and purchasing through longer runs and quantity discounts. So some costs go down.

To find the best level of inventories, you want to balance all costs until you get to the point of lowest total costs. You must deal with all costs, and do this systematically. Costs can be determined objectively, that is, from records or time studies, with one exception: the value of money. This must be determined subjectively. It is a matter of inventory policy, to be established by the president. The value of money has more influence on the size of your inventories than any other cost or economic factor. This brings us to the second suggestion.

2. *Set the value of your money high enough so the money will work hard for you; that is, so that it will give you a good return on your investment in*

inventories. When you have inventories, you tie up money. How much is that money worth to you?

Some companies may say 5 percent a year, others 10 or 15 percent, still others 20 or 25.

What does it mean to say money is worth, for example, 20 percent a year to you? It means that when you put your money into a project, you expect that project to pay off at a rate of 20 percent annually. If it does not pay off at 20 percent or more, you would prefer to have your money back to put into a project that will provide a 20 percent or more return on investment. If there is no 20 percent project at the moment, you would rather hold the money in cash to be ready when a 20 percent opportunity comes along.

How much is money really worth to you? This is a subjective decision the company president has to make. The trouble is that he often does not realize (and is not told) the consequences of his decision. He may say the value of money is 5 or 10 percent a year without realizing the implications of his decision. The higher the value he places on company money, the harder that money will work for the company. The higher the value of money, the smaller the order quantities will be and the lower the inventories.

The opposite is also true; low value of money, larger order quantities, higher inventories.

Here is an example of the importance of establishing the value of money correctly: A company had a product with a high value per pound. It considered air shipments to avoid inventories. But then it set the value of money so low there was no incentive to reduce inventories. The company therefore could not justify the extra transporation cost for shipment by air.

You might remember this rule: When you double the value you place on money, the formula for the economic order quantity will lead you to reduce your operating stocks 29 percent. Your money then works 41 percent harder for you. For example, if you have been saying that money is worth 5 percent a year to you, and you then decide it is really worth 10 percent, that change in the economic order calculation will reduce operating stocks 29 percent, and make your money work 41 percent harder.

Similarly, when you triple the value of money, operating stocks are reduced 43 percent, and money works 76 percent harder. When you quadruple the value of money, for example going from 5 to 20 percent a year, operating stocks are cut in half and money works twice as hard as it did.

There is nothing mysterious about the figures. They are simple calculations from the economic order formula. (See Figure 1.)

3. *Reduce lead times.* Short lead times have many advantages. You can get by with less stock, because you can replenish quickly.

When it comes to ways of reducing lead times, investigate the possibilities of faster communications, faster transportation, and faster processing of orders through the office and the warehouse.

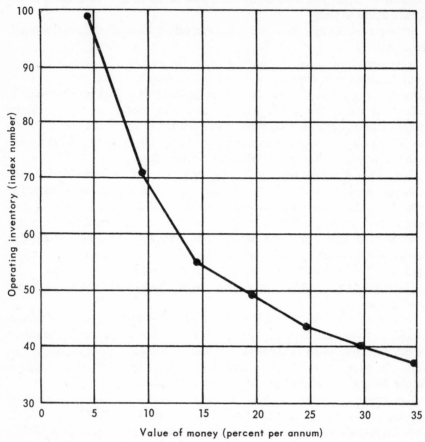

Figure 1. How Operating Inventory Decreases as Value of Money Increases.

Note.—In this example, the index number for operating inventory is set at 100 when the value of money is 5 percent per annum.

4. *Observe the 80-20 rule.* This rule says that 80 percent of your business is done with 20 percent of your items. These numbers are not exact, of course, but the principle is sound.

The important few items, those that give you most of your business, are worth more time and attention than the relatively unimportant many items.

5. *Use your computer as a tool, not a crutch.* Instead of taking corrective action on inventories, many people are letting problems go in the hope that some day a computer will solve them. A computer can be very useful, but it is not a magic wand, and is not necessarily the best solution for every inventory problem.

6. *Remember that inventories are part of physical distribution.* Make sure

your inventory policy is coordinated with policy on transportation, warehousing, packaging, and other distribution functions.

For example, when you set up a new regional warehouse, you increase your inventories and storage costs, but you may save on transportation. Some of these distribution costs go up, others go down. You have to look at all of them together.

7. *Sharpen your sales forecasting.* Inventories are produced and held in anticipation of sales. The more accurately you predict future demand, the better the job you can do on inventories.

Sales forecasting is a systematic procedure for looking ahead to see what will happen, so you can be ready for it. Here are three suggestions regarding sales forecasting:

First, in making a forecast, use a blend of historical data and judgment. Don't rely on one and exclude the other. You need history, but you also need judgment to apply that history to the present situation.

Second, whenever you get new information from the field, revise your forecasts. This is where many companies fall down. They make a forecast and let it stand until it's completely out of date. Get as much feedback from your markets as you can, and use this feedback promptly to keep your forecasts up to the minute.

Third, at the end of each period, check back to see the relation between sale and forecast. If you were off, find out why, so you can do better next time.

8. *Measure your inventory performance.* The company president is a busy man, but he should spend some time, regularly and systematically, on inventory policy and performance.

How much time? At least a couple of hours each month, tying this in with his complete review each month of physical distribution activities.

Every month, the company president should ask *six questions* on inventories, and his staff should answer with regular systematic reports.

First question: "How hard is our inventory money working for us?" The report to be given to the president should show items (perhaps grouped) with sales, inventories, and a turnover rate or months of supply for every item or group.

Second question: "What are we doing to make our inventory money work harder for us?" The report answering this question should be similar to the first, but the report should also show the exceptionally bad items, that is, those with very low turnover or many months of supply. It should give reasons for this poor performance and tell the corrective action being taken on each item.

Third question: "Is our inventory money working hard for us at every point where we have inventories?" This report, also similar to the first, should show turnover or months of supply at each regional and branch warehouse. Data on this report, as on all others, should be in enough detail to point up problems and to guide corrective action.

Fourth question: "Are we losing sales because of stockouts?" The report for the president should show every item out of stock during the month, with information on how long it has been out, the number of line items affected, the number of orders affected, and the reasons for the stockout with corrective action taken.

Fifth question: "Are we losing sales because of inadequate supplies?" This report should show every item that is in short supply to the point where it has to be rationed or allocated, and should show reasons for the shortage, and the action taken to remedy the situation.

Sixth question: "How accurate is our sales forecasting?" This report should compare actual and predicted sales for every item, with explanations for wide discrepancies. For the president, the information should be summarized in a frequency distribution.

With these six reports, the company president has the basis he needs for establishing sound inventory policies. and for following up to make sure these policies are observed throughout his organization.

So far as inventories are concerned, with an approach like this, the president can be sure that his will be a successful company.

19

The Most Influential Factor
in Distribution Economics

AARON J. GELLMAN
The Budd Company

Transportation thoroughly pervades a nation's economic activity.

It is a universal input—perhaps the only one in economic terms.

As such, transportation warrants special attention from governments, from private enterprises in both the transportation and non-transportation sectors of the economy, and from all persons interested in the welfare of a particular company, city, region, nation; in fact, the well-being of the world.

Put another way, the leverage exerted by transportation is so very great that this sector of an economy demands special treatment.

It should not be difficult to convince transportation experts of the significance of transportation costs in the delivered price of commodities. Perhaps this explains why there are so very few data to permit us to pinpoint the relationship.

To be sure, there are numerous estimates of the grossest sort found in the literature of our times. An example is the statement . . . "for manufactured products, distribution costs generally range from 5 percent to 35, even 50 percent of the total cost."

There is precious little research to support any estimates given in the example. Few transportation planners today know the ratios between transportation costs and the final market value for a variety of commodities.

Research needed. At once then, a recommendation can be advanced that economic research be undertaken to study the significance of value added by transportation in the final pricing of various types of goods, with emphasis placed upon determining changes in the relationship as an industry or a nation continues to develop.

A bit more can be said about this matter. For example, the Interstate Commerce Commission published a report entitled *Freight Revenue and*

Table 1. Proportion Formed by Transportation Costs in the Delivered Value of Selected Commodities.

Commodity	Percentage of transportation cost in delivered values
Products of Agriculture:	
Wheat	8.77
Corn	10.34
Straw	47.16
Cotton seed hulls	38.88
Apples	13.60
Cabbage	43.30
Onions	26.75
Animals and Products:	
Horses	5.87
Poultry	4.72
Eggs	4.91
Wool and mohair in gross	2.23
Leather, n.o.s.	2.64
Products of Mines:	
Anthracite coal	25.74
Bituminous coal	40.33
Sand, industrial	54.08
Stone, finished	28.25
Salt	27.20

Adapted from Meyer, et al, *Economics of Competition in the Transportation Industries.*

Wholesale Value at Destination of Commodity Transported by Line haul Railway, in which the percentage of transportation costs in delivered values is given for selected commodities (See Table 1).

A different sort of *fix* can be observed from material published in the United Nation's *1962 Yearbook of National Accounts Statistics*, which shows the relationship of transportation investment in a total gross national product (GNP) for a number of countries (See Table 2). These data clearly support the hypothesis that transportation is a very important factor in economic activity. It represents, in all cases, a significant proportion of the total fixed investment of the countries included.

Whatever you buy, you buy transportation! It is a disarmingly simple observation that transportation is literally part of the value of every commodity and of most services available in any economy. This is far more important and dramatic than any data which would precisely pinpoint the proportion of transportation costs embodied in the final market value of commodities.

Table 2. Transportation Investment in Relation to Gross Fixed Investment and Gross National Product [a]

Country	Gross Fixed Investment as a Percentage of Gross National Product	Transport Investment as a Percentage of Gross National Product	Transport Investment as a Percentage of Gross Fixed Investment
Colombia	19.6%	5.3%	26.9%
India	11.5%	2.1%	18.7%
Israel	26.5%	4.5%[b]	17.3%[b]
Japan	42.6%	4.9%	11.4%
Mexico	13.8%	2.4%	17.2%
Nigeria	13.8%	4.9%	49.0%
Pakistan	11.9%	1.8%	15.4%
Sudan	13.3%	2.0%	15.6%
Thailand	16.6%	2.8%[b]	16.5%[b]

Source: Statistical Office of the United Nations, Department of Economic and Social Affairs, Yearbook of National Accounts Statistics (New York: United Nations, 1962).
[a] All estimates pertain to one year in the period 1959–62.
[b] Including communications investment.

The methods by which decisions to ship goods are reached are of considerable importance. A few years ago, it was still common practice to find freight traffic routing decisions being made on the basis of the lowest transportation cost.

Since that time, the traffic manager has increasingly been placed under supervision of the *distribution manager*, reflecting industry's desire to minimize its total costs, and thereby maximize its profits. There is evidence that entrepreneurs recognize transportation routing decisions, if made in a vacuum, can result in higher-than-necessary costs for the company and, in terms of the requirements, for the economy as a whole.

PDM. The physical distribution manager is concerned with those factors which interact with transportation, and with each other. These factors always have an effect upon the implications for the transportation decision and also are affected by the traditional traffic considerations. Among the principal elements in the physical distribution process, there are:

1. Transportation.
2. Warehousing and storage.
3. Inventory policy and control.
4. Packaging.
5. Purchasing.
6. Insurance.

7. Documentation.
8. Communications support.

Proper decisions. The correct physical distribution decisions from the point of view of the shipper are those which minimize the total cost of the enterprise. It is at once obvious that the degree of skill required to reach the proper decisions is higher when distribution principals govern than when the traffic segment operates alone. This can be seen in Table 3, which sets forth the general relationships between the major elements of the distribution process.

The matrix is constructed to show the degree of interaction in the other elements of distribution when a decision is taken in any one element. The active (affecting) elements are shown in the left-hand vertical column; the elements affected are arranged across the top.

Several features of this matrix are worthy of mention. First, transportation decisions interact with all other components of the distribution process and they in turn interact with transportation in each case. The top row and the left column are filled with *important action* elements. The lower right portion of the matrix displays largely *possible* and *little or no action*, This reflects the more influential character of the first of the elements listed in the matrix.

Specific interactions. It is interesting to review, in more detail, some of the specific relationships which have been found to exist between the various components of the distribution system.

Perhaps the most publicized have to do with transportaiton routing decisions and inventory policy. Well known is the case of the California manufacturer of high-priced women's swimsuits who found it less expensive, and thoroughly profit maximizing, to ship virtually all product by air at substantially higher transportation cost than before. In this instance, as in some others, savings on warehousing costs and from inventory reduction were more than sufficient to justify the decision.

Noteworthy too is the fact that this manufacturer also reaped market benefits by being able to introduce a highly perishable style of goods more rapidly, and over a far greater geographic area, than could its competitors.

The international shipment of large-scale computers by air on a routine basis dramatically demonstrates a number of interactions within the distribution system, including that between *pure* transportation costs and packaging expenses. Ocean movement of such items is far less expensive from a strict transportation point of view, but typically the reduced level of packaging required for air shipment fully offsets the added transportation costs. Of course, less time in transit, more reliable service, reduced documentation, and lower insurance costs contribute additionally to the savings inherent in routing by air.

Modern management literature is replete with instances where the joint consideration of purchasing and transportation routing factors has resulted in distribution decisions different from those that would have been made were the lowest-transportation-cost criterion alone employed. Indeed, the entire concept

Table 3. A Distribution Matrix

Affecting Elements	Affected Elements							
Distribution Elements	Transportation	Warehousing	Inventory Control	Product Packaging	Purchasing	Insurance	Documentation	Communication
Transportation		●	●	●	●	●	●	●
Warehousing	●		●	●	●	●	◉	●
Inventory control	●	●		●	●	●	◉	◉
Product packaging	●	●	●		◉	◉	○	○
Purchasing	●	●	●	◉		◉	◉	○
Insurance	●	●	◉	●	◉		◉	○
Documentation	●	◉	○	○	◉	◉		○
Communication	●	●	●	○	◉	○	○	

● – Important action upon the above   ◉ – Possible action upon the above   ○ – Little or no action on the above -

189

of *economical order quantities* in the purchasing and inventory management fields owes much to the emergence of the physical distribution manager as coordinator of transportation and related factors.

The principal point of the preceding examples is to demonstrate once more the myriad mutual interdependencies found among the various functions involved in physical distribution. Those concerned with transportation can overlook this crucial point only at their peril—and that of their employer, be it private enterprise or governmental agency.

Unitization, a link to economies. One specific that will more closely bind all elements of distribution, causing far greater interactions, is unitization.

Unitization, it should be noted, includes:

1. Glueing together boxes or case goods on pallets.
2. Steel-strapping heavy machinery on pallets.
3. Shipping bulk liquid or dry commodities in compatible units.
4. Moving 'permanent' metal or plastic containers having a cross-section of about 8 X 8-feet, with lengths up to about 40-feet.
5. Transporting trailers on railway flatcars.

Obviously, the heart of unitization is in assembling or organizing loads to promote their speedy, routinized handling in order to realize all the benefits such practices offer.

It is interesting to consider the likely effects of a decision in favor of unitization, including containerization, upon the various elements of the physical distribution process.

Effect on Warehousing. With respect to warehousing policies, sturdy containers that are watertight can reduce reliance on permanent structures for storage. Otherwise, the decision for unitization can be expected to have little effect upon warehousing requirements except as the unitization decision itself may influence the choice of mode of transportation. This may in turn lengthen or shorten the transit time, affect the 'pipeline' quantities, and influence the reliability of service to a point where the unitized method requires a different warehousing decision to maintain the same standard of customer service.

Again, if unitizing requires a break-bulk operation prior to final delivery, it is conceivable that additional warehousing would be required.

Effect on Inventory Policy. Except as the decision for unitizing affects model choice, it should have very little effect upon inventory policy. But, very frequently, a decision will influence the choice of conveyance. It is not unusual to find freight being shifted from one mode to another in accordance with a least-distribution-cost criterion simply as a result of a shift to containerization. As noted earlier, it is where the decision influences modal choice that the ramifications are greatest for the rest of the distribution system. That is, once again, the result of transportation being the most influential single factor in the full distribution process, although it is by no means the only factor to be considered.

Effect on Packaging. Relative to packaging commodities to be shipped, other things being equal, the protective requirements can probably be relaxed, especially if the unitizing technique that is selected employs containers.

On the other hand, should the commodities move considerable distances and receive harsh treatment beyond the break-bulk point, it may not be possible to reduce packaging cost or standards.

Effect on Insurance. In the majority of instances, where unitizing has replaced more conventional techniques, insurance coverage and costs have been substantially reduced. This is especially true where the high insurance rate was the result of a substantial probability of pilferage or malicious damage. The international movements, particularly the cost savings in this area, can be substantial.

Effect on Communications. For the present, it is not likely that selecting a unitized method will influence communications support costs. However, in the future, this may change because it is anticipated that ultimately each transportation vehicle and each container or similar unit in the transportation network will be marked electronically. The presence of the shipment will be sensed automatically at various locations and reported promptly to the owner, the shipper, or the carrier who needs to know its whereabouts.

When such automatic vehicle and container identification systems become ubiquitous, unitized shipping could in fact substantially reduce the present costs of communications in support of distribution functions. The communications system will likely be very different in many ways from that used today for distribution control purposes.

Effect on Documentation. Where international shipments are concerned, unitizing substantially reduces documentation costs.

Moreover, such cost reductions will become greater in the future as the various nations become increasingly aware of the possibilities for document simplification attendant to unitized methods of shipping, and as shippers place increasing pressures on governments to set more rational paperwork requirements. Indeed, unitization in and of itself provides the most important single impetus to simplified documentation in international trade. This is a precious by-product of the growing trend toward unitization in international trade.

Effect on Purchasing. Purchasing policies and practices can be substantially affected by decisions to 'go unitized.'

The whole question of the most economical order quantities is often reopened where unitized shipment becomes a possibility. Again, with the expansion of container services, the number and location of candidate suppliers is likely to be expanded. Also, especially where the containers are shipper-furnished rather than carrier-provided, purchasing policy may be modified to an f.o.b.-origin basis rather than the f.o.b.-destination. Perhaps it will remain f.o.b.-destination if the supplier provides the containers.

One of the most appealing features of unitization, particularly in the container field, is the strategic mobility it affords the transportation planner within the distribution process. This, of course, stems directly from the intermodal capability of unitization which, in turn, gives versatility not only to the shipper and carrier, but also to the transportation facilities planner in government and in private industry.

20

The Role of Information
Systems in Physical
Distribution Management

BERNARD J. LA LONDE
Ohio State University

JOHN F. GRASHOF
U.S. Army

Businessmen have demonstrated increasing interest in management information systems as the techniques and technology of data processing and data communication have developed. As firms acquire computer capability, their managements become interested in deriving the greatest benefit from the investment. It is not surprising, therefore, that firms began to study the development of information systems for various functional areas of business.

The following discussion is concerned with the concept of distribution communications and the role of information systems in physical distribution. The focus is on the relationship between information flows and physical distribution management, using the basic tasks of management as a framework for the discussion.

The Relationship Between Information Flows and
Physical Distribution Management

Physical distribution, as is the case with most business activities, does not automatically function to provide the necessary services for the firm and its customers. The distribution system must be managed. What is involved in managing the basic tasks of a manager may be summarized by the diagram in Figure 1.

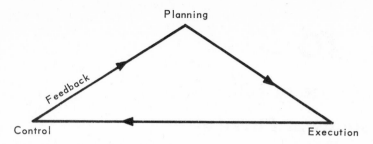

Source: E. J. McCarthy, *Basic Marketing: A Managerial Approach,* 3d ed. (Homewood, Ill.: Richard D. Irwin, Inc., 1968), p. 17.

Figure 1. The Three Tasks of Management.

Information in Planning

One of the three primary tasks of management is planning. In physical distribution this planning will encompass at least two areas. First, the distribution system itself must be planned. The management of a firm must plan the location, size, and design of the system's plants and distribution centers, the transportation of goods between single or multiple production facilities and stock locations, and the content of the inventories at each of the storage points within the system.

To effectively accomplish the design of the physical flow, two types of information must be made available by the firm's information system. The first type is historical—that is, information on past sales of each of the items the firm produces, including where the item was made, where the item was delivered, the size of the order, the content of the order (other items on the same order), and the time allowed to process the order and deliver the item. The historical information gives the systems designer a picture of what happened in the past which can be used as a model for what will probably happen in the future. Thus, the historical information sets some of the constraints on the system.

The second type of information is current information. Two forms of current information are needed by the systems planner for the development of the physical distribution system. One of these is external information on the availability and costs of possible components of the distribution system, including such factors as the costs and availability of alternative modes of transportation, the costs of public warehousing in each of the needed locations in the system, and the costs of constructing and operating warehouse facilities. The other category is internal information. Perhaps the most important of the several types of internal information is that which specifies the objectives of the firm with respect to the physical distribution system. The desired service level, one of the objectives established by top management, must be among the information the systems planner has available. Also included is any information the firm has that will indicate what will happen in the future—for example, the firm's plans for the future, analysis of economic and industry business conditions, and marketing research information concerning the activities of competitors and customer reaction to both our products and our distribution policies.

A second area needing planning is the communications (information) system that supports the physical flow of goods through the physical distribution system. The location and types of communication terminals and paths among the terminals must be designed to provide the necessary information when and where it is needed. The development of the communications aspect of the system is predicated, then, on studying and developing the information relevant to the flow of goods through the system and deciding what kinds of decisions must be made, where they must be made, who is going to make them, and the criteria to be used in the decision. Once these decisions have been made, the information needed at any point in the system can be identified and the system planned so as to provide the specified information. The planning is based on having the information available that describes the system.

Although they are discussed separately, the above two aspects of a firm's distribution system cannot be planned separately. There is a direct and important link between the physical flow of goods through a physical distribution system and the quality of the information system component of that system. That link is centered on the relationship between the speed of the flow of correct information through the system and the amount of inventory that must be held at various points in the system.

Figure 2 is a diagram of a hypothetical inventory as a function of time. Notice in the diagram that the actual inventory at any point in time is made up of two

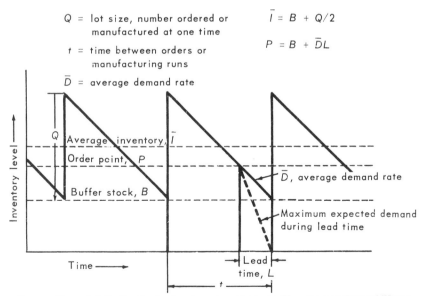

Q = lot size, number ordered or manufactured at one time

t = time between orders or manufacturing runs

$\bar{D}$ = average demand rate

$\bar{I} = B + Q/2$

$P = B + \bar{D}L$

Source: Elwood S. Buffa, *Production-Inventory Systems: Planning and Control* (Homewood, Ill.: Richard D. Irwin, Inc., 1968), p. 75.

Figure 2. Inventory Level as a Function of Time.

components—the inventory needed to cover the expected demand between any point in time and the receipt of the next order and the buffer stock. The buffer stock is that quantity of inventory carried to cover the unexpected demand that might occur between the order point and the receipt of the order. The lead time (L) in the figure is what many physical distribution analysts call the *order cycle*. The order cycle is generally defined as the number of days required from the placement of an order to its receipt by a customer. Thus defined, the order cycle can be subdivided into three components: (1) order transmittal time; (2) order-processing time; and (3) shipment of the order to the customer (warehouse withdrawal and transportation time). The first two components of the order cycle, the order transmittal time and the order-processing time, are both directly related to the information system segment of the firm's physical distribution system. As illustrated in Figure 3, both of these activities are primarily related to the flow of information. On the other hand, the time required for the shipment of the order to the customer is a function of the physical flow component of the physical distribution system.

The size of the buffer stock is a function of the length of the order cycle (lead) time and the expected rate of demand. Thus,

$$B = D_{max} L - \bar{D}L = L(D_{max} - \bar{D})$$

where

$$
\begin{aligned}
B &= \text{buffer stock} \\
D_{max} &= \text{maximum expected demand} \\
L &= \text{order cycle time} \\
\bar{D} &= \text{average expected demand}[1]
\end{aligned}
$$

If we define L in terms of its components we have:

$$L = OT + OP + OS$$

where

$$
\begin{aligned}
L &= \text{order cycle time} \\
OT &= \text{order transmittal} \\
OP &= \text{order processing} \\
OS &= \text{order shipment}
\end{aligned}
$$

The equation for the buffer stock then becomes:

$$B = [(OT + OP + OS)(D_{max} - \bar{D})]$$

Since OT and OP are functions of the speed of the information system, any improvement in the information system to provide for faster flow of

[1] Elwood S. Buffa, *Production-Inventory Systems: Planning and Control* (Homewood, Ill.: Richard D. Irwin, Inc., 1968), p. 77.

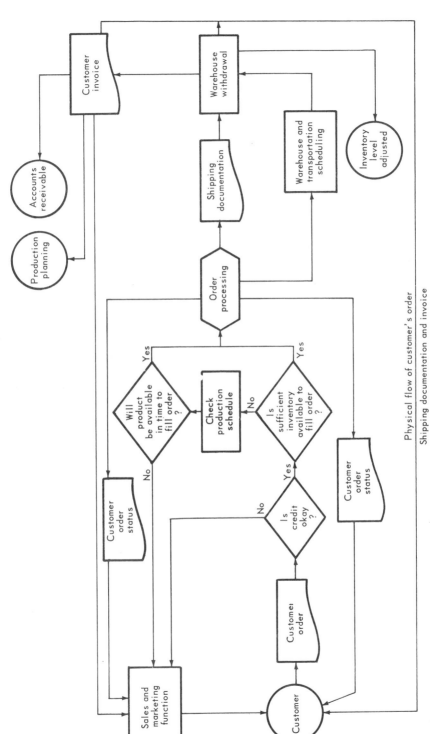

Note: All of the connecting lines in the figure are flows of information except the "Physical flow of customer's order."

Physical flow of customer's order

Shipping documentation and invoice

Figure 3. The Path of a Customer's Order.

197

information will decrease either *OT* or *OP* and will result in a decrease in the buffer stock required.

The problem of the physical distribution systems planner is to select the quality of the information system to use such that the marginal cost of improvements in the information system are equal to the marginal costs of the extra inventory carried because the improvement was not made. Most improvements in information systems, such as the use of wire rather than U.S. Mail for the transmittal orders, come at some increase in cost, both in installation and in operation. These cost increases must be offset by cost reductions at other points in the distribution system or by improvement in customer service levels which justify added cost outlays.

The Role of Information in the Operation of a Physical Distribution System

The execution of the plans mentioned above results in the normal operation of the physical distribution system. Just as in planning, information plays a key role in the operation of a physical distribution system. Much of the planning of the physical distribution system is devoted to the development of an information system that will adequately support the physical flows component of the system.

Information performs two distinct tasks in the operation of a physical distribution system. One of these tasks is controlling the operation of the system so that the desired service level, in terms of both delivery time and filling of the order, is maintained at minimal expense. Whereas the service level for any distribution system could only very rarely (and probably never) reach the 100 per cent level, the reporting and control of the physical distribution system must always be at the 100 per cent level. That is, the physical distribution system performs such an important function for a firm, and the customers of that firm, that it is necessary for the information component to provide for a continuous monitoring of the physical and information flows within the system. The control function of information is discussed in greater detail in a later section.

The other task of the information system is to act as a triggering mechanism for the physical flows component and other portions of the information flows component of the physical distribution system. The operation of a physical distribution system is initiated by the input of a customer order into the system. Once this order is put into the system by the sales and marketing department, or perhaps by the customer himself, the rest of the sequence of activities that result in the customer receiving the right items, shipped via the proper mode of transportation from the proper warehouse, arriving at the right time, and delivering an invoice for the goods shipped, are triggered by some flow of information. In fact, if the order is routine, and the information system performs properly, the sequence of physical distribution activities should take place almost automatically. For nonroutine orders the information system should provide to a manager the information he needs to make the necessary decisions in a way that will be satisfactory to the firm and the customer.

The Path of a Customer's Order

In order to structure the discussion of the triggering activities performed by the information component of the physical distribution system we will organize our discussion around the path of a customer's order. This path is diagramed in Figure 3. In the diagram, every connecting line indicates the flow of information either between the customer and the firm or within the firm. The only physical flow of goods in the diagram is represented by the line connecting the warehouse withdrawal box and the customer, a line which also indicates the flow of the invoice to the customer. Although the flow of a customer's order in any specific firm can differ from the pattern illustrated, Figure 3 illustrates the general functions performed in most physical distribution systems.

The starting point in the diagram, as in any physical distribution system, is the ordering of goods by a customer. The order is obtained by the sales and marketing function and then transmitted either directly or through the sales and marketing office to the firm's headquarters. The time required for the transmission of the order from the customer to the headquarters is what was called order transmittal time earlier in the discussion and is one of the components of the order cycle.

The vehicle for the transmission of the order is generally the order form and a customer order can be relayed from point of origin to point of action by a variety of methods. Recently, the vehicle for the transmission of the orders has been increasingly an electronic impulse or punched card or tape with the data being transmitted over wires. The transmission of an order over wire is more expensive than through the mail but often results in saving several days time with the corresponding reduction in the inventory level necessary to maintain customer service in the system.

The wide variety of information contained on an order form is illustrated in Figure 4. The information from the order form initiates and provides the basis for control of every activity of the physical distribution system that takes place in the sequence of activities resulting in the filled order being received by the customer. It is, therefore, of the upmost importance that the information contained on the order form be complete and accurate. The control mechanism of the system should be able to locate errors later in the system. However, errors in the input data to the system will only be located when a dissatisfied customer calls to inform you of "your" error, and frequently these types of orders are extremely expensive both in terms of order adjustment costs and lost customers.

Once received by the firm, whether by wire, mail, or hand, the order triggers the first activity of the physical distribution system—an activity that deals entirely with information. This activity is the credit check to determine whether the customer is judged financially responsible for the amount of the order.

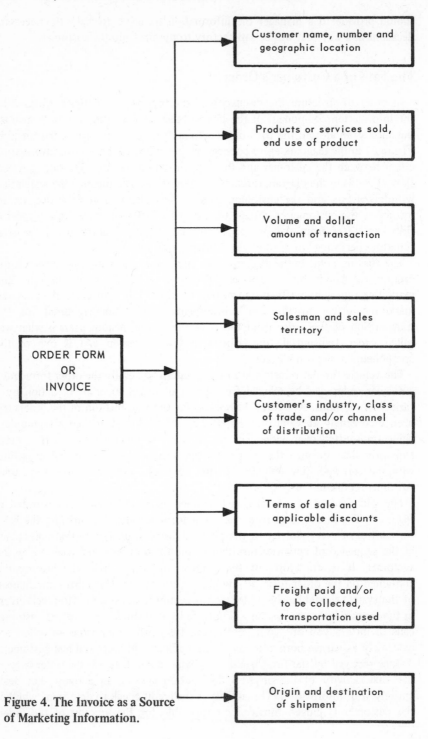

Figure 4. The Invoice as a Source of Marketing Information.

Although credit checking should more logically be a part of the sales and marketing activity and orders should not be officially received unless they have been credit cleared, this is frequently not the case. Occasionally the field sales organization, in their zeal to get an order, will do an incomplete credit check or neglect it completely. Thus, it is often up to the physical distribution system to provide for this credit check. However, it should not be allowed to disrupt the operation of the physical distribution system. In those firms where the order processing activity is mechanized or computerized the credit check can be accomplished routinely by the system.

The credit check will result either in clearance or in a question concerning the credit of the customer. In those few cases where the credit of the customer is in question, the order is sent to the sales and marketing function for further checking and a decision. In most cases, credit clearance is obtained and the order is transmitted to the next stage or step in the distribution system.

Once the order has been cleared the next step is to determine whether the order can be filled in time to satisfy the customer. The order can be filled from one of two sources—from the inventory of the firm or from a production run that will be completed in time to ship the item. The first source checked is the firm's inventory of the item. If the item is not available in the firm's inventory, then the production schedule is checked.

If the order can be filled from the inventory or from current production, the order processing cycle is continued with the development of the shipping documentation and the scheduling of warehouse withdrawal and transportation. When the order cannot be filled from either source, the customer is notified through the sales and marketing function. Hopefully, the customer will allow the order to be backordered for him and filled at a later date. If not, the customer will probably use an alternate source of supply and his order will be lost. As the preparation of the shipping documentation is begun, the customer and the sales and marketing function are notified of the status of the customer's order.

Once prepared, the shipping documentation triggers the filling of the order at the warehouse and the shipment of the order by the proper carrier. As the warehouse withdrawal is accomplished, the final set of information flows relative to the customer's order begins. One of the information flows results in the updating of the inventory through an adjustment for the order.

The other information flow generated the invoice, usually in multiple copies. One of these is sent to the customer, either with the goods or separately, for payment. The other copies remain within the firm, generally within the information system. Included in the other copies of the invoice are a copy for production scheduling to inform them of the withdrawal from the inventory, and a copy to the sales and marketing function to indicate that the order has been shipped and to provide information for their marketing research and sales analysis.

This description of the path of a customer's order has illustrated the role of information in triggering the functioning of a firm's physical distribution system.

In addition, the description has pointed out the wide variety of information that flows within the distribution system and between the distribution system and other functional areas of the firm.

The Role of Information in Controlling Physical Distribution

In addition to triggering the activities of the distribution systems, two types of control are necessary for the efficient operation of the physical distribution activities of a firm. The first of these is the operational control of the system to make sure that the desired service level is maintained. Except for the customer's order, which is clearly beyond the scope of the system, all other flows of information and all of the physical flows in the system should be subject to continuous monitoring. This monitoring should test whether, at all times within the system, the correct items in the proper amounts with the proper information attached are flowing through the system.

Within the path of the flow of a customer's order checks should be made at any point at which a decision is made or information is transcribed. Thus, at the inventory check and the check of the production schedule, the items being checked should be compared with the customer order to make sure that the correct items are being located. Further, at all points through the inventory check, order processing, and the shipment of the order the timing of the order should be checked with the customer's desired date of receipt of the order. If the flow is ahead of the desired date, the order can be held until it should be shipped. Or, if the order is late, it can be expedited—something that could not be done unless there was a monitoring of the timing of the flow of the order through the system. Checking of the timing and location of the order should continue right up until the time the order is received by the customer.

An example of the developments in the information component of physical distribution systems resulting in better control through better information is the development of computerized rail car tracing. Under such a system the location of all rail cars and their contents would be stored in the memory of a computer. When a shipper or his customer wanted to find out the location of an order they would contact the computer, input the car number, and the computer would respond with data on the location and status of the shipment in question.[2]

The second type of control of the physical distribution system is managerial control—that is, the control of the various levels of responsibility by the managers at each level. Whereas the control of the execution was accomplished by 100 per cent monitoring of the activities, the level of managerial control is never 100 per cent. Rather, managerial control is accomplished through periodic summary reports combined with exception reports as needed during the period.

Different factors and different ranges of activity must be controlled at each of the several levels of activity within the distribution system. For example, the

[2] Paul E. Jamison, "Computerized Car Tracing," *Transportation and Distribution Management*, June 1968, pp. 33–36.

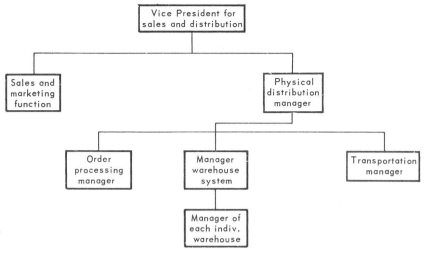

Figure 5. The various levels of control in a physical distribution system.

problems of the warehouse manager and the activities he must control are significantly different from the level of the activities that the physical distribution manager must control. Thus, each of the various levels of control should be discussed separately. Figure 5 indicates the three levels of control that exist in a typical physical distribution system. These levels will be used as the focal point for our discussion.

The lowest level of control in the diagram is the level of the individual warehouse manager. On a routine basis, the warehouse manager would receive reports indicating:

1. The number of labor hours used.
2. The amount of product moved.
3. The amount of product moved per labor hour.
4. The labor cost.
5. The amount of spoilage, damage, and theft.
6. Operating costs such as heat, light, and water.

The manager would also receive reports on any of the above on an exception basis if, during a period of operation, any of the factors deviated excessively from budgeted levels.

The warehouse system manager is one of the three managers at the second level of control. On a routine basis the warehouse system manager should receive reports concerning the operations of the warehouse system. The reports would summarize the information received by the warehouse manager. In addition, the warehouse system manager would typically receive routine reports on equipment cost, building repair costs, and other aspects of the operation of the system. These reports would be on a system basis with reports on an individual warehouse being developed on an exception basis. The warehouse system manager would also receive reports on the service level achieved by the system. Such reports would be on a routine basis unless during the period the service level went below the preset standard. In this case, if any of the aspects of the system deviated from the budgeted levels, the system manager would receive an exception report.

The manager of the order processing function would receive the routine and exception reports that reflected the operation of his activity. Included in the reports would be:

1. Labor costs.
2. Equipment costs.
3. Output reports.
4. Operating cost reports.

Of particular importance among the reports the order processing manager would receive would be a 100 per cent reporting of any errors. Since the order processing activity is generally responsible for the transfer of customer order information from the original customer order to the warehouse withdrawal and shipping documentation, it is in the order processing activity that errors may occur that would result in the shipment of an incorrect order to a customer. This is one of the most serious and costly errors in the entire physical distribution system and as such is reported on a 100 per cent basis.

The transportation manager is the third manager on the second level of control illustrated in Figure 5. One of the factors that makes the transportation manager unique is that part of the information he receives is external and part is internal. The transportation manager has to have available complete and up-to-date information on transportation rates and schedules. Thus, he must receive, as part of the routine information flowing to him, reports of any changes in the rates of particular carriers, changes in the rate structures that might affect the type of goods he ships, and changes in the schedules of any of the common carriers he uses.

In addition, the transportation manager must receive the internal information that is necessary to efficiently manage the transportation of the firm's goods. Included in this information would be changes in the customers' requirements for transportation, changes in the type of packaging or the design of the product, and changes in the policies of the company with respect to the shipment of customer's orders. An additional type of important information that the manager must receive is that information necessary for carrier analysis. The transportation manager, if he is to make intelligent selections of the carriers to use to ship orders, must know how well the various carriers perform in relation to expected performance.

The third level in the control sequence of the physical distribution system is the physical distribution manager. At this level the routine control reports that are received are summaries of the activities of each of the areas discussed above.

More importantly, at this level, are the exception reports that indicate that something in the distribution system is malfunctioning. By far the most important of these kinds of reports are the reports that indicate that a customer received incorrect merchandise, late merchandise (either because of inventory shortage or delays in the distribution system), or damaged or spoiled merchandise. Although such reports would come under the general category of exception reports, each of them must be followed up quickly and completely, the necessary explanations for the trouble developed, and provision made for the correction of the cause of the problem.

The other kinds of exception reports within the distribution system are more typical management reports including:

1. Excessive labor costs in an area.
2. Lack of control of operating expenses.
3. Labor problems.
4. Excessive equipment costs.
5. Excessive repair or maintenance.

Each of these reports indicates a problem that must be investigated and corrective action taken.

Summary

In recent years management has become increasingly cognizant of inventory costs and, therefore, of the benefits of sound inventory management procedures. As a result of this increased focus on inventory management, effective distribution communication has been thrust into the role as an element in the overall marketing strategy of the firm. That is, the firm that can deliver a product in a reliable and damage-free manner now often has an identifiable competitive advantage in the marketplace. Hence, the ability to reduce inventory investment of customers by ensuring rapid and reliable delivery has become part of the sales and merchandising strategy of some firms. This is particularly true in those industries where products are mass merchandised to consumer markets.

In the future, as pressure mounts to push inventory back into the channel and demand rapid inventory replenishment, effective distribution communications will become a necessity rather than a competitive edge. Those firms which do not choose to design flexible and responsive communication networks will require increased inventory burden in order to cushion sudden shifts in market requirements. The cost of increased inventory will require higher prices to customers or reduced profit margins. In either case, a competitive disadvantage could result.

On the other hand, the firm with a sound distribution communications system can reap the advantages of lower inventory costs and improved customer service and relations.

21

The Total Cost
Approach to Distribution

RAYMOND LeKASHMAN
Knight and Gladieux, Inc.

JOHN F. STOLLE
Booz, Allen and Hamilton, Inc.

The more management focuses the company's efforts on cutting distribution costs, the less successful it is likely to be in reducing the reals costs of distribution. This apparent paradox is no abstract or armchair play on phrases. It explains why so many companies have diligently pruned distribution costs—in the warehouse and in inventory, in order processing and in transportation—only to find that these hard-earned savings are somehow not translated into improved profit margins. They have been watered down or actually washed out by increases in other costs scattered throughout the company.

It is these "other costs," motley and miscellaneous as they first seem, that turn out on closer analysis to be the *real* cost of distribution. They never appear as distribution costs on any financial or operating report, but show up unidentified and unexplained at different times and in assorted places—in purchasing, in production, in paper-work processing—anywhere and everywhere in the business. When these gremlin-like costs are traced to their roots, however, one finds that they are, in fact, all intimately interrelated, linked together by one common bond. They all result from the way the company distributes its products.

It is this aggregation of distribution-related costs—rather than what managements usually mean when they complain about the cost of distribution—that represents the important and increasing drain of distribution on earnings. These are the costs—rather than those usually defined and dealt with as distribution costs—that have eluded even the most earnest cost-cutting drives. Because of its size and its elusiveness, this cost complex remains for many companies a promising profit-improvement potential.

The Total Cost Approach

When to Use It

For earnings-minded managements, the dimensions of this profit potential, and a practical technique for tapping it, have now been tested and proved. A handful of companies have faced up to the across-the-board impact of distribution on costs and profits. They have accomplished this by applying an approach—we call it the "Total Cost Approach"—that is designed to convert these intangible and intricate cost interrelationships into tangible dollar-and-cents improvements in profit margins.

A major food manufacturer, after applying effectively an assortment of rigid cost-cutting techniques, has found that this new approach is enabling the company to add 1.7 per cent to its margin on sales.

A major merchandiser, already enjoying the benefits of advanced distribution techniques, found that this same new approach could cut from its corporate costs an additional $7.5 million—3 per cent of the sales value of its products—while at the same time significantly improving service to customers.

At Du Pont, a company well known for its general management excellence, this same new approach underlies the announcement that programs recently instituted are expected to cut $30 million from its total cost, a 10 per cent reduction of the costs attributed to distribution.

These success stories shed some light on how distribution drains profits—and on what can be done about it:

The real impact of distribution on profits is much greater than most managements think. In companies in which distribution-connected costs have been studied, they turned out to be significantly greater than management estimated—as much as from a third to a half of the selling price of the product.

This untapped profit-improvement potential exists because these costs lie in a managerial no-man's land, where they can increase because they are outside the scope of responsibility or control of any operating executive. These distribution-related costs are not strictly the responsibility of the man in charge of distribution, because they are costs of purchasing, manufacturing, or some other function of the business. But they cannot be dealt with effectively by the executive in charge of these other functions because they are actually caused by distribution decisions, for which only the man in charge of distribution has any responsibility. They are the result of complex interrelationships involving all of the functions of the business. Distribution lies at the crossroad of these complex interactions, and that is what is so different about distribution. In no other function of the business can decisions made at the operating level look so right and be so wrong.

The Real Cost of Distribution

Warehousing

Transportation

Production or
supply alternatives

Alternative
facilities use

Communications and
data processing

Inventory carrying

Inventory obsolescence

Cost concessions

Channels of distribution

Customer
service

The real cost of distribution includes much more than what most companies consider when they attempt to deal with distribution costs. In a sense, any major distribution decision can affect every cost in the business and each cost is related to all the others. Our experience indicates that the following ten cost elements and interrelationships are the ones that are most likely to prove critical in evaluating the impact of alternative distribution approaches on total costs and total profits.

Warehousing. To provide service through the company's chosen channels of distribution, some warehousing is required, involving from one in-plant warehouse to a multiple-unit network dispersed across the country. Service usually becomes better as the number of warehouses is increased, at least up to a point. However, as the number of warehouses increases, their average size decreases, this will begin to reduce the efficiency of service to customers. Also, costs increase. Thus, any change in the three variables—number, type, or location of warehouses—will affect both service and costs.

Inventory Carrying. The ownership of inventory gives rise to costs for money, insurance, occupancy, pilferage losses and custodial services, and sometimes inventory taxes. Depending on the business involved, this group of costs may range from 10 per cent to 30 per cent of average annual inventory value. Customer service will be improved by keeping inventory at many storage points in the field near to customers, but this will increase total inventory and the cost for carrying that inventory. Thus, inventory carrying cost is closely linked to warehousing cost and customer service.

Inventory Obsolescence. If (at a given level of sales) total inventory is increased to provide better customer service, then inventory turnover is decreased. Also, the greater the "pipeline fill" in the distribution system, the slower the inventory turnover. This automatically exposes the owner to greater risks of obsolescence and inventory writedown. This is a particularly important cost for companies having frequent model change-overs, style changes or product perishability.

Production or Supply Alternatives. Production costs vary among plants and vary with the volume produced at each individual plant. Plants have different fixed costs and different unit variable costs as volume is increased. The decision of which plant should serve which customers must give weight not only to transportation and warehousing costs, but also to production and supply costs; these will vary significantly with the volume allocated to each plant.

Cost Concessions. A special aspect of production or supply alternatives arises from the fact that distribution decisions can affect costs otherwise incurred by suppliers or customers. For example, when a retailer creates his own warehouse this may free suppliers from packing and shipping small quantities or from maintaining small local warehouses in the field. A retailer who establishes his own warehouse network may be able to recoup some of these costs by negotiation with the supplier.

Channels of Distribution. The choice of distribution channels profoundly affects the nature and costs of a company's sales organization, its selling price and gross margin structure, its commitment to physical distribution facilities. These in turn will affect production and supply costs.

Transportation. Changing the number or location of warehouses changes transportation costs, sometimes in unanticipated and complex ways. For example, an increase in the number of warehouses may initially reduce total transportation costs; but past some determinable point, the cost trend may reverse because of the decreasing ratio of carload to less-than-carload tonnage.

Communications and Data Processing. These costs vary with the complexity of the distribution system and with the level of service provided, including costs for order processing, inventory control, payables, receivables and shipping documents. These costs rise as more distribution points are added to the system. Additionally, as the cycle time or response time of the communications and data processing system is shortened, costs of this service are increased.

Alternative Facilities Use. Changes in inventory requirements or in other aspects of the distribution operation will change space requirements and utilization in a plant-warehouse facility or a retail store. Space used for distribution may be convertible to selling space which yields incremental sales and profits. In the case of retail business, this is actually a variation of the customer service factor since it increases the availability of goods with which to fill customer requirements.

Customer Service. Stock-outs, excess delivery time, or excess variability of delivery time all result in lost sales. Any change in the distribution system will influence these elements of customer service, and therefore must either gain or lose sales for the company. These effects, while difficult to measure, must be considered part of the real cost of distribution.

These costs will not respond to the usual cost-cutting approaches. Management has achieved near miracles in cutting costs in one function of the business after another, including costs within the distribution function, notably in warehousing, transportation, and order-filling. But conventional cost-cutting approaches are limited to costs that fall within any one operation of the business; for cutting these costs, management can hold some executive responsible. Distribution-related costs are organizational orphans, beyond the reach of even the most diligent, skillful cost-minded executives.

These costs will respond only to a high level across-the-board re-examination of how distribution affects the total costs and total profits of the business, and of what management action is necessary to tap this profit opportunity.

Thus the problem and the opportunity are deposited squarely on the desk of the chief executive. The pursuit of these added profits has to get its start, its support, and its sanctions at the top management level. With this high-level effort, even companies that have tightened and tidied their distribution operations can greatly increase earnings by a frontal attack on the basic framework of their distribution decisions and practices.

This broad, basic approach has a continuing payoff, for once the most profitable pattern of distribution has been defined for the present operations of the business, management has in its hands a yardstick for measuring the impact on total profits of any proposed management moves. This makes it possible to define the impact on total profits of a new plant or a new product, or a cluster of new customers, and so makes it possible to determine what changes in distribution—if any—will ensure peak profits from these new ventures.

What is this total cost approach? What is new about it? Why have we not heard more about it?

The Approach Simply Stated

This approach sounds simple. *First*, analyze the distribution impact on each cost of the business, and select for more detailed study those activities the cost of which is significantly affected by distribution policies and practices. *Second*, develop the data necessary to measure the profit impact that alternative distribution decisions would have on each of these activities. *Finally*, determine which distribution decision will maximize profits.

Obviously, if it were as simple as it sounds, more companies would long ago have beaten a path to this better mousetrap. Three sets of facts explain why this has not been so:

1. The impact of distribution on costs is more difficult to unravel than is the effect of other business decisions. All functions of a business are somewhat interrelated, but distribution is more complexly intertwined with each. And it is these interrelationships—rather than the costs of the distribution functions per

se—that are the cause of high distribution costs and the key to understanding and reducing these costs.

2. Because corporate accounting has historically been oriented to finance and production, rather than to marketing or distribution, the operating reports that guide managerial action do not tot up in any one place the full impact of distribution on costs. The real cost of distribution never stares management in the face.

3. Even where managements have become aware of these costs and their impacts on profits, there was until recently very little that anyone could do about the pervasive effects of distribution. Even a relatively simple problem in distribution system design can involve hundreds of bits of information that interact in thousands of ways. So there was no way of dealing with the distribution cost complex until techniques were developed to manipulate this mass of material as a single integrated entity.

This last is, in fact, the major reason why these distribution-related costs have continued to rise and to depress profit margins throughout our economy. And for that same reason the total cost concept remained until recently a topic for textbook discussion theoretically provocative but of little practical use. But techniques have been developed to deal with information in these quantities and with interrelationships of such complexity. They have converted this sound but previously unworkable concept into a practical management approach.

The examples that follow are composites of a number of companies. The relevant facts and figures have thus been disguised without in any way changing the practical significance of the results. The first example traces the step-by-step process involved in the analysis of the factors that enter into the application of the total cost approach in a business engaged primarily in the retail distribution of a wide range of consumer products; the second shows how this complex array of information is analyzed and manipulated to provide management with profitable answers to some familiar distribution problems.

What Makes Distribution Different

Consider the problem facing the management of a large company whose business consists of a widely dispersed chain of retail stores and a few factories that produce some of the merchandise sold in these stores. This company has shipped directly from its suppliers and its factories to its stores, but wants to determine whether there would be any profit advantage in shifting to a national system of field warehouses.

When this company looked at the combined cost of warehousing and of transportation that would result from introducing various combinations of field warehouses, it appeared, as shown in Figure 1, that the lowest cost system was one with six warehouses. But this would *increase* its distribution costs by $12.9

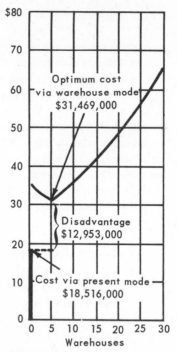

Figure 1. Distribution Cost Solution.

million. Thus, on the basis of apparent distribution costs alone, there was no profit advantage in any field warehouse system.

However, when this study investigated how alternative distribution networks would affect other costs in the company, the answer was quite different. As shown in Figure 2, the most efficient warehouse system turned out to be one with five, rather than six, field warehouses. And this five-warehouse system would cut the total costs of the company by $7.7 million; an increase of 1.4 per cent on sales.

Looking at distribution from a standpoint of total costs, this company discovered an opportunity to increase its profits that it could not have identified or taken advantage of in any other way. What explains the difference? What legerdemain turned up this handsome profit potential that represented a 22.4 per cent return on the investment required to design and install this field warehouse system? The answer, in this case as in other similar corporate experiences, involves following through the various steps of the total cost approach—that is, to determine the total cost of the present operation and then compare it with the total costs that would follow from alternative distribution systems.

At its very inception, the total cost approach is different in a number of ways from the traditional functional approach to distribution management. In the

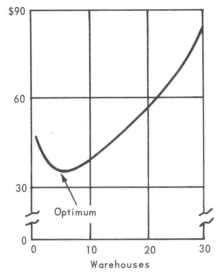

Figure 2. Total Cost Solution

first place, it deals with the impact of distribution decisions on business costs wherever these costs appear. Secondly, many important cost factors and many critical relationships between distribution and other parts of the business are not usually translatable to quantitative terms. Customer service is a classic example.

The first step was to determine what distribution-related factors contribute significantly to total costs, trace the interrelationships of these factors and then quantify both the factors and the interrelationships. This process has to be repeated anew for each company because of the important differences from industry to industry and even from one company to another in the same industry.

Then each of these have to be translated into a common denominator, so they can be measured and compared. If impact is measured in dollars, a unit that meets these requirements, it is possible to reduce all of the cost and profit considerations and all of these intricate interrelationships to one final total dollar cost for each alternative course of action.

The significance of this for management is seen in Figure 3; graphs show, for each major activity affected, the impact of different field warehouse systems (indicated by the numbers along the base of each graph) on the total cost of this operation. These graphs clearly show that for each factor of costs, a certain number of warehouses would yield the lowest costs and the maximum profit. Because each of these factors has its own built-in logic, each curve takes on its own configuration. The sum of all of these curves—each with its own optimum—is one final curve that defines the total cost. That in turn defines the optimum number of warehouses for this operation, when all considerations are taken into account. Except by chance coincidence, this point will differ from

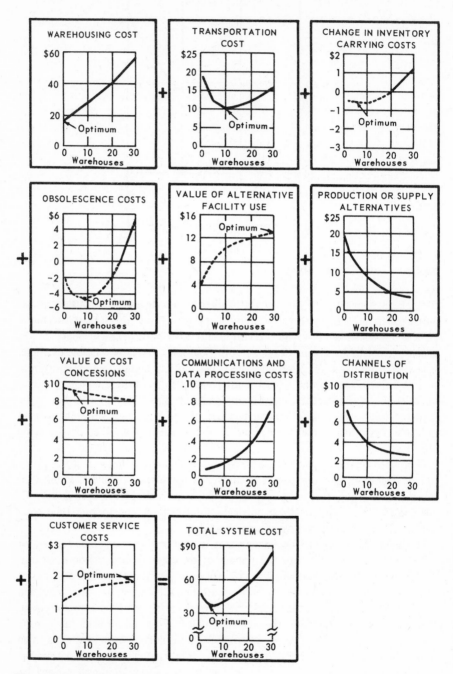

Figure 3. Total Cost Approach.

the optimum of each of the component curves. Obviously, a piecemeal approach to cost reduction will not yield the maximum profit impact achieved by this total cost approach.

These graphs show that even though one or several elements of distribution cost are cut to their lowest practical level, total costs may actually increase, and dealing with these costs one at a time will not produce the best result. They show the pitfalls of considering these various factors as single and static, instead of as interrelated and dynamic. The first and second graphs in the series make apparent the process whereby the consideration of distribution costs alone—the cost of warehouse plus the cost of transportation—led to the conclusion that no change in distribution could add to the profitability of the business. Only the final graph, summing up all of the interacting factors involved, demonstrates unmistakably that a shift to the five-warehouse system would be a very profitable move for this management.

Actually, in this case as in so many others, a reduction in warehouse and transportation could in fact lead to increases in other distribution-related costs, with the result that total costs would be increased and this significant profit opportunity missed. Only by increasing these distribution costs could total expenses be cut and total earnings increased in this company. By this kind of trade-off the total cost approach brings a company closer to achieving its maximum potential profit. The actual figures from this company's calculations for the five-warehouse system are shown in the accompanying table.

Table 1. Profit Impact of Distribution—Gains (Losses)(in millions of dollars)

Warehousing	(14.4)
Transportation	0.5
Total distribution costs	(13.9)
Inventory	
Carrying costs	1.4
Obsolescence costs	4.3
Value of alternative use of facilities	7.8
	13.5
Production and purchasing	
Production and raw materials costs	0.2
Reduced cost of purchased	
finished goods	6.7
	6.9
Data processing	(0.2)
Marketing	
Channels of distribution	0.2
Customer service	1.4
	1.6
Total profit impact of distribution-	
related items	21.8
Pretax Profit Increase	7.9

It is difficult to conceive of a distribution problem in a company of any substantial size that could not show near-term benefits from this kind of analytical approach: the approach does much more than offer a one-time solution to what is actually a perennial problem. Because this company distributes mostly through its own retail outlets, the channels of distribution are not currently an important variable. They involve only the small amount of its product that it makes in its own factories but sells to other customers. The availability of field warehouses, however, would make it possible to sell and ship more of the output of these plants direct to customers rather than through local jobbers. As it turned out, the $200,000 it added to profitability was just about what it cost to design and engineer this whole new distribution system.

In this case, the company had good reason for considering the significance of distribution channels. Looking ahead, it could see the possibility of integrating backwards, then becoming more heavily involved in manufacturing. In that case, alternative channels of distribution might become more important. The point is that in this kind of analytical exercise it is essential to consider all possible directions for company growth. Otherwise, a new distribution system, however profitable it may be under present conditions, might freeze the company into a set of cost factors that would preclude an otherwise profitable growth opportunity. The total cost approach offers management this built-in flexibility in assessing alternatives.

Every time management makes a decision of any magnitude, it ought to be in a position to get an answer to the question, "How will it affect distribution costs throughout the company?" The total cost approach puts the company in a position to make continuing gains by applying a rigid yardstick to any proposed corporate venture. Whenever manufacturing management designs a new plant, develops a new production process, or turns to a new source of raw materials, the pattern of distribution-related costs will be changed throughout the business. Similar far-flung changes will take place whenever marketing management adds a new product or a promising new group of customers. The total cost approach enables management to define how these changes will interact with distribution to affect the company's total cost and its total profits. It tells management what distribution decisions need to be made to avoid the loss of potential profits, or to add to them.   So both short-term and long-term benefits result from management's recognition of these complex cost and profit relationships.

From Data to Decision

How these complex interrelationships and the mass of related data enable management to put a dollar value on alternative courses of action can be seen quite readily in the following case. The total cost approach was used by a division of a large manufacturing company. This division does an annual business of about $45 million, with over 3,000 customers located in every state. It has manufacturers and warehouses at five points across the country, shipping to customers via both rail and truck.

The profit problems this management posed have a familiar ring; some are long-range problems:

Without any major investment, can we increase our profits by changing our distribution system?

Can total costs be reduced by shifting some of our available equipment from one factory to another?

Can we further reduce costs and increase profits by changing our marketing approach?

Is there any profit advantage in changing the capacity of one or more of our present plants, or perhaps building a new facility at another location?

Could we further improve profitability by changing our warehouse capacities or locations?

An analysis of this company's business showed quite readily what factors and what interactions determined the total profit of the product delivered to the customer.

Finding Relevant Facts

Every distribution study has to start with a definition of where the customers are located and what requirements they impose on their suppliers. In this case, some customers requested that they be shipped to by rail, and others stipulated that they be served by truck. Some buy FOB, others at a delivered price. Options, consolidation requirements, or other ingredients of the customer service package are often relevant.

Different companies will have differing requirements for details. In this case, it was important that the data be broken down by sales districts. Therefore, it was determined for 160 sales districts what percentages of sales came into each district by rail and by truck, and percentages were found in each sales district for FOB and delivered prices.

The company then knew where the products were going and how they were going to get there. Next, information was needed that would help determine from which of the five plants and warehouses each sales district should be supplied. This involved an in-depth analysis of the cost of production and warehousing per unit in each of the plants and warehouses for various volume levels.

Figure 4 shows the total plant and warehouse cost for the Indiana installation of this division, for amounts from zero to 2,100,000 hundredweight. The total plant cost is built up by analyzing the cost for varying production volume of materials, inbound freight, direct labor, and plant overhead. Each of these cost elements will, of course, differ at each plant, even within the same company. Total warehouse costs over this same volume range were similarly analyzed. The same calculations were made for each of the company's five facilities.

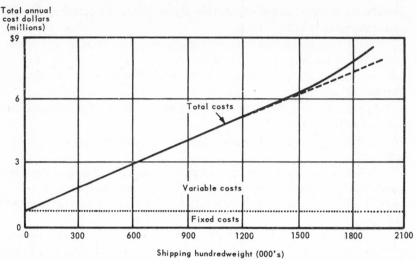

Figure 4. Total Plant and Warehousing Cost, Indiana Plant.

Figure 5 shows these total cost curves for all of the plants and warehouses. These costs are, of course, different for each facility at each point on the curve. Not only does each curve start at a different point, reflecting different overhead costs, but the rate of increase is also different, reflecting different variable cost factors at increasing volumes for each installation. These cost differences play an important role in the calculations. It then became necessary to know the cost of shipping from each warehouse to each sales district, by train and by truck. This information is readily available, though gathering it is often a time-consuming

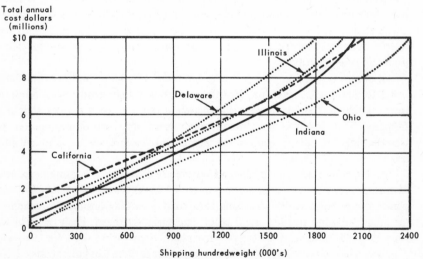

Figure 5. Total Plant and Warehousing Cost, Five Plants.

chore. Any other factors influencing profitability have to be studied similarly, in relation to each of the other cost factors. In this case, management, as a matter of policy, eliminated from consideration any changes in data processing, customer service, and channels of distribution, so these were held as constants. Under other circumstances these factors might have been evaluated as significant variables. Similarly, in other company situations, other cost factors might have required analysis so that their impact could be introduced into the final decision.

Manipulating the Data

At this point, available information showed for each unit of product and for each customer the profit contribution under all possible combinations of production and distribution. The problem that remained was to put all these possibilities together into a single solution that will maximize the company's total earnings.

While this could be done by a series of pencil and paper calculations in which each combination of factors could be worked out and the profitability of each pattern determined, it would represent an enormous and costly chore. That, of course, is the reason why the total cost concept has not found its way into management thinking until recently. To make the process practical requires a computer to process the data. And to introduce this data into the computer calls for a range of mathematical techniques known as nonlinear programming and simulation modeling. The technical aspects of these techniques are not important for their managerial implications. What is significant is that they do exist, that they do work, and that once the computer program has been written, this kind of distribution problem can be solved in a matter of minutes.

Concerning the questions confronting the management of this company, the total cost approach was able to provide a very precise answer to each of them:

1. *By rearranging the company's distribution pattern and making appropriate shifts in production and warehousing loads, it was possible without any change in facilities to increase this company's profits by $492,000 a year.* The largest ingredient in this change would come from reduced materials cost at $126,000, with warehouse savings contributing $138,000, direct labor saving in the plants adding $57,000, and plant overhead $27,000. Transportation, so often over-stressed in distribution decisions, contributed only $54,000 to this total profit improvement package.

2. *Additional savings of $180,000 could be effected by shifting equipment from one plant to another at minor cost.* To determine this, it was necessary to develop new production cost curves for alternative arrangements of equipment and run these through the computer, comparing them with the most profitable way of using the equipment as presently located.

3. *Further savings of $447,000 a year would result if about half of the customers could be persuaded to shift from truck to rail delivery.* These reduced

costs could be added to earnings or passed on to the customer, thus giving the company a competitively significant price advantage.

4. *It was determined that there was no plant addition that would provide an acceptable return on investment.* Although building a new plant in Michigan would result in lower production and warehousing costs amounting to $225,000, the return on the investments would be only 2 per cent, and the "other costs" discussed above more than offset any possible gains, so that this investment would not be a wise one.

5. *On the other hand, an addition to the capacity of the warehouse at the Delaware plant would add $75,000 a year to profits and represent a sound investment.* This was determined by setting up new warehousing cost schedules and running them through the computer alongside the costs under existing conditions. The comparison showed that the investment in the added Delaware warehouse capacity would return almost 25 per cent a year.

The total addition to profits adds up to almost $750,000 a year, from changes in distribution and facilities that were well within the company's capabilities. These would add 1.7 per cent to this company's margin on sales. The important point is this: these profits could not have been generated by decisions based on the insight or the experience of the most competent line executive. Only the total cost approach could have established, for example, that the earnings of this business could be increased by supplying its customers in the Dakotas from a plant in Ohio rather than from a much nearer facility in Illinois. Yet when total profits were calculated, this turned out to be an element in the most profitable use of the existing facilities of this company.

Similarly, only a total-cost calculation could provide the background for estimating the return on investment that could be expected from building a new facility in Michigan. Actually, that new plant would have reduced production and warehousing costs by an appreciable figure. However, other costs would be incurred in serving customers from this facility rather than from the present plant in Illinois; these other costs substantially reduced the potential savings and made the investment an unsound one. This ability to put precise price and profit tags on each pattern of alternatives makes the total cost approach a particularly effective management tool.

Making the Total Cost Approach Work

The successful applications of the total cost approach illustrated by these examples leave no doubt that this approach can, for many companies, uncover profit opportunities previously obscured by established ways of looking at distribution costs and by existing methods of managing distribution functions. But the experience of the successful companies also serves as a warning to those who are tempted to use the term "total cost" lightly. Understanding of many factors is required in order to undertake the kind of analysis required to define what all these costs are and what they really amount to, to develop a way to recover the profits they represent, and then to translate that solution into actual practice.

Though experience shows that the approach works out differently in every practical application, the sequence of steps that management has to take is always the same and it always involves the same inexorable logic:

To succeed, the total cost approach must have the active endorsement of top management. The total cost concept can be initiated at any place in the company, but unless it receives strong support from the top, it will not progress successfully for the simple reason that only top management can insist that the real cost and profit impact of distribution be defined and measured, and at regular intervals. Only top management can see to it that there is a senior executive actively concerned with doing something about this impact of distribution on costs and on profitability. And only top management can assign to this executive the authority necessary to tackle this problem across organizational lines, in order to identify and take advantage of this profit opportunity.

Only a carefully conceived feasibility study can determine whether or not a restructuring of the distribution system is likely to be profitable. This thorough kind of study requires a wide range of technical and managerial skills. The team that can do such a study has to include transportation, production, and materials handling specialists, warehousing and logistics experts, as well as analysts with backgrounds in economics, mathematical decision making and operations research.

Some companies have found it appropriate to assemble these skills within the company, while others have preferred to bring the necessary talent in from outside; this is a decision that management must make. But one fact cannot be avoided: this kind of study involves a much wider range of talents than is usually brought to bear on distribution problems, as well as a broad experience in the application of these capabilities to these total cost problems.

A more substantial and more time-consuming study is then required to determine in detail what changes are indicated, what profits can validly be expected from alternative ways of effecting these changes and what improvement in profits can be anticipated from the most practical solution.

To succeed in this effort the firm must develop quantitative information on the variables that affect each cost factor and the interrelationships among the various factors. Much of this information may be available in company records, and some of what is not available can usually be derived from existing reports. In most cases, it will be necessary to generate additional data.

Then, all of the significant interrelationships must be traced through the operation, the significant correlations defined and quantified, and all of this data subjected to mathematical analysis.

Next, the appropriate mathematical models must be constructed and then tested against past experience to validate their effectiveness. Then, alternative solutions to present and foreseeable problems have to be developed, and these studied by putting them through the model. This puts dollar values against each alternative and defines the optimum solution—the one that is most practical and most profitable.

Finally, the business implications of this solution need to be checked against organizational requirements, implications for competitive strategy, and ultimately for practicality in terms of timing and return on investment.

The final stage in the application of the total cost approach is the actual implementation of the solution. Initially, this involves putting into place the distribution system that matches the company's existing needs and its requirements for the short term future. Since the business itself and its external environment are both changing inevitably with the passage of time, with changes in product and in marketing policies and practices, as well as in response to changes in competitive forces and strategies, it is likely to prove profitable to rerun the problem at regular intervals. This process will redefine optimum distribution decisions and adjust plant loads and shipping schedules.

The companies that have been successful in using this approach have found that along with this restructuring of their distribution system, certain additional steps are likely to be critical. The assignment of responsibility for distribution has to be clarified. An information system has to be developed that will provide data on distribution costs and performance to whomever is responsible for controlling these activities. The company's data-gathering and data-processing system must be adapted so that it will pick up routinely the necessary informational input. Procedures must also be established to feed into the information system intelligence concerning conditions in the marketplace, and notably a continuing reassessment of prevailing customer service levels.

Thus the accumulated experience not only confirms the practicality and profitability of the total cost approach, but it also defines some clear-cut guidelines for managements who propose to put this approach to work. Experience in applying this approach suggests, too, that a number of additional considerations need to be clarified.

The fact that this substantial profit opportunity exists in a company is no implicit criticism of its operating management. No traffic manager or transportation specialist can be expected to deal with a problem the roots of which extend far beyond his sphere into manufacturing and marketing. Nor can the best warehouse manager be expected to come up with solutions to problems the causes and conditions of which extend from purchasing and supplier relationships at one extreme, to customer service considerations at the other. Even those companies that have centralized distribution responsibility in the hands of a single high-level executive rarely can provide this executive with the wide range of supporting capabilities and in-depth experience necessary to deal with this profit potential.

Nor does the fact that the necessary action requires top management support mean that the chief executive has to become an expert in the complexities of the mathematical tools involved, any more than he has to become knowledgeable in computer technology or the relative merits of the hardware and software. No one intends to suggest that management has to do or know anything specific or technical about distribution. What is required is management's insistence that something be done, by someone with the appropriate capabilities and experience.

In this sense, the challenge of the total cost approach has another interesting management meaning. The relentless and increasing impact of distribution on profits is one of a growing category of management problems that are not going to be solved satisfactorily within the framework of traditional organizational and decision-making approaches. The most effective solution to any company's distribution problem requires looking at the company as a whole and dealing with the profitability of the entity. More and more, management is being faced with problems requiring this kind of across-the-board attention.

At the same time new concepts, new techniques, and new technology are becoming available that are peculiarly able to cope with this very kind of problem. The more we learn about the computer and about such techniques as simulation, the more apparent it is that they are used to fullest advantage when they are used to deal with problems like these for which no other problem-solving technique is truly appropriate.

There is every reason to believe that with the increasing complexity of modern businesses and the mounting competitive pressures in their environment, the ability of companies to forge ahead and to grow profitably may have a direct relationship to the ability of management to put these new tools and their vast new capabilities to work. In the days ahead, competition between companies may in large measure reflect the skill with which competing managements take advantage of these new management tools.

22

Total Cost Approach to Physical Distribution

MARVIN FLAKS

Booz, Allen and Hamilton, Inc.

In recent years, retailers, wholesalers, and manufacturers all have exhibited an increasing awareness of the significant effect which physical distribution has on their company's profit picture. The exposure of this long-neglected phase of business activity to scientific analysis is derived from the need to satisfy two objectives. One objective is to reduce distribution costs, usually brought about by the ever increasing profit squeeze. The second is to improve marketing effectiveness, necessary to remain competitive.

Accomplishment of these objectives presents a difficult problem, since each tends to move operating costs in opposite directions. To improve marketing, companies frequently utilize additional field warehouses, commit additional funds to maintenance of field stocks, or make extensive use of premium transportation. However, to reduce distribution costs, companies may restrict field operations and use only the most economical modes of transportation.

Although these and similar physical distribution problems have been analyzed by many companies, most studies have looked only at segments of the problem. Some studies have considered only customer benefits, some considered only warehousing costs, while others have been traffic oriented. These partial evaluations result from responsibility for distribution frequently being spread among numerous functions, including manufacturing, traffic, sales and accounting.

This split responsibility has become apparent to corporate managements as they have devoted more attention to their distribution problems. Thus, there is now a tendency to view physical distribution as a single integrated system stretching from factories to customers with "physical distribution" emerging as a separate function. However, there still remains the question, "What factors must be considered before altering our present distribution methods?"

224

Certain considerations are usually present in varying degrees in most comprehensive distribution analyses. These can be grouped into five categories:

1. Operating costs.
2. Marketing factors.
3. Data processing considerations.
4. Mathematical techniques required to obtain optimum solutions to problems.
5. Management considerations necessary to make the required decisions and implement the proposed changes.

Together these comprise a total cost approach to physical distribution. Analyzed jointly, a basis for solution to this complex problem is provided. Let's now examine each of these basic considerations.

Operating Cost Consideration

Any proposal to alter existing distribution methods must deal with the following matters.

Transportation Costs

Transportation is a major expense item in almost every distribution system. The magnitude of this expense is related directly to the number and location of warehouses.

Generally, the manufacturer finds that adding warehouses reduces the distance his goods must travel between his factories and his customers. Cost thus tends to lower as distance is reduced. However, as the number of warehouses increases and the total business is divided among them, the volume handled by each decreases. Hence, the manufacturer finds that where before he could ship carload or truckload lots from his factories to a small number of warehouses, he is no longer able to do this. Consequently, his transportation costs begin to increase.

Chart 1[1] illustrates this situation, as shown by the curve labeled "Transportation Cost: Suppliers to Warehouses." As the number of warehouses increases, the inbound transportation cost decreases to a minimum, then begins to increase as the number of carload movements decreases.

Also of concern is the transportation cost outbound from warehouses. As shown in Chart 1, this cost decreases continually as additional warehouses are added. Theoretically, this cost is minimized when every store has its own warehouse. A critical point, of course, is the number of warehouses for which total transportation cost is minimized.

[1]The charts contained in this article reflect the situation typically found by the chain store operator.

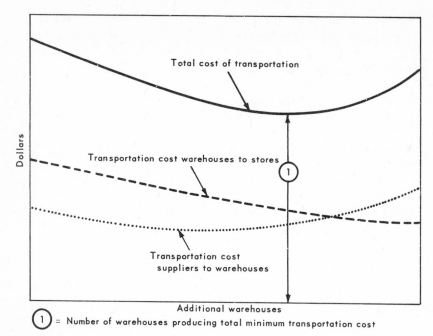

Chart 1. Transportation Cost.

The manufacturer faces much the same dilemma as the retail chain operator. However, the retailer generally has more flexibility in selecting alternate suppliers. Thus, as warehouses are established in areas of retail store concentrations, suppliers may be located in the vicinity of those warehouses thereby reducing the distance the merchandise must move and, consequently, the cost of transportation. The chain retailer may feel that he requires daily shipments from his warehouses to his stores. However, this restricts the amount of merchandise moved in each shipment and, to the extent that bulk shipments are reduced, transportation costs are increased. Also requiring analysis are the modes of transportation used and the frequency of shipments. It is usually true that the most rapid service is also the most expensive.

Warehouse Cost

An important factor affecting the cost of operating warehouses is size. Each warehouse has certain fixed and semivariable expenses. Thus, for a given volume of business, a smaller number of large warehouses will involve a lower total of fixed and semivariable expenses. This is illustrated in Chart 2 by the curve marked, "Fixed and Semivariable Costs."

Also, in larger warehouses, automatic handling devices can be justified with a resulting reduction in operating costs. Thus cost reduction has become quite

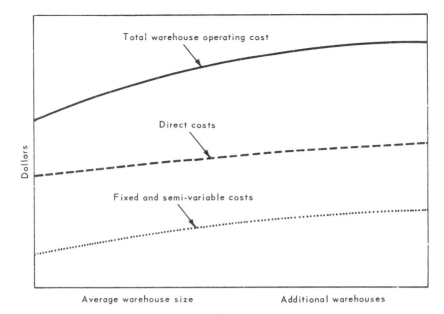

Chart 2. Warehouse Operating Cost.

significant in highly-automated warehouses. For example, devices now are available to perform the following key functions:

1. Incoming merchandise can be automatically directed by a receiver to an assigned storage area.

2. Customer orders can be converted to punch cards or magnetic tape to activate a mechanism for automatic order picking.

3. Outbound customer orders can be automatically sorted and routed to preselected truck or freight car loading docks.

The effect of mechanization is demonstrated by the "direct cost" curve in Chart 2. Direct costs, by definition, are those which vary directly with the quantity of merchandise handled. However, on a unit basis, these direct costs are less in a large (high volume) warehouse compared with a small (low volume) warehouse, since one finds that additional automatic, labor-saving devices can be justified in the larger warehouse.

Another important factor is the location of the warehouses. Major factors that must be analyzed in this regard are state and local taxes, labor rates, construction costs, and land costs.

Inventory Costs

Carrying inventory is a major expense item. The components of this cost are: insurance, taxes, space costs (including heat, watchmen and maintenance), spoilage, pilferage and interest on investment, all of which increase with added exposure.

Manufacturers, wholesalers, and retailers find that as the number of warehouses increases, the turnover in each decreases. Thus, for a constant sales level, average inventory levels increase with the number of warehouses. This is true for the following two reasons:

1. As the number of customers served by each warehouse decreases, the beneficial "balancing" effect is reduced. To illustrate, a warehouse serving a single customer must be prepared to meet that customer's peak demands. However, if the warehouse serves two customers, it is unlikely that the peak demand of each, for the same product, would coincide. Hence, the warehouse need only be prepared for a peak demand somewhat lower than the sum of the peak demands of the customers.

2. The average warehouse inventory level for each stock-keeping unit can be reduced as the volume through a given warehouse decreases. However, a practical limit is reached when the order quantity is reduced to the minimum factory pack (or to a minimum economic order quantity). Hence, for some stock-keeping units, subsequent reductions in volume will *not* be accompanied by reductions in inventory.

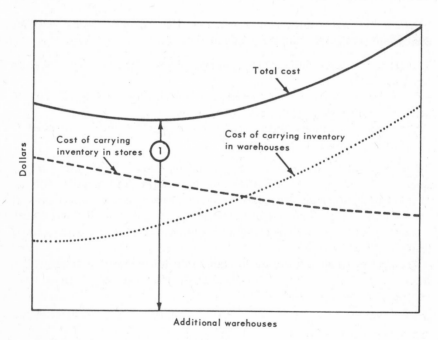

Chart 3. Inventory Carrying Cost.

The retail chain operator also is concerned about the stock levels which must be maintained in his stores. As the number of warehouses increases, the transit time from warehouses to stores is reduced. This permits the stores to operate with lower stocks. This, in turn, produces significant benefits to be later discussed.

Chart 3 illustrates the cost of carrying inventory as a function of the number of warehouses. A critical point to note is the number of warehouses producing total minimum inventory carrying costs.

Marketing Considerations

Warehouse networks generally are expanded to achieve certain marketing values. An evaluation of these benefits normally can be made in terms of the following:

The Value of Improved Service

Service improvement can be equated to changes in time utility and place utility. In some lines, customers have come to expect a given time availability of merchandise. For example, delivery within two days after ordering. Failure to provide this expected level of service results in a competitive disadvantage.

Place utility involves having the goods available where the customer wants them. For instance, in some lines wholesalers know that their customers operate with little or no inventory of their own and consequently, customers must have access to a local wholesaler who stocks a full range of merchandise available for immediate delivery.

A change in distribution practices intended to improve service must be expressed quantitatively in terms of both added sales to be achieved and the profit engendered by those sales. Contrarily, any change intended to reduce cost must be equated to the possible curtailment of service and the concomitant effect on profits.

The Cost of Lost Sales

A sale may be lost each time an order is presented at a warehouse and is not filled because the requested item is out of stock. This is well recognized by the wholesaler or the manufacturer whose customer may have immediate need for the product and can easily obtain a substitute from a nearby competitor. The retail chain operator knows that when demand for a given item is heavy, he must be able to keep his stores supplied with that item or suffer a loss of sales opportunity.

For either the manufacturer or retailer, he runs the risk of a permanently lost customer once the customer is compelled to use a competitor and perhaps form new shopping habits.

The risk of lost sales can be reduced by maintaining a high inventory level; yet costs are decreased by keeping inventory levels low. To determine an optimum inventory level, one must assess the probability of a run-out and resultant effect on sales and profits, weighing decreased costs against higher sales.

Improved Turnover and Reduced Inventory Obsolescence

Turnover is of particular importance to the retailer because of the well-known relationship to markdowns: Namely, as turnover increases, markdowns decrease. Changes in distribution can have a major influence on store turnover since, as noted previously, (1) mode of transportation affects replenishment time and (2) proximity of field warehouses can permit reduction of store inventories. Hence, a quantitative relationship is required between turnover and markdowns.

The same problem plagues the manufacturer. The longer merchandise is held in storage, the more susceptible it is to inventory obsolescence. The premium which can be paid to improve turnover should be measured against the possible savings attributable to reduced obsolescence losses.

Data Processing Considerations

The nature and degree of administrative controls frequently spell the difference between a mediocre distribution system and a highly efficient one. Therefore, a comprehensive distribution study should consider the following points related to data processing.

Receiving and Processing Orders

Many automated devices are available, and additional devices are in advanced stages of development, for the efficient processing of quantities of orders. These devices may yield economies, not only in the receipt of orders, but also in the physical handling operations. Warehouses can be planned to segregate case lot picking from less-than-case lot picking and to accommodate grouping of items based on their activity, with specialized treatment accorded each group.

Devices also are available to permit manufacturers to offer various forms of automatic replenishment to their customers. A typical example is the punched card which some manufacturers attach to each unit of merchandise shipped to a customer's sales outlets. When a unit of merchandise is sold, a punched card is returned to the manufacturer. This represents an order to replace the particular item, enabling the sales outlet to maintain pre-established stocks.

Handling Invoices

The preparation of invoices, shipping documents, and accounting inputs also lend themselves to efficient electronic data processing. The costs and benefits of these operations must be considered as an integral part of any distribution survey.

Controlling Inventory

The maintenance of appropriate inventory levels is a major consideration in operating a multiwarehouse network. An approach should be developed to assure that the desired merchandise is available when and where required, while at the same time holding inventory investment to a minimum. Recent data processing system developments permit a degree of sophistication not heretofore obtainable.

Mathematical Considerations

Analysis of the elements comprising the *total cost* approach to distribution is a complex undertaking. It would include analysis of such variables as merchandise in transit from producing points, goods in warehouse stock, products in transit to customers, and store inventories. Until quite recently, required solutions for some distribution problems had not been developed. Currently, better answers are being obtained for these complex problems by using operations research techniques such as linear and non-linear programming, and simulation. Some typical mathematical applications are listed below.

Model Design

It is possible to construct a mathematical model which represents the proposed system. Through use of a high-speed computer, the inputs to the model can be manipulated to produce the equivalent of many years of actual experience with the proposed system. Other proposed systems can be tested in a similar manner to arrive at an optimum solution.

The model design technique can be used to solve complex problems of warehouse design such as determination of: the optimum number of truck spots, or the best width for picking aisles, the optimum material-handling system, and other considerations.

Sample Design

One must usually secure data from some detailed source such as customer orders, invoices, or bills of lading. A mathematically designed sample can reduce the data collection job substantially while maintaining a prescribed level of accuracy.

Multiple Correlation Analysis

One frequently needs to determine to what extent changes in variables A and B can be used to predict changes in variable C. Multiple correlation techniques permit this determination. Further, one can determine what change in C is likely to take place for a given change in A or B.

This technique, for example, was used recently to determine the relationship between retail sales and inventory (hence, turnover) and retail markdowns. The result was an expression permitting estimation of changes in retail markdowns as a function of changes in store inventory levels.

Management Considerations

After all of the preceding questions have been answered, there still remain several additional determinations before management has adequate information upon which to make a proper decision.

The Organization Required

A major change in a company's distribution system usually requires organizational realignment. If a new distribution network appears necessary, new responsibilities are created and old ones are altered. Management must assign responsibilities for transportation, warehousing and inventory control. These functions must be properly coordinated with manufacturing (or buying) and selling (or merchandising).

The Probable Effect on Sales Volume and Profits

Additional warehouses may increase sales and profits for any or all of the following reasons:

1. Improved delivery may open a new market where the company now is not competitive.
2. Sales may be increased by reducing out-of-stock situations.
3. Increased inventory turnover may reduce obsolescence losses.
4. Reduced inventories in retail stores could release space which might be converted to productive selling space.
5. Reputation could be enhanced when customers recognize the consistent early availability of current products. This, in turn, could produce more sales.

These questions are frequently overlooked in the analyses of distribution systems. The reason for this neglect is the difficulty of quantitative analysis. However, techniques now exist for the evaluation of these questions.

Chart 4 illustrates the typical effect of added warehouses on profits. As shown, gross profit increases. Usually, a higher than normal rate of profit can be attributed to incremental sales because of higher volume on the same overhead base. Gross profit will continue to increase with additional warehouses.

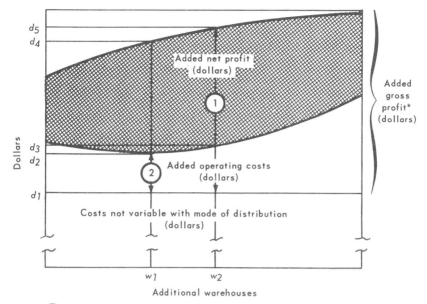

① = Number of warehouses w_2 producing maximum increase in net profit d_5-d_3

② = Number of warehouses w_1 producing minimum operating cost d_2-d_1

* Reflects an improved profit percentage on incremental sales

Chart 4. Effect of Additional Warehouses on Total Profit.

As warehouses are added, for example, total operating costs usually will decrease to a minimum and then proceed to rise and accelerate quite rapidly.

Chart 4 permits certain important observations:

1. If the illustrated distribution study has been concerned only with operating costs, the solution would be to operate with w_1 warehouses, since, at this point, operating costs, numeral 2, are minimized.

2. However, a study of all factors reveals that the optimum number of warehouses is w_2. This results in higher operating costs $(d_3 - d_2)$, but also results in higher net profit, indicated by numeral 1.

3. Added net profit is maximized: $(d_5 - d_3)$ instead of $(d_4 - d_2)$.

4. Although gross profit would increase when operating with more than w_2 warehouses, operating costs would increase more rapidly than gross profit, resulting in a diminishing of net profits.

The Investment Required and the Probable Return on Investment

Another critical determination remains. Analyses of each of the preceding questions will have produced an expected economic benefit if the changes in the distribution system are consummated. Management needs next to determine the required investment in additional facilities as well as the one-time costs of implementing the changes. At this point the expected return on the required investment can be calculated and a decision reached on the desirability of pursuing the proposed course of action.

Summary

The cost of distributing merchandise continues to mount every year. As competitive pressures increase, companies will continue to feel the necessity of offering their customers additional services. Yet, in the years to come, the pressures of mounting costs and service demands will cause many companies to consider both modifications and restrictions of their distribution systems. As described herein, the questions arising in the conduct of a comprehensive distribution study are numerous and complex. However, to arrive at a correct conclusion, it is absolutely essential that all of the pertinent questions be answered. It is essential that the ultimate judgment be based upon an examination of the *total costs* involved and their interrelationships. Modern techniques of distribution analysis make this possible.

23

Quantitative Methods —
What They Are and How
You Can Use Them

RONALD H. BALLOU
Northwestern University

Many of physical distribution's problems can be solved by quantitative analytical methods. Suppose, for instance, you had five retail outlets supplied by a single warehouse as pictured in Figure 1. Could you figure out the fastest truck route from warehouse through all five outlets and back, by any means other than expensive trial-and-error? You could if you used the analysis technique called "the assignment method," which will show you the best of the 720 possible routes with only a fraction of the time investment required to try each one out. This analytic method and others (some just as simple, some more complex) form the basis of the entire physical distribution concept. It's important that you know what these methods are, so you can use them to help solve your problems.

The framework for analysis is a good place to begin this discussion of techniques, because we can define our objectives and concepts. A physical distribution system is, very simply, several inventories interconnected by a transportation network, as Figure 1 depicts. A product moving from raw materials origins to points of consumption may pass through one, or several, such segments, depending upon the complexity of the system of which the segment is a part. Your goal, as physical distribution manager, is to find a way to get the lowest costs (or the highest return on investment) of providing movement and storage services that create time and place utilities in a product. It isn't quite as simple as it reads, though, because attainment of your objective is hampered by several constraining factors. Two major limitations are customer service standards and inventory location. Determine these constraints (for example, select warehouse locations), and you've partly established the design of

235

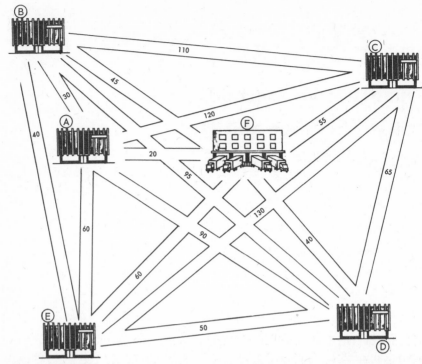

Figure 1. Problem: Find the fastest truck route from warehouse through each outlet and return. Travel times are shown in minutes. Hint: The assignment technique (a quantitative method) will help you solve the problem quickly.

your physical distribution system. But you've also limited your system's cost improvement possibilities because you've fewer alternative courses of action.

To make a useful analysis of your physical distribution system's two major elements (inventories and transportation alternatives), you must also analyze supporting activities. Called the subsystems, these include warehousing, material handling, order processing, supply scheduling, customer service standards, and facility location. The techniques discussed can also be used to analyze these subsystem activities.

Philosophy for analysis. Quantitative methods used to analyze real-world problems are often criticized because they don't consider all the factors influencing the situation being analyzed. This criticism isn't very worthwhile because these methods aren't designed to produce an all-encompassing solution to the problem. Instead, quantitative models use only the measurable factors of a real problem to produce the best solution for an abstraction of that problem. They give an approximate solution which you must modify to account for the problem's intangible or un-measurable factors. The modified solution is your desired course of action.

Further, a mathematical model can't encompass the broad point of view required for a total-cost analysis. As a physical distribution manager, you must consider the effects of any quantitative solution to your problem on overall company objectives and the goals of other departments or divisions.

Considering all these shortcomings, you may doubt that the quantitative model has any value at all. It does, though, because even the simplest model is based on one or more of your problem's most important factors (inventory models, for example, include carrying and procurement costs). You're thus assured that your decision considers these important factors.

Then too, solution of the model may be only a first stop, a point of departure for a more thorough investigation. Many problems are far too complex to be solved by judgment alone, but models can find good initial solutions, thereby bringing the final answer within the range of judgment.

Analysis of transportation problems. Selection of carriers and selection of routes are two transportation problems susceptible to mathematical analysis. Model application may give only a slight cost improvement for each decision, but multiplied by the great volume of such decisions, significant cost reduction results.

A carrier can be described for analytical purposes in terms of service cost and operating characteristics (speed and dependability). To intelligently choose a carrier, you must know what effect its operating characteristics will have on inventory costs of both shipper and receiver (for instance, the least expensive carrier is often the least dependable one). Greater service dependability means lower safety stock requirements for the inventory into which the goods are being shipped. You can quantitatively determine which carrier offers the best balance between freight and inventory costs.

Another common problem for distribution activities is the routing of trucks from warehouse to retail outlets. As pointed out before, a warehouse with five outlets offers 720 possible round-trip routes. Mathematical procedures (which can also be used to route material handling equipment through warehouses, select least-cost highway routes through cities or states, or find the most efficient way to transmit orders) will determine the best route more quickly and efficiently than will complete enumeration of all possible routes.[1,2]

Lets illustrate by solving the problem presented in Figure 1. We'll use a technique called the assignment method to find the fastest truck route.

Travel times between the points are first set down in matrix form as in Table 1. Next, subtract the smallest value in each *column* of the matrix from all other values in that column. Repeat the process with each *row* of the revised matrix.

[1] Sasieni, Yaspan and Friedman, *Operations Research—Methods and Problems*, (Wiley, 1959) pp. 185-192 and pp. 264-267.
[2] Zoints, "Methods for Selection of an Optimum Route," in *Papers—Third Annual Meeting, American Transportation Research Forum*, American Transportation Research Forum, 1962, pp. 25-36.

Table 1. Matrix of Travel Times for the Network Shown in Figure 2.

From			To			
	W	A	B	C	D	E
W	–	30	45	55	40	60
A	30	–	30	120	90	60
B	45	30	–	110	95	40
C	55	120	110	–	65	130
D	40	90	95	65	–	50
E	60	60	40	130	50	–

The assignment technique at work. Easy computation eliminates expensive trial-and-error.

Your result is the opportunity-time matrix shown in Table 2. Because the problem was simple, the best solution is produced at this point; all that remains is to read it out. Beginning with the "W" on the "from" side of the matrix, box a zero in that row (at "C"). This gives you your next point of departure, so return to the "from" side and find another zero in row "C". Continue the

Table 2. Matrix of Opportunity Travel Times with Routing Problem Solution Partially Indicated by Arrows.

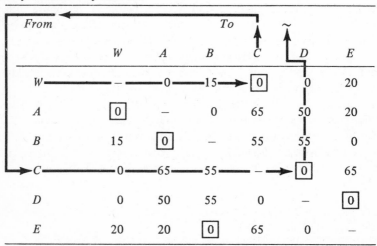

From			To			
	W	A	B	C	D	E
W	–	0	15	[0]	0	20
A	[0]	–	0	65	50	20
B	15	[0]	–	55	55	0
C	0	65	55	–	[0]	65
D	0	50	55	0	–	[0]
E	20	20	[0]	65	0	–

The assignment technique at work. Easy computation eliminates expensive trial-and-error.

procedure until all rows have been examined. Your best routing plan as described by the boxed zeros is: W→C→D→E→B→A→W. This plan (or the reverse of it) is feasible; the route W→D→C etc., (you probably tried it) is not. The minimum total time is 255 minutes.

Inventory models. Inventories are buffers between sales and production. They help smooth production output while helping you meet customers' service requirements. In a physical distribution system they represent a balance between the cost of additional inventory and the cost of more premium transportation.

The many models designed to help control these inventories answer two basic questions: how often and in what quantities should orders be placed to get the lowest total costs of buying and holding inventories. Common inventory models find the best balance among the costs of placing an order, stockouts, and inventory storage (Figure 2). Simplest of these models (used when cost and demand data aren't accurate enough to justify a more sophisticated formulation) is the familiar economic order quantity formula, which considers inventory

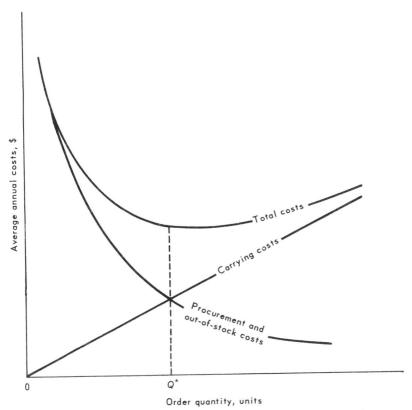

Figure 2. Common inventory models find the best balance among the costs of placing an order, stockouts, and inventory storage. They may be simple or very complex; either way, they help you keep costs low.

demand and replenishment time known and constant, and doesn't permit stockouts.[3]

Inventory levels are better controlled through use of more representative models which consider the variability of both demand and replenishment, include quantity discounts, and sometimes even have dynamic features built into them.[4] To solve a more sophisticated model, you'll need greater mathematical skill, but this is the price you must pay for its use.

Because your transportation activity must ultimately move the order volume suggested by the inventory model, you must know how that volume will effect transportation efficiency. The final decision on quantities to flow through the physical distribution system should be based on cost trade-offs between inventory and transportation activities.

Location models. Warehouse and plant sites must be chosen carefully, both because location effects the cost level of the entire physical distribution system, and because large investments are at stake. Existing location models of two types, optimum-seeking, and heuristic, help in your site selection decision.

Optimum-seeking models attempt to determine on a geographic or time map which location will give mathematically the lowest cost or highest profit. Only a limited number of cost factors can be included in these models because they must examine a very large number of possible sites. Transportation costs are most often included in these models as the major locational force.

The "center-of-gravity" technique is probably the simplest of these models and easiest to apply.[5] Here, the volume and transportation rate associated with each source or destination point is treated as a weight. Solution shows you the one site (called "least transportation cost point") at which all the weights are balanced. This model's construction and solution procedures have been slightly modified to afford greater accuracy because it hasn't always yielded the least-cost location.[6]

Other optimum-seeking location models include the sophisticated Mossman–Morton,[7] and Bowman–Stewart[8] models. In the former, "time-to-market" is an important factor because it effects the revenue the system can produce. The Bowman-Stewart model yields both the size and number of warehouses needed to serve a region.

Heuristic models are so named because, unlike the optimum-seeking models,

[3] Hadley and Whitin, *Analysis of Inventory Systems*, (Prentice-Hall, 1963).

[4] Cahn, "The Warehouse Problem," *Bulletin of the American Mathematical Society*, Vol. 54 (1948), p. 1073.

[5] Smykay and Fredericks, "An Index Based Method for Evaluating Warehouse Locations," *Transportation Journal,* Fall, 1963, pp. 30-34.

[6] Bergin and Rogers, "An Algorithm and Computational Procedure for Locating Economic Facilities," *Management Science*, Feb., 1967, pp. 240-254.

[7] Mossman and Morton, "A General Model for Computing Elasticity of Demand for Service," in *Logistics of Distribution Systems*, (Allyn and Bacon, 1965) pp. 245-256.

[8] Bowman and Stewart, "A Model for Scale of Operations," *Journal of Marketing*, Jan., 1956, pp. 242-247.

managerial judgment is used at the outset of solution so that greater realism can be added to the problem definition. For example, computational complexity of the location problem is reduced by considering only those sites that managerial judgment considers most likely to be chosen as the final site. With fewer sites under consideration, additional cost factors can be included in the model, such as warehousing, land, and delivery delay costs. The heuristic model, then, offers near-optimum solutions to more realistic problem definitions whereas the optimum-seeking model gives the optimum mathematical solution to a limited problem definition.

Kuehn and Hamburger developed an heuristic model (probably the best-known of its type) for locating warehouses, which uses the computer to analyze the costs of multiple-warehouse location patterns.[9] The heuristic approach is also used in models based on linear programming techniques.[10] Most existing location models don't account for changing demand patterns or economic conditions, but this shortcoming can be overcome by using the technique called "dynamic programming" with these models.[11]

Warehousing analysis. Quantitative methods can help solve problems of the many activities of warehousing, such as warehouse size,[12] internal physical layout of merchandise,[13,14] number of docks,[15] truck scheduling, conveyer design,[16] and improved space utilization.[17] Lets look at two of these.

Merchandise layout, or stock arrangement within the warehouse, directly affects material-handling costs. Several methods exist to help you find the layout plan that will produce the lowest total stock-handling costs.

The popularity method locates high turnover items nearest the shipping dock, and is based on the assumption that you'll ship these items in units, smaller than the units in which they're received. The object is to keep order-picking travel distance as short as possible.

The volume (size) method locates merchandise by size, and may produce the lowest material-handling costs because more small-sized items than large ones can be located near the shipping dock.

The cube-per-order-index, a third method, combines both previous techniques.

[9] Kuehn and Hamburger, "A Heuristic Program for Locating Warehouses," *Management Science,* July, 1963, pp. 643-666.

[10] Baumol and Wolfe, "A Warehouse-Location Problem," *Operations Research*, March-April, 1958, pp. 252-63.

[11] Ballou, "Dynamic Warehouse Location Analysis," unpublished.

[12] Bowman and Stewart, *op. cit.*

[13] Armour and Buffa "A Heuristic Algorithm and Simulation Approach to the Relative Location of Facilities," *Management Science*, Jan., 1963, pp. 294-309.

[14] Ballou, "Improving the Physical Layout of Merchandise in Warehouses," *Journal of Marketing*, July, 1967, pp. 60-64.

[15] Sasieni et al., *op. cit.*, and Zoints, *op. cit.*

[16] Morris, *Analysis for Materials Handling Management,* (Irwin, 1962), pp. 129-169.

[17] Moder and Thorton, "Quantitative Analysis of the Factors Affecting Floor Space Utilization of Palletized Storage," Journal of Industrial Engineering, Jan.-Feb., 1965, pp. 8-18.

This method guarantees movement of the greatest stock volume over the shortest possible distance.

Finally, linear programming has been used as a more sophisticated approach to layout problems. In preliminary comparisons materials-handling costs were 11 to 23 percent lower than the foregoing methods.

Dock requirements can be determined if you use the queuing (waiting line) theory method. Waiting for service (waiting to be loaded or unloaded) generates costs just as performing the service does. The queuing theory finds the best balance between waiting and service costs, from which you can figure how many docks you need for a least-cost operation.[18]

Computer simulation is an analytical tool set apart from the other quantitative techniques already discussed because it is probably your most powerful tool. Simulation simply describes a part of the real world in terms of algebraic formulae. Solving these formulae with the help of a digital computer shows you how your decisions will effect your entire physical distribution system and even other company operations *before* those decisions are implemented and without interrupting work in progress.[19] As examples of simulation applied to physical distribution systems, Forrester[20] observed the effect of customer demand patterns on inventory levels by simulating an entire physical distribution system, and Shycon and Maffei[21] used simulation to analyze a system's warehouse location pattern.

In summary, the increasing use of scientific management techniques by all functions of business is clearly indicated. This trend will continue under the impetus of improved computer technology and growing management interest in operations research. Accordingly, I have presented brief descriptions (an overview, if you will) of some of the quantitative models and techniques you can apply to your physical distribution problems.

[18] Schiller and Lavin, "The Determination of Requirements for Warehouse Dock Facilities," *Operations Research*, April 1956, pp. 233-243.

[19] McMillan and Gonzales, *Systems Analysis—A Computer Approach to Decision Models,* (Irwin, 1965).

[20] Forrester, *Industrial Dynamics* (M.I.T. Press and Wiley, 1961).

[21] Shycon and Maffei, "Simulation—Tool for Better Distribution," *Harvard Business Review,* (Nov.-Dec. 1960), pp. 65-75.

24

Simulation—Tool for Better Distribution

HARVEY N. SHYCON
Booz, Allen and Hamilton, Inc.

RICHARD B. MAFFEI
M.I.T.

Recently a vice president of the H. J. Heinz Company, recognizing that proper warehousing was one of his company's biggest problems, asked himself these pertinent questions concerning his distribution system:

1. "How many warehouses should we have?"
2. "Where should the warehouses be located?"
3. "What customers should each warehouse service?"
4. "What volume should each warehouse handle?"
5. "How can we best organize our entire distribution function?"

In a firm like Heinz—with a dollar sales volume in the hundred millions, with several factories, with many mixing points where products from several factories are assembled for large shipments, with dozens of warehouses and thousands of customers—lowering the costs of distributing products to market, while still maintaining good customer service, is no easy trick. Moreover, the rising costs of distribution make maximum mileage from the distribution dollar absolutely essential.

How can answers to difficult questions like these best be obtained? The problem can be resolved through the use of simulation, one of the great advances in the science of business management developed in the past decade. Simulation provides the ability to operate some particular phase of a business on paper—or in a computer—for a period time, and by this means to test various alternative strategies and systems. Distribution, sales and marketing, production problems—taken separately or in combination—have been solved in a remarkably accurate fashion by simulation. In the case of the H. J. Heinz Company, simulation worked with such effectiveness that a whole new approach to achieving the lowest practical costs of distribution resulted.

How Simulation Works

In this article, we hope to describe the way we applied simulation to solve, to a considerable extent, Heinz's distribution problems. It should be of special interest, for this simulation is perhaps the most complete, comprehensive, and accurate study of a national distribution system ever carried out.

Some readers, of course, are much more sophisticated about simulation and its uses than are others. Those who are, I hope, will bear with us as we explain each step of our method. They should remember, also, that our object here is not to write a lofty treatise on simulation theory but to share with practical businessmen, in as clear and simple terms as possible, the logic of how we went about our simulation of Heinz's distribution system. While this information can hardly be expected to enable, say, a marketing executive to tackle a simulation study completely on his own, we do hope that it will enable businessmen to understand, in general, how such a procedure could be used to help their companies test various marketing and distribution strategies.

What we are describing is a general-purpose tool—a mathematical representation of a company's distribution system. It takes into account each of the important factors involved in the operation of a distribution system: transportation rate structures, warehouse operating costs, the characteristics of customers' demand for products, buying patterns of customers, costs of labor and construction, factory locations, product mix and production capacities, and all other significant elements. These factors, taken together, make up the distribution system. Each of these elements is represented in a way which simulates its actual effect in the national distribution pattern and its effect on costs, with proper weighting and consideration given to the interrelationships among the various factors.

Since the simulation represents the essential parts of the actual distribution system, it permits the operation of the system in such a way that a whole year's transactions can be run through under close scrutiny. "Goods" flow through the system, from factory to mixing point, to warehouses, to the customer; and transportation and operating "costs" are incurred, just as they would be in real life.

But because it is only a synthetic representation, it permits the testing of various schemes for developing better distribution methods and achieving lower operating costs. Different cost trends incurred by the alternative distribution arrangements are compared, leading ultimately to a plan of distribution at lowest cost.

For the H. J. Heinz Company, the simulation has provided a unique tool for determining the number of warehouses and mixing points which should exist in the national distribution system. It also has determined where they should be located to achieve a minimal over-all operating cost. In addition, it has provided information on how best to service the many thousands of customers by an optimal combination of service direct from factory and service from area warehouses. Further, it has given a detailed plan for allocating merchandise to given warehouses and to particular customers for each product line and from each factory. With this cohesive national distribution plan in hand, management has now proceeded to make future marketing plans with assurance of lowest actual distribution costs.

The Heinz Problem

Heinz is typical of many manufacturers with large-scale distribution requirements. From multiple manufacturing plants across the nation, from a system of mixing points and warehouses spread across the country, the company must service all of the national marketing areas. As with many other manufacturers (both in the food and in the nonfood fields), Heinz's distribution setup has been undergoing substantial changes over the past few years.

Specific factors which have influenced traditional distribution methods are shifts in population centers and principal markets, the emergence of brand identification as a prime marketing factor, technological changes in distribution methods, the growth of large retail operations, and other changes in marketing. Added to these, of course, is the fact that the cost of physical distribution of product to market has been rapidly increasing.

As a result of these changes, the Heinz management recognized some years ago the need for a careful re-evaluation of its marketing plans and has had in process a program for streamlining and improving the marketing and distribution system nationally. More recently, it became evident that a re-examination of the transportation and warehousing system was required so that modern methods of physical distribution could be fitted to the new marketing plans in a way that would achieve a minimal over-all cost of distribution.

Heinz considered it important that a cohesive plan be developed which would combine the best features of direct plant-to-customer distribution with those of a national warehousing network. By an optimal combination of these, management hoped to minimize inclusive costs of distributing products to market and, at the same time, to maintain its policy of excellent service to customers.

Growth and Costs

Problems of distribution involving both the length of distribution time and the increasing cost of getting the product to market are felt in many major segments of industry. Heinz is hardly unique in this sense. Consumer products of all kinds—hard goods as well as soft goods, appliances, automobiles, electrical goods, clothing, the entire food industry—all are subject to increasing distribution costs.

The problem faced by the management of the Heinz company was even more complex than most. Not only were the costs of physical distribution of product to market growing, but the distribution system was increasingly being dated by a streamlined marketing program instituted at the company over the past few years to accommodate the needs of the market better and to provide improved service to customers. Included in this program were a greater recognition of the function of jobbers and distributors and a reorganization of the marketing program to build up the distributors function in the marketing framework. Whole marketing areas had been converted from direct retailer selling to distributor areas, and, finally, an ever increasing portion of volume was moving through the distributor channels.

With changes of this nature taking place, it was inevitable that a warehouse system originally designed to handle one type of market would eventually require basic changes in order to service properly the new marketing system. Originally, the national market had been served by some 68 warehouses placed geographically to handle the many low-volume customers in the system. With the marketing structure changing, it became evident that some warehouses were located incorrectly in relation to the market now being served, and that some warehouses were simply no longer needed.

Management faced squarely the problem brought about by these changes, developed plans for the reallocation of customer volume to other warehouses, and closed some of the lower volume branches. This resulted in a reduction in the number of warehouses in the system. The company wanted to know if it had gone too far, if it had gone far enough, and, indeed, if it had retained the right locations in the system.

Chain Reactions

Management soon became convinced that the conventional methods were inadequate for analyzing (a) which warehouses to retain and (b) how best to allocate customer volume among warehouses, mixing points, and factories. In a large system of this kind changes in distribution pattern—even at the local level—tend to have chain reactions throughout the national system. A change which may appear to yield a lower cost of operation at the local level can, in fact, cause an increased cost of operation when all relevant costs are considered on a national basis. For example: When a warehouse is placed close to a given customer, the cost of delivering merchandise to that customer may well become lower. But the over-all effect on cost of transportation of merchandise from the various factories to the warehouse, and costs of delivery to other customers still farther away—all these, combined with the cost of operating the given warehouse, make the problem complex indeed.

What was needed, management decided, was a bold new approach to studying the distribution system as a whole, on a national basis. The many interrelated costs, the many source points and many thousands of customers throughout the country, all had to be taken into account in establishing a distribution pattern of warehouses and mixing points which would yield the lowest over-all cost.

Simulation Requirements

Our complete representation of Heinz's complex, high-volume national distribution system had to be detailed enough to handle each of the thousands of customers in the Heinz system. Specifically:

1. It had to take account of each customer's order sizes, his ordering patterns, the various types of shipments he receives, and his product mix.

2. Provision had to be made for handling the costs of the various kinds of shipment made—i.e., carload, less-than-carload, truckload, less-than-truckload, and various shipment sizes within the lower classifications.

3. Variation in warehouse operating costs—i.e., labor costs, rentals, taxes for different geographic areas—had to be considered.

4. The many different classifications of products which Heinz manufactures, the alternative factory source points for each of these products, and the factory capacity limitations on each—all had to be examined.

5. Finally, when such a representation was designed, it had to be in such form that it could be synthetically operated, using real operating figures, for a year's time, over and over again.

In this way, various configurations of warehouses and mixing points could be tried so that costs might be observed for different conditions, and the lowest cost pattern achieved. And since the number of transactions required for one year's operation of the national system would be so great, the representation had to be in such form as to be operable on a high-speed computer.

Logic of Simulation

A distribution system exists in order to link production activity (which, of course, *cannot* exist everywhere) and consumption activity (which *does* exist almost everywhere). A company interested in studying its warehouse location problem could start by specifying where production takes place and where the majority of its customers are located. It could, initially, assume arbitrary locations of warehouses. If proper cost information, consumption information, and production information are available, then the costs of distribution associated with a given *assumed* configuration of warehouses could be determined. These results could be compared with costs accruing under other assumed configurations.

This idea is simple enough, but the question that immediately suggests itself is this: *How can sufficient detail be designed into such a representation to provide genuine assurance that the lowest-cost distribution plan developed on paper would be realized during actual operations?*

This question is not only legitimate but is of crucial importance when analysts talk of studying and simulating systems. The answer lies in the nature of the simulation developed. Properly designed, the simulation takes account of all relevant aspects of the problem as they interrelate with one another, and operates much as the real system does.

It might be said that simulation, in providing the means for testing the various alternative courses of action available, simply evaluates all of the "What if?" questions frequently asked. It tests those things that businessmen would like to try if time, money, and manpower permitted. For example: Without simulation, Heinz would have done a cost analysis for each of a number of distribution systems under various assumptions as to sales patterns. Each such analysis would have been rather costly to conduct. Analysis of a single national distribution configuration, yielding one year's operating results, required some 75 million calculations by the computer—and these were performed in less than one hour. By conventional methods, this would have taken two clerks almost 50 years!

Further, the number of alternatives which could be economically examined in this way would have nowhere nearly exhausted all of the possibilities. Analysis of just 20 such possibilities would have required 2,000 clerks working one year! Moreover, management could not feel any great confidence that its final decision was "correct," because of the probability of human error and the great passage of time during which things would change.

Basic Factors

To assure that the results of this study would be meaningful, we first had to specify the characteristics of Heinz customers and factories. Each customer's characteristics were specified according to:

1. Geographic location.
2. Order sizes and frequency.
3. Volume of purchases.
4. Variety requirements.

And each factory's characteristics were specified according to:

1. Geographic location.
2. Production capacities by product line.
3. Product mix.

Between these two basic factors—customer location and needs, and factory location and production characteristics—lies the distribution system. The problem, then, becomes one of determining the number, size, and location of warehouses and additional mixing points which would properly serve customers at a minimum cost nationally.

In a dynamic distribution system of this type many forces exist which influence warehouse number, location, and size. The nature of each customer order—its product mix, its timing, the effect of special promotions and pricing policies on customer ordering and stocking, and other factors—all are influential. In similar fashion, every applicable freight rate from each geographic point to every other geographic point, the freight rate "breaks," and similar transportation specifications have their effect. The cost of operating a warehouse at each potentially alternate location has its influence. Finally, the precise product mix of each factory, along with the capacity limitations by product line, affects warehouse location and the cost of distribution.

To evaluate properly each of these characteristics—for the many thousands of customer orders, for the thousands of alternative sources and routings possible, for the multiplicity of alternate possibilities of warehouse and mixing point configurations—it was necessary to construct a mathematical "model" of the distribution system. Adding high-speed computing ability completed the requirements necessary to a solution of this problem.

Included in this "model" are all the essential parts of the distribution system which influence warehouse location. But which parts of the distribution system are essential and which are not?

The answers were found only after considerable research into the actual distribution records of the company. Specifically, these are the factors that had to be taken into account in setting up the model:

1. How frequently customers order, how much they order, what they order, where they are located, and how they prefer to take receipt of ordered goods.

2. The kinds of goods that can be supplied from any given factory point, the quantities that can be supplied, and the location of the factories.

3. The relationship between shipping rates and points of origin and destination, for truck and rail transportation, and for different types and sizes of orders.

4. The relationship between total handling costs and total volume handled at warehouses and mixing points.

5. The knowledge of where these relationships differ, so that adjustments to cost and volume estimates might be made.

Once this information was obtained, we then had to establish some basic working definitions of the terms *customer, factory, warehouse,* and *carrier.* And for our work at Heinz, the definitions had to be in precise numerical terms.

A. What Is a Customer? In terms of distribution requirements, a customer can be defined according to the following criteria:

By *specific geographic location.*

By *business type* (that is, whether it is a chain, distributor, wholesaler, jobber, vendor, or a hotel and restaurant distributor).

By *product-mix consumption pattern*—As a result of a thorough search of internal product records by customer account, some 50 different consumption patterns were isolated. Each customer in the national system was assigned that pattern which best reflected his product usage.

By *frequency, quantity, and patterns of ordering*—Each customer has his own way of ordering and of taking inventory. Some may accumulate requirements and take only large quantities; others may order frequently and in relatively small quantity shipments. The option is theirs. It was considered essential to reflect each customer's ordering patterns explicitly since this aspect was felt to have a great bearing on the distribution system.

By *proximity to Heinz's various warehouses.*

B. *What Is a Factory?* In terms of distribution requirements, a factory can be defined like this:

By *geographic location that produces various company products.*

A *product-mix pattern*—Not all factories turn out every product that the company makes. Therefore, in the Heinz study we defined a product as having both food and location characteristics.

In Exhibit 1 you will see that Product #1 was defined as a class of varieties that were produced only at Factory #1. Product #2 was a member of a class of products that were produced at Factories #1, #2, #3, and so on for Products #3, #4, and #5. This process of classification covered all the products in the Heinz line.

A *production capacity pattern*—Capacity by product lines is difficult to conceive and to measure in a multiproduct, multiequipment plant. Therefore, in order to get an idea of system costs, production restraints must be imposed. This was done in the Heinz case, and a production capacity pattern was established for each of the factories in the system.

A *controllable source*—It is important to note that management has within its direct control the power to expand or contract capacity, to add or subtract product lines, and so on.

A *cost area for transportation purposes*—That is, the costs of shipping to an area of 100 miles around Chicago will probably not be the same as the costs of shipping to a 100-mile area around Denver.

With the simulation now completed, management has the means for testing various changes in production or marketing strategy. It can better answer questions as to whether additional factories should be allowed to produce a given product, or whether economies would result if certain products were removed from a given factory's production schedule. Let us take a simple

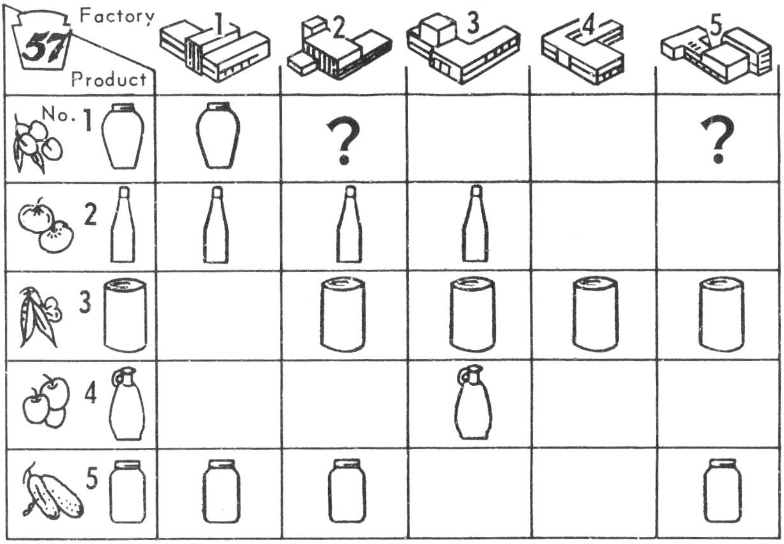

?To see how costs are affected when Factories #2 and #5 are added see the explanation below.

Exhibit 1. What Products Are Produced Where?

example, and illustrate it with Exhibit 1: In the case of Product #1, which currently is produced only at Factory #1, we might wish to know what over-all costs would be if we were also to permit Factories #2 and #5 to manufacture Product #1. How do we find out? Simply by adding production capacity for Product #1 to our simulated Factories #2 and #5, and once again operating the system within the computer. A new cost of distribution will then indicate whether such a change is desirable.

We find this an excellent way to bring to management's attention the potential savings to be had under various assumed conditions.

C. What Is a Warehouse? For the purposes of our study, we defined a warehouse as:

A geographic, gathering, sorting, and redistributing point—A warehouse performs work, owns or rents space, employs people, pays taxes, and in general accumulates costs. In a study of this kind, it must be assumed that any geographic area in the United States is a potential location of a warehouse. And costs differ by geographic area.

A cost accumulation point—Geographic area cost differentials must be recognized in any study of warehouse numbers and locations. In a simulation of a national system it is most feasible to build into the model cost-adjustment factors by geographic area for the various cost elements.

For Heinz, the country was divided into a large number of "cost areas," and cost-adjustment factors were developed by area for warehouse labor, taxes, rentals, or depreciation. Hence, when a warehouse was placed in a given geographic area, its cost of operation was computed using the local area costs. When, in the study, the same warehouse was moved into another geographic area, the cost of operation was computed using the new area's costs. By this method a given warehouse might be more or less attractive for serving certain customers, based not only on the transportation cost for serving them, but also on the operating cost of that warehouse versus other warehouses in other areas which might have different operating cost structures.

D. *What Is a Carrier?* For our purposes, carriers were defined as:

Either a trucking firm or a railroad.

A cost for moving goods between geographic points; in effect, a geographic movement-cost relationship—It is extremely difficult to analyze transportation rate structures. Yet when we wish to determine distribution costs, we must draw a pattern of freight costs which accurately reflect the national rate structure with all its differences depending on size of shipment, type of carrier, and other important factors.

Nevertheless, after much effort, basic regularities governing rate structure have been determined and have been made part of the simulation now accomplished. When, after careful consideration in the study that we made of the Heinz distribution system, it was decided to use relationships rather than point-to-point costs, we did this with the assurance that there was genuine regularity, and that the results were indeed authentic.

It is worthy to note that the transportation rate structures are frequently further complicated by other factors. Some consumers cannot or will not accept certain types of shipments; some cannot accept rail. Some, for reasons of their own inventory policies, will not take shipments above certain sizes; others prefer not to accept small shipments. All these factors complicate the analysis problem and make necessary the use within the simulation program of fairly complex rate structure relationships based on type of shipment, shipment sizes, geographic area, and other pertinent factors.

Program Characteristics

A sequential flow of subcomponents and components representing the flow of raw materials and finished goods through the many processing and transfer points forms the simulated distribution system. Basically, customers place requirements on a system and the system responds. Demand thus usually "explodes" backwards through the production and procurement system. But this backward explosion of demand will vary somewhat in the channels used among different industries. For example:

In the distribution of automobiles, customers in an area place orders first with dealers. The dealers then refer orders back to an assembly plant which, in turn, places demands for subcomponents back on suppliers and factories.

In the case of food and pharmaceuticals, on the other hand, customers place packaging demands back on warehouses or manufacturing plants of container companies. These companies then place orders with suppliers of raw materials or with other manufacturers.

In the Heinz system, as we conceived it, customers place orders with the company and the company responds by delivering in one of three basic ways, depending on which way or combination of ways offers the least cost. These three are:

1. Direct shipments from a given producing factory to large customers.

2. Shipments from various factories to a so-called mixing point located at a factory and then to customers.

3. Shipments from factory points to a warehouse and then to the customer.

Warehouse Function

Let us focus our attention now on the warehousing aspect of the system and ask a basic question: Why do warehouses exist? Under what conditions might they be unnecessary? If all customers were very large, if all of them gave sufficient lead time when ordering, and if all factories produced the full line of the company's products, then all shipments to ultimate consumers could be made directly from the factory. Thus the main reasons why warehouses exist are that customers are not large enough to warrant direct shipment, and do not all give sufficient lead time when ordering, and that individual factories are not always full-line.

Since our objective, however, is not only to determine the number and location of warehouses but, even more important, to design a total distribution system which will operate at lowest total cost, it is necessary that we assign customer shipment volume to its highest distribution classification. Thus: If a given customer's volume is such that he qualifies for shipments direct from producing factories, and if he is willing to accept shipments by this method, then we should ship that way. Similarly, if part of a customer's volume might most economically be shipped from a mixing point, then this method is proper.

Hence, only after other volume has been allocated do we consider warehouses for shipment. And our simulation must be designed to make these determinations automatically.

Direct Shipments Removed

Some customers in the system can take part of their total demand in direct shipments. Because shipments direct from producing factories to customers bypass the mixing point and warehouse system completely, direct shipments of this kind, as Exhibit 2 shows, have no effect on the optimal placement of mixing

THE ACTUAL DISTRIBUTION PATTERN IN ABSTRACT FORM

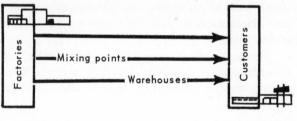

THE SIMULATION VIEW OF THE DISTRIBUTION PATTERN

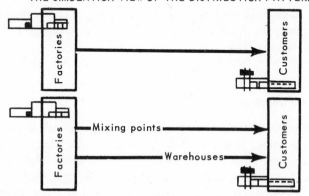

Exhibit 2. Actual and Simulated Views of Distribution.

points and warehouses. Therefore, all direct shipment customers are eliminated from consideration when we are concerned with warehouse location.

Similarly, direct shipment volume is removed from the order patterns of those customers who take only part of their demand in direct shipments. That is, when the computer found a customer whose volume of given items was large enough to take shipments direct from producing factories, it made separate record of the volume so delivered and listed only the remaining volume for delivery from warehouses or mixing points.

This adjustment needs to be done only once and can be done by simulation. After removal of direct shipment volume for every customer, a single run on the computer will make available the resultant consumption patterns of the national system. This, then, is the information used to study the warehouse location problem.

The Computer Program

When talking in terms of large-scale computers, we should bear in mind one thing. Although computers are frequently called "electronic brains," they are by no means thinking machines in the human sense. A computer is merely a mathematical "beast of burden" which will do only what it is specifically told to do. But it does its assigned job with a speed and accuracy far beyond any other known means, human or mechanical. Instructions to the computer, therefore, must be precise and in detail. These instructions on how to proceed are called the computer "program."

In concept, the program for the simulation described is quite simple. Stored on tape is all information relating to transportation, handling, and delivery costs, geographic adjustment factors, factory locations, factory production specifications, and the volume remaining after elimination of direct shipment volume. Even the program itself is stored on tape.

The basic process is to vary warehouse configurations and to observe and compare the resultant effects on distribution costs. To do this, we must compute in detail the annual costs for operating the proposed nondirect distribution system for a year. Included are such costs as those for each of the warehouses and mixing points, for all shipments (both from factories to warehouses and warehouses to customers), and for each of the several thousand customers. Further, these costs must be broken down for each product class and each type of shipment.

Optimizing the System

Now the simulation is ready to accomplish its twofold objective: (1) to enable management to close in rapidly on the number and approximate locations of warehouses which will achieve lowest costs of distribution, and (2) to discover where changes can be made in warehouse locations which will lower costs still further.

When the simulated one-year operation of a complete warehouse configuration has been completed and all costs computed, the following results are shown in detail as computer output (see, for example, Exhibit 3):

1. Costs are shown for all pertinent items indicated in accounting terminology familiar to management. For each factory, warehouse, and mixing point, there are three major categories of distribution costs determined in the simulation:

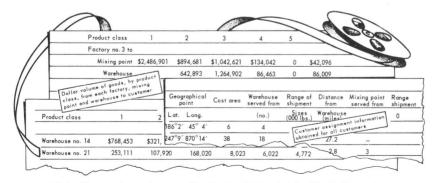

Note: Figures shown here are disguised and intended for illustration only.

Exhibit 3. Sample of Computer Output.

- Costs of direct shipments, factory to mixing point, mixing point to customer, and factory to warehouse shipments.
- Costs of operating both mixing points and warehouses at specified locations.
- Costs of shipping from warehouses to customers.

2. All these costs are further classified by size of shipment, and include a volume-by-product-line breakdown for each warehouse.

3. Customer-warehouse affiliations are given so that accurate service areas are built up for each warehouse, mixing point, and factory. All this is based on a lowest cost for operating the entire distribution system.

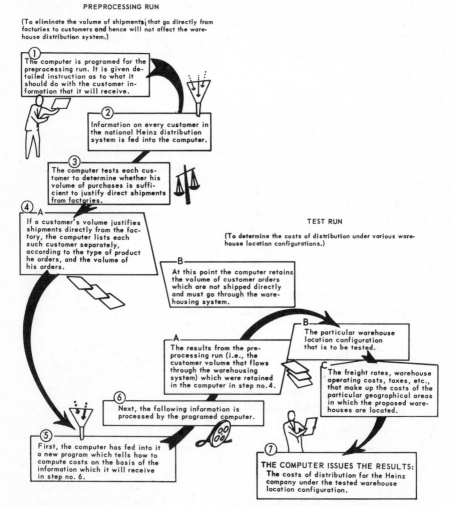

PREPROCESSING RUN

(To eliminate the volume of shipments that go directly from factories to customers and hence will not affect the warehouse distribution system.)

1. The computer is programed for the preprocessing run. It is given detailed instruction as to what it should do with the customer information that it will receive.

2. Information on every customer in the national Heinz distribution system is fed into the computer.

3. The computer tests each customer to determine whether his volume of purchases is sufficient to justify direct shipments from factories.

4. A — If a customer's volume justifies shipments directly from the factory, the computer lists each such customer separately, according to the type of product he orders, and the volume of his orders.

B — At this point the computer retains the volume of customer orders which are not shipped directly and must go through the warehousing system.

TEST RUN

(To determine the costs of distribution under various warehouse location configurations.)

B — The particular warehouse location configuration that is to be tested.

A — The results from the preprocessing run (i.e., the customer volume that flows through the warehousing system) which were retained in the computer in step no. 4.

C — The freight rates, warehouse operating costs, taxes, etc., that make up the costs of the particular geographical areas in which the proposed warehouses are located.

6. Next, the following information is processed by the programed computer.

5. First, the computer has fed into it a new program which tells how to compute costs on the basis of the information which it will receive in step no. 6.

7. THE COMPUTER ISSUES THE RESULTS: The costs of distribution for the Heinz company under the tested warehouse location configuration.

Exhibit 4. How the Simulation Tests a Particular Warehouse Configuration.

In short, a great deal of useful information about any distribution configuration is provided by the simulation developed.

Exhibit 4 may prove helpful at this point as a summary of the step-by-step action we took in using the simulation to test one particular warehouse pattern. A similar process, you will realize, took place for each warehouse and mixing point configuration we tested.

With the design of the simulation described, and the substantial research performed, the results showed a very distinct cost minimum. The cost of distribution which was minimized was that broad concept which includes costs of transportation between Heinz factories and warehouses, costs of operating the warehouses in various locations, and the cost of final delivery to the Heinz customer.

The results showed clearly that for the distribution requirement of the H. J. Heinz Company (a given optimal configuration of mixing points and warehouses, with given locations, and serving given customers in accordance with prescribed procedures) a lowest over-all cost of national distribution would be realized. The results are logical and attainable.

An area map is shown in Exhibit 5 to illustrate hypothetical warehouse locations obtained. For Heinz, a complete national map of actual warehouse

Exhibit 5. Hypothetical Example of Customer Assignments and Warehouse Locations Obtained from the Simulation.

locations recommended was drawn to provide a visual identification of the new distribution system. In addition, we were able to draw precise warehouse-to-customer assignments, specifying which warehouse would best serve each customer in the national system for each type of shipment received. Further, where shipments were large enough, we specified which mixing point should be used and, if a direct-from-factory customer, which factories should ship. These precise customer assignments then indicated exact area outlines for each warehouse. Samples of warehouse area assignments are shown in Exhibit 5.

Evaluating the Results

While the simulation does indicate such things as the optimal configuration of warehouses in exact figures, it is by no means a substitute for the judgment of management. As shown in Exhibit 6, for example: The results indicated clearly that for most efficient operation it was necessary to have M warehouses, but that it did not matter much, from a dollars-and-cents point of view, whether there were as few as L or as many as M. Costs were about equal under either alternative or any alternative in between. From the point of view of customer service, we recommended M, although a good case could have been made for some number in between. L and M differed by some few warehouses.

In making choices within ranges such as this, solid judgment, experience, and knowledge of local conditions in given areas come to the assistance of the

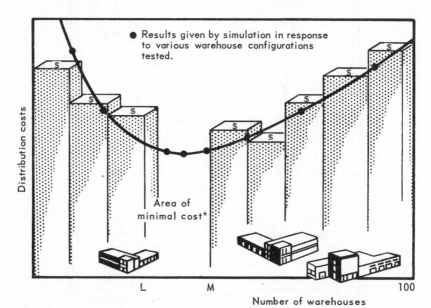

* Here management must make decisions as to whether the number of warehouses should be closer to the L or the M limits of the minimal cost area.

Exhibit 6. Arriving at the Number of Heinz Warehouses That Would Minimize Total Distribution Costs.

simulation. And, as we did in the Heinz simulation, trends in the industry and economic arguments beyond the scope of the simulation should be examined carefully to determine whether the recommendations of the simulation were indeed proper ones.

Other Uses

The method for performing the Heinz study has provided great facility for studying other aspects of the business which are at least as important as the development of an optimal distribution system. When the simulation was developed, it was thought important to build a general-purpose tool, one which management could use at any time, future as well as present, to study questions of major concern. It was not, however, until the simulation was designed that it was fully realized that the tool provided such facility for studying a wide range of perplexing management problems. Specifically:

Distribution cost studies—Customers can be separated by areas, types, shipment sizes, salesmen, type of carrier, channels of distribution. We could get estimates of distribution costs on the basis of each or any combination thereof.

Locational studies—The number and location of factories could be changed, for example, rather than altering the warehouse configuration. Then, too, the effect on the company's operations of a sudden shift in customer type or location could be studied.

Studies related to products—The product mix at each factory can be changed arbitrarily to observe whether adding product capacity would change distribution costs appreciably. Similarly, customer consumption patterns can be altered to see what effect such changes will have on distribution costs.

Studies related to time—Customer data can be altered in order to reflect gross annual volume changes by product line. These data would then be used to determine distribution costs. Thus, it can be seen what effect proposed changes in sales policy, prices, or new products would have on customer purchasing frequency, order size, or volume. The possible effect on distribution costs and on profitability can be estimated experimentally.

Limitations in Use

While the simulation is a remarkable management tool, it does have its limitations:

1. Resources can only be stretched so far. Some compromises obviously have to be made, although any compromise that might seriously reduce the meaningfulness of major results must be avoided or the project may be worthless.

2. The technical characteristics of the equipment set bounds. The program we used was written to be fast and versatile. This meant that much had to be stored

in the computer's internal memory, and in a problem of this size it does not take too long to jam up against a 32,000-word ceiling.

3. The accuracy and adequacy of input information impose limits on the program. If any one maxim developed out of this study, it was this: Know your customers (i.e., get control over your input data). Results are only as good as the data that are used to create them.

Conclusion

Great advances in the science of business management have taken place in the past decade on a scale unprecedented in the history of business planning. Perhaps one of the most useful techniques developed is simulation. Simulation provides the ability to operate some particular phase of the business, on paper or in a computer, for a period of time and by these means to test various alternative strategies. Distribution, sales and marketing, production, or even all in combination, can yield to this new science.

Every major decision-making executive has long wished he might, by some means, test the various alternatives open to him before making a final decision on a complex problem. With the development of simulation, a major breakthrough has been achieved in providing this insight into the future. To be able to test many alternative courses of action and to obtain documented evidence of the operating results of such proposed action, places in the hands of the agressive businessman a tool of inestimable value.

The use of high-speed computers is a principal element contributing to the feasibility of examining the various alternatives. In order to put the problem on a computer, it is first necessary to express the problem and the characteristics of distribution in mathematical form, that is, to construct a mathematical model of the distribution requirements. Once it has been designed, however, the model may be looked on as a form of capital investment which makes possible economies in analysis, both present and future.

The importance of this accomplishment must be considered not only in the light of more profitable distribution, but also as a basic adjunct to policy determination and the study of profit achievement. Regardless of whether a company is in hard goods or soft, in food manufacturing or electrical applicances, in consumer or industrial products, it can conduct, through simulation, a wide range of basic studies. Area profitability, product line and type of customer profitability, the effects of pricing "breaks," all these can be studied just as the factory and warehouse location problems have been by the Heinz company.

Certainly, though, we do not mean to imply that all the major logical difficulties of simulating a distribution system have now been solved. The remaining tasks of embellishment and increased accuracy are great. But we do want to assert that such simulations are powerful tools. In the business of the future, perhaps, every company will have one.

25

Logistics of Physical Facilities in Distribution

ALFRED A. KUEHN

Carnegie Institute of Technology

Characteristics of Distribution and Transportation Problems

Distribution and transportation problems tend to require the examination of large quantities of data. Simple rules are seldom available to compute the large bulk of information needed in solving such problems. For example, transportation rates from point to point are generally the result of a long process of negotiation, competition and historical circumstances rather than a convenient function of air-mile or even road-mile distances. Special commodity rates are generally negotiated prior to the construction of a new plant or warehouse. Price breaks at various volumes are frequently open to bargaining between large volume shippers and transport firms.

Even greater volumes of other types of data are likely to be required in the solution of many distribution problems: expected demand of individual or groups of customers, warehouse operating costs, effect of delivery delays upon lost sales, etc. For example, in the scheduling of airlines it is necessary to know the daily and hourly distribution of traffic demand between city A and city B as well as the attractive potential of competitors' planes and flight schedules. All of these factors result in a very complex problem both in terms of data requirements and in terms of a model capable of capturing the essence of the problem.

Alternative Approaches to the Solution of Distribution Problems

Two general classes of quantitative methods have been used to solve distribution and transportation problems: 1) optimizing algorithms such as linear and integer programming, and 2) heuristic programs. The use of heuristics in the solution of such problems is the older of the two methods, businessmen having used such an approach for years. The main shortcoming of the average businessman's use of heuristics is his dependence upon his personal computational abilities rather than that of a high speed electronic computer. (Another shortcoming of the businessman is his failure to coin and/or use the term "heuristics." The term heuristics has made respectable a method still known by most businessmen as "cut and try" or "trial and error.") To be sure, recent developments in heuristic programming have improved greatly upon the rules of thumb used by many businessmen, but this would appear to be only of secondary significance. If businessmen once attain command over the computer, they too are likely to develop improved guides for decision-making.

Optimizing models, developed and put into business practice largely since World War II, have been the province of operations researchers. Recently, however, heuristic methods have also been adopted and promoted by this group of "management scientists" as providing a means of solving business problems which have resisted solution by the available optimizing methods. All too frequently, business problems cannot be cast into the framework required by optimizing models.

Conditions Affecting Choice Between Heuristic and Optimizing Models

The most desirable attribute of optimizing models is the guarantee that the computational method they prescribe leads to the best possible solution (or set of solutions) of the problem *as it has been stated in the model.* Knowledge that the optimal solution has or has not been obtained can be a valuable bit of information.

Heuristic methods do not as a rule guarantee reaching the optimal solution (or set of solutions) and, furthermore, do not provide an indication as to whether or not the optimal solution has been obtained. The value of heuristic methods lies elsewhere:

1. *Complexity*—Heuristic methods can be used to solve much more complex problems than can be treated by existing optimizing models.
2. *Size*—Heuristic methods can be used to solve problems which are much larger than those which can currently be solved on existing computing equipment with the available optimizing models.
3. *Cost*—Heuristic methods can solve problems economically which could only be solved at prohibitive cost by available optimizing models.

Heuristic methods are tools that can be very valuable in solving today's business problems. The standards of comparison in such cases are current practice and other available alternatives—not the unattainable guarantee of an optimal solution. Heuristic methods can be used in solving all business problems which can be explicitly and unambiguously stated and for which procedures can be specified to search for (generate) and evaluate alternatives. Heuristic programs can be developed to solve such problems faster, with greater accuracy, and with better results than human problem solvers insofar as we are capable of identifying (or improving upon) methods in current use.

For the future, there is reason to believe that heuristic and optimizing models will be integrated into individual programs. Heuristic methods might be used to develop advance starting points for subsequent analysis by optimizing models, or the latter might be used merely to test whether an optimal solution has been reached. Even greater integration is likely insofar as optimizing algorithms are incorporated as subroutines within heuristic programs. This approach, for example, would appear to be one of the alternative ways in which certain types of capacity constraints could be introduced into the plant and warehouse location problem discussed briefly in the next section.

Warehouse and Plant Location Problem

Several versions of this heuristic program have been in use for more than four years. Consequently, it has been documented in more detail than the other two problems and programs which are outlined in the following sections. Much of the program structure as is exists today is comparable to that originally published in "A Heuristic Program for Locating Warehouses."[1] Some of the more recent revisions and additional details in its application have been documented by P. L. Flannery in "Heuristic Warehouse and Plant Location Program: Application Guide,"[2] Consequently, the discussion in this section will be limited to certain general observations about the performance of the program in practical application, the experience of some of the firms who have used it, and the problems and costs of data processing and the preparation of input data.

The performance of the program has exceeded our wildest expectations in terms of the quality of solutions provided. Although a large amount of research has been done in additional testing of the general form of the heuristics used in the original program, only very limited success has been achieved in terms of improving the quality of solutions. Much more progress has been made in reprogramming the problem for greater computational efficiency, application to much larger problems, and development of improved input and output formats to facilitate practical application. Also, in reprogramming, the program was prepared so that it could be adapted quite easily to a much wider range of problems than had been originally anticipated. Every application appears to require some program modifications and, consequently, a variety of new cost functions, constraints, and the like have been developed for use with the various

[1]A. A. Kuehn, and M. J. Hamburger, "A Heuristic Program for Locating Warehouses," *Management Science,* 9, No. 4, July 1963.

[2]P. L. Flannery, "Heuristic Warehouse and Plant Location Program: Application Guide," Market Science Associates, Inc., Pittsburgh, Pennsylvania, 1964.

individual versions of the program. It was discovered that the program was not only useful in analyzing warehousing networks but also multiple locations of plants (e.g., refineries, assembly plants, etc.), alternative types of warehousing or plant facilities, and different modes of shipping. Mixing points at plants can also be evaluated.

The experience of firms using the program has been very favorable in that great opportunities have been uncovered for improvement of distribution systems. In large complex networks, management is likely to have considered only localized changes in operational procedures and so is unlikely to uncover the desirability of major changes in its distribution system. Another result of the program has been to focus management's attention on existing transportation rate structures which are out of line. In several cases, solutions provided by the program appeared to be completely unreasonable, but further inspection identified the problem as peculiarities in rate structure. In some cases, identification of such factors can provide direction to management in the renegotiation of rates. The program can then also be valuable in the evaluation of the total impact on costs of any proposed rate changes.

One firm has also made much use of the program in the evaluation of the various stages of their distribution network as it might change from the current existing system toward the best system originally developed by the heuristic approach. Organizational and transition problems required a step-by-step adjustment. Also, since only half of the proposed changes are likely to result in 85% to 90% of the total potential cost savings, even neglecting transition costs, it is likely that all of the proposed changes will never be instituted. The errors in input data, coupled with transition costs and the fact that the actual problem is changing over time, tend to suggest that management should not arbitrarily attempt to institute the "best" solution developed by the program but rather only move in that direction, reevaluating its position along the way.

The major problem in the use of the program is the collection of data. Problems as large as ten factories, 46 intermediate transfer points and 287 district warehouses have been run through the computer at a computational cost of only $400 to $500. The evaluation of specific networks is substantially less expensive. Consequently, the major problem apart from defining the problem is collecting the needed data and preparing it for use with the computer. Although this can be an enormous task, the response of the firms that have gone to the effort of doing so indicates that the result that can be achieved from a reevaluation of warehouse locations and operating patterns represents a very good return on the investment. Some firms now look upon the reevaluation of warehousing and distribution systems as an item to be reviewed annually rather than only when costs are already out of line.

Local Truck Routing and Scheduling

The routing and scheduling of trucks is a problem which must be solved very rapidly once orders have been received. For a local distributor with 35 ten-ton and twenty-ton trucks, and a total of 400 customers, it has been established that even a crude heuristic program can meet all delivery requirements and substantially reduce the overtime costs of the drivers and helpers.

The problem in this case is to group the orders and route the trucks to minimize costs, given the available truck capacities, union rules for drivers and helpers, travel time between customers, unloading times, and state regulations on axle weights. Orders must be processed rapidly and instructions provided to the warehouse order fillers, dock loaders, and drivers and helpers. The time period currently available for these decisions is so short that management has relied upon the use of relatively stable route structures as a means of meeting the customers' delivery requirements. Nevertheless, changes in the daily order sizes on these routes offer the opportunity for the development of a more flexible scheduling procedure to make better use of the available facilities and manpower resources. It appears that a substantial increase in the delivery capacity of the firm could be achieved in this manner, providing savings in the investment in trucks as well as in daily operating costs.

A computer program now operating but still under development in conjunction with R. L. Hayes, Carnegie Institute of Technology, approaches the truck routing problem by identifying extreme points to which deliveries must be made and then filling out the truck capacity and guaranteed union working hours in a near-optimal way. Orders to be added to the delivery route on any given day are chosen probabilistically, the probability of any given order being selected for addition depending upon its suitability as a filler order, the ease with which it might be added to the routes, and the incremental cost of adding it to the route in question. The total scheduling program is reprocessed a number of times, in effect resolving the problem on each cycle, until there is reasonable assurance that a good solution has been developed.

Airline Scheduling

A number of optimizing models for use in solving this problem have been reported in the literature in recent years. Interestingly enough, however, the airlines are not using the techniques that have been published. Several of the major airlines have pointed to the major problem—the techniques do not recognize the time distribution of demand between specific cities. The "solutions" merely schedule planes to provide the number of daily flights requested by management but do not schedule these flights with a view toward the time distribution of demand or competitive schedules.

Most of the proposed solutions are recognized by their developers as not solving the complete problem. It has been suggested, for example, that the solutions provided are only suggested solutions which must be "hand-massaged" to develop practical operating schedules. This does not really appear to be desirable in practice, however, since only a very limited number of minor local changes could be made without disrupting the entire schedule. When one flight is changed, it is likely to conflict with the future deployment of that plane.

A heuristic program now in development for the airline scheduling problem recognizes explicitly (1) the size and time distribution of passenger demand between each pair of cities on the airline's CAB flight authorization, (2) CAB restrictions on route structures and flight requirements, (3) plane maintenance requirements, and (4) competitive schedules, including types of planes. Not yet included are two important issues which will be considered at a future date, the scheduling of flight crews and the effects of pattern scheduling upon consumer choice (e.g., a flight between New York and Chicago every hour on the hour). Within the framework of the above variables, the program is designed to schedule an airline's planes to "near optimize" management's criterion function (e.g., profits, share of market on individual routes subject to some minimum profit constraint, etc.). Thus the program determines how many flights to schedule and when to schedule them in an attempt to best satisfy management's objectives. If management wishes to add additional flights (or reduce the number of flights) on particular route segments, this can be incorporated into the problem as a constraint much as can changes in CAB directives.

The program begins operation by scheduling a plane from some major terminal on the airline's route structure to some other city consistent with CAB restriction. In choosing which city to fly to, the program considers all the available alternatives over the next two stages. That is, consideration is given not only to the profitability of the alternative flights that might now be scheduled out of City A but also the profitability available in scheduling the plane over the subsequent leg of its journey out of the destination city. An additional alternative is offered if no flights are profitable and if the plane is not needed in another city, namely, delaying the flight until a more profitable level of demand is available.

The daily distribution of demand is identified as 48 values, representing half-hourly intervals beginning at 12:15 a.m. each day. It appears that the time distribution of demand over all city pairs can be classified into no more than 25 sets of values. The passengers attracted by a given airline's flight from City A to City B at time t with a stop at City C will then depend upon the total demand and its distribution, the availability of competitive flights at various departure times, the time delay enroute of each competitor, the type of plane, and the airline's connecting route structure at cities A and B. The available traffic is divided among competitors according to a mathematical relationship previously found useful in describing consumer preferences and choice behavior in the purchase of grocery products differing with respect to certain physical characteristics. In the airline problem, the times of departure, times enroute and types of planes would appear to be the most significant variables. (Note that the types of planes and times enroute can incorporate much of what would otherwise appear to be a significant effect—the number of stops. Additional empirical evidence is necessary to establish whether the number of stops must be considered as an additional variable to take into account effects above and beyond that of the plane type and route times.)

While this is still a matter of conjecture, there is reason to believe that the program now under development will prove useful in the development of airline schedules. Much more work is, however, required to incorporate maintenance and crew scheduling, matters of serious concern to the airlines. These too, however, should be solvable.

Other uses of the program could include evaluation of the probable effects of CAB route changes, the determination of fleet sizes, and questions related to the mix of planes. Extension of the program should also permit improved solutions to the deployment of planes when schedules must be violated due to weather, mechanical failure, and the like.

Conclusion

This brief review of research in the location and scheduling of physical distribution facilities has pointed to the promise shown by heuristic methods. The location of warehouses was discussed as an example of an application already implemented with favorable results by a number of major firms. Truck and airline scheduling were presented as large, complex problems which will soon be solved by heuristic computer programs, operating programs now being available for test purposes. Each of these applications has been demonstrated to have the potential of producing significant reductions in distribution and transportation expenses.

The prime hurdles restricting the development and use of heuristic programs are (1) sound statements or models of transportation and distribution problems are not generally available, (2) the quality of heuristic solutions is difficult to establish, being dependent upon comparison with other known solutions, with no guarantee of an "optimum" or even good solution, and (3) procedures by which useful heuristics might be developed or identified are not well-established. At this stage of the development of heuristic programming, research with heuristic methods is more of an art than a science. Nevertheless, the great potential of heuristic programs in helping to solve the complex problems of distribution and transportation management is likely to insure the widespread use of such techniques within the next few years.

26

Linear Programming:
A Straight Line to
Distribution Efficiency

B. F. ROWAN

Walker Manufacturing Company

Are we operating our physical distribution program at the lowest possible cost consistent with satisfactory customer service?

This was the basic question of our (or anyone's) physical distribution analysis. To answer it, we immediately had to ask more basic questions, such as:

1. How many warehouses should we use?
2. What locations and sizes?
3. Which markets should each warehouse serve?
4. Which products should be made at which plants and in what quantities?
5. Which plants should serve which warehouses?
6. Should an additional plant be built?
7. What customer service levels are desirable and at what cost?

To answer these we needed information on current physical distribution operations. We developed this under five heads: (1) Market locations (this was readily available). (2) Alternate warehouse locations (we made logical choices based on car registrations). (3) Types of shipment (used present practice). (4) Freight costs. (5) Warehouse operating costs.

Market locations. We took the sales data by product class and customer and converted it into sales totals for each county in the United States. We grouped these counties into metropolitan trading areas. Those areas accounting for about 85 percent to total sales were designated major markets. Interestingly, we found that less than 100 metropolitan areas accounted for more than 85 percent of sales. The remaining 15 percent was widely scattered. We totaled them by state and assigned them to the next largest trading area within each state. In this way we reduced the total number of market locations from thousands to 140 without significantly misrepresenting the actual geographical dispersion of our markets.

Alternate warehouse locations. We first studied the locations of the company's markets, their relative importance, and the location of cities which were important transportation centers. We then selected a list of possible warehouse sites. In addition, we included the four plant sites and some of our personal preferences. After crossing off the duplicates, we had 31 alternate warehouse locations to include in our model system. Around each site we drew a circle to show one day's transit time.

Freight costs from each plant to each warehouse and from each warehouse to each market: We used an IBM 1401 to compute these. We considered first the number of times each warehouse would have to be supplied to keep desired stock levels with the smallest inventory investment. Next, the annual weight of product for each type of shipment (LTL, TL, and CL). We then programmed the computer to calculate the annual volume of shipments in pounds for each plant-warehouse combination.

Type of shipment (TL or LTL) to each market was calculated from an analysis of bills of lading. Next we found the freight rates for each warehouse market combination. Finally, we programmed the computer to calculate transportation costs based on units × weight × proper freight rates.

Warehouse operating costs divide up into rent, labor, inventory carrying charges, and miscellaneous costs. To complicate matters, unit costs would

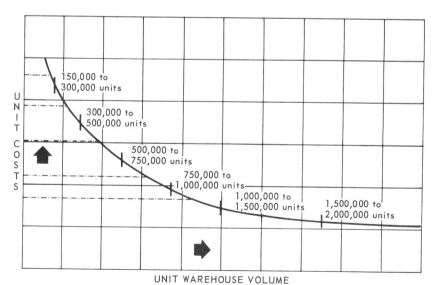

UNIT WAREHOUSE VOLUME

Figure 1. Warehouse Operating Costs.

naturally vary with the annual volume of throughput for any given warehouse. Also hourly labor rates and required warehouse space vary for each location. To solve this problem, we developed standard curves for any given warehouse for each element of cost. (Figure 1 is a typical curve.) To straighten out this curve we selected certain unit volume ranges from these curves for which we could assign median costs. (On the chart, the dotted lines show the median range for each volume range—150,000 to 300,000 units, and so on. By this method, we established standard unit costs for each cost element at the varying volumes of throughput. We developed geographical multipliers and added these to the input data so that we become linear again. The multipliers provided a percentage relationship between the average hourly rate for non-manufacturing order pickers at each alternate location. We used Bureau of Labor statistics and our own experience to develop these rates. Applying the geographical multiplier to the base unit labor costs gave us individual labor unit figures for each of the selected volume throughput ranges at each of the 31 alternate warehouses. For each alternate warehouse location, we now had unit operating costs at select unit volume ranges.

Logical or linear? We decided against a logical computer program or simulation approach in favor of linear programming. Simulation is basically a trial and error method and we felt linear programming would offer the closest to the optimum solution. But we had to find a method of integrating the non-linear factors with the linear program. As it worked out, the approach required six computer runs compared to the single run needed for a straight linear program. However, it was well worth the effort.

The next step was to develop a mathematical model of the distribution system consisting of linear equations which we could use with an existing computer code. (The code was called the LP 90; the computer was an IBM 7090). In this model, we had to include these factors:

1. Size of the market in terms of the number of units of each product class.
2. Locations of the selected alternate warehouses.
3. Transit times from each alternate warehouse to each market.
4. Product mix in each market and the products made exclusively at each plant.
5. Average weight for each product class and the proportion moving TL and LTL to each market.
6. Plant capacities for each plant for each product class.
7. Unit manufacturing cost for each product class of each plant.
8. Unit freight costs for LTL, TL, and CL from each plant to each alternate warehouse, and from each alternate warehouse to each market (for each product class).
9. Unit cost for warehouse operating and inventory expenses at varying volumes of unit throughput.

The matrix of the model had more than 700 rows (equations) and 5,000 columns (variables), making up a data input of nearly 38,000 punched cards. In effect, the computer simulated every conceivable combination of plants, warehouses, and markets. The optimum solution we finally selected was the one pattern of distribution that provided each and every market with its requirements at minimum laid down cost. We included all manufacturing and distribution costs.

First run. As we had no idea of the actual volume throughput which would be assigned to any particular warehouse, we arbitrarily picked a starting point for the first computer run. We selected a throughput range of 1 to 1½ million units a year applied to each of the warehouses. On this first run, we were in effect ignoring the influences of warehouse volume on operating expenses and plant-to-warehouse transportation costs. On this basis, we would have had a distribution setup of more than 20 warehouses serving the territories shown on the map above.

Re-runs. Next we analyzed the actual unit throughput that the computer had assigned to each warehouse in this first run. For example, one warehouse had an actual throughput of more than 2 million units, while others had throughputs less than 300,000 units. We therefore adjusted the unit operating expenses and plant-to-warehouse transportation costs to the actual unit throughput of each warehouse and reran the problem on the computer. The result was that some warehouses increased in volume while others disappeared from the solution completely. We were left with eleven warehouses. We again analyzed this pattern, made adjustments to obtain more accurate costs and reran it on the computer. Repeating this sequence four more times brought the unit costs for each warehouse to agree with the actual unit throughput.

Where, what, how much? Our final solution told us:

1. The number and location of warehouses.
2. The markets each warehouse would serve.
3. The volume of throughput for each warehouse.
4. The products and volumes each plant would produce.
5. The volume of each product which each plant would ship to each warehouse.
6. The total cost of the proposed physical distribution system.

Briefly, the computer solution was to have distribution centers at Harrisonburg, Virginia; Aberdeen, Mississippi; Chicago, Illinois; and Bakersfield, California. At Harrisonburg and Aberdeen, our company has plants with integral warehouses. This eliminates double handling.

But some of the warehouse territories seem strange. For example, you would probably not decide to supply most of Illinois out of Aberdeen, Mississippi, when there's a warehouse in Chicago. However, we did manually spot check several such situations and were forced to agree with the computer. Perhaps the moral here is that the obvious answer is not always the right one. So many inter-related factors go into this kind of study—production costs, plant capacities, transportation rates, warehouse operating costs, and so on—that in fact there's no such thing as an obvious answer. Although the proposed physical distribution system demanded ample capital, the rate of return seemed more than adequate. We therefore built a $1¼ million Chicago area distribution center in Batavia, Ill.

Physical distribution is a sales satisfying force complementing marketing as a sales generating force. The ultimate goal of any well-managed company is to produce and market a product or service that will reach, or is available at a destination, at a cost and in the time and condition desired by the customer. We should not over concern ourselves with academic practicality in our research to reach this goal. If a lower cost method does present itself, we can compare it with pre-determined policies or fixed methods and then decide if it is practical as well as being economical.

Our primary management goal is profit. If the total bill for the physical distribution of American products could be reduced by as little as one percent, industry could cut costs by an estimated $1½ billion annually.

In the early part of this century, public demand for goods and services far outpaced our productive capacities. Production, or manufacturing management then came to the fore. When sufficient output to meet demand was finally available, it then became necessary to cultivate and expand sales.

Marketing really matured in the 1940's. The large percentages of available profit had already been tapped from manufacturing. It was now necessary for marketing to generate additional consumption. The marketing people have done a good job. Nationally, managers began to look for other largely untapped pools of profit within the corporate structure. They found it in the functions and responsibilities linking manufacturing with marketing. These were consolidated and called physical distribution.

Part Three

ORGANIZATION, ADMINISTRATION, AND CONTROL

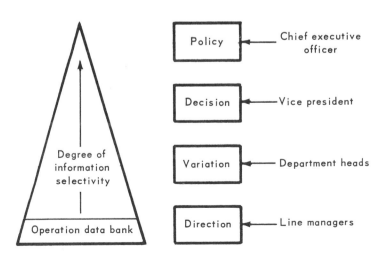

Editors' Introduction

Regardless of how good the basic design of a physical distribution system may be, results will not meet expectations unless the operation is properly organized and administered. The subjects of organization, administration, and control are among the most elusive of physical distribution topics because relatively little has been written about them in comparison with other areas.

In actual practice, a paradox appears to exist between organizational arrangements and results. Some firms with ideal organizational arrangements seem to have difficulty in achieving desired results. Others with less ideal organizations seem to enjoy very high performance. This situation seems to support the conclusion that a proper management philosophy toward integrated physical distribution operations is a basic prerequisite to good performance.

The impact of computers on operational control and organization is just reaching a point where the entire management process is undergoing rapid change. New concepts and techniques of control are now at the disposal of management. The ultimate impact of computer technology and information system control can be expected to alter dramatically the traditional concepts of administration.

At this point in the development of the physical distribution discipline, questions appear more abundant than answers. The articles contained in Part Three provide background discussion for these emerging issues.

27

Emerging Patterns of Physical Distribution Organization

DONALD J. BOWERSOX
Michigan State University

One of the most interesting things about real life physical distribution management is the way in which most companies administer the product flow process. More often than not, they have split the responsibility for product flow and assigned it to several departments. Because of this fragmented responsibility, they can not coordinate the movement of goods throughout their distribution systems.

Since each of the departments with a chunk of distribution responsibility somehow managed to get the goods through its part of the system, no one questioned the administration of product flow. The fact that many companies budget for physical distribution on a segmented functional basis (department by department) has, in effect, stymied any given department head's initiative for a re-evaluation of the existing organizational set-up. Each department head would naturally devote most of his effort, time and budget to improving the productivity of his particular department. Unfortunately, an action that makes the department look good may not be in the best interests of another department or even the company as a whole.

Fortunately for some companies, a limited number of exceptionally broad-minded departmental executives have envisioned the impact of physical distribution decisions beyond individual departments. Such executives foresaw the trade-off relationship among the various physical distribution activities not only within their own departments, but between other departments throughout the company.

In one particular firm, for example, a manufacturing executive realized that an increase in transportation expenditures would exceed the standards established by finance for the manufacturing function. However, this increased expenditure could achieve two beneficial results: inventories (accountable to finance) would be reduced, and customer service (a marketing responsibility) would be improved. The question was, how could these trade-off benefits be achieved? Once the overall corporate benefits became clear, new standards based on corporate goals and objectives were established. Actual manufacturing expenditures for transportation are officially no longer singly important. While this firm was able to realize one particular improvement, its executives felt this coordinated effort constituted only a first step toward tapping the real potential of integrated physical distribution management. As a result, they insituted a major review of current practices which resulted in a complete reorganization of all physical distribution functions into a single department.

Unfortunately, many firms still have not devoted special attention to the feasibility of a physical distribution organization. Internal pressures favored not upsetting the apple cart. So the functions of physical distribution in these firms remains neatly housed throughout the marketing, manufacturing and financial departments. In such a status quo situation, a single functional responsibility is overlooked even though the potentials of operating an integrated and balanced system of physical distribution in coordination with marketing, manufacturing and finance are significant.

Under the traditional organization structure each physical distribution management function, such as protective packaging, transportation and warehousing, must be relegated to a role of secondary importance in the major mission and responsibility of its parent department. For instance, manufacturing traditionally has been concerned with achieving economies of scale through longer production runs and lower cost procurement. The distribution function in manufacturing has been concerned with utilizing low speed, low cost delivery even in acute marketing situations. Marketing, on the other hand, has been concerned with customer service. Like manufacturing, marketing has its affect on distribution costs. Rather than waiting to consolidate shipments into truckload and carload shipments, marketing creates diseconomies by shipping in LTL and LCL quantities to achieve customer satisfaction. In addition, marketing favors broad product line inventories close to customers. This lack of a corporate-wide awareness and sensitivity to the economic potentials realizable in integrating physical distribution functions into one department is a major deficiency of the traditional organization. Physical distribution seeking an integrated system questions the total cost commitments of these independent functions.

Departmental Conflicts

Conflict is not new in the corporate scene and neither is the need to reconcile such conflict. Historically, finance and manufacturing gained corporate recognition in resolving the conflicts between financial policies and production economies. Marketing then stepped into the corporate limelight. Here again, compromise was in order to resolve the conflicting policies of marketing, manufacturing and finance.

In all instances of corporate conflict, top management has been forced to select the combined viewpoint that was capable of meeting the total corporate objective most effectively. After each parlay, however, something better emerged. The corporation in total became better equipped for long-range survival.

In organizing for physical distribution, many companies follow a pattern of grouping physical distribution responsibility within an existing organizational unit. For example, transportation is renamed physical distribution and specific distribution activities found in marketing, manufacturing and finance are merely transferred to the new department. The new department, however, continues to operate in the same manner as before and with the department manager still reporting to a senior executive in marketing, manufacturing or finance.

The corporate reshuffle, while often an improvement, more often than not is a failure in actual practice. Management has not truly recognized the full potential of an integrated physical distribution department. In fact, it appears very evident that the proper atmosphere for physical distribution is lacking.

In such limited reorganization, the real problems of expenditure, trade-off and performance measurement continue to exist. The quasi-physical distribution department still remains primarily interested in the functions it must perform for its parent organization. For instance, the transportation function if renamed physical distribution is primarily concerned with freight rates, rate reductions, classifications and low cost movement rather than service, reliability and system design. Physical distribution in this situation still remains subservient to its administering department. This prevents the physical distribution department from being influential in corporate policy formation, for such considerations often would lead to conflict with the responsibilities and objectives of the parent department.

Thus, physical distribution as a functional area of management now has arrived at the point where top management should review its company's organization to determine the benefits available. In an increasing number of cases it has found that the establishment of a specialized physical distribution organization will improve the corporate profit picture through lower total costs and better customer service capabilities. What seems to be the pattern of such specialized organization and what new issues have been created as a result of such reorganization?

Establishing the Organization

The setting up of a specialized physical distribution organization should include the grouping of all related functions into a newly conceived department. Each firm must evaluate the feasibility of such a reorganization based upon the merits of its own situation. However, there are some guidelines which may be helpful in evaluating the desirability of a reorganization move.

First, the cost of performing physical distribution must be a significant expenditure in relationship to total corporate sales. A firm spending 40 percent of each sales dollar on physical distribution is a far more serious candidate for reorganization than one spending less than 10 percent. Thus, sheer size of expenditure is one valid check-point concerning the desirability and potential for an integrated approach.

Second, the importance of customer service to the overall marketing program of the firm offers another viewpoint for evaluation of a general reorganization. If customer service performance is critical, the chances are that more consistent operations will result from an integrated organization. The establishment of a physical distribution department in no way challenges the importance of the firm's commitment to a high degree of service capability. However, it is natural that a degree of antagonism and suspicion will accompany the reorganization move. The shakeup to improve the viability of the firm will force change upon the status quo and reduce marketing's direct control over customer service performance. All departments affected by the change should be reassured that the reorganization will allow the overall firm to more readily achieve its goals. The creation of a specialized physical distribution department should strengthen the firm's customer service capability.

Finally, top management should appraise its own willingness to fully support the new organizational concept. Whatever happens, care should be taken to prevent the newly created organization from becoming a political football or a hot potato. The ideal environment is for the new organization to receive corporate-wide understanding that top management is behind the move. The most logical way to assure such support is to provide the new organization equal structuring with other major groupings such as marketing, manufacturing and finance. From such a position in the overall corporate organizational structure, physical distribution can exercise comparable authority and responsibility to act as an effective corporate support unit unless top management is willing to go the full route with the new organization, the desirability of reorganization is questionable.

Line and Staff Considerations

A traditional organizational distinction is made between line and staff activities. A line organization is generally conceived as performing day-to-day operational duties related to the firm's product or service offering. Specifically for a specialized physical distribution department, the activities would consist of warehousing, order processing, inventory management, protective packaging, material handling, and traffic and transportation. In contrast, a staff organization exists for developing new techniques and providing assistance to the line organization so operational objectives can be achieved. Some of the activities the staff provides are system design, warehouse planning, warehouse layout, inventory analysis and material handling engineering.

In the initial development of the new physical distribution organization staff, assignments will in most cases dominant line assignments. Before the integrated physical distribution concept can be implemented, considerable planning is required in advance of separating line activities from manufacturing, marketing and finance. Basically, the staff should develop a system design wherein the line activities are placed in proper perspective to one another. As line activities are initiated, the staff will continue to exist in order to evaluate and assist the functioning of these line activities. As time passes the balance of operational activity will swing primarily from staff to line activities.

In most cases, the change from a traditional organization to a specialized physical distribution organization requires a considerable time period. The staff in this initial reorganization often provides in-house consultants to aid management in establishing a coordinated physical distribution function.

Development of a physical distribution organization is initially staff oriented rather than line. The relative newness of the physical distribution concept renders a need for substantial work of a staff nature prior to line reorganization. Thus, the separation of physical distribution staff activities from traditional departments offers a convenient way to initiate and evaluate organizational change. Under this arrangement the new staff initiates research and development of distribution activities while the old functional departments handle the line operations.

In many cases establishment of a physical distribution staff department may constitute sufficient reorganization. The staff capacity provides internal consultants to aid in development of co-ordinated logistical performance. However, for the vast majority of companies such an arrangement while perhaps sound on paper, has problems in performance. The staff group, lacking in authority and responsibility, may find substantial resistance to implementation of system modifications. The fact remains, that when retained in traditional departmental groupings, the line activities of physical distribution remain secondary activities to the primary mission of its parent organization.

To eliminate the secondary status of physical distribution, top management must continue with its organizational reshuffle. The establishment of a line physical distribution function will increase the status of physical distribution. To make it effective though, as noted earlier, executives responsible for distribution management must be situated at a level equal in stature to other top executives in the firm. As a general guideline in establishing a physical distribution department, the line function should not be created unless supported by a competent staff function.

With both a line and staff organization, close coordination is required if system effectiveness and efficiency are to be achieved. The staff must advise and design the system. The line must operate and administer the system.

In summary, the responsibilities of physical distribution are conveniently divided between line and staff. In certain instances, reorganization at a staff level may be sufficient to achieve improved distribution performance. In most cases staff activities should be performed in advance of line grouping. The combination of both in the proper balance will result in the most positive advancement of distribution capabilities. Physical distribution then no longer remains a secondary function encompassed within another departmental grouping. Its importance is now shown on an equal footing with manufacturing, marketing and finance.

Centralized Versus Decentralized Organization

An issue of sufficient magnitude is the question of centralized versus decentralized organization. Many firms are organized by division, each of which has a profit responsibility related to a specified product or service grouping. Each of these divisions may in turn have marketing, manufacturing, physical distribution and finance operations.

The contrast between centralized and decentralized organizations is normally based upon the degree of direct operating responsibility over specified operations and not geographical location. Two divisions of a given corporation may be located in the same building as the corporate headquarters and be classified as decentralized.

Corporations that are decentralized normally maintain corporate staff groups to assist in the coordination of separate divisional operations. Thus, while each division may have marketing line and staff organization, corporate headquarters will also have marketing staff. Under such organizational arrangements the divisional staff will normally be of a limited size and will assist in marketing that particular division's product line. Broader issues of marketing tactics and strategy will be reserved for the corporate staff group.

Physical distribution line and staff operations can be fitted into this general structure of decentralized operations. However, unlike marketing and manufacturing, certain aspects of physical distribution encourage greater centralization. In general, economies of product flow are directly related to volume. Grouping of physical distribution line responsibilities of a number of different divisions into one centralized unit can result in elimination of duplicate facilities, economies of scale and more effective performance.

The centralization of physical distribution responsibilities offers the potential of a single network of distribution warehouses, one order processing system and the operation or purchase of a single transportation service. Thus, while decentralization may be the order of the day in marketing and manufacturing, physical distribution organization tends toward centralized organization.

Centralized physical distribution will benefit a company with small divisions while it may only hinder the operation of a large division. The question of centralization is related to volume. The smaller the individual divisional volume the greater the tendency to centralize. Such centralization is also limited by congruency of marketing efforts. It is difficult to develop an efficient distribution system for two products sold through different channels to divergent markets.

Regardless of the degree of centralized line operations, divisionalized corporations normally find that physical distribution staffs gain an advantage in performance efficiency when grouped on a centralized basis. The planning of logistical activities can best be performed from the overall corporate vantage point where it is possible to evaluate multi-divisional product flow in distribution system design. Such centralization of staff responsiblity allows maximum freedom in evaluation of needs and capabilities. The most logical organization is one that mixes centralized staff and decentralized line operations among individual divisions in multi-divisional firms. The operations of a number of divisions will be centralized to combine volume and mixed product delivery while other divisions will enjoy sufficient volume to operate on a decentralized basis. Such combinations represent the prime objective of integrated physical distribution analysis.

Conclusion

Successful reorganization must move physical distribution from the structure of existing departments that are primarily concerned with other responsibilities. Only then will the benefit of integrated logistics be fully realized. The physical distribution department should stand parallel to marketing, finance and manufacturing. To develop a successful organization, management will have to evaluate staff and line relationships. While development of a staff offers a way to get started, the degree of centralization of physical distribution desirable in multi-divisional firms depends upon size and compatibility. In general, emphasis will be on centralized staff with line operations seeking a degree of centralization depending upon operational requirements. Regardless of final organizational arrangements, the full benefit of a physical distribution organization will not be realized unless the management of such operations is afforded a voice in corporate planning and policy formation.

28

How to Manage
Physical Distribution

JOHN F. STOLLE

Booz, Allen and Hamilton, Inc.

More opportunities for cost reduction are seen by businessmen than are captured. Nowhere is this truer than in the area of physical distribution. The following examples are representative:

●A packaging materials manufacturer with annual sales of $100 million identified a $1.5 million cost-reduction opportunity in its distribution operations.

●A pharmaceutical house with sales of $200 million annually had an opportunity to reduce distribution costs by $2.5 million a year.

●A machinery manufacturer selling $180 million annually found an opportunity to save $2 million and at the same time make available $3 million in capital through disposition of excess distribution facilities.

●A drugstore chain (a division of a billion dollar retailing company) saw an opportunity to save $800,000 a year among its 40 stores and avoid the need to invest $2 million in distribution facilities.

But none of these companies could capture these dollars!

Why was this the case? Each was a highly successful, well-managed business. The packaging materials manufacturer had succeeded in a segment of the industry where many other companies had failed. The pharmaceutical house had successfully met the problems of manufacturing and marketing one of the most complex product lines in the industry. The machinery manufacturer was making steady inroads on the industry leader. And the drugstore chain had doubled in size in the past three years and would probably double again in the next three. In the face of such success in every other aspect of these businesses, inability to realize physical distribution improvement was a paradox.

282

The reason was the same in all four companies. Their distribution activities were inter-related in a complex way, and responsibility for them was scattered throughout each organization. No one individual was responsible for distribution, and no one had the authority to coordinate these various distribution tasks. *In short, while these companies had developed the ability to make an advanced total distribution analysis, they were not organized to do a total distribution job.*

Many other companies today are in exactly the same position. As a result, they face a competitive disadvantage both in distribution costs and in service.

Later we shall return to the cases of the four companies just mentioned. Let us turn now to some of the problems, trends, and solutions which characterize business in general.

Focus on Techniques

By applying management science techniques to the physical distribution problem, businessmen have identified billions of dollars of profit improvement opportunities. However, only some of these opportunities are appearing on the P & L statement. A part of the reason may be found in the following explanation: Having recognized that physical distribution is a large part of the total cost and that proficiency in physical distribution is an important competitive weapon, management has developed the ability to analyze and design distribution systems that minimize the total of all the costs involved. However, executives are finding that it is much easier to *analyze* the total costs of distribution than it is to *manage* them.

To some extent, business has become entranced with the analytical tools—linear programming, nonlinear programming, and simulation, for example—and for good reason, since they add greatly to management's capability. But the very power of these management science techniques is deceptive in that it obscures the fundamental requirement that companies also do a better job of organizing and managing distribution activities.

Even when the organization problem is recognized, it is often oversimplified. For example, people ask, "Is a distribution manager needed?" This is not the proper question. *The real issue concerns the extent to which distribution activities need to be coordinated—and the extent to which this coordination should be achieved through a formal distribution organization rather than through formalized procedures and operating practices in a traditional organization pattern.*

If we take this view of the organization issue, and then hark back to some organization fundamentals that have been applied successfully in other areas of the business, we should be able to find the best way to organize for effectiveness in physical distribution.

Traditional Approach

"Value added" by manufacture, selling, and distribution accounts for the total value of goods. These acts impart tangible properties, desirability, and

Manufacturing	Selling	Distribution Channels
Materials	Advertising	Production and supply alternatives
Labor	Promotion	Warehousing
Overhead	Packaging	Transportation
Depreciation	Sales activities	Carrying inventory
Research	Extension of credit	Inventory control
Development	Profit taking	Communications and data processing
Engineering		Customer service

Exhibit 1. Components of Total Value.

availability to goods; these qualities add up to "worth." Seen from the customer's point of view, manufacturing creates product quality; selling generates attraction; and distribution provides service. Altogether, the various kinds of value added generate demand.

The elements that make up each kind of value added are shown in Exhibit 1. Value added by distribution accounts for everything not accounted for by manufacturing or selling. Viewed in this perspective, distribution value is a significant part of the inherent total value of goods, and as business leaders know, distribution costs exert a major influence on the total value of goods.

A change in any one of the elements of distribution listed in Exhibit 1 is likely to affect all others, some favorably and others unfavorably. However, while the elements are closely interrelated, in the traditional organization, responsibility for them is scattered. In a typical company, no one executive has responsibility for managing all distribution activities; this pattern is shown in Exhibit 2. Each element of distribution tends to get lost among the other activities of marketing, finance and accounting, and manufacturing. Exhibit 2 also highlights the inevitable conflict of objectives that results from this organization pattern. Only the president really seeks maximum total company return on investment, and the individual objectives of executives in marketing, finance and accounting, and manufacturing often conflict with this overall objective—and with each other (as the arrows denote).

In the light of these aspects of traditional physical distribution organization, it is small wonder that companies are having difficulty capturing the large profit-improvement opportunities which exist.

Building Blocks

Even when the need to organize for physical distribution *is* recognized, a less-than-adequate organization plan frequently results. The most common

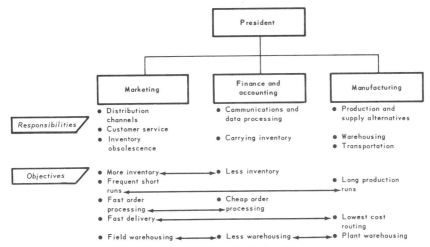

Exhibit 2. Organization in a Typical Manufacturing Company.

inadequacy stems from a poor definition of distribution, such that the organizational grouping is incomplete and thus fails to accomplish the total coordination job. There is also a tendency to include some extraneous functions that are unrelated to physcial distribution but for which management has had difficulty finding a home. And, on occasions when all of the proper activities *are* included, their grouping within the physical distribution organization often fails to reflect adequately the existing interrelationships.

The organization task for physical distribution is no more difficult than for marketing and manufacturing, which have been so successfully handled by businessmen in the past. The need is to hark back to the basic principles of organization which, in this instance, begin with the distinction between line and staff distribution activities.

Traditionally, management has distinguished between line and staff activities as follows: Line activities are those directly associated with producing or selling goods or services. Staff activities are primarily analytical, advisory, supplementary, or consulting, and exist to provide facilities or services in assisting the line people to produce and sell.

If we add "distribute" to the "produce" and "sell" in the above definition, it is apparent that just as marketing has line activities (e.g., field sales) as well as staff activities (e.g., market research); and just as manufacturing has line activities (e.g., assembly) and staff activities (e.g., industrial engineering)—so distribution has line activities (e.g., field warehousing) and staff activities (e.g., materials-handling engineering).

Several line and staff distribution activities are shown in Exhibit 3. While there are others, and while the terms used vary from company to company, these activities are representative. They are the building blocks of our physical distribution organization. And how we group them—either with their traditional

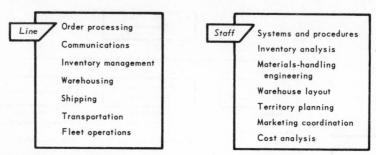

Exhibit 3. Line and Staff Distribution Activities.

counterparts in marketing, finance, and manufacturing or in some new pattern—is the issue at hand.

Emerging Patterns

Having made this distinction between line and staff distribution activities, it becomes apparent that there are three *basic* ways in which to group distribution activities. Naturally, these three patterns seldom exist in a pure form. However, most companies which have successfully come to grips with their physical distribution organization problem have done so by using one of the three basic patterns.

1. Grouping Line Activities

Many companies are grouping line distribution activities only, thus forming another line function comparable to sales and production. When this is done, one individual is made responsible for "doing" the distribution job. As shown in Exhibit 4, a physical distribution manager is responsible for each action that the company must take to meet the customer's service requirements. Following receipt of the customer's order, his department handles the order-processing steps which must be taken, inventory management to ensure that the product is available, physical warehousing and shipping activities, and transportation or delivery of the product to the customer. In short, failure to give distribution

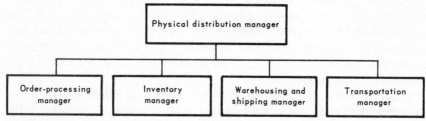

Exhibit 4. Grouping of Line Distribution Activities Only.

service, if it occurs, is the responsibility of one man who is also responsible for the total cost of distribution.

Under this organization pattern, the staff distribution activities identified earlier remain with their traditional counterparts in other organization units. For example, materials-handling engineering in the distribution system is done by the manufacturing industrial engineering group.

2. Grouping Staff Activities

Another pattern of distribution organization is to group only the *staff* distribution activities. In this form of organization, the line distribution activities are performed by their traditional counterparts—warehousing and shipping by the manufacturing group, for example. As shown in Exhibit 5, this approach pulls together all distribution activities needed to help the line activities perform most effectively. Because the line activities remain scattered, this organization also includes a coordination function.

The staff distribution activities can be grouped in various ways, one of which appears in Exhibit 5. Here, the planning unit uses advanced management science techniques to determine optimum geographical distribution patterns and facilities requirements. The planning unit is also responsible for budgeting the total cost of distribution, programming the distribution of new products, and introducing new distribution services. The analysis unit measures the performance of each of the line distribution activities against the plans and budgets developed by the planning unit. The coordination unit works with the various line distribution activities in sales, production, and finance and accounting to ensure that the total cost of distribution is minimized and to avoid a situation where each line distribution function goes its own way. The engineering unit

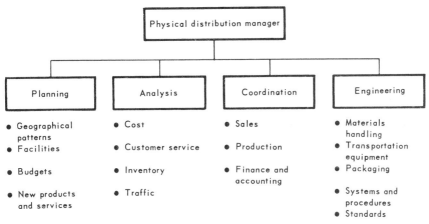

Exhibit 5. Example of Grouping of Staff Distribution Activities Only.

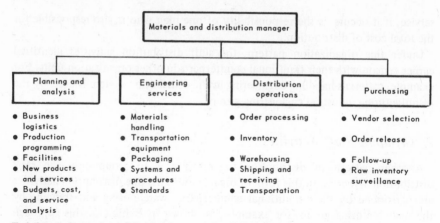

Exhibit 6. Grouping of Both Line and Staff Distribution Activities.

provides a complete set of distribution-engineering skills to establish methods and standards that can be utilized by the planning unit.

3. Combining Line and Staff

Obviously, the third organization pattern is to combine both line *and* staff activities previously mentioned, and, in addition, it frequently includes the materials-purchasing function. When purchasing is included, the physical distribution manager's job is expanded to cover the total management of materials and distribution; he has the total materials management responsibility, from the point of acquisition of materials from suppliers through to the delivery of the product to the customer.

In this organization, the individual line and staff distribution activities can be grouped in any of several ways, as dictated by the circumstances of each company. One grouping that has proved efficient is shown in Exhibit 6. A key feature of this grouping is that all the line distribution activities are placed under a single manager, thus pinpointing the total "doing" by responsibility in one individual.

Choosing a Pattern

As indicated earlier, only rarely do the three physical distribution patterns just described exist in a pure form. Most companies possessing a physical distribution organization have tailored it to their specific needs. This, of course, is good planning. There are sound reasons for using one or another of these basic forms, and their selection and modification should be made to accomplish certain specific objectives.

Before examining this choice in detail, I want to emphasize that the new patterns are not the only ones that management may properly consider. There is a fourth alternative—to leave things in the traditional pattern. For many companies, this is the best choice. They may be able to achieve the coordination needed without special organizational action, using instead specific and formal procedures and operating practices. When this is possible, distribution management can be accomplished at less cost. Here is a case in point:

A bakery produced its products in a single location and distributed them nationwide. The distribution pattern and practice of this company was well established, and the opportunity to improve profits by better planning and coordination of distribution activities was limited. Setting up a physical distribution organization would have accomplished nothing more than the addition of several individuals to the company payroll. When this conclusion emerged from a review of the facts, company top executives were disappointed because they hoped that the distribution manager would be a long-sought answer to a recurring operating problem between sales and production. What the needed improvement required was (a) better sales forecasting and (b) more disciplined coordination of sales and production, neither of which in itself was a valid reason for establishing a distribution organization.

Although the traditional "unorganized" pattern of physical distribution organization has been the best choice for many companies, this has not been the case with any of the four companies cited at the outset of this article. Each of them needs one of the three alternative groupings. Let us turn to that matter now.

Line Organization

The machinery manufacturer requires a line distribution organization to capture the $2 million annual savings and $3 million release of capital. This company's business is highly seasonal, and failure to maintain inventory and to make on-time delivery results directly in lost sales and profits. Distribution effectiveness "in the heat of the season" is so important that all "doing" distribution activities need to be grouped under one executive. The total cost of distribution for this company represents 12% of sales, or $20 million, and the grouping of line activities provides for one executive to have responsibility for this total cost.

Another type of situation calling for grouping of line distribution activities is that of a large multidivisional company where costs can be reduced by establishing a single warehousing and transportation capability serving all of its divisions. Any company where the execution of the distribution function is critical in terms of either service or cost should consider grouping its line distribution activities.

Thus the line grouping of distribution activities is generally made when coordination is vital to (a) doing the distribution job at lowest cost and (b) giving the required level of customer service. It follows that grouping only the line activities, as opposed to grouping both line and staff activities, is best when the staff activities can be performed effectively and at a lower cost when combined with their traditional counterparts elsewhere in the organization.

Staff Group

The packaging materials manufacturer and the drugstore chain have found the grouping of staff activities best suited to their needs. The packaging materials manufacturer is composed of several autonomous geographical divisions, each having total profit responsibility in its area. The drug chain, as was pointed out, is one division of a large retailing company. Establishment of a staff distribution group at the corporate level in each of these companies is the best organizational approach.

In these highly decentralized companies, the line distribution activities should be retained in each autonomous division since line activities vary greatly from division to division, have a major effect on profits, and must be tightly coordinated to be efficient. However, it is uneconomical for each division to maintain the full-time engineering and analytical skills required. Formation of a staff distribution group at the corporate level provides the needed staff skills to each division at low cost, and also avoids diluting the responsibility of division line executives for profits.

This organization pattern is being adopted by many multidivisional companies.

Line and Staff Unit

The pharmaceutical house is adopting the line and staff organization structure to obtain its $2.5 million annual profit improvement. This company's management has decided that with these large dollar opportunities, it should give the distribution function all the tools needed to do a total job. The staff skills required could be provided (at no added cost), except that systems and procedures is retained in accounting and finance where it has traditionally resided.

This line and staff grouping would seem to be the pattern that most companies would establish, since it places the total distribution responsibility on one individual and gives him all the authority and skills required to meet this responsibility. Only when there is a compelling reason to choose another pattern—as when, for instance, staff activities can be performed more economically elsewhere, or when there is no reason to form *any* distribution organization—should a pattern other than the line and staff grouping be chosen.

The discussion so far has focused on organization structure, which is important, but this is only a part of the total organization question. There are other vital matters to consider—the availability of capable people to staff the organization, the degree of cooperation and working relationships to be established with other groups in the company, and the problem of how best to implement the new organization. Implementation is usually a difficult problem since the new physical distribution group is formed by taking activities away from other organizational groups which may resent this violation of their traditional functional fortresses.

All these additional, practical considerations should influence the organization form selected. However, it is important that the basic line, staff, and line and staff grouping alternatives be identified first and the pattern best suited to the company determined. Then a modification for practical reasons can be made most effectively.

Conclusion

The four companies cited in this article had these things in common:

1. All had developed the ability to apply advanced techniques in the analysis and design of distribution systems to minimize the total of all costs involved.

2. All had been able to identify major profit improvement opportunities.

3. Each was unable to seize these opportunities as long as it lacked the organization that was needed to manage all the elements involved in distribution.

4. But when such an organization was created, the picture for each improved radically.

Prior to 1960 most companies had their backs turned to the tremendous profit-improvement opportunities available through improved management of physical distribution. But in a few short years, the situation has completely reversed; and physical distribution management is now recognized as perhaps the last area of opportunity for *major* cost reduction and profit improvement.

As with most developments as dramatic as this, many mistakes have been made. The inevitable fad aspect has tended to produce an "if you don't have a distribution manager, you aren't progressive" rationale for organization action. Other problems have resulted from haste and a tendency to focus more attention on the techniques of analysis than on good management practices.

However, industry's perspective on physical distribution management is rapidly maturing. The function is achieving the same stature as manufacturing, marketing, and finance. The same kind of sound organization thinking that has been applied to those important areas needs also to be used in physical distribution.

29

Why Not Truly Integrated PD Management?

WALLACE I. LITTLE

University of Washington

There is a general impression that distribution management has made great strides forward in recent years. Many articles have been written on improved integrated management of the distribution functions. Other articles have lauded improved performances in speed of service, and savings in the cost of total service, through new techniques of operation.

It is my belief that most achievements in distribution have been in the application of new or improved technical facilities—and not through more scientific management. Certainly, there have been improvements in the efficiency of distribution performance. But the credit should be attributed more to scientific and mechanical breakthroughs than to improved management technique.

The science of integrated management has hardly been broached. The potential of integrated systems planning—which technical improvements have made feasible—has not been exploited. But this is understandable, since the complexity of the potential of integrated systems management is awesome.

Improved technology has made greater efficiency possible in all phases of distribution. Some managerial changes have succeeded the technological improvements. For example, improved communication and information services have made possible the reduction of the number of storage facilities. Faster handling and lower ton-mile transport costs have induced many managers to shift from slow ground transportation plus storage to air transportation and less storage.

However, it should be observed that most managerial changes in distribution operations have usually involved only one or two distribution functions. In most instances, improved management has changed only a single distribution function—consolidated storage, a change in the mode of the carrier or a change in the packing procedure. The more complex possibilities of distribution change through inter-functional planning have yet to be exploited.

It is in this more complex realm of opportunity that management should be encouraged to plan and experiment. It will be in the improved coordination of purchasing, transportation and storage—as a distribution whole—that the less obvious, more subtle opportunity lies for integrated distribution management.

Integrated distribution management consists of planning the total performance of distribution functions so as to maximize total company objectives. This is appreciably different from attempting to minimize unit purchasing costs, total transport costs, average storage costs and/or total costs. It is even different from minimizing total distribution costs. It necessitates a computation of optional combinations of distribution services with their cost and profit effects on total firm operations.

The Primary Difference

The difference between good and bad management is greatest under those circumstances in which the number of variables managed is greatest. The primary difference between a management operation that is predominately administrative, rather than one of planning, centers on the number of management options that are both available and exploited.

Distribution can be converted from a complex management operation, controlling many functions, into a simplified series of administrative operations by departmentalization of responsibility. This is what has happened to defeat planning in many business firms; the planning role has been departmentalized away.

Since the Industrial Revolution, integrated planning in the business firm has been forestalled by the allocation of functional responsibility to department managers. The opportunities for improved management through centralized planning have been concealed by a series of factors:

1. Improved administration of departmentalized functions seems to infer improved management.

2. Discussion by departmental leaders to reduce areas of conflict suggests that optimum combinations of conflicting functions will be worked out.

3. The complexity of inter-functional planning for many firms that are confronted by thousands of purchases (which must be transported, stored and fed through a complex assembly line operation) had defied complete systems planning.

4. The establishment of responsibilities and objectives for each of the operating departments seems to suggest that a maximization of fragmented firm-wide goals will be maximized.

The Computer's Role

In an address before the Fifteenth Annual Meeting of the Pacific Railway Club, Karl Ruppenthal of Stanford University made the statement that the computer will have a more profound effect on the management operations of the railroad industry than dieselization. This forecast should not be taken lightly, for electronic data processing is the key to integrated management. The primary reason integrated management has not been instituted in years gone by has been the absence of this technological facility, which can perform high speed calculations on mass data.

The reasons why the computer is the key to integrated management might be summarized as follows:

1. Integrated management requires the selection of the optimum combination of functional activities for the maximization of total profit.

2. Linear programming and conventional mathematics are too slow and costly to permit the array of all combinations of costs available in an inter-functional management planning operation. Furthermore, many of the cost relationships are not linear anyway.

3. Costs change so frequently that the solution to an integrated management problem requires continuous re-computation to determine the most current solution and the trend for long-range planning.

4. The computer of tomorrow will have the technical capacity to store and keep current the mass of optional costs in purchasing, transportation and storage. It will compare and select combinations of costs, forecast the trends of costs, and suggest the outcome of alternatives through simulation.

5. Integrated management is too costly without computerized assistance, even if it could be done.

Electronic data processing will convert management from a fragmented administrative art to a complex management science. The increased complexity of inter-functional planning will permit the application of many sciences long regarded as theoretical but not practical. Intricate statistical and economic models which have long been theoretically sound—but practically inapplicable— will finally be employed.

Before pursuing the opportunities for integrated management in distribution, terms and functional classification should be clarified.

Throughout this article, distribution refers to the functional areas of purchasing, transportation and storage—with their inherent shipping and receiving functions. Obviously, these three major functional areas embrace a host of administrative and semi-managerial functions.

Divide by Three

For sake of discussion and planning, let's divide the total operations of the firm into distribution, production and marketing. This functional and terminology distinction is necessary since marketing specialists sometimes prefer to include the distribution functions as defined above in marketing—though they seem to prefer to leave the development of distribution to specialists.

Sometimes, distribution is made synonymous with marketing. Classification of the operation sections of the firm into distribution, marketing and production should eliminate much confusion in semantics. The multi-functional area of distribution provides a unique opportunity for implementing integrated management.

There are several reasons why distribution offers so much opportunity for inter-functional planning. First, much of distribution negotiation and planning is very short-range, rather than long-range. Carriers are called daily for initiation of the transportation service. Purchasing is frequently performed only when needed—though sometimes also on a long-range, order-when-needed basis. Mixed car movements may be planned on the day of multiple and widespread purchase. Storage may be planned within hours of purchase time. This considerable amount of frequent and current contracting provides opportunity and need for inter-functional planning. It is not forestalled by long commitments.

In contrast, many of the production functions are committed over a long-range period. Production equipment is used long-range; its layout is planned long-range and rarely altered. In marketing, the channels are not altered without considerable review. Even advertising might be contracted on a long-range basis.

Conflicting Functions

Second, distribution functions are highly substitutional in some degree for one another. Substitutional functions are managerially conflicting functions. For example, storage may be performed by the purchasing source and result in high unit purchase prices. It might be performed in part by a slow carrier, supplemented by a storage operation enroute to the production facility.

Or, storage might be largely eliminated by air transportation, which would substitute higher rates for consignor storage operations. The high costs of air transportation are likewise a substitute for the considerable inventory-in-transit costs by a slower carrier mode. High packing costs usually associated with a slower carrier may be regarded as a substitute for both loss and damage costs, as well as higher air transport rates. Containerization's cost may reduce the costs of tracing, packing, loss of time enroute, and some theft loss and damage.

It becomes increasingly apparent that distribution functions represent either a planning opportunity—if jointly controlled—or a nightmare of conflicting and substitutable functions when separated through departmentalization.

Versatile Functions

Integrated planning is inter-functional planning, and inter-functional planning is most rewarded in those distribution functions highly substitutable for one another. Distribution functions are also substitutable for functions in production and marketing. Storage costs, for example, are substitutable for production costs when continuous production is instituted for goods having a seasonal or fluctuating demand.

The functions of distribution in the firm are more fragmented and departmentalized than those of marketing and production. Advertising, selling, product planning, channel planning and the like are normally controlled by the marketing department of the firm.

But rarely are the distribution functions of purchasing, transportation management, storage, and shipping and receiving controlled by a single department of the firm. They may be controlled somewhat independently or jointly by a traffic department, a purchasing department and/or some form of a warehousing department. Some of the distribution functions, such as purchasing and storage, may be controlled by the production department or the marketing department.

Outside Contracting

Responsibility for the planning and performance of other distribution functions may be contracted to organizations outside the firm. For example, the F.O.B. contract terms may commit the responsibility of carrier selection to the seller. Storage may be rented rather than provided by firm-owned facilities.

In short, the many distribution functions are more likely to be subject to fragmented jurisdiction than are the functions of marketing or production. This suggests the need and opportunity for integrated management.

It is difficult to understand why a concept as obviously valid as that of integrated management has been so long waiting in the wings to be implemented.

Long-run profit maximization requires inter-functional planning. The decisions implemented in any given functional area have a profound influence on the decisions in successive functional areas—as well as in the choices available and costs involved in successive functional areas. This is illustrated in Table 1 which follows.

It will be observed by reviewing Table 1 that a functional decision involves both the direct costs of the immediate management decision as well as the indirect cost influence on decisions in functional areas that must follow.

For example, Table 1 shows that the direct costs in a purchasing decision are the costs specified in the purchase contract. The terms and conditions of the contract are spelled out in the contract itself. However, the indirect costs of the purchase contract are extensive. They appreciably influence, if not determine, the decisions and the costs in functional areas which succeed the purchase function.

The purchase contract may determine the cost and procedure for storage of the commodities purchased, which may pre-determine the carrier mode selection and the transport rates. This may determine the in-transit inventory costs as well

Table 1. How Purchasing–Transportation–Storage Interrelate.

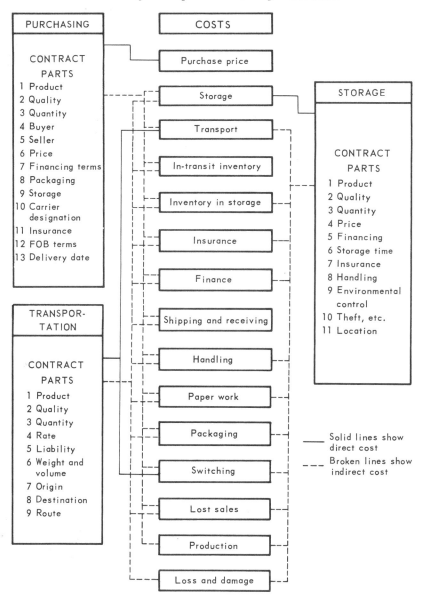

as the inventory-in-storage costs. It soon becomes apparent that a purchasing decision should involve much more consideration than the direct purchase price.

Certainly, these economic truisms could not have been overlooked by the great theoreticians and managers of the past. The immediate question is: Why is integrated management not applied in the business firm and theoretically developed in the business school today? There are a number of reasons.

Discussion vs. Action

In the first place, many business firms believe they are effecting integrated management by resolving the functional conflicts through coordination and planning discussion. However, discussions rarely resolve anything except the direction of the balance of power of the discussion group.

Given a conflict of objectives between departmental managers, the individual with the greatest seniority, keenest wit, most dominant personality—or the most influence with the top management—will prevail in his views. Integrated management is computational—not discussional—in its *modus operandi.*

A second reason most firms have not instituted integrated management is that they believe such scientific procedure is only applicable to firms larger, or richer or more vertically integrated than their own. The theory of integrated management seems sound, but inapplicable to their own well-established management procedure.

A third factor affecting installation of integrated management has been the profound influence it would have on responsibilities and powers of the personnel. Many managers would soon be performing predominantly administrative management operations. Unfortunately, while they don't know it, this is largely what they are doing today.

A Centralization Need

It must be recognized that departmentalization, which fragmentizes management, will always have value for administratives purposes. However, a move in the direction of integrated management is an acknowledgement of the validity of centralized planning.

Unfortunately, without the tools and know-how for a systems-computational application, centralized planning is an insecure exercise. Judgment management "feels more secure" in a narrowed area of simplified responsibility. Top management also feels less oppressed with the responsibility of functional management fragmented off to the second level of department management.

The fourth and most significant reason for the failure to recognize the value of integrated management—and to put it into effect—is the failure of management and academicians to develop this science of sequential integrated planning. The depth and diversity of experience, and tooled capacity required to develop the theory and implement it, are deceptively much greater than would seem to be necessary.

Management problems that require a total cost and profit approach cannot be developed in a piecemeal manner by a group of specialists. The sequential approach requires an understanding of the interrelationship of costs and profits.

Furthermore, the typical academician and business manager lacks the depth of training required to apply statistical, mathematical, economic and computer tools.

The extent of capacity which might be required in a typical distribution problem might be illustrated by considering an inventory control problem. A considerable amount of excellent groundwork has been accomplished in inventory control; unfortunately, most of it resolves only a piece of the problem. The challenge of determining the effect of varying inventory options on distribution, production and marketing costs, and the contingent effect on profits, has yet to be merged into a sequential solution.

Many-Faceted Costs

Storage, for example, is only one aspect of total inventory costs. Inventory-in-transit costs might be considered another part of inventory costs. Furthermore, different optional purchase volumes represent varying opportunities to buy in quantity, use containers, expedite shipments, apply for reduced rates, achieve minimum carload rate volumes, coordinate mixed carload shipments with other shippers, consolidate intra-firm mixed carload shipments, change packing procedures and institute many other methods of altering distribution costs.

The computer may be of particularly great value in two ways in an inventory control problem:

1. For purpose of simulating the effect of varying inventory levels on purchasing, transportation, storage and production costs.

2. To facilitate the storage of cost data and permit a rapid computation of combinations of costs under varying inventory circumstances.

One of the most common and valuable usages of the computer in the science of management will be in simulation exercises. The practicality of this application of the computer is apparent when it is recognized that it merely determines the independent and cumulative effect of a superimposed operational change on existing functional operations.

For example, the order cards for the previous years' inventory control can be made available. The purchasing costs, transport costs, inventory-in-transit costs, insurance costs and the like, can be associated with each order of the previous year. The effect of a change in inventory level on each of these costs can be simulated by the computer, and the net cost and profit can be estimated.

This expensive organization of cost data would be valuable to the firm in many other ways besides inventory control. It could be used in a comparative product-addition study. Here again, the simulated effect on existing functional costs of different product-addition alternatives could be computed from the same data cards.

More Than Awareness

Integrated systems management is more than recognizing an interrelationship of costs—and then acquiring a computer. The science of inter-functional planning has yet to be developed. It will require much more depth and breadth of capacity for the business managers and management academicians of tomorrow.

I contend that the area of distribution is the most promising starting point for the introduction of integrated planning in a firm. The high degree of available alternatives, the frequency of short-range decisions, and the erratic changes in the costs of distribution suggest: Distribution management offers the most lucrative immediate potential for the institution of integrated management.

30

The Management of
Physical Distribution:
A Dilemma

ROBERT E. WEIGAND

De Paul University

During the last ten years businessmen have increasingly expressed an interest in what might be called an "integrated viewpoint" toward business operations. This term implies two things. First, it suggests that the executive has achieved sufficient perspective to understand the wide range of factors which influence his decision and appreciates the implications of his decisions once they have been made. The factors which are strategic to the success of an operating decision frequently are difficult to identify, complex, and numerous. Accurate evaluation of a problem situation must be preceded by gathering sufficient information about these factors so that an accurate decision can be made. The implications of a decision, meaning the impact it will have on various areas in a business, is difficult to determine both because it involves an element of futurity and because other areas which may bear part of the force of a decision are seldom as familiar to an executive as his own area.

Second, the term suggests that organizational responsibility often accompanies the manager who has such considerable authority to make decisions which influence others. Virtually every executive decision in a firm has at least some small though often immeasurable influence over the other people in a firm. Some decisions are so significant, however, that specific organizational steps must be taken to assure that a decision made in one area does not have a disastrous influence elsewhere within the firm.

The purposes of this article are to demonstrate the interrelationship between what is usually called Sales (or more recently Marketing) and the physical supply functions of transportation and storage, to present empirical evidence which shows that organizational provisions have *not* always been taken to assure a blending of effort of these two areas, and to cite some causes for this lack of integration.

Marketing literature seldom expresses a doubt that the physical supply functions are a part of the marketing process. Implicit in most definitions is the thought that physical movement is as much a part of marketing as the better-known process of selling through a personal sales force, advertising, or sales promotion. Where authors have chosen to list the activities generic to marketing, transportation and storage are virtually always included. From the viewpoint of an academician, there is no question concerning the scope of the marketing process: it clearly includes transportation and storage, which create place and time utility.

A Vital Interrelationship

There is a considerable literary void, however, in specifying the reasons why physical supply decisions are so closely related to the other activities of marketing. The "integrated viewpoint," meaning a reasonably full understanding of this relationship, is not clearly presented in the marketing literature. For an executive to achieve such an understanding through job experience is time-consuming and difficult; some never see the blending of the two areas as they should in order to make fully effective decisions. The following circumstances exemplify the need for appreciating the interrelationship of sales and physical supply.

Speed of Delivery

First, there is almost universal recognition that ability to deliver goods on the date that they are promised and in the condition implied by the salesman has a substantial influence on the capacity of the sales force to do what is expected of it. The sales force generally views volume as the principal measure of its success. One of the major tactical weapons available to the salesman is the promise of quick delivery. This weapon is particularly important where his customers look upon the product he is selling as substantially the same as that of his competitors. It is really not very important whether either management or the sales force sees differences among brands. If the buyer sees no differences, whatever differences there may actually be are interesting but tactically useless. In an industry characterized by relative homogeneity of product, speed of delivery can be a major competitive weapon.

On the other hand, physical distribution must be attained at a reasonable cost. Attempts to cater to the needs of the market would include, for example, shipment by faster means and the use of regional warehousing through company-owned or public warehouses. These efforts tend to increase volume and consequently are viewed with sympathy by the sales force. Simultaneously, however, they increase costs. The manager of physical distribution obviously acknowledges the importance of sales, but he is held accountable for his own department's costs.

If the sales force manager is not also responsible for physical distribution, the situation just described contains the elements essential to a philosophical and operational conflict. Relatively greater emphasis on volume by the sales manager and relatively greater emphasis on costs by the manager of physical distribution present a dilemma.

Cost of Delivery

Second, the geographic market area a firm can cover effectively is strongly influenced by the costs incurred in making a sale and distributing the product. In heavy goods industries, meaning those groups of firms in which delivery costs are a relatively high proportion of sales price, there is an economic limit to the area that can be served profitably by a single manufacturing plant. But neither the cost of a sales force nor the costs of physical distribution alone are the determinants of the optimum boundaries of a market area. For example, the sales force may experience relatively little economic disadvantage in soliciting sales a considerable distance from the point of manufacture. But the cost of delivery, if borne by the seller in order to price competitively, may render such sales unprofitable. Therefore the boundaries of a firm's geographic market frequently are determined by its ability to distribute its products economically.

The ability of a manager of physical distribution to manipulate carload or pooled car shipments, to choose the method of shipment, such as train versus truck, and to know when to use central versus regional or "spot" stocking, significantly influences the size of market a firm can serve profitably. Again, a dilemma is presented. Central to the dilemma is the fact that there may be little similarity between the optimum sales force territory and the point where delivery costs become too great for the firm to compete with other firms more favorably located.

A Coordinated Inventory

Third, the capital of a firm is used more effectively when inventory levels are closely matched with sales expectations. There is probably considerable temptation in many firms to maintain inventory at about the same level because sales follow no established pattern and are highly unpredictable. To the extent, however, that the marketing executive can forecast either long-term or short-term changes in sales there is merit in coordinating inventory levels with anticipated sales. Except where sales or economic forecasting has become a specialized staff activity, the chief marketing executive often is best fitted to predict what his sales force will sell during the period ahead. (To reduce the likelihood of an overly optimistic bias, some firms have taken the sobering step of holding the marketing executive responsible for selling his predicted volume at a profit.)

The inventory position of a firm not only is affected by the sales forecast, but marketing strategy is also affected by inventory levels. This view carries the unfortunate implication of the tail wagging the dog. In an ideally operated firm, the market dictates what will be manufactured, held briefly in inventory, and sold. But misinterpretation of market tastes and preferences can create undesirable inventory build-up. This build-up, though not planned, becomes a major determinant of short-term marketing tactics. Another dilemma becomes readily apparent. In any firm in which the marketing executive is not fully aware of changes in inventory levels the speed with which he can adjust his department's effort is seriously impaired.

Empirical Evidence

The ideas just presented indicate that there is a close relationship between sales and physical distribution. This relationship, though often ignored in the literature of marketing, must be recognized if profitable decisions are to be made. The individual who consistently sees such relationships is one who has achieved the integrated viewpoint already mentioned.

Such perspective is not likely to be gained, however, unless specific organizational steps have been taken to provide an organization and an atmosphere in which this understanding will grow. These conditions seem *not* to be present in a substantial number of firms. Contrary to what is implied by the definitions of marketing, there is little indication among five industries which were studied that sales and physical distribution are viewed as closely related activities. Furthermore, in relatively few firms have organizational steps been taken to assure that a decision in either sales or physical distribution will not have a serious and unfortunate effect on the other. The evidence presented here is taken from a study of the marketing organization of firms with a net worth of at least one million dollars, operating in the electrical machinery, non-electrical machinery, fabricated metals, chemicals, and instruments industries.

A total of 220 firms replied to a mailed questionnaire. One part of the questionnaire concentrated on the extent of the chief marketing executive's responsibility for traffic and warehousing decisions and the extent of his participation in discussions concerning these activities. Fewer than 10 (9.09) percent of the top marketing executives were fully responsible for traffic decisions, and in only a slightly greater (10.95) percent of firms were they fully responsible for warehousing decisions. These figures are probably not too surprising to traffic or warehouse supervisors who are accustomed to reporting to someone other than the top marketing executive. In the majority of firms (50.25 and 53.32 percent respectively) the top marketing executive at least participated in discussions concerning traffic and warehousing although he did not always assume responsibility for these activities.

Although the above is gratifying evidence that efforts are being made to coordinate sales and physical distributions in many firms, a substantial share of the respondents indicated that the top marketing executive neither assumed any responsibility nor participated in discussions concerning physical distribution. The figures were 43.06 and 35.26 percent respectively. (The remaining 6.69 and 11.42 percent indicated that the activities were not a formal activity in their firm.) There is ample cause to wonder how a balanced decision can be made concerning physical distribution when the views of the chief marketing executive are not considered.

Evidence of Change

In order to gain perspective concerning change which may have occurred over a ten year period, the same questions were asked for both 1950 and 1959. There was little indication that the top marketing executive was more frequently assuming full or partial responsibility for these two activities: the figures for 1950 were about the same as for 1959. On the other hand, there was evidence that the top marketing executive was increasingly asked to participate in discussions concerning shipping or storing. The percent of firms in which the top marketing executive participated in discussions (but did not assume any responsibility) changed from 21.54 percent in 1950 to 29.20 percent in 1959 for traffic and from 16.02 percent in 1950 to 21.42 percent in 1959 for warehousing. This appears to be a small but healthy tendency.

Difference According to Firm Size

The firms which responded to the questionnaire were divided into those with sales under $10 million, those with sales between $10 and $100 million, and those with sales over $100 million. There was little difference between the small and medium-sized firms, but the large firms were considerably different. In a greater percent of the large firms the top marketing executive assumed either full or shared responsibility for decisions concerning physical distribution. More specifically, the top marketing executive in 43 percent of the large firms either shared or took full responsibility for physical supply decisions; the figures for medium and small-sized firms were 24 and 26 percent.

This difference is not surprising and can be explained by another significant difference in the responsibilities of top marketing executives in large firms. In about half of the large firms the chief marketing executive was not responsible for supervision of the sales force. His activities were confined to management of staff duties. It would appear that relief from such a time-consuming job as supervision of the sales force affords time for integrating sales and physical distribution.

Reasons for This Dilemma

It has been suggested that there should be a close relationship between decisions made in the marketing department and physical distribution activities. Yet the empirical evidence indicates that in many firms the top marketing executive does not assume responsibility for transportation or storage decisions and only infrequently participates in decisions concerning these areas. The suggestion is now made that the reasons for this dilemma can be identified and that they are not defensible under current conditions.

Complexity

First, traffic decisions traditionally have been considered complex and not easily supervised by an executive trained in marketing. This is an understandable view. It is not easy for a manager to assume responsibility for an area totally unfamiliar to him.

On the other hand, the manager does not need to understand the detailed operations of every individual with whom he is expected to work. It is essential, however, that he have the managerial ability to integrate the actions of the various specialized individuals who report to him. This concept permits a strong argument in favor of the traffic manager reporting to the top marketing executive.

Decentralization

Second, in many firms the top sales executive spends more time working with the sales force than he does managing his marketing staff. Inasmuch as the efforts of the sales force are naturally decentralized the manager of the sales force often feels that he must travel in order to perform his duties effectively. Where such travel is frequent and extensive, management of other activities is impaired.

On the other hand, to an increased extent in recent years marketing executives, particularly those who have achieved the integrated viewpoint referred to earlier, seem to be spending more time planning and organizing a complete marketing system than in daily supervision of marketing activities. Sales supervision is still the responsibility of the marketing executive in the majority of firms, but he often has an assistant who assumes a considerable share of the burden. To the extent that this gives the top marketing executive additional time, he can spend his time managing a wider range of activities than before. And it is suggested here that physical distribution should be among the activities that are within his area of interest. While some will argue that he should not assume responsibility for transportation or storage policies, at the very least he should be consulted because of the influence these areas have on the marketing department.

Interrelationship

Finally, the interrelationship of sales and physical distribution has not always been fully appreciated by those responsible for organization planning. Organizations often have grown with less than adequate regard for structuring activities that should be closely integrated under the same executive. Because most individuals arrive at a middle or top management position through a series of relatively specialized positions this lack of perspective is understandable. Although perhaps understandable, it does not excuse the frustrating results which occur when one part of the organization seems not to know what the other part is doing. Obviously decisions often have an effect throughout the firm; their impact is not restricted to a single department. But some decisions have such a substantial impact on other areas that the interrelationship cannot be ignored. The suggestion is made here that an "organizational audit" would reveal serious structural deficiencies in many firms. One aspect of an organizational audit would consist of reviewing the activities which should be most closely coordinated. The formal organization structure and responsibilities of executives should correspond to this interrelationship. The empirical evidence suggests these steps have been taken too infrequently in American industry.

31

Management Intuition Plus Mathematics and Logic Equals Effective Distribution

HARRY J. BRUCE
Spector Freight System

Distribution either has a history going back to the beginning of trade when sea shells were toted across the hill to swap for arrow heads—or it has no history at all. That is to say, distribution has existed as long as commerce has existed. But until it was recognized to have an identity of its own, distinct from manufacturing and selling, and until it was given a name, no historian could write about it. And none did. All we had were stories of transportation—the camel caravans, the sailing ships, the railroads. These were not distribution. They were only devices to aid in distributing.

You might ask, "How can anyone be so pedantic as to say what distribution is and what it is not?" The answer is simple—it is the right of primacy. The inventor of a word signifying an idea has the right to define it, and to defend it, until someone with a better definition knocks him from his pedestal.

This is what is happening now. A broad definition of distribution has been tacked down, but it has not yet been firmly nailed to the framework of business theory and practice. There really hasn't been time. Distribution theory in its present form is scarcely ten years old, unless you want to be scrupulously rigorous and report that someone thought of it back before the Depression... and note that some of it came to attention in the development of the systems approach to weaponry planning during World War II days.

The definition of distribution is being made *now*... and the history of the theory and practice is being made *now*. We are on a new path, probably the last path to cost reduction and profit maximization. The temptation is to dash madly ahead and stake out areas of domain. But, if we are not careful, we may be crushed—or lost—in the stampede like latter day Oklahoma Sooners. And some fine theories and expensive programs have already been crushed.

So, paradoxically, distribution is as old as time and as new as computers. To get our bearings, it is necessary to distinguish between distribution as the economist views it, and distribution as the company president views it.

For the broader concept, the noted economics and business writer, Peter Drucker, put it this way in 1965:

> Physical distribution is simply another way of saying the whole process of business. You can look at a business—particularly a manufacturing business—as a physical flow of materials. This flow, is interrupted when we take the stuff and cut it or shape it, handle it, store it, etc. These are turbulences that interrupt the flow. . .and materials may flow from the iron ore to the galvanized garbage can. But the flow runs through all functions and all stages, and this is the fundamental reason why it isn't being managed. It does not fit into the traditional structure of a functional organization.

The basic truth of that definition hasn't changed, except that the function of distribution *is being managed* today in an increasing number of corporations. For a current definition that provides a guide both to organizational structure and operations, let's take the one of the National Council of Physical Distribution Management:

> Physical distribution is the term employed in manufacturing and commerce to describe the broad range of activities concerned with efficient movement of finished products from the end of the production line to the consumer, and in some cases includes the movement of raw materials from the source of supply to the beginning of the production line. These activities include freight transportation, warehousing, material handling, protective packaging, inventory control, plant and warehouse site selection, order processing, market forecasting and customer service.

Now that is a big order; so big in fact that only a few of even our largest corporations would dream of analyzing the job, let alone doing it. The distribution division of a company may, for example, exercise some control over its purchase of steel, but none at all over factors governing the initial mining of the iron ore.

So the concept of total control of physical distribution must be qualified with such words as "within possible and practical limits." And there go a squad of theorists to the wailing wall!

So where does distribution fit in the business organization? What does it do? How does it do it?

In the traditional business organization, distribution is hard to find. It isn't fitted into any one place. To find it you need to take the new definition of distribution in hand and go a-hunting. For, as we said, no one was able to summon it until it had a name.

The Third Leg of the Stool

Until recently, distribution was the shipping clerk, the traffic man, the warehouse manager, the order processors—all the people down the line who took orders from staff people in manufacturing and sales. Distribution was many kinds of thing-moving-activities. So distribution—whatever name it bore—was usually attached as closely as possible in space and organization to the things that had to be moved.

Few, if any, executives thought of transportation or warehousing as contributing to the value of the company's product. Accountants placed the expenditures for distribution under the total figures for manufacture or marketing, if they bothered to segregate them at all. Even today, in most companies, it is extremely difficult to compile relevant data about distribution.

But a new day is dawning. Sophistication of manufacturing management is of a high order. Marketing has pulled together the necessary functions and developed the concepts and techniques to prove its maturity as a division for top management concern. And now comes distribution up the same ladder.

Few managers today deny that distribution is the third leg of the stool of maximum customer service—manufacture and marketing being the other two. And, like the other two, it is essential to the maximizing of profit for satisfactory return on investment.

Companies that are taking the total cost approach to their distribution operations are surging ahead of their competitors. This is understandable when we realize that costs of distribution can be as high as 40 percent or more of the final price of a product.

In many cases, the selling effort also costs 40 percent of the price charged the final consumer. Add those two percentages together and you have 80 percent of what is paid for merchandise at the corner store. Of course, these percentages apply to products that go through the many stages of factory, merchandising representatives, wholesalers and retailers.

These figures are not meant to be the average, the mean, the median or the mode of all the things we produce in this country. But study of the pricing background of many of the articles sold at the neighborhood drugstore or supermarket reveal percentages of this kind popping up again and again. Often, it should be emphasized, distribution adds as much value, or price if you prefer, to a product as does selling. And selling—depending upon the particular accounting system—includes a great deal more than salesmen's mileage allowances and hotel bills. Sales costs include things like advertising, promotion, research, consumer surveys and a good many others.

Now the importance of distribution to profits becomes clearer. All management should be interested in paring a few percentage points off that distribution cost. Easier said than done? Definitely! Many a brilliant, imaginative hypothesis has dissolved in the effort to make it a theory. And many a theory has collapsed under the strain of practical application.

Change the Environment

What the distribution manager must do in his job may seem impossible. But the difficulty of thought and execution will not serve as an excuse of avoidance. None of us any longer can be content—or successful—in adapting to the business environment around us; we have to get up on our hind legs and change that environment. Isn't that what has made our species dominant on this planet? When we couldn't adjust to things we didn't like, we did what we could to change the environment that displeased us.

This is the challenge of the new distribution. The old order has to give way to the new. In this year of 1968, fortunately, astute management knows the profit potential in scientific control of distribution. Many corporations have tested it and proved it.

All organization, as all organisms, are resistant to change. People, because they can think ahead, are especially resistant to change that may upset the familiar routine of their lives. This applies as much to the corporation president as to the shipping clerk.

Intellectually, we all may agree that continuous change is the nature of things. But, really, we don't like it very much.

There are other obstacles, however. Given the greatest good will of every segment of an organization, the new concept of distribution controlling every physical movement from raw material receipt to delivery of the finished product at the customers' door may prove to be ridiculously illogical. While it could be the success of one company, it could be the ruin of another. This obstacle must be faced with a good, healthy measure of common sense, whatever the systems analyst or the computer may say.

Managing Distribution Costs

Let's turn for a moment to look at the alternative ways a company could approach the management of total distribution costs.

First, a vice president of distribution could be named with complete control over the eight basic divisions of the distribution function: (1) distribution channels, (2) production and supply alternatives, (3) warehousing, (4) transportation, (5) inventory, (6) order processing, (7) management information flow, and (8) customer service. This approach really means that all staff functions in these areas are consolidated under one executive responsible—and cost accountable—for results.

The second alternative is to start at the other end of the organization and coordinate distribution function at the line level. This could mean that the plant manager remains in charge of shipping, but is responsible to a staff vice president for overall costs as well as for the most expeditious delivery, consistent with customer demands, as reported by sales and made possible by manufacturing.

The third alternative is a combination of the other two. A top level distribution staff would do the research, planning and so on. The line departments would remain under their traditional control but would work under staff direction in solution of problems arising through conflict with other distribution departments or divisions of the company. For example, traffic would normally follow its usual rate, routing, etc., routine, but would follow staff directives or call on the staff for help in case of a conflict of interest or "conflict of possibility." That is, transportation might be caught between the demands of sales for immediate delivery and an inventory "out of stock" report, a situation that it would have neither the means nor the authority to resolve.

Can there be a fourth alternative? Yes, the one sometimes forgotten. Leave everything just as it is.

What is the best choice? Experience has shown there isn't any optimum solution that's good for everybody. A company with operating divisions spread across the country could hardly integrate all its line functions. But it could profit from having a top level distribution staff to rely on for planning and technical assistance. It would not be economical or practical, for instance, to have highly expensive computers and staff in every branch plant.

Integration of distribution at the line or working level, on the other hand, could be the answer for the organization that could save money by combining its warehousing and transportation activities to get directly to the goal of providing better service to the customers.

The combination arrangement has the advantage of being a single, unified apparatus under the control of an officer reporting directly to the president. In this setup, personnel and equipment can be more easily shifted in usage and placement to the areas of optimal operational value. And, of course, a standardized reporting and auditing system becomes easier to construct and operate. This program of total integration of distribution has seemed to work best for most companies.

And, finally, the "leaving well enough alone" concept often makes sense. It implies the use of normal procedures to cut costs and raise efficiency. But it avoids the error of building an apparatus requiring additional people and equipment at an expense not warranted by the savings that could be effected.

Distribution Today

So, business today is looking at distribution in a new light. It is a top management profit responsibility to provide inventory and transportation at the right time and the right place to assure the kind of service that profits the customer in his enterprise.

The achievement of this goal may require the closest coordination and control of marketing plans and forecasts, purchasing, production scheduling, packaging, warehousing and inventory, material handling, transportation and—because of the overwhelming mass of statistical data required—data processing and computerization.

It is a gargantuan task. Companies have spent months—even years—in gathering the information needed for decision-making, for building and testing a model, and putting a program into operation. By and large, the investment in this thorough and cautious approach has paid off.

From what has been outlined here in general terms, it can be seen that little will be gained by using old rules of thumb or patchwork remedies. The approach must be scientific in the sense that word is used in business. First, as in the basic sciences, relevant factors must be carefully observed, recorded, put in order, grouped into classifications of similarity, and assigned symbols and numbers that can be manipulated in mathematical formulas and electronic brains. Thus, out of randomness and confusion, order appears. And order leads to knowledge, and knowledge to effective action.

The physical distribution manager can know this and yet be incapable of logical, timely action because of the vast quantity of data that he must put into order and analyze. There is vital information about when the product is scheduled to come off the production line, about the quantity in inventory and its location, about the availability of transportation, to mention but a few.

And these facts of time and place mean nothing unless they are organized to fit the rule of lowest cost consistent with maximum customer service. It is obviously bad business to search out the cheapest form of transportation if a resulting delay in delivery costs the company the loss of a good customer. And yet, on the other hand, perfect service to every customer everywhere could easily turn profit into loss. So distribution, in fact, exercises—or should exercise—some control over sales; the tremendous expense involved in creating a customer is not justified if the cost of serving him is greater than the amount of money his business produces.

How can a human brain—or group of brains—recall or pull together all this information, weigh one alternative against another, and produce a profitable course of action? The answer is: unaided human brains can't. Distribution of the kind we are discussing didn't come of age until the development of data processing and electronic computers.

Today, the effective distribution man must talk the language of computers and the language of mathematics that computers understand. The new machines and the techniques behind them provide the only possible way that thousands upon thousands of numerical facts can be stored, updated, retrieved in a desired order, and compared—all in the flash of a speeding electron.

Fortunately a PhD in mathematics or electronics is not required. Competent personnel can be hired for that. What the physical distribution manager must know is how to ask the right questions with the right vocabulary. Terms like systems analysis, simulation and model building must be understood.

To share a secret, it isn't as difficult as it may seem. The term "simulation" for instance, is just the new name for a way of thinking that is second-nature to us. The child who asks: What would happen if the sky fell down or the ground disappeared? is simulating. He is asking "what if?" That is, he is setting up a non-existent situation in his mind and asking what would happen if one or another alternative should really happen.

It is no different when a distribution man asks a computer to compare the cost of various modes of transportation between two points and relate the answer to the shipment time involved.

The answers that computers give, provided they have been fed the right data and asked the right questions, are generally used for larger purposes. One of the most important is model building. . .again a word that means little more than drawing a blueprint of the most effective way for the company to operate. The model is a realistic image of the actual business system. Because this model is on paper, it can be repeatedly changed as one alternative after another is tested and either retained or discarded. No physical operation of the company is disturbed.

This kind of problem solving is called systems analysis and the technique is called operations research. It is a way of handling virtually limitless numbers of bits of information in a methodical way. But it is only as good as the information stored in the memory bank and the imagination of the man who asks the questions. No machine, for example, can answer a question such as: What would happen to our export business if war were declared? The computer would blow a fuse unless someone had foreseen the need to feed in information about past war experiences and projections of anticipated conditions.

What goes into the computer determines what comes out. Or, in the language of computer people, "GIGO," garbage in—garbage out. Perhaps you have heard about the two zoologists who wished to cross a crocodile with an abalone fish in order to produce a new creature called an "abadile." Knowing that nature's process of propagation couldn't possibly work, they decided to blend the genes of the two animals in the laboratory. But the complexity of the spirals of DNA and RNA molecules was far too complex for their solution. They had to call in a computer expert to program their problem. Somehow he asked the wrong questions and instead of getting an "abadile" the zoologists received a "crock-a-balone."

It happens. The emphasis is on the importance of the modern distribution man thinking in terms of the whole business system with which he is concerned. He must not only think of a flow of materials within his company, but thoughts must go beyond the shipping dock to the customer's doorstep—sometimes backward to the sources of supply. His thinking must cut across traditional organizational lines. It must reach out to include competitors, potential markets; in short, the physical distribution manager must think big.

Yes, the kind of distribution management that is fast coming into being requires a new breed of manager. Not only must his observations be extensive and thorough, he must be familiar with the scientific processes and tools that translate raw data into directions for meaningful action. He must know how to think within the framework of mathematical logic. He can not afford to take the position that Winston Churchill once did when he said:

> I had a feeling once about mathematics—that I saw it all. Depth beyond depth was revealed to me—the byssus and the abyss. I saw—as one might see the transit of Venus or even the Lord Mayor's show—a quantity passing through infinity and changing its sign from plus to minus. I saw exactly how it happened and why the tergiversation was inevitable—but. . .it was after dinner. . .and I let it go.

We can't let it go. And that is the meaning of $[MI + (M \cdot L)] = E.D.$ Management intuition plus mathematics and logic equals effective distribution.

32

Strengthening Control of
Physical Distribution Costs

RONALD J. LEWIS
Northern Michigan University

Historically, accountants and industrial engineers have concentrated on production costs. As a result, detailed cost control and planning are the rule rather than the exception in production.

The same cannot be said for distribution. Despite a growing management emphasis on marketing and on physical distribution, these subjects have been neglected by accountants, both in theory and in practice. Accountants have given some attention to selling costs, but conventional accounting methods and procedures do not provide adequate differentiation of physical distribution costs, and there is little evidence that accountants are making much effort to provide the information necessary to identify and isolate these costs for centralized management and control.

This is particularly surprising because many of the well-known problems of distribution cost accounting do not apply to physical distribution. "Distribution costs" as used in accounting textbooks and in most other literature mean marketing costs. Marketing embraces two basic functions, the obtaining of demand for the products or services of a company and the servicing of that demand. Costs of obtaining demand include advertising, personal selling, merchandising, sales promotion, and market research. Costs of servicing demand include warehousing, transportation, order processing, inventory holding costs, and customer servicing costs.

Accounting for distribution costs has been hampered by the difficulty of determining bases for allocation and of developing standards for cost control and analysis. As many accountants have recognized, however, these problems arise in accounting for the demand-obtaining activities, such as direct selling and advertising, rather than in accounting for the demand-servicing activities. In comparison with selling activities, physical distribution activities are relatively

316

easy to quantify and to subject to mathematical analysis. In this respect, physical distribution activities are more like production activities than they are like the demand-obtaining activities of marketing.

Yet accountants for the most part have failed to capitalize on the relative ease with which physical distribution costs could be determined. In part, at least, this failure is the result of historical patterns of organization.

Some components of physical distribution have been treated separately since the nineteenth century. Plant location theory dates back to such early German writers as von Thunen and Weber. Transportation and warehousing were subjects of early marketing literature. Long-established organizational patterns provide for separate control of these components. Assignment of responsibility has been spread in varying ways to different levels of management, both vertically and horizontally. Relationships among the components have been obscured by the established organizational framework.

Yet physical distribution functions, while divided managerially and physically, have closely interrelated cost implications. These functions—materials handling, packaging, traffic, transportation, inventory control, terminal management, and warehousing—are more closely related as cost centers than production and sales. They connect the customer to the production line geographically and temporally.

Since World War II there has been increasing recognition of the uniqueness of physical distribution. Physical distribution has emerged as a distinct, identifiable function requiring an integrated approach and a separate organization. Even where physical distribution has been given organizational recognition, however, accounting for it has lagged, as the following case example illustrates.

Need for Control

The data in this case study were obtained from a Midwestern company considered progressive in the area of distribution. It has an advanced understanding of physical distribution, with a separate department to control physical distribution functions. Yet the expense allocation practices of its accounting system, when analyzed by an outside consulting firm, were found to show little understanding of the control needs of the distribution manager.

Table 1 presents a list of accounts showing twelve-month actual operating costs as recorded in the accounts. These are the total costs of manufacturing, excluding raw materials, for the entire plant operation. The consultants were shocked to learn that a full three-fourths of these costs were charged to overhead. Under the existing method of recording the expenses, only $53,390, or 25 per cent of the total operating expense, was charged to direct labor, and $161,229 (75 per cent) was charged to overhead.

An interview with the company's physical distribution manager disclosed that he was unable to control the expenses under his jurisdiction since none was assigned functionally to his activities. He was aware that some of the charges for

Table 1. A Midwestern Company—Functional Redistribution of Plant Costs; Actual Operating Statement Prepared for a 12-Month Period.

	Amount	Per Ton	Std.
Direct Labor:			
Mfg. Super	$10,359	.41	.29
Mfg. Base	8,343	.43	.34
Mix. & Bag.	12,974	.52	.49
Shp. Bulk	4,458	.28	.26
Shp. Bag.	15,150	.66	.49
Mfg. Gran. Base	2,106	.56	.58
TOTAL	$53,390		

	Overhead Expense:	Amount
33	Supplies	$ 6,143
42	Indirect Labor	20,663
43	Premium Time	2,950
44	Salaries	34,240
45	Off-Duty Comp.	5,606
46	Assoc. Payroll Costs	15,940
51	Depreciation	15,060
55	Taxes & Insurance	19,658
56	Repair Materials	18,194
57	Repair Labor	11,930
58	Electrical Power	4,315
59	Fuel	4,171
60	Defects & Losses	1,689
85	Other Expense	12,231
86	Standard Prorates	0
87	Chgs. from Others	0
89	Chgs. to Others	(11,561)
	TOTAL	$161,229
	GRAND TOTAL	$214,619

Cost Redistribution Functionally

Manufacturing & Shipping:	
Unloading	$ 9,846
Handling in Process	30,227
Shipping	52,849

Delivery	(1,098)
Manufacturing	53,385
TOTAL	$145,209
Overhead Expense:	
Custodial	$ 9,942
Administrative	22,468
Misc. Overhead	37,000
TOTAL	$69,410
GRAND TOTAL	$214,619

supplies, indirect labor, premium time, and depreciation, for example, were assignable to unloading, handling in process, and other physical distribution activities, but the existing accounting system did not provide him with the allocations.

After the accounts were redistributed functionally, as shown in the second part of Table 1, it was found that $145,209, or 68.1 per cent of the total operating expenses, could be charged to manufacturing and shipping, leaving only 31.9 per cent for overhead. The 68.1 per cent was further broken down into $53,385, or 24.8 per cent, for manufacturing; $51,751, or 24.6 per cent, for shipping; $30,277, or 14.1 per cent, for handling in process; and $9,846, or 4.6 per cent of the total, for unloading raw materials. The redistribution is shown in detail in Figure 1 and Figure 2.

With these accounts redistributed functionally, the distribution manager was able to identify and control 43.3 per cent of the total operating expenses as in-plant materials movement. Formerly he could isolate none of these physical distribution costs for managerial control.

Even after the analysis, 17 per cent of the total plant costs shown were allocated to miscellaneous overhead. The consulting firm's analyst agreed that this was too large an amount to remain unidentified and that further investigation would probably reveal additional physical distribution costs in the miscellaneous overhead category.

Criticisms

There is growing demand for improvement in physical distribution cost accounting. This demand is coming from the physical distribution specialists, not the accountants. Executives and academicians in the field of physical distri-

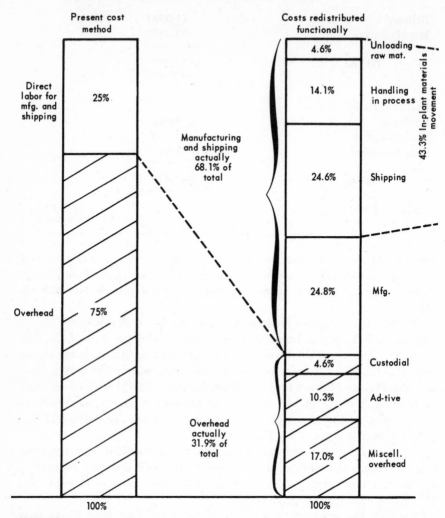

Figure 1.

bution, moving into cost analysis by default, have taken the lead in this area, urging accountants to give them the data they need for adequate control and meanwhile trying to design cost accounting systems of their own.

Examples of pressure from the distribution side of the organization are numerous:

H. G. Miller, distribution manager of Diamond Crystal Salt Company, charges, "Traditional accounting methods tend to hide true distribution costs, create illusory savings, and relocate costs rather than reduce them."[1]

[1] H. G. Miller, "Accounting for Physical Distribution," *Transportation and Distribution Management,* December 1961, p. 7.

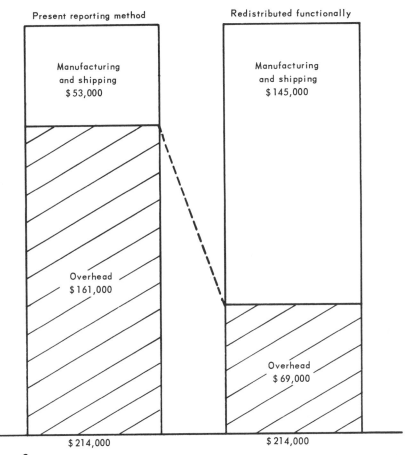

Present reporting method | Redistributed functionally

Manufacturing and shipping $53,000

Manufacturing and shipping $145,000

Overhead $161,000

Overhead $69,000

$214,000 | $214,000

Figure 2.

Donald W. Drummond, vice president, Olin Mathieson Chemical Company, complains, "The accounting department is generally working to the advantage of everyone except the marketing department. Only if this service function (accounting) can be more fully utilized by this department (marketing) can their full contribution to profits be realized."[2] In response to this problem, Mr. Drummond has devised his own method of accounting for physical distribution costs, designed to pinpoint more precisely the costs that are the responsibility of the physical distribution manager and can be controlled by him.

In an unpublished doctoral dissertation,[3] Richard J. Lewis, assistant professor, Michigan State University, has pointed out specific accounting deficiencies.

[2] Donald W. Drummond, "A Marketing Yardstick," *Transporation and Distribution Management,* February 1962, pp. 13-16.

[3] Richard J. Lewis, *A Business Logistics Information and Accounting System for Marketing Analysis,* unpublished doctoral dissertation, Michigan State University, 1964.

Conventional methods used in accounting for distribution costs ignore the geographical variability of costs, he asserts; by allocating total costs among the various activities of marketing on the basis of standards or standard costs, rather than building up the individual charges at the source of their incurrence, the accountant fails to allow for the variability of marketing costs that results from locational differences. Instead, Professor Lewis proposes geographic cost control units for the accumulation of costs at their point of origin.

Other critics support this view. Speaking of averages such as those used in applying standard costs to distribution cost analysis, Edward W. Smykay, Frank H. Mossman, and Donald J. Bowersox argue, "If. . .variations within the average are neglected, then a standard uniform cost is assessed against all geographic markets. Neglecting the variations of spatially separated markets will mean that no market is precisely measured as to the precise cost of servicing it."[4]

Accounting procedures, these critics contend, are designed to serve the needs of financial officers, inventory valuation, the Securities and Exchange Commission, and tax officials, often without regard for the needs of important internal control functions. As a result, the customary accounting treatment of distribution costs does not provide adequate information for their control, and physical distribution managers lack the data they need to make enlightened decisions.

Actually, as has been indicated before, physical distribution costs are not difficult to identify and analyze. A number of possible systems could be developed; the model that follows is offered for the consideration of the accounting profession as a solution to the problems placed before it by the managers of physical distribution activities.

According to J. L. Heskett, Robert M. Ivie, and Nicholas A. Glaskowsky, Jr.,[5] the principal problems in cost analysis under the "total cost" concept are as follows:

1. Separating and identifying logistics costs.

2. Establishing accounting cost centers that are capable of providing the type of information necessary for continuing logistics cost analyses.

3. Analyzing the results of changes in the performance of a system after new concepts have been implemented.

These are the principal problems of which distribution executives complain. They want an accounting system that permits complete control of distribution costs and provides for comparisons among various years' performances and among installations of similar type.

[4]Edward W. Smykay, Frank H. Mossman, and Donald J. Bowersox, *Physical Distribution Management*, The Macmillan Company, New York, 1961, p. 77.

[5]J. L. Heskett, Robert M. Ivie, and Nicholas A. Glaskowsky, Jr., *Business Logistics Management of Physical Supply and Distribution*, The Ronald Press Company, New York, 1964, p. 455.

An accounting system for physical distribution costs must incorporate characteristics that will overcome these obstacles, yet it must remain simple and operable. It must start at the point of separating and identifying physical distribution costs; this is where the most important changes must be adopted. Traditional accounting procedures would be affected mainly in three different areas:

1. Bases and methods of allocating costs.
2. Classification of accounts.
3. Financial statements.

The model described here was designed for a manufacturing firm in the chemical industry. However, it could be modified to apply to other industries.

Allocating Costs

In the unit functional analysis method used in distribution cost accounting the expenses are originally accumulated in the natural accounts, e.g., auto expense, commissions, etc., and then assigned to functions (activities), e.g., selling expense. Then a unit rate for each function is developed in terms of the function's factor of variability, and the total expense is allocated by manner of application, e.g., product, customer, territory. This process of cost analysis is followed to identify profitable or unprofitable customers, products, sizes of orders, or territories.

The bases for allocating these expenses by manner of application (segments) are often arbitrary. That is, the basis may not be representative of the factor of variability. Furthermore, the unit rate is in effect an average. The use of an average without statistical analysis provides only spurious accuracy. An average of 50 may be obtained from 40 and 60 or from 5 and 95. Where the use of averages is desirable in assigning unit costs by manner of application, e.g., product, customer, a measure of dispersion such as the standard deviation could be applied to the data. Thus, wide dispersion might indicate that the use of the average would result in inappropriate allocations.

Another major deficiency in distribution cost methods as now applied is the assumption of independent causation for each of the segments analyzed, e.g., product, customer, order size, and territory. The segments are analyzed independently; that is, inferior customers are isolated, then inferior products are isolated. There is no attempt to assess the interdependence of these four segments. For example, customer A may be found unprofitable when total costs are allocated by customer alone. But customer A may order in large sizes, may order only the most profitable product lines, and may be located in a low-cost territory.

These four segments are interrelated and should be considered concomitantly for the cost analysis to be fruitful. The objective would be to show something like this: Customer A buying product A with order size C in territory C would be unprofitable whereas customer A buying product A with order size D in territory B would be profitable.

Professor Richard Lewis has experimented with a system that attempts to solve some of the problems inherent in current physical distribution cost analysis methods. His system would obviate the arbitrary bases for allocation and the averaging techniques. It would accumulate costs at homogeneous geographical cost centers identified by customer, product, etc., at the source of incurrence. Homogeneous geographical grid blocks are coded for the entire United States. These control unit members are reported on the various marketing records, such as the sales orders, showing the location numbers for the origins and destinations of shipments. The control unit location number for each manufacturing point, distribution point, and customer must be determined.

Electronic data processing equipment makes possible a continuous flow of information from the coded documents. If Professor Lewis' system were incorporated into an accounting system, it would provide the cost centers for accumulating the geographically variable physical distribution costs. Identification of the customer, the product he buys, the size of his order, and the geographical control unit could all be interrelated with this system. So far this system has been applied only to geographically variable logistics costs, such as freight and pipeline inventory, but it has additional application in distribution cost accounting.

Classification of Accounts

The second accounting practice that requires modification to satisfy the needs of distribution executives is the traditional method of classifying accounts. The bases for allocating charges to the functional accounts in servicing demand are more precise than in the marketing area of obtaining demand. Professor Lewis' system is designed primarily to control geographical variability. Within the production and warehousing facilities there are logistics activities with no geographical variability. The main problem in this area is that many accounts which reflect logistics activities are charged to production (or cost of sales) accounts.

The model set of physical distribution accounts that follows represents a system that is already in the process of being implemented. It is not merely hypothetical or a theoretical ideal; it is soon to become a reality.

The following accounts will be assigned to physical distribution control:

A. Now assigned to production department control:
1. Packaging labor.
2. Packaging material.
3. Material handling equipment depreciation (or rent) and maintenance.
4. Handling labor.

5. Warehouse space cost (depreciation, maintenance, taxes).
6. Taxes and insurance on inventories.
7. Order handling costs at the plant.
8. Transportation equipment cost—net rental on shipper-owned or leased equipment (such as tank cars, barges, ships) plus cleaning and maintenance.
B. Accounts controlled by the distribution and traffic department:
1. Terminal and warehousing expenses outside the plant. (This includes the analogue of accounts 1-7 in A above.)
2. Freight—plant to customer (or terminal) and terminal to customer. (This includes miscellaneous charges such as demurrage, pump and line costs for tank trucks and barges, tolls, insurance, and others.)
3. Administration of distribution function.

To complete the system the physical distribution manager would require the following:

1. Customer-absorbed freight.
2. Supplemental information of the same type on inbound purchases (vendor-absorbed and vendee-absorbed) along with such information as origin, commodity, tonnage, type shipment, etc., for a complete inbound analysis.

Financial Statements

Some distribution managers do not see any need to alter the formal financial statements. They feel that the information they require can be obtained from supplementary reports. Others feel that the present financial statements are misleading by reporting in such a way that some physical distribution costs are assigned to production and cost of goods sold.

In a model system of accounting for physical distribution costs two changes would be made in the income statement:

1. Freight should be shown as an expense rather than netted against gross sales. This would eliminate the possibility that net sales will increase or decrease because of a change in the logistics system.
2. The accounts listed in A above, normally charged to production, would become distribution expenses, thus changing the face of the income statement.

An example of this modification is given by Donald W. Drummond.[6] The purpose of his proposal is to disclose some of the costs of marketing obscured by conventional accounting procedures. His analysis, confined to a single product or a small group of products, contains all relevant marketing cost elements. He compares the present method of presenting income statement information (in Table 2) with his suggested new method (in Table 3).

[6] Drummond, *op. cit.*

Table 2. Present Financial Statement Method.

Net Sales:	$
Cost of Goods Sold	_____
Manufacturing Profit	
Operating Expenses:	
General and Administrative	
Selling Expenses	
Research and Development	
Advertising and Sales Promotion	
Other Income and Deductions	
State Taxes	_____
Pre-Tax Profit	$

Proposed New Method

The present method starts with net sales and subtracts costs of goods sold to show gross profit. Operating expenses, other income and deductions, and state taxes are accounted for to obtain earning before income tax. Mr. Drummond argues that if the calculation begins with net sales, as in Table 2, many significant cost elements relevant to the total cost analysis of the various marketing segments may be overlooked. Examples given are deductions for freight equalization or allowances, price allowances, and sales commissions.

Mr. Drummond further points out that some of the costs conventionally charged to cost of goods sold are actually physical distribution or promotional costs. He mentions shipping, warehousing, tank car rentals, and bad debts as examples.

This proposed method starts with gross sales, which he defines as the maximum revenue that could be realized for the product (see Table 3). From this figure the cost of goods sold is subtracted, but this is not the conventional cost of goods sold. All elements of physical distribution or other marketing activities have been eliminated so that only true production costs remain. The result is called manufacturing profit. From this figure operating expenses excluding those considered sales-controllable are deducted; state taxes and other income and deductions are subtracted (or added); and the result is termed "profit before selling."

The purpose is to show the true diminution of the revenue obtained by the

Table 3. Drummond—New Method.

Gross Sales	$
Cost of Goods Sold:	
Raw Materials	
Operating Expenses	
Plant Overhead[*]	
Manufacturing Profit	$
Operating Expenses Excluding Sales Controllable	
General and Administrative	
Research and Development	
Other Income and Deductions	
State Taxes	
Profit Before Selling	$
Sales Controllable	
Shipping	
Freight Equalization or Allowance	
Sales Commission	
Price Allowances	
Cash Discounts	
Tank Car Rentals	
Warehousing	
Direct Sales Costs	
Sales Administration	
Advertising and Sales Promotion	
Bad Debts	
Pre-Tax Profit	$

segment (e.g., product) under observation that is attributable to costs controllable by the executives assigned the responsibility. Those items that follow "profit before selling" in Table 2 should be controllable by a marketing executive, such as a sales manager or a physical distribution manager.

In summary, a model accounting system for physical distribution would be the present accounting system with these recommended modifications:

A. General Recommendations

1. Refinements in selecting bases for functional cost allocation where necessary.

2. Analysis of present plant overhead charges to isolate functionally costs of either production or physical distribution that may be buried there.

3. Application of more sophisticated statistical tests to averages used in allocating costs, where appropriate.

B. Specific Innovations

1. Implementation of Professor Lewis' system of collecting cost information for the geographically variable costs, such as freight and pipeline inventory time.

2. Revision of present account classifications to remove physical distribution activities from the production accounts.

3. Revision of the income statement to reflect the above refinements, e.g., freight.

Research Study

There is great need for additional research in the area of accounting for physical distribution costs. An exploratory research study conducted by the author[7] showed clearly both the dissatisfaction of the distribution managers and the relative indifference of the accountants.

Several questions were raised in the study regarding the physical distribution concept and its implications for the accounting profession. Two of these questions and the conclusions drawn in the research study from responses to these questions are discussed here.

1. *Does the recognition of physical distribution as an unique marketing concept by marketing executives and academicians demand a corresponding response from accounting executives and academicians?*

Yes, say the physical distribution managers. In order to solve the problems that many distribution managers are encountering as a result of traditional accounting practices, accountants must recognize and understand the marketing concept of physical distribution and its accounting consequences. Evidence presented in this research study indicates that serious obstacles to the correct decision-making interpretation of cost information are embodied in existing accounting procedures and practices.

Failure to make the classification of accounts coincide with cost control centers may lead to misleading managerial interpretations. Also, the preponderant lumping of physical distribution charges to overhead at the plant level provides insufficient information for total cost control.

Where the correction of these deficiencies is feasible and does not result in serious loss of comparability and consistency, it behooves the accountant to

[7] Ronald J. Lewis, *Accounting Consequences of Physical Distribution System Changes*, unpublished doctoral dissertation, Michigan State University, 1965.

respond to the demand of the physical distributionists. Accounting serves the needs of the whole company as well as the interests of stockholders and others outside the internal structure of the company. The informational demands of these groups must be balanced. This requires considerable discretion on the part of accounting management. It would appear that accounting executives and academicians can improve this balance by a response to the requests of the physical distribution people.

CPAs Lack Awareness

2. Is there an awareness by the firm's accounting management, public accounting firms, and academic accountants of the informational needs of the executives responsible for physical distribution activities?

This research study found little evidence of such awareness, despite some contrary evidence in published literature. One of the companies from which data were received for this study complained that accounting management was not cognizant of the needs of the distribution manager; this complaint was based on the inadequacy of intracompany communications. Another company also reported that the accounting department did not provide satisfactory information to the managers of physical distribution activities.

Preliminary observations indicate that few public accounting firms are aware of any problems in the area of physical distribution. Among six local offices of well-known public accounting firms contacted for the study, only one could produce or even acknowledge the existence of a change in a physical distribution activity that resulted in a change in accounting procedures or that required attention by the public accounting firm. Yet this kind of a change in distribution systems frequently occurs.[8] It can be deduced from this evidence that the public accountants are not aware of the concept. Perhaps they are too occupied with other demands to acknowledge it, or perhaps they have too little contact with marketing personnel to become aware of their problem.

Academic accountants are not ostensibly concerned with this marketing problem. This observation is based on the almost complete absence of literature in accounting journals dealing specifically with the physical distribution concept.

The accounting profession at all levels has failed to emphasize or even in some cases to recognize this problem area for the distribution manager. Understandably the accounting profession cannot shift emphasis at the command of each functional area of the business firm. Such decisions are made only at the top management level. Apparently the distribution manager's message has not yet been effectively communicated to top management. When this is done the accounting profession may respond with a solution.

[8] See Arthur Andersen & Co., *Operations Research in the Firm*, February 1961, pp. II-7, II-14, II-23, and II-32, for examples of physical distribution changes that engaged the attention of certified public accountants.

It may be concluded that the accountant not only lacks familiarity with the relatively new physical distribution concept but also faces demands from many specialized areas: tax, auditing, financial, legal reporting, manufacturing, product costing, administrative budgeting. Distribution costing to the accountant is just another specialized area—and one that is not making as pressing demands as tax and financial accounting.

Distribution managers themselves are at least partly to blame. All too often they are not able to tell the accountants just what it is that they want; they only know that they are not happy with the accounting data that come to them. Or they are not willing to accept the burden of working with the detailed data necessary to produce useful control information.

Accounting, already attempting to satisfy many masters, is reluctant to reshuffle the accounts without considerable persuasive evidence that it is necessary. The physical distributionists must first persuade top management of their need for better cost control. Then the accountants will be only too happy to make adjustments.

33

Pathway to Profit: The Management Information System

BERTRAM A. COLBERT

Price Waterhouse and Company

What has information to do with profitability? Every chief executive knows it has a great deal to do with it. Information plays a major, usually a crucial, role in achieving profits—the profits which are one of the main indexes of successful business operations in our economy.

Obviously, the manager must understand and evaluate a wide range of information about his operations in order to reach sound, profitable decisions. Concise, complete, and timely management information thus forms the basis for effective planning, decision making, and control.

As the complexity and magnitude of business decisions have increased, the typical corporate manager has found that existing systems do not have the capability to deliver the significant data required at the time they are required. Too often the manager has found himself overwhelmed with masses of data or long listings of historical information which were of little help in the decision making and planning processes.

The need for a better way was clearly evident. Therefore, many companies, both large and small, are seeking ways to improve their information and data flow and its end use—the generation of profit. The result has been the group of techniques called the management information system.

Let us consider some basic questions:

What is a management information system? How does it differ from such existing systems as accounting, sales, or production? Should you have one? What is its value? How do you obtain one or put one in a specific company?

This article attempts to answer these questions, to show graphically the management process and the part information plays in it, and finally to provide a frame of reference within which each executive, by further analysis, can obtain more complete specific answers, tailored to his company's needs.

We may begin by noting the functions of management: to plan, to organize, to direct, and to control, as indicated in Chart 1 and by illustrating the role which information plays in this process (Chart 2). Information which is internal is necessary to provide communication in the management process. Information which is external is necessary to assure that management is aware of, first, the outside events which may influence the plan and, second, the effect of the operation on this outside world. As information is received, we may recycle through the management process: RE-plan, RE-organize, RE-direct, with the measurement in the control process.

To provide a framework for discussion, let us consider the organization of a typical company (Chart 3). The company has five principal functions: administration, marketing, research and development, manufacturing, and finance. The relationship to the board of directors and the specific departments which we might find in each function are depicted in Chart 3.

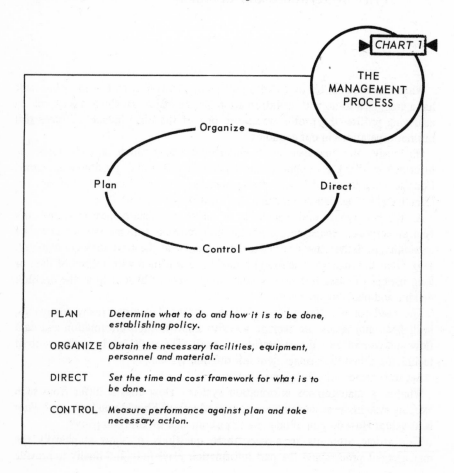

CHART 1

THE MANAGEMENT PROCESS

Organize

Plan   Direct

Control

PLAN   Determine what to do and how it is to be done, establishing policy.

ORGANIZE   Obtain the necessary facilities, equipment, personnel and material.

DIRECT   Set the time and cost framework for what is to be done.

CONTROL   Measure performance against plan and take necessary action.

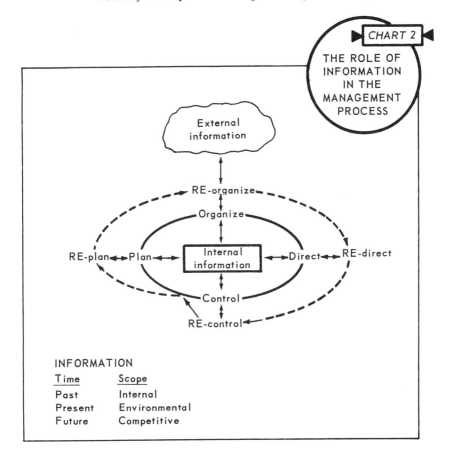

CHART 2

THE ROLE OF
INFORMATION
IN THE
MANAGEMENT
PROCESS

Management Information System

A management information system, simply, is an organized method of providing each manager with all the data and only those data which he needs for decision, when he needs them, and in a form which aids his understanding and stimulates his action.

Such a system:

1. Considers the full effect of a decision in advance by supplying complete, accurate, and timely data for use in the planning and decision making processes.

2. Eliminates from the planning and decision making processes the problems associated with the use of inconsistent and incomplete data by providing a means for preparing and presenting information in a uniform manner.

3. Uses common data and methods in the preparation of long-range and short-term plans.

4. Identifies, structures, and quantifies significant past relationships and

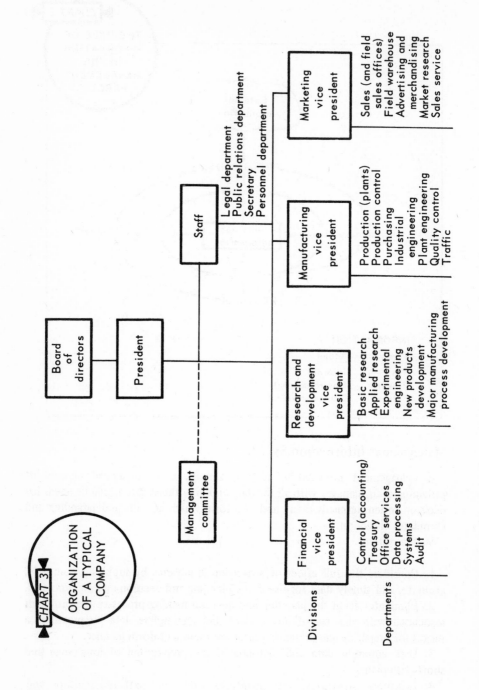

CHART 3

ORGANIZATION OF A TYPICAL COMPANY

Board of directors

President

Management committee

Staff

Legal department
Public relations department
Secretary
Personnel department

Divisions

Financial vice president

Research and development vice president

Manufacturing vice president

Marketing vice president

Departments

Control (accounting)
Treasury
Office services
Data processing
Systems
Audit

Basic research
Applied research
Experimental engineering
New products development
Major manufacturing process development

Production (plants)
Production control
Purchasing
Industrial engineering
Plant engineering
Quality control
Traffic

Sales (and field sales offices)
Field warehouse
Advertising and merchandising
Market research
Sales service

forecasts future relationships through the use of advanced mathematical techniques in analyzing data.

5. Merges financial and production data to produce significant measures of performance to facilitate control of present costs and to facilitate planning decisions with minimum processing of data.

6. Recognizes the needs of all corporate units so that the requirements of each are met with a minimum of duplication while serving the corporation as a whole.

7. Reduces the time and volume of information required to make decisions by reporting to each level of management only necessary degrees of detail and usually only the exception from the standard or norm.

8. Utilizes personnel and data processing equipment effectively so that the optimum in speed and accuracy is achieved at the lowest cost.

9. Requires that the data be presented to those responsible for the decision making and planning processes in a form which minimizes the need for analysis and interpretation.

10. Provides flexibility and adaptability to change.

The concept of management information is one that would be equally valid if the company were small or large or if the data were obtained and processed through the most simple manual means or through the most sophisticated computer. Management must, to design a system, select at each level of control only the data that are required. The data must be presented in a manner which facilitates understanding and action and provides a measure of the effectiveness of the action which has been and is being taken.

Most growing companies and many mature companies show certain symptoms or clear indications of what we can call "information hunger." Some of these symptoms may, of course, arise simply from poor management, even when the information system is adequate, but we have listed them here because they are so common and often so baffling even to competent managers. Many managers just do not realize that the information on which they are basing even their most routine decisions may be dangerously inadequate or misleading because their information system is not geared to the needs of their company. Let us turn to Chart 4 and consider the 25 symptoms any or any combination of which may indicate an inadequate information system.

In the operational aspect of the business, they range from large inventory adjustments to a sterile R&D program; in the human aspect, from inability to note the significance of certain financial indicators to overloaded briefcases and poring over reports at midnight.

Any executive will do well to study these symptoms and note whether his organization exhibits one or more of them. A study of the present scope of management information in the typical enterprise (Chart 5) and a comparison of the typical management informational efforts with the values to be received through each (Chart 6) show that in the typical organization management is either using its information facilities too narrowly or has not developed facilities

OPERATIONAL	PSYCHOLOGICAL	REPORT CONTENT
Large physical inventory adjustments	Surprise at financial results	Excessive use of tabulations of figures
Capital expenditure overruns	Poor attitude of executives about usefulness of information	Multiple preparation and distribution of identical data
Inability of executives to explain changes from year to year in operating results	Lack of understanding of financial information on part of nonfinancial executives	Disagreeing information from different sources
Uncertain direction of company growth	Lack of concern for environmental changes	Lack of periodic comparative information and trends
Cost variances unexplainable	Executive homework reviewing reports considered excessive	Lateness of information
No order backlog awareness		Too little or excess detail
No internal discussion of reported data		Inaccurate information
Insufficient knowledge about competition		Lack of standards for comparison
Purchasing parts from outside vendors when internal capability and capacity to make is available		Failure to identify variances by cause and responsibility
Record of some "sour" investments in facilities, or in programs, such as R & D and advertising		Inadequate externally generated information

CHART 4

SYMPTOMS OF AN INADEQUATE MANAGEMENT INFORMATION SYSTEM

of the necessary scope and significance to ensure the enterprise's future. As indicated, most managements devote 90 per cent of their efforts to obtaining information which will enable them to operate and control and only about 5 per cent of their efforts to obtaining the necessary information to meet competition and another 5 per cent to obtaining the information needed to meet future needs. These proportions do not make the organization adaptable to change and may lead to such stagnation or such poor preparation that a competitor's new product or a change in consumers' tastes and needs may knock the enterprise right out of the ball game.

Kinds of Information Needed

What, then, are the kinds of information which managers need? They can be grouped into three major categories: information which various company executives require for operation and control, information required to assess future action, and information required to assess or compare performance by the company in competition or within the industry.

Let us look first at information required for management operation and control. A great deal has been written on this subject, and most organizations of any size or sophistication have developed fairly good and reliable information-generating systems for operations (production, inventory, efficiency). Where they often fall down is in the selection, organization, and processing of this information. The best method of employing such information is that of rigid selection by need—that is, sending key information to executives, information processed purely for the management requirements as indicated and requested by the recipients. A system called *Key Item Control* (described in *Management Services,* January-February, '67, p. 21) gives a detailed discussion of such a method.

Control, of course, is obtained by comparing actual performance for each given activity with pre-established goals set at each level. The principal value of presenting key items to management using exception techniques is that it focuses management attention on the important areas of operation which require action. A typical operating report of this type (Chart 7) shows how the tabular information normally presented in a company could be re-presented to enhance understanding and provide data for decision. This is done through a blending of narrative, graphic, and tabular techniques of presenting information.

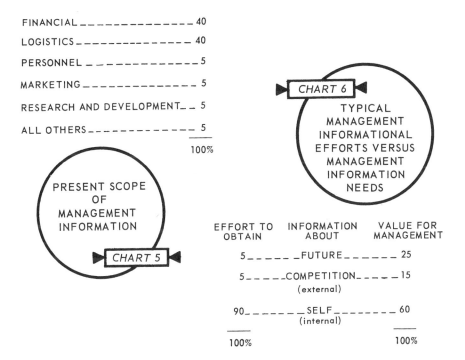

FINANCIAL _ _ _ _ _ _ _ _ _ _ _ _ _ 40

LOGISTICS _ _ _ _ _ _ _ _ _ _ _ _ 40

PERSONNEL _ _ _ _ _ _ _ _ _ _ _ 5

MARKETING _ _ _ _ _ _ _ _ _ _ _ 5

RESEARCH AND DEVELOPMENT _ _ 5

ALL OTHERS _ _ _ _ _ _ _ _ _ _ _ 5

100%

PRESENT SCOPE OF MANAGEMENT INFORMATION

▶ CHART 5 ◀

CHART 6

TYPICAL MANAGEMENT INFORMATIONAL EFFORTS VERSUS MANAGEMENT INFORMATION NEEDS

EFFORT TO OBTAIN	INFORMATION ABOUT	VALUE FOR MANAGEMENT
5 _ _ _ _ _ _	FUTURE _ _ _ _ _ _	25
5 _ _ _ _ _	COMPETITION _ _ _ _ (external)	15
90 _ _ _ _ _ _	SELF _ _ _ _ _ _ _ (internal)	60
100%		100%

EXAMPLE OF A
KEY ITEM
MANAGEMENT
INFORMATION
SYSTEMS
REPORT

CHART 7

PERIODIC MANUFACTURING REPORT
PERFORMANCE HIGHLIGHTS

Shipments increased as expected this month. However, Herron Manufacturing Co., one of our principal motor suppliers, was on strike until four weeks ago. Accordingly, we were not able to build inventory as planned in preparation for the added shipments. As a result, we had to go to a partial third shift for the assembly department and add a number of new employees throughout the plants this month. The inexperience of the new employees and the lack of adequate supervision on the partial third shift led to decreased delivery performance and labor productivity, particularly in the machining department. These problems have been largely corrected and we expect improved performance next month.

KEY INFORMATION

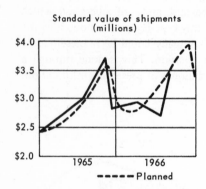

Standard value of shipments
(millions)

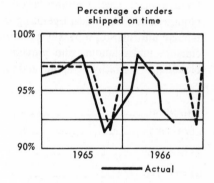

Percentage of orders
shipped on time

	ACTUAL AS PERCENTAGE OF		
	Actual	*Plan*	*Last year*
YEAR TO DATE EXPENDITURES (millions)			
Operating—controllable	$15.61	102%	122%
Operating—uncontrollable	$ 5.95	101%	109%
Capital	$ 1.10	104%	81%
% OF TOOLS PASSED INSPECTION			
Month	97.6%	98%	99%
To date	99.4%	99%	100%
% OF LABOR PRODUCTIVITY			
Month	91.5%	93%	94%
To date	98.1%	101%	103%
INVENTORY TURNOVER	3.9 times	98%	100%

The overall highlights of the operations are given in a narrative summary. Graphs present comparisons of present performance with planned performance in the framework of trends to provide current perspective, and tables provide key figures of detail information.

Let us now suggest the kinds of information which should be generated in two key areas, financial and research and development (Chart 8 and Chart 9). Some 23 items are suggested in the financial area in Chart 8, and 15 items in the R&D area in Chart 9. It can be seen that the data vary widely from an analysis of sources and availability of capital in the financial area to a research personnel analysis in the R&D segment. Nevertheless, top management must consider all the kinds of information its operations require and then turn to the task of processing this information to achieve maximum use from it.

The financial information available to management is usually quite complete. Often, however, the accounting data are not as integrated with operating control information as would be practical or desirable. Frequently the chart of accounts

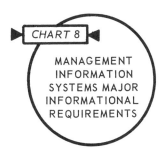

CHART 8

MANAGEMENT INFORMATION SYSTEMS MAJOR INFORMATIONAL REQUIREMENTS

FINANCIAL

Cash and working capital positions, forecasts, analyses

Current ratios

Line of credit utilization

Temporary investment opportunities

Accounts receivable turnover, age, collection status, problem accounts

Inventory investment analysis

Debt to equity status

Adequacy of reserves

Analysis of surplus

Long-term spending requirements

  —R & D

  —new products

  —capital assets

Sources and availability of capital

Short-term requirements

Money market developments

Stock

  —ownership changes

  —prices and P/E trends

  —analyst opinions

Lease obligations

Financial guarantees and other contingent obligations

Adequacy of insurance coverage

Tax situation

Internal accounting control situation

provides information for audit, internal control, or tax purposes but not specifically for management control. Often major improvement would result from integrating operating management information with cost management information. In this approach, the source documents used to provide information for operating statistical purposes would provide cost and financial management information as direct products.

Techniques of Improvement

Substantial improvement in most companies' management information would result from the following:

1. Increased use of ratios to provide improved understanding of the effects or results of operations, including graphic presentations of the ratios to provide analysis of both short-term and long-range trends. The data would also provide

RESEARCH AND
DEVELOPMENT

Knowledge of research discoveries
and advances in existing knowledge

Research opportunities

Research goals and balance of effort

Research proposal evaluation

   —product improvements

   —new products

   —new materials

   —process improvements

Research projects

   —status—technically

   —status—cost

Research personnel

   —qualifications

   —experience

Scientist support

Research space/person

Research cost as % of sales

Historical evidence of value
of research to company

CHART 9

MANAGEMENT
INFORMATION
SYSTEMS MAJOR
INFORMATIONAL
REQUIREMENTS

an improved basis for forecasting probable future events, particularly in the cost area.

2. Use of information developed from using work sampling, work measurement, and work simplification techniques. This would provide improved measures of the effectiveness of personnel in the clerical and production groups. In addition, these techniques would permit costs of specific operations to be determined and would enable management to determine the most efficient and least costly way to perform them. A further benefit of using such techniques would be the development of cost data which would be integrated with operating statistical data and thus improve management information.

3. Increased use of network techniques of presentation. Specifically, this would place in focus all of the events that would be involved in a particular management activity and would define their relationship to each other. This technique could be of great value in determining the chain of events which must take place in order to implement a management of decision which was made on the basis of improved management information. It would also provide understanding of the time and personnel which would be involved in such an implementation.

4. Increased use of PERT techniques in the cost system. The PERT technique places cost information in relation to the event occurrence. This approach would incorporate the principles of flexible budgeting.

5. Increased use of incremental cost concepts. These would improve the decision making related to costs of operating facilities at various production levels. This cost concept would provide management with an improved tool for determining the cost effect of operating a given facility at different specific levels or volumes of production by measuring the cost effect in major steps or increments rather than only by an average slope or trend.

6. Increased use of data processing equipment as a means of securing vital data in a timely and effective manner to implement the new concepts involved.

7. Increased attention to the development of a stimulating incentive which would serve as a motivation to management to take action on the basis of the information provided by an improved management information and control system.

Range of Information

Each chief executive represents a different company of different size in a different location. To a large extent, his problems are individual. He does, however, operate within the framework of a certain industry and can make decisions based on analyses of the data in a specific industry.

To illustrate the range of information which might be significant to the management of a typical company, let us now turn to a study of information of the second category: information required to assess future action. For our purposes let us call our illustrative company Company X (although they do not make the well known "Brand X"). This company markets a product in the consumer industry and is affected by consumer patterns of spending. What kind of information would management review to plan and assess future action? Let us consider the following data:

Population Growth Effect

First, management might look at the effect of growth in population (Chart 10). In 1910 the population of the United States was about 90 million people. The population now is close to 200 million; the population has doubled in less than the lifetime of most managers. As you can see from the projection for 1975, population is expected to increase another 30 per cent to 40 per cent in this shorter time. We are in an era of rapidly changing, rapidly increasing population.

The growing population has very interesting characteristics for our Company X. Perhaps the most significant is shown in Chart 11. This is a measure, since 1900, of per capita disposable personal income. Income for the individual has gone from less than $1,000 per person in 1900 to almost $3,000 per person and is rising at an increasing rate; it is expected to approach $4,000 by 1980. Such predictions have often proved to be conservative. We have a rising population which is living better.

Now Company X management might consider the effect of this increase in per capita income and the additional increase in the working population as reflected in per household disposable income (Chart 12). As noted, this income has gone from $4,000 to $6,000 per household since 1939 and is expected to exceed $10,000 in ten years. Gross national product, which has nearly tripled since 1950, is likely to pass the $1,000-billion mark by 1975 (Chart 13). Next, management of Company X can note that, in the period since 1950, our total of consumer expenditures in the United States has gone from $200 billion to $400 billion (Chart 14). The population in this period has not doubled, but our per capita income has just about doubled.

What does this mean for Company X? It means people have much more money to spend individually and, therefore, in total. One of the most interesting things is that, with this income, expenditures have become more discretionary. People have more money, but they have begun spending it in different ways even in the short span of ten to fifteen years. Chart 15 indicates that in 1950 our population was spending almost 23 per cent of its total income for food. By 1962 this had dropped to 19 per cent. This growing population which has more money is spending it increasingly in areas other than for food—spending it for clothing, shelter, transportation; for moving to suburban areas of larger homes where people have an average of almost two cars per family; spending it on increased recreation—or better living.

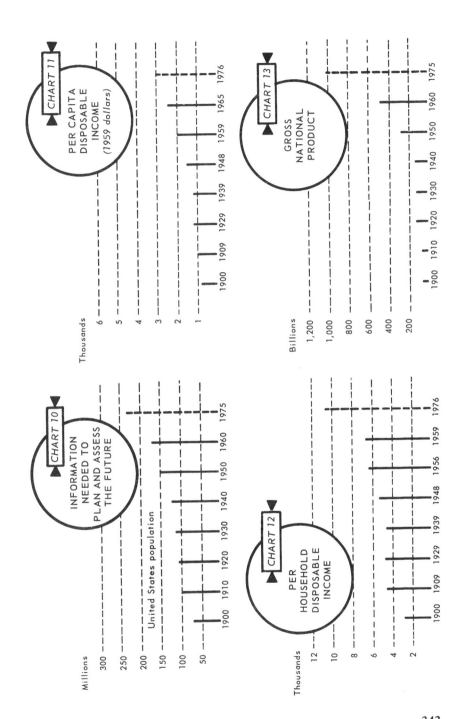

CHART 10 — INFORMATION NEEDED TO PLAN AND ASSESS THE FUTURE

United States population (Millions): 300, 250, 200, 150, 100, 50 — 1900 1910 1920 1930 1940 1950 1960 1975

CHART 11 — PER CAPITA DISPOSABLE INCOME (1959 dollars)

Thousands: 6, 5, 4, 3, 2, 1 — 1900 1909 1929 1939 1948 1959 1965 1976

CHART 12 — PER HOUSEHOLD DISPOSABLE INCOME

Thousands: 12, 10, 8, 6, 4, 2 — 1900 1909 1929 1939 1948 1956 1959 1976

CHART 13 — GROSS NATIONAL PRODUCT

Billions: 1,200, 1,000, 800, 600, 400, 200 — 1900 1910 1920 1930 1940 1950 1960 1975

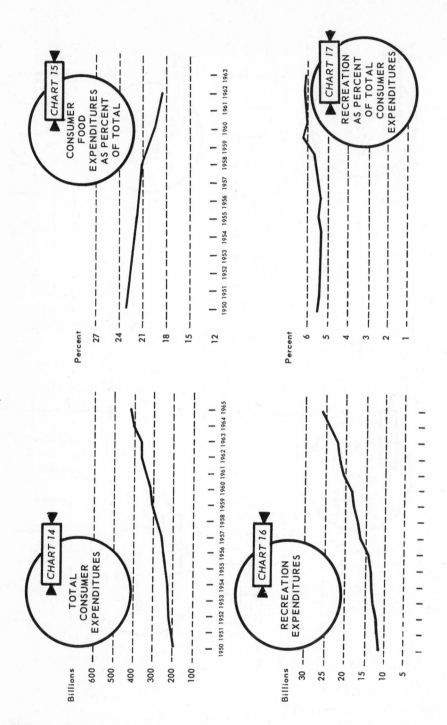

CHART 15

CONSUMER FOOD EXPENDITURES AS PERCENT OF TOTAL

Percent

27
24
21
18
15
12

1950 1951 1952 1953 1954 1955 1956 1957 1958 1959 1960 1961 1962 1963

CHART 17

RECREATION AS PERCENT OF TOTAL CONSUMER EXPENDITURES

Percent

6
5
4
3
2
1

CHART 14

TOTAL CONSUMER EXPENDITURES

Billions

600
500
400
300
200
100

1950 1951 1952 1953 1954 1955 1956 1957 1958 1959 1960 1961 1962 1963 1964 1965

CHART 16

RECREATION EXPENDITURES

Billions

30
25
20
15
10
5

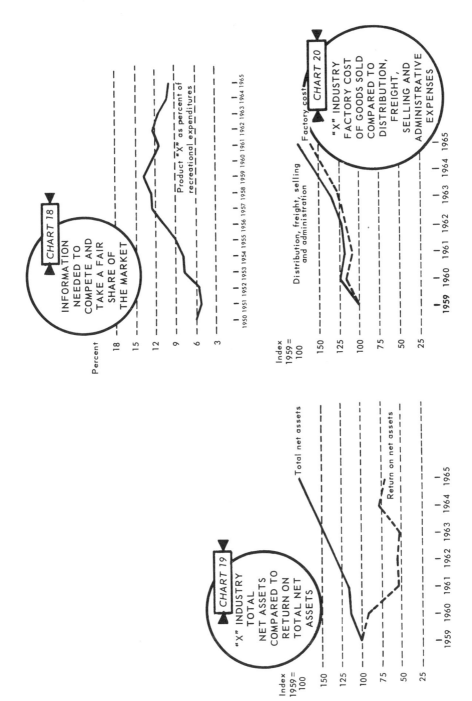

CHART 18

INFORMATION NEEDED TO COMPETE AND TAKE A FAIR SHARE OF THE MARKET

Percent

18
15
12
9
6
3

Product "X" as percent of recreational expenditures

1950 1951 1952 1953 1954 1955 1956 1957 1958 1959 1960 1961 1962 1963 1964 1965

CHART 20

"X" INDUSTRY FACTORY COST OF GOODS SOLD COMPARED TO DISTRIBUTION, FREIGHT, SELLING AND ADMINISTRATIVE EXPENSES

Index 1959 = 100

150
125
100
75
50
25

Factory cost

Distribution, freight, selling and administration

1959 1960 1961 1962 1963 1964 1965

CHART 19

"X" INDUSTRY TOTAL NET ASSETS COMPARED TO RETURN ON TOTAL NET ASSETS

Index 1959 = 100

150
125
100
75
50
25

Total net assets

Return on net assets

1959 1960 1961 1962 1963 1964 1965

345

Recreation Expenditures

Perhaps the most significant characteristic of the economy for the industry in which Company X operates is shown in Chart 16 which charts the expenditures on recreation. This chart indicates that these expenditures have increased from about 12 billion to 27 billion dollars, more than doubling in the past 15 years.

As Chart 17 indicates, in this period the consumer expenditures on recreation as a per cent of total expenditures have risen from 5 per cent to over 6 per cent as a result of the shift in consumer interests.

We now come to that third category of information—the information needed to compete in an industry and to obtain a fair share of the market. Here we present some of the kinds of information in this category and show how the managers of our Company X might use it to place themselves in the industry.

We can start with some calculations for Product X made by our company showing the expenditures for Product X as a per cent of total recreational expenditures (Chart 18). This ratio indicates that, while there was a rise from the 1950 to 1959 period, there has been a downward trend in the past six years, with a reduction from 12 per cent to 9 per cent, or almost a 25 per cent change in the ratio. For planning purposes in this industry, this should be a significant area of concern.

One of the measures of profitability of a company is that of return on net assest. It reflects the return on this protion of the investment in the company. As shown on Chart 19, the return from the period of 1959 to just recently has definitely gone down about 30 per cent in a period where the net assets themselves were rising over 50 per cent. This indicates weakness in cost control, a key requirement in remaining competitive.

Another measure which might well affect competitive position is the change in cost of goods sold as compared to selling, distribution, and administrative expenses (Chart 20). This analysis indicates a significant increase exceeding 50 per cent for the period, with the trend increasing for the overhead costs in relation to factory costs. This indicates a need for review of manpower utilization and distribution cost controls.

A third measure might be the pre-tax earnings as a per cent of sales for the "X" industry compared to twelve major industries for the past year (Chart 21). The chart indicates that in relative ranking, the "X" industry has the lowest per cent of earnings.

Fourth, management might look at the annual inventory turnover rate for the same group of industries (Chart 22). The desirability of management action to improve its cash position as indicated by this measure of performance is clear.

Next let us observe the measure of sales change from 1964 to 1965 (Chart 23). The chart indicates that "X" industry is average as compared to the group.

Moving Out Ahead

Up to now we have been speaking generally about industry averages. Perhaps the most significant item noticed in Company X's relationship with companies in

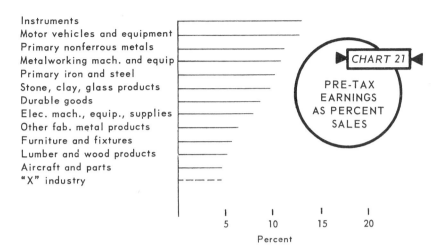

Instruments
Motor vehicles and equipment
Primary nonferrous metals
Metalworking mach. and equip
Primary iron and steel
Stone, clay, glass products
Durable goods
Elec. mach., equip., supplies
Other fab. metal products
Furniture and fixtures
Lumber and wood products
Aircraft and parts
"X" industry

CHART 21

PRE-TAX
EARNINGS
AS PERCENT
SALES

5   10   15   20

Percent

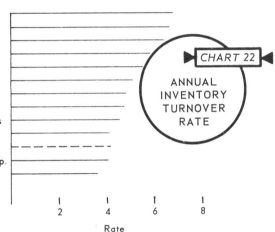

Stone, clay, glass products
Furniture and fixtures
Lumber and wood products
Motor vehicles and equip.
Primary iron and steel
Other fab. metal products
Primary nonferrous metals
Durable goods
Elec. mach., equip., supplies
Instruments
"X" industry
Metalworking mach. and equip.
Aircraft and parts

CHART 22

ANNUAL
INVENTORY
TURNOVER
RATE

2   4   6   8

Rate

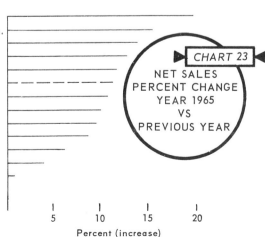

Primary iron and steel
Metalworking mach. and equip.
Instruments
Primary nonferrous metals
Other fab. metal products
"X" industry
Durable goods
Motor vehicles and equipment
Elec. mach., equip., supplies
Furniture and fixtures
Lumber and wood products
Stone, clay, glass products
Aircraft and parts

CHART 23

NET SALES
PERCENT CHANGE
YEAR 1965
VS
PREVIOUS YEAR

5   10   15   20

Percent (increase)

its industry is the effect of individual management ability and action. One can go along with the crowd. A company can become profitable as its industry becomes profitable, or it can lose money as the industry loses money if it acts only as the average company does. There have been dramatic instances which show that when management of a specific company takes dynamic aggressive action, it can (despite what has happened on the average to the industry in general) make its company more profitable than average. It can use the information in an improved management information system for management action.

Let us then consider the case of Company X as an instance of this kind of action. To protect the identity of our illustrative company, we will not identify specific years or the specific industry.

Let us look, however, at this actual industry and Company X. Chart 24 shows industry average sales for a recent eight-year period compared with sales for Company X. The industry sales increased through the period as shown in previous charts, rising 20 per cent in the eight-year period. The sales of Company X doubled in the same period as a result of the policy that it had adopted.

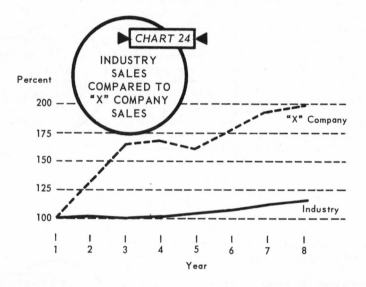

Turning to the ratio of net profits on sales for a recent four-year period in Chart 25 we note that industry profit on sales has stayed generally about 2 per cent, declining slightly as shown in earlier charts. Profit on sales for Company X, however, rose from 2 per cent to almost 5 per cent in the same period as a result of the individual actions which management in that company had taken.

In the ratio of net profit to invested capital (Chart 26), the industry in the recent four-year period has shown a rate of about 10 per cent and slightly decreasing. The profit picture of Company X is considerably more attractive than the industry average, increasing from 17 per cent to almost 25 per cent in the same period.

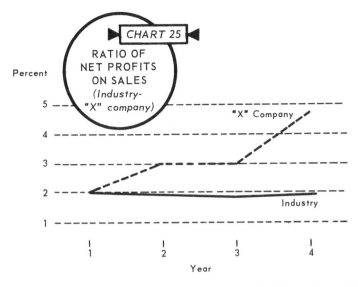

With regard to the ratio of current assets to current liabilities (Chart 27) for a recent three-year period of Company X as compared with eight individual companies representative generally of companies in the industry, the ratio of assets to liabilities for the companies in the industry has changed very little, while in the three-year period Company X has rapidly increased its ratio to a more and more attractive figure.

These charts show clearly the effect when individual management takes action, based on information available through its information system—when a company does not merely follow the trends in the industry, but makes its own trend. There are many factors to consider in improving profits. By itself, no system, no

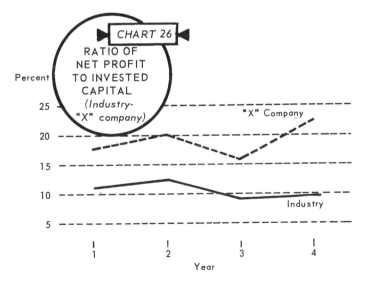

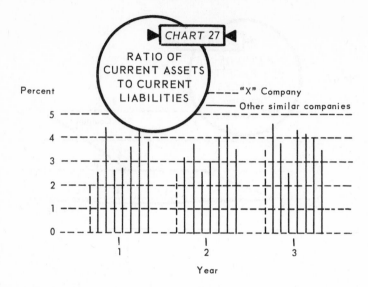

data processing installation, no plant modernization can do the whole job. Each must, to be effective, operate within the framework of good management, and good management always and everywhere depends on good information.

The manager in industry operates in the present in influencing his profit picture. Knowledge of past and present operations, as shown in our charts, is one of his basic tools. However, the manager must plan for the future to assure continuity of profits. To do this, he needs a good forecast of future demands on materials, labor, facilities, and capital, and good forecasting again requires good information.

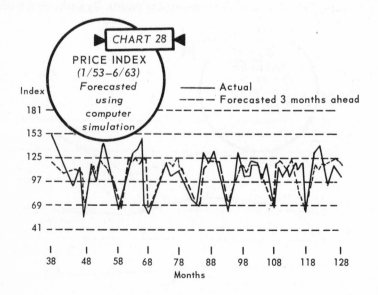

In recent years, tools for prediction have been greatly improved. The use of mathematical techniques for quantifying and analyzing probability have provided important contributions to the management decision making process. Increasingly, the use of computers for rapid solution of mathematical "models" of business problems has provided a tool which can increase profitability of operations.

To illustrate, in Chart 28 results are shown which were obtained from forecasting using a simulation technique recently developed by a Price Waterhouse & Co. mathematician, J. L. Ray. The solid line shows the actual price index for the 128-month period from 1953 to mid-1963. The dotted line shows the price index forecast by the model three months in advance of the actual month.

The computer program is designed so that, for example, at month 40, the computer reviews the predicted price index for month 40, the actual price index reported for month 40, the deviation from prediction for month 40, and the deviation pattern for each previous month of actual to forecast. The program then calculates the best prediction for month 43 based on all past history. This forecast simulator is a general purpose tool which has proven to be remarkably effective in a wide variety of predictions. It provides the manager of today a technique for improvement of his decision making.

In summary, the profit picture in any company in the future will be to a significant extent a result of the gathering and intelligent use of good information. Each company should be concerned that it is providing its managers with the kind and quality of information they need to do their job well.

34

The Organizational
Impact of Computers

HAK CHONG LEE
State University of New York at Albany

From the earliest days of electronic data processing there has been general agreement that the new information technology would have a profound impact upon the structures and personnel of the organizations that adopted it. There has been much less agreement about the nature of that impact.

Predictions of widespread labor displacement, the elimination of middle management, and increasing centralization of decision making have not yet come true. On the other hand, they have not yet been conclusively disproved. Despite more than a decade of rapid expansion of the use of computers and growing sophistication in their application, the patterns of change are not yet clear.

A number of research studies have supplemented the speculation and opinions about the impact of the computer on business organizations, but their results differ to such a degree that it is difficult to gain a clear understanding of exactly what is happening. The purpose of this article is to summarize and evaluate the present knowledge of how computers are affecting organizational structure, administrative decision making, employment, and the skill content of employees' jobs; to determine the extent to which individuals agree on these effects; and, if conflict is found, to analyze the arguments.

The first question about which there has been a great deal of discussion is whether computers are going to centralize or decentralize the organizational structure and the process of administrative decision making. The best known and perhaps most controversial view on this question was expressed by Harold Leavitt and Thomas Whisler in their famous *Harvard Business Review* article, "Management in the 1980's."[1]   In that article they made three important predictions.

[1] Harold J. Leavitt and Thomas L. Whisler, "Management in the 1980's," *Harvard Business Review*, November-December 1958, pp. 41-48.

First, they forecast that electronic computers would change the organizational structure drastically by forcing the regrouping of activities carried out in various functional divisions and at various levels of the organization. Because computers would make it possible to integrate on the basis of the organization as a whole a large volume of business information that was formerly segmented, a computer-using company would find it expedient to standardize operational procedures throughout the organization. This would lead to a great deal of consolidation of activities that had been functionally and geographically separate.

Secondly, Leavitt and Whisler predicted increased use of computers to process more and more of the routine management decisions. Assuming that the bulk of middle managers' work consisted of rather routine decisions, these authors concluded that middle management jobs would gradually be automated and taken over by computers. Thus, the magnitude of the computer's impact would be proportionately greater at the middle management level than at the clerical level.

They also foresaw a shift to top management of a larger proportion of innovating, planning, and creative functions, with concomitant centralization of the organization structure and the decision making process. All these changes would have a drastic effect on the shape of the organizational structure. Top management would "bulge" as middle management would "thin out." The overall organizational structure would change from the traditional pyramid shape to a shape looking something like a "football balanced upon the point of a church bell."

A number of actual research studies have tended to support the views of Leavitt and Whisler. Ida Hoos, for example, found in her study of nineteen business organizations[2] that computer applications in these companies had led to some radical changes in the organizational structure and in managerial decision making. Many jobs at middle management levels had been either combined or eliminated. Communication systems and decision making patterns in the organizations were undergoing changes, generally in the direction of centralization. As more and more operations were programed in the data processing department, the functions of operating departments were often undercut and the authority of many department managers truncated while the power and status of new computer personnel expanded.

Acceptance of Leavitt and Whisler's views is far from unanimous, however, Melvin Anshen,[3] for example, agrees with them about the increased use of computers in the areas of managerial decisions. But he takes issue with them on the question of how computers are going to affect the organizational structure and the locus of decision making.

Anshen believes that computers will be limited to repetitive decisions based on

[2]Ida R. Hoos, "When the Computer Takes Over the Office," *Harvard Business Review*, July-August 1960, pp. 102-112.

[3]Melvin Anshen, "Manager and the Black Box," *Harvard Business Review*, November-December 1960, pp. 85-92.

already quantified records of existing accounting, cost, and financial data and will leave relatively untouched such managerial decision areas as finding problems, setting objectives, implementing decisions, and evaluating results, all of which require a great deal of management imagination and creative thinking. As a result, instead of gradually eliminating middle managers, computers will relieve them of repetitive decision making and related paperwork and thus give them more time to concentrate on creative and judgmental tasks. Instead of being shifted upward or absorbed completely into computers, the work of middle managers may become more like that of top managers.

Anshen denies that computers will necessarily lead to centralization of the organization structure or the decision making process. The trend toward decentralization may be slowed down, he says, but if this happens it will be caused by the geographic relocation of decision centers, not by abandonment of efforts to decentralize managerial responsibilities.

Anshen's views have also been supported by research studies. Donald Shaul,[4] for example, found in a number of companies that had installed electronic computers that middle managers had not been seriously threatened but rather that their roles in the organization had become more important than ever. The organization structure had not changed a great deal, offering little indication that greater centralization follows the installation of computers.

There is general agreement that computers, with their vast capacity to manipulate management information, will affect the process of managerial decision making. There is much less agreement, however, on the scope of the computer's potential in automating decisions and on the vulnerability of middle managers to displacement by computer programs. It is also recognized that the use of computers tends to require standardization of operating procedures and integration of data. Opinions differ, however, as to whether these changes necessarily mean more centralization of decision making and a change in the conventional pyramid form of organization structure. The evidence so far on all these points is inconclusive.

Manpower Displacement

Another hotly debated question is the effect of computers on employment. At issue are both the effect on total employment—in the company and in the economy—and the effect on the relative proportions of various types of employees, such as managers, technical personnel, and clerical workers.

Technological employment has been a controversial subject since the time of the Industrial Revolution, but concern has heightened in recent years because of the growth of computer "automation." Reduction in the number of employees (usually clerical) in that part of the organization immediately and directly related to the computer operations has been widely anticipated. This

[4]Donald R. Shaul, "What's Really Ahead for Middle Management?" *Personnel*, November-December 1964, pp. 8-16.

anticipation has proved correct for the most part, as is shown by a number of research studies.[5] However, there has been no reduction in clerical employment in the economy as a whole and often none in the individual companies affected. The effect of the computer seems to have been to slow rather than reverse the rate of growth in clerical employment.

The computer's effect on the relative proportion of various types of employees is less clear-cut. As was previously discussed, Leavitt and Whisler expect that, since much of the work of middle managers can and will be programmed into computers, manpower reduction will be greater at the management than at the clerical level. On the other hand, Anshen's belief that computerization will be limited to routine, repetitive decisions implies the reverse.

Actual research findings so far seem to support Anshen's view rather than that of Leavitt and Whisler. Indications are that manpower reductions have been greater in the clerical than in the managerial work force, both in absolute terms and in proportion to the total employment in the organization.[6] In some cases, indeed, the total number of managers in computer-affected departments has increased rather than decreased. Whether this trend may be expected to continue is far from certain at this time, particularly in view of the growing sophistication with which the computer is being applied to managerial decision making.

The only personnel change that seems to be more or less certain is that the installation of a computer increases the number of staff positions, mostly technical, directly associated with the computer operations. This increase is both absolute, in terms of total numbers, and relative, in proportion to the total employment.

Job Content

Another problem is how computers change the work content of those jobs that remain. The questions include how computers affect the overall skill level required in a job; how they affect specific work skill aspects of a job, such as mental, clerical, physical, etc.; and how they affect the distribution of work skill content among various types of jobs, such as clerical and managerial.

Because of the assumption that technology tends to mechanize unskilled and routine tasks, it is generally thought that computers tend to reduce the unskilled work component and increase the skilled task work component of affected jobs. There is considerable support for this view.

As was discussed earlier, Anshen believes that the jobs of computer-affected middle managers will be upgraded when computers take over the routine tasks,

[5] For example, see Hak Chong Lee, *The Impact of Electronic Data Processing Upon the Patterns of Business Organization and Administration,* School of Business, State University of New York at Albany, 1965, pp. 27-29.

[6] For example, see U.S. Bureau of Labor Statistics, *Adjustments to the Installation of Office Automation,* Bulletin No. 1276, Department of Labor, Washington, D. C., May 1960, and Edgar Weinberg, "Experiences with the Introduction of Office Automation," *The Monthly Labor Review,* April 1960, pp. 367-380.

leaving the managers free for more creative and more analytical work.[7] Shaul's previously cited study also supports the idea of increased skills for managerial personnel.[8]

George Delehanty found in his study of several insurance companies[9] that the general skill level of clerks was shifted upward after computers began to be used. After the installation of computers in these organizations, as compared to before the computer, there were fewer clerical jobs distributed over low-grade classifications and more jobs over high-grade classifications. There also are other studies that generally support the existence of a tendency toward increased skill requirements in clerical jobs as well as managerial ones.[10]

Other studies, however, have indicated a different tendency. Some researchers, finding that computers upgraded some jobs while downgrading others, concluded that it was difficult to find a consistent pattern one way or the other.[11] Other studies have found the skill level of the affected jobs largely unchanged; upgrading was limited to so small a number of jobs that there was practically no change in the overall work skill requirements after the computer installation.[12]

A study by James Bright,[13] however, showed a definite—and different—trend of change in work skills as a result of technological change. Through intensive analyses of different stages of computer-integrated manufacturing technology, he found that work became easier and less demanding at high stages of technology. Thus, he suggests a pattern of decrease rather than increase in the overall level of skill requirements.

Here again, the verdict must be "not proven." Much more research needs to be done on the computer's effect on skill requirements; existing observations on the subject are largely in generalities, lacking precise measurement of the magnitude of changes.

Special Problems

Why do opinions and research findings about the organizational impact of computers differ so sharply? One obvious problem is semantics. Frequently those whose opinions differ also differ in the meanings they attach to such key words as centralization, decentralization, decisions, work skills, managers,

[7] Anshen, *op. cit.*

[8] Shaul, *op. cit.*

[9] George E. Delehanty, "Office Automation and the Occupation Structure: A Case Study of Five Insurance Companies," *Industrial Management Review*, Spring 1966, pp. 99-110.

[10] For example, see Harold F. Craig, *Administrating a Conversion to Electronic Accounting*, Harvard Graduate School of Business Administration, Boston, 1955, pp. 68-70.

[11] C. Edward Weber, "Impact of Electronic Data Processing on Clerical Skills," *Personnel Administration*, January-February 1959, pp. 20-26.

[12] Jack Stieber, "Automation and the White-Collar Worker," *Personnel*, November-December 1957, pp. 12-16.

[13] James R. Bright, *Automation and Management*, Harvard University, Boston, 1958, pp. 186-189.

clerical workers, and technical employees. This, of course, magnifies the differences among the opinions and also presents serious methodological problems in the conduct of research studies and the evaluation of their findings. It is crucial that a common understanding of these vital terms be attained by everybody.

Another, perhaps more important, problem is the discrepancy among evaluations of computer technology. "Experts" differ not only about future developments in computer science and the possibility of programing currently "unstructured" decisions but even about the current capability of computers in decision making.

Furthermore, the results of research studies in different organizations may differ because of differences in the way computers are used and the length of time they have been used in these organizations. For example, in companies that have been using computers primarily for accounting and financial purposes for a relatively short period of time the organizational changes may not be as drastic or as extensive as in companies where computers have been used for managment decision making purposes and/or for a longer period of time.

A final source of conflicting opinions is the failure of researchers to recognize the importance of managerial philosophies, objectives, and policies toward both the computer applications and the changes that these applications are expected to bring about in the organization. The managerial attitude toward initiating and accommodating the changes is also a major variable governing the nature and magnitude of changes in the organizational structure, in employment, and in the work content of affected jobs.

Clearly, understanding of how computers affect the organization is essential to effective manpower and organizational planning. It is important, therefore, that the various opinions and research findings on the impact of computers be evaluated and interpreted with adequate cognizance of (1) the variations in the meaning given to key terminology used in describing the changing organizational patterns, (2) the nature and maturity of computer applications in an organization, and (3) the managerial attitude toward introducing and handling the changes in the organization. Recognition of the semantic problems and of the variables conditioning the organizational changes will promote better understanding of the nature of the computer's impact.

It is also important to realize that computer technology is always advancing, that computer applications are continually expanding, and that managerial philosophies and policies are continually adapting to changes in the techno-logical environment.

Thus, the organizational impact of computers is changing all the time. As a result, continuing study is needed to clarify the issues and search for major organizational variables that may underlie the definite patterns of change that may be common to all computer applications.

35

'Interface'— Computerized Management Information Systems and Corporate Management-Staff Relationships

ROBERT L. JOHNSON
Stanford Research Institute

The Environment

The corporate organization for the generation and transfer of management information is in a constant flux. Steady state is neither expected nor desired, since both the content and nature of information are in continuous change.

Maturation and growth of a business enterprise introduce changes in personnel and methods of operation. Responsibility is redistributed to make use of the number and type of skills available. Each change in organization or methods is accompanied with predictions of doom and gloom. (The change itself is often a reaction to warnings of disaster to befall unless the suggested changes are made.)

The corporation characteristically survives, in some fashion, despite its introduction of the new organization or process or its failure to introduce the change. Corporate management often must choose between the inefficiencies of changes that are "too early" or "too late." In the one case, resistance to change and job (or status) protection activity interferes with the efficient modification of the corporate structure or methods. In the other, the overloading of staff and facilities introduces excessive costs.

The executive often is faced with the problem of timing to satisfy the admonition, "Be not the first by whom the new is tried, nor yet the last to cast the old aside." Competition dictates a level of efficiency; guts alone often determine whether the decision is made in time to reach and keep that level, since the executive usually lacks good information on which to base a decision or choice.

Management attempts to correct the information deficiency underlying many changes in organization and methods. Attempts by those in the management communications system to avoid or subvert change—to maintain the status quo—create additional problems for management.

Changes are made in response to problems, and they create new problems. One problem attending any major change in the flow or distribution of management information is that of organizational structure and extrastructural relationships. Unless faced and planned for as part of the information system design and implementation problem, this aspect is likely to be more detrimental than any other technical or administrative problem.

Activity

Specialization of the information processing function appeared early in social organization. When time, distance, or number prevented the manager from direct observation and control of his subordinates, delegation of authority brought a distinguishable reporting system into being.

As the scope of reporting activity broadened, functional specialization began in information handling. Financial, engineering, production, and marketing reports and records took on individual identities. Within the operating organizations, the task of collecting, assembling, and reporting information was segregated from the "mission" tasks, and was delegated to clerks. The shop clerk, for example, was made responsible for keeping shop records and for reporting to the foreman or production manager. This trend bothered some shop foremen or managers, who feared that their job security was threatened; but others accepted it as an opportunity to shed the burden of paper work. Both points of view polarized as the clerical job broadened into work planning, machine load scheduling, and order dispatching—and became an identifiable production planning and control organization.

The effect on the organizational structure, and on personnel relations, was obvious at this stage. Shop clerks were moved from the direct supervision of the section foreman into a new group under a "planning foreman" on the same managerial level. As the concept and the organization developed, the function broadened and moved upward until the shop clerk—section foreman relationship had been reversed, with the former clerk now giving direction to the foreman (in the name of the production manager, of course).

At the corporate management level, a similar phenomenon developed. The profusion of reports saturated the reading and reaction capability of upper management, and a staff function appeared on the organization chart. The management staff was given responsibility for the collection, analysis, and interpretation of reports from operating and functional staff organizations and for the development of reports and recommendations for upper management.

The organizational chart graphically described the planned network of information communication within the enterprise. The systems and procedures function developed and became an organizational entity. This group was made responsible for the development of standards for the form, language, and timing of reports and for monitoring or controlling adherence to company procedures. This activity most often became a function of the financial accounting or comptroller's organization.

Information processing, as an operating function, also fell into the accounting organization, primarily because of the financial nature of much of the data (inventory accounting, labor hour accounting, payroll calculation, and so on) and because the personnel and equipment in the accounting organization were appropriate for the job.

The introduction of computers brought a major change in organization. Where punch card equipment "programming" was normally a relatively minor part of the machine operator's (or the supervisor's) job, the new computers required special talents, and the programming staff developed. Organizational conflicts developed as operating program requirements (engineering and production technical systems) clashed with accounting requirements and computer-programmer staff resources. Concurrently, as more computer-produced reports engulfed the management staff, they became less useful due to contradictions and differences in timing or scope. The concept of Integrated Data Processing (IDP) became popular, and the organization was again modified to reflect the change in the information flow. The major change in a number of corporations was the congealing of the activities attending data systems design, computer programming, computer operations, and management data analysis, and the placement of the "management information" function at the top level of organization, with its head reporting to the president or a vice-president, as a staff and management support function.

Mathematically oriented programmers introduced or responded to operations research and management science techniques in the management area, and the management information system expanded to provide management with decision assistance based on statistical forecasts rather than mere historical reports. Opportunity was provided for managers to pretest (through computer simulation) the probable effect of a decision (or choice) before committing company resources, and to select the alternative providing the best potential return on investment.

Expected Impact

The history of organizational development in modern business corporations makes prudent the assumption that the introduction of the Management Information System (MIS) will be accompanied by a major change in the corporate organization. Changes in the form and channels of management communication will drastically modify existing relationships among management staff and operating and support personnel. Status and job security undoubtedly will rank as major concerns for individuals. Some resistance can be expected, with attendant personnel frictions and obstructions to system implementation and effective operation.

It appears reasonable to assume that *information* will be recognized as a major resource, and that the functions attending its management deserve major consideration in the corporate organization.

Likely, the information function will move from staff to operative status collateral with the financial, production, and marketing functions. Specialists in information processing (including those performing information handling functions in staff, operating, and support organizations) will be organizationally assembled and managed. Information management will be a top management functional responsibility (vice-presidential, coequal with finance, marketing, and operations). Major changes will be necessary in the definition of cost centers, product costing, and overhead. Properly established, managed, and operated, the system should increase corporate profits.

As with earlier changes, resistance can be anticipated from those most immediately affected. Reflection will indicate that each major change has affected a higher level in the organizational structure. Middle management was most affected by the implementation of information systems integration. A staff organization (and its support operations) took over much of the administrative monitoring and reporting activities and exposed operational inefficiencies to upper management. The functional organization manager was forced to adjust to a staff-dominated control system. The result, in most cases, has been a forced improvement in technical management and operations. Functional managers at all levels, provided with feedback information about their operational efficiency, have been enabled to make better plans or to take better corrective action than in the pre-IDP era. Those who have made the transition, and who have accepted IDP as an aid rather than as an opponent, have become better (and more valuable) managers.

The planning function is most affected by MIS. The greatest impact will be on the managers and staff personnel at the corporate and functional planning level. They will now be provided with better techniques and information for planning and forecasting.

Again, many may feel their status and security threatened. Some will resist the change (ultimately futile), while others will perceive the opportunities in it. Since the change will affect upper management, preparation for change is a top management responsibility. The corporate executive can acquaint the next lower echelon with the structure and concepts of the new organization, define organizational relationships, and point out opportunities for present executives.

Generally, MIS will provide the top level functional manager with better planning and control information and techniques. It will allow for functional specialization in his present specialty or in information management. It will require that he work more effectively as a member of a top management team, with a new team member (the information manager) and a more rapid response requirement.

The specific impact on individuals at the upper management level probably will fall into a pattern much like the following description.

First, the size of his organization and the scope of his managerial jurisdiction will shrink as his information specialists (planners, record-keepers, reporters) are shifted to a new organizational element outside his functional control.

Next, the nature of his relationship to his organizational peers and to his immediate subordinates will change significantly. Since most planning, including contingency planning, will be done in the corporate context and since control will be based on outside analysis of information (reports), there will be little interchange of such administrative information. Contrary to expressions in popular magazine articles, it is neither likely nor necessary that the executive become an expert in computer technology, operations research, mathematics, or management science. (Specialists in the information function area will provide these skills as needed to assist him in his job.) Planning will become a process of choosing between alternatives tested and evaluated by an agency outside his jurisdiction, but the manager will be expected to choose between offered alternatives on the basis of his technical competence, experience, and judgment. Guts and human relations skills will dominate. Leadership and cooperation will be essential in meeting corporate objectives.

Relations with coordinate functional managers will hinge on the exchange of nonquantitative information (experience, judgments, political interactions, and so on) related to advisories or choice alternatives from the planners, to provide balance and the required management subjectivity in decision-making and execution.

Leadership will involve two major aspects—first, evidencing acceptance and support of corporate objectives, plans, and programs; and second, maintaining effective human relations within the organization to alleviate frictions induced or aggravated as a result of "outsiders' interference" in functional operations.

Realistically, at the executive level, the job of the manager is not changed greatly by the introduction of MIS; but his organizational relationships are changed significantly. He must provide executive leadership, which now must become more personal, since he will be closer to functional (technical) operations divorced from paper work specialists. (Most contacts at present are buffered by the information specialists within the functional organizations.)

Most executives have already delegated (to staff or support personnel within their organizations) the routine duties associated with planning and control. Decision-making, or choice, has been the principal function of the executive. MIS merely transfers the staff work outside the functional organization. Whether it is done principally by computers or by staff personnel should mean little to the executive so long as the results are appropriate in content and time.

What Has Happened

Few companies prepare well for organizational change, even major change. Most organizations grow like Topsy, and human relations suffer with the impact of each change. When change affects the lower levels of a company, or only some departments, the detrimental effects of nonpreparation wash out with time, and the organization eventually adjusts to the change.

The development of information systems crossing organizational lines makes lack of preparation dangerous. The health and survival of the corporation is in the balance. There must be preparation for the change, and those affected must participate in the transition from one organizational structure and mode to its successor.

A recent *Dun's Review* article ("Middle Managers vs. the Computer," November 1966) sets up managers and the information staff (including the computer and the techniques employed) as opponents, and suggests that managers are locked in combat for organizational survival in this environment. This attitude appears prevalent among nonexecutives in the management environment. It is unfortunate and unrealistic. It is the result of incomplete or nonpreparation for change by those responsible for change. This is disruptive to corporate harmony.

Concurrent with the technical aspect of systems change, the organizational aspect, including the human factor, must be considered. The impact of each change on processes and data flow, as well as on the organizational structure and functional relationships, must be analyzed with the active participation of those affected, and the transitional interface provided for in systems design and implementation.

The scope of the management system study should be expanded to include an analysis of the human factor and to provide for the effective integration and optimal use of the human and information resources.

36

Physical Distribution Development, Current Status, and Potential

DONALD J. BOWERSOX

Michigan State University

During the past two decades the discipline of physical distribution has evolved as a major facet of business administration.[1] The objectives of this article are: to highlight some major developments which have served as catalytic forces to the emerging field, to provide a synthesis of contemporary physical distribution thought, and to offer a brief diagnosis of some areas providing research opportunities.

A Decade of Crystallization

Physical distribution consists of those business activities concerned with transporting finished inventory and/or raw material assortments so they arrive at the designated place, when needed, and in usable condition. Economists have long recognized this process as a vital aspect of value added through the distribution process. However, in the typical commercial enterprise and within the study of business administration, the overall process of physical distribution has traditionally received fragmentary and most often secondary consideration. The concept of integrated physical distribution emerged during the 1950s. The following quote from a 1954 speech of the late Professor Paul D. Converse provides a general appraisal of physical distribution as recently as fifteen years ago.[2]

---

[1] Other common titles used to describe what is here called Physical Distribution are Business Logistics, Logistics of Distribution, and Materials Management.

[2] Paul D. Converse, "The Other Half of Marketing." *Twenty-Sixth Boston Conference on Distribution*, Boston Conference on Distribution (Boston, Massachusetts, 1954), p. 22.

In the study of marketing and the operation of marketing departments and businesses a great deal more attention is paid to buying and selling than to physical handling. In fact the physical handling of goods seems to be pretty much overlooked by sales executives, advertising men and market researchers. Problems of physical distribution are too often brushed aside as matters of little importance. I have for many years been reading business and economics magazines. Such publications over the years have devoted relatively little space to physical distribution.

A logical explanation for the neglect and subsequent late development of physical distribution can be attributed to at least two major factors.[3] First, prior to the time that computers emerged from infancy and before applied analytical tools were generally at the disposal of business, there was no reason to believe that an overall attack on physical distribution activities would accomplish improved performance. The 1950s were destined to witness a major change in traditional orientation since neither computers nor quantitative techniques were to be denied the fertility of physical distribution applications.

A second major factor contributing to a reexamination of traditional viewpoints was the prevailing economic climate. The prolonged profit squeeze of the early 1950s, highlighted by the recession of 1958, created an environment conducive to the development of new cost control systems. Integrated physical distribution provided a productive arena for new methods of cost reduction.

Thus, technology and need abruptly changed during the 1950s. After a great many years of relative obscurity, the period from 1956 to 1965 was to become the decade during which the integrated physical distribution concept would crystallize. An interpretation of the literature reveals that the physical distribution concept congealed as the product of four significant developments. Each is briefly discussed in this section. A synthesis is provided in the next section.

The Notion of Total Cost

In 1956 a specialized study of air freight economics provided a major new orientation to physical distribution costing.[4] The study, while explaining the economic justification for high cost air transport, introduced the concept of total cost analysis. Total cost was developed as a measure of all expenditures required to accomplish a firm's physical distribution mission. The authors illustrated that high freight rates required for air transport could be more than justified by trade-offs in reduced inventory possession and warehouse operation costs.

[3] For an expanded treatment see Donald J. Bowersox, Edward J. Smykay, and Bernard J. LaLonde, *Physical Distribution Management: Logistics Problems of the Firm*, Revised Edition (New York: The Macmillan Company, 1968), pp. 8-15.

[4] Howard T. Lewis, James W. Culliton, and Jack D. Steel, *The Role of Air Freight in Physical Distribution* (Boston, Mass.: Division of Research, Graduate School of Business Administration, Harvard University, 1956).

The concept of total cost, while basic in logic, had not been previously applied to physical distribution economics. Probably because of the economic climate of the times, the immediate reaction was a flurry of attention to physical distribution problems. Subsequent refinements provided a comprehensive treatment of physical distribution cost characteristics and related functional analysis of available trade-offs.[5]

Application of the Systems Concept

It is difficult to trace the exact origins of the systems approach to problem solving. However, the notion of total integrated effort toward the accomplishment of predetermined goals rapidly found a home in physical distribution analysis. The systems concept provided a research posture, and total cost analysis offered a method of evaluating among alternative system configurations.

The first general articles directed to the subject of physical distribution relied heavily on systems technology.[6] In particular, it became apparent that the great deficiency of the traditional viewpoint was the prevailing practice of treating the many physical distribution activity centers as isolated performance areas. The result was a failure to capture the benefits obtainable only from integrated control.

When viewed from a systems viewpoint, integrated physical distribution creates a new requirement for compromise between traditional business activities. For example, manufacturing traditionally desires long production runs and lowest procurement cost, while physical distribution raises questions concerning the total cost commitment of these practices. Finance, traditionally favorable to low inventories, may force a physical distribution system to adjust components in a less than satisfactory total cost arrangement. With respect to marketing, traditional preferences for finished goods inventory staging and broad assortments in forward markets often stand in conflict to economies offered through total system evaluation.

The basic belief that integrated system performance can and most often will produce an end result greater than possible from non-coordinated performance rapidly became a primary focal point in development of the physical distribution concept. The logic of systems technology offered a regimented way to penetrate the traditional viewpoint.

[5] In particular see: Marvin Flaks, "Total Cost Approach to Physical Distribution," *Business Management*, Vol. 24 (August, 1963), pp. 55-61. and Raymond LeKashman and John F. Stolle, "The Total Cost Approach to Distribution," *Business Horizons*, Vol. 8 (Winter, 1965), pp. 33-46.

[6] For example see: Harvey N. Shycon and Richard B. Maffei, "Simulation—Tool for Better Distribution," *Harvard Business Review*, Vol. 38 (November-December, 1960), pp. 65-75; Donald D. Parker, "Improved Efficiency and Reduced Cost in Marketing," *Journal of Marketing*, Vol. 26 (April, 1962), pp. 15-21; J. L. Heskett, "Ferment in Marketing's Oldest Area," *Journal of Marketing*, Vol. 26 (October, 1962), pp. 40-45; and John F. Magee, "The Logistics of Distribution," *Harvard Business Review*, Vol. 40 (July-August, 1962), pp. 89-101.

Beyond Cost

By the early 1960s the horizons of the emerging field of physical distribution began to expand. Peter Drucker stimulated top management's attention to the emerging new dimension of business administration.[7] During this period, emphasis began to shift toward a more penetrating appraisal of the improved customer service capabilities gained as a result of a highly integrated physical distribution system. Another 1962 article which made a major impact was authored by Professor Lazer; it served to provide a synthesis of developments between physical distribution and managerial marketing.[8] Lazer and Drucker thus made a particularly noteworthy contribution by adding new posture to the field of physical distribution. Attention was now directed to issues of demand cultivation and to the overall importance of physical distribution to corporate vitality on other than a purely cost orientation that dominated earlier treatments.[9]

Physical distribution now came into focus as representing a balanced effort between product delivery capabilities and related system alternatives. Given a programmed level of service, several alternative systems might be capable of accomplishing the stated goals but at various levels of total cost expenditure.

Emphasis upon Temporal Relations and Physical Commitments in a Channel Context

An additional development in physical distribution thinking relates to the dynamic elements of channel management. The majority of physical distribution systems have been studied from the vantage point of vertically integrated organizations. A more useful viewpoint is that physical distribution activities and related responsibilities seldom terminate when product ownership transfer occurs. Many significant costs of physical distribution are experienced between firms linked together in cooperative vertical marketing systems. The interface of two or more individual firm physical distribution systems may well lead to excessive cost generation and customer service impairment for the total channel. Even under conditions of system compatibility, the total cost of physical distribution for the channel may rapidly accumulate as a result of efforts duplicated by various firms within the total channel.

A more realistic approach to channel-wide physical distribution performance evolved from an evaluation of information lags and product assortment

---

[7]Peter Drucker, "The Economy's Dark Continent," *Fortune,* Vol. 72 (April, 1962), pp. 103-104.

[8]William Lazer, "Distribution and the Marketing Mix," *Transportation and Distribution Management,* Vol. 2 (December, 1962), pp. 12-17.

[9]For an outstanding review of the customer service impact of physical distribution see Wendell M. Steward, "Key to Improved Volume and Profits," *Journal of Marketing,* Vol. 29 (January, 1965), pp. 65-70.

commitments inherent in channel organizations. In 1958, Jay Forrester provided a new view of business operations. In terms of physical product flow, the Forrester treatment dramatically illustrated the impact of information dynamics upon fluctuations in inventory accumulations.[10] The impact of time delays had been generally neglected among early treatments of physical distribution in deference to a primary emphasis upon spatial relationships. During more recent years a more balanced approach considering the interrelated impact of spatial and temporal relationships has emerged.

With respect to product assortment commitments, it is now generally accepted that the strategies available to a single firm or a cooperative vertical marketing system are directly related to the quantity of inventory nodes contained within the system. A great deal of the impetus in this direction resulted from the classical work of the late Professor Alderson.[11] The functional approach that he provided served to revive, expand, and update the contributions of early marketing scholars concerning the risk and degree of commitment involved in physical supply.[12]

Physical Distribution 1969: a Synthesis

Thus, by 1965 management was afforded a rather segmented—but theoretically sound—approach to the development of physical distribution planning. The years since 1965 have been characterized by a refinement in basic concepts and development of greater precision in tools of analysis. While 1961 saw the first book devoted to the subject of physical distribution, today a wide variety of text and reading collections are available.[13] Currently, four trade journals are exclusively devoted to practical applications in physical distribution, and articles frequently appear in leading academic journals.[14] The field is represented by an active professional association, the National Council of Physical Distribution. The physical distribution course has become a common offering among many leading business schools. Thus, the flurry of attention that Professor Converse saw as a critical need in 1954 has by 1969 become a reality. In this section contributions regarding physical distribution noted earlier are synthesized.

[10] Jay W. Forrester, "Industrial Dynamics," *Harvard Business Review,* Vol. 36 (July–August, 1958), pp. 37-66.

[11] Wroe Alderson, *Marketing Behavior and Executive Action* (Homewood, Ill.; Richard D. Irwin, Inc., 1957).

[12] In particular see Percival White, *Scientific Marketing Management* (New York: Harper and Brothers, 1927), and Fred E. Clark, *Readings in Marketing* (New York: The Macmillan Company, 1924), Chapter 15.

[13] The initial book in the field was: Edward W. Smykay, Donald J. Bowersox, and Frank H. Mossman, *Physical Distribution Management* (New York: The Macmillan Co., 1961).

[14] The four trade journals exclusively devoted to physical distribution are: *Transportation and Distribution Management, Handling and Shipping Illustrated, Distribution Manager,* and *Traffic Management.*

At the Individual Firm Level

For the most part, physical distribution is viewed in a micro context wherein attention is directed to the managerial aspects of a single firm's integrated system. To this extent, physical distribution management can be defined as that responsibility to design and administer corporate systems to control the flow of raw materials and finished inventories.[15] This systems orientation stands in direct contrast to the traditional approach of treating the many activities integral to physical distribution on a separate or diffused basis.

The main strength of physical distribution seems foremost to evolve from the development of techniques and concepts for treating the range of inherent functions on an integrated basis. Systems technology provides the framework for studying alternative system designs and evaluating feasible system arrangements on a total cost basis. High speed computers provide the tool required to evaluate complex system designs plus to keep track of the multitude of details engaged in geographically dispersed physically distribution operations.

In a strategic context, the central or focal point of physical distribution is the corporate commitment to inventory. Individual products are properly viewed as a combination of form, time, place, and possession utilities. The product has little value until form is placed in a temporal and spatial context which will provide the opportunity to enjoy the physical and psychological attributes related to possession. If a firm does not consistently meet the requirements of time and place closure, it has nothing to sell. On the other hand, if a firm does not *efficiently* meet the requirements of time and place closure, profits and return-on-investment are placed in jeopardy. Excessive inventory stockpiles can compensate for errors in basic system design and may even overcome poor administration of physical distribution activities. The proper objective in inventory commitment is to deploy the minimum quantities consistent with specified delivery capabilities and management's willingness to underwrite total cost expenditures.

To achieve these managerially specified goals the inventory allocation must be integrated within a system of facility locations, transporation capability, and a communications network. The capacity of such a system is measured in terms of the dual standards of total cost and customer service.

Managers should keep in mind that excessive commitments to high levels of customer service can be extremely expensive. System attributes of fast and consistent customer service both have related costs. The higher each of these qualities of performance, the greater will be the required cost. In fact, individual physical distribution studies support the conclusion that physical distribution cost and related improvement in customer service have a nonproportional relationship.[16] Each additional unit of customer service capability requires a greater incremental expenditure. For example, a firm that strives to support a service standard of overnight delivery at 95% consistency may confront nearly

[15] Same reference as footnote 13, p. 3
[16] Same reference as footnote 13, pp. 314-321.

double the total cost of implementing a program of second-morning delivery with 90% consistency.[17]

The typical firm must seek that balance between reasonable customer service and realistic cost expenditures which will achieve managerial goals. Two factors concerning the cost-service relationship are significant. First, seldom will such a balanced relationship result in the lowest possible total cost physical distribution system. Second, in terms of the temporal aspects of customer service, consistency of delivery can be expected to be viewed among customers who buy for purposes of resale as a greater virtue than pure speed of delivery. This premium upon delivery consistency is directly related to available techniques of inventory control. While sophisticated forecasting techniques and more rapid order transmitting systems have improved the ability to predict sales during leadtime and thereby reduce safety stocks, inconsistency in delivery has the net result of introducing the need to apply probabilistic methods to the delivery time portion of the order cycles. Unlike sales patterns, consistency in delivery performance can be controlled. Among buyers of substitute products it is reasonable to assume that preference will be afforded those sellers who can promise and provide consistency in delivery, if other factors are equal.

Beyond the Firm

Today increased attention must be given to the rapidly advancing extension of physical distribution subject matter to the broader issues of channels and to the emerging concerns of macro-distribution.

Early treatments of physical distribution seemed to rely upon assumed vertical integration for the conception and development of total cost systems. The more realistic viewpoint is that physical distribution operations and responsibilities seldom terminate when ownership transfer occurs. Many significant costs of physical distribution occur between firms linked together in a marketing channel. The interface of two or more physical distribution systems operated by individual firms may well lead to excessive cost generation and customer service impairment. Even under conditions of system compatibility the total cost of physical distribution for the channel may rapidly accumulate as a result of efforts duplicated by various firms within the total channel. The net result of duplication may well be a weakening of overall competitive posture of the total channel.[18]

---

[17] Same reference as footnote 13.

[18] For some representative treatments dealing with physical flow in marketing channels see: Louis P. Bucklin, "Postponement Speculation and the Structure of Distribution Channels," *Journal of Marketing Research*, Vol. 3 (February, 1965), pp. 26-31; J. L. Heskett, "Costing and Coordinating External and Internal Logistics Activities," unpublished paper presented before joint seminar, The Railway Systems Management Association and The Transportation Research Forum (Chicago, Ill.: October 6, 1964); and Donald J. Bowersox, "Changing Channels in the Physical Distribution of Finished Goods," in Peter D. Bennett, editor, *Marketing and Economic Development,* Proceedings American Marketing Association (Chicago, Ill.: American Marketing Association, 1965), pp. 711-721.

Two facets of viewing physical distribution performance on a channel-wide basis illustrate the nature of issues that arise. First, when product flow is viewed on a cooperative channel basis, it is interesting to observe that individual enterprises having the greatest impact upon channel performance often enjoy the smallest risk in total channel destiny. For example, negligent and sporadic performance by a common carrier may well negate consistent service capabilities for the channel with little or no corresponding penalty to the carrier. Consequently, the range of intermediary specialists must be expanded beyond the traditional institutions of marketing to include all influential parties. The performance of these low risk specialists must be calibrated in terms of impact on total channel effort.

Second, there appears to be no justification to support the traditional assumption that an outstanding network of marketing intermediaries will have the requisite capability to achieve efficient physical distribution performance. Differentiated marketing to a wide variety of market segments may have the inherent weakness of forcing small shipment diseconomies and related disadvantages in physical flow. The specialized institutions proficient in performing marketing functions may be different from those most capable of outstanding physical distribution support.

The development of multi-firm physical distribution channels raises a need for careful review of traditional concepts of marketing channels. The social justification for intermediaries has always appeared questionable and has led to the widespread promulgation that the elimination of middlemen will result in increased marketing efficiency. However, middlemen appear to have increased in numbers and importance.[19] Perhaps reevaluation of the transaction generating and physical distribution support functions of middlemen will yield significant returns toward a more general understanding of marketing channels.

Beyond questions of channel structure, dynamics, and efficiency remain a series of interesting broader issues. For this article, suffice it to acknowledge that applications of systems technology hold significant potential toward greater precision in policy formulation to guide public resource allocation. Issues of a macro-distribution nature seem on the verge of greater attention when one considers the degree of population congestion predicted for this nation during the years ahead. Our aggregate capability to perform physical distribution activities under the demands of expanding city-state and revitalized urban centers will, to a great degree, rest upon well-planned public transit and carrier networks.

Some Issues for Research

A rapidly expanding field such as physical distribution naturally offers a vast array of potential research topics. This final section outlines some areas and

---

[19] Reavis Cox, *Distribution in a High-Level Economy* (Englewood Cliffs, N.J.: Prentice-Hall, Inc., 1965), p. 51.

issues that appear most germane to subject matter expansion during the immediate future.

Some Remaining Questions of Cost

As noted earlier, a great deal of initial concern with physical distribution was cost orientated. Emphasis was placed upon finding ways to reduce prevailing physical distribution costs. However, many questions regarding cost remain unanswered. The most pressing issues can be divided in terms of aggregate expenditures in the economy and in terms of deficiencies in managerial accounting.

What are the true aggregate costs of physical distribution in the United States? Does physical distribution really account for one half of total marketing costs? Is relative cost increasing or decreasing as a result of renewed interest in the physical distribution process? What are the prospects for improved aggregate performance in the economy during the decades ahead? The above questions highlight the current lack of data regarding the magnitude of national expenditures on physical distribution effort.

At the individual firm and channel level, traditional accounting does not generally provide the necessary information for physical distribution decision making. While considerable effort has been made to isolate and classify cost accounts, managerial accounting models to guide decisions concerning alternative system designs at various throughput volumes remain deficient.[20] Some of the following questions require more detailed answers. Are adequate cost accounting procedures and understanding of account structures available to perform true total cost analysis? How do current costing techniques stand up to the problems of total channel design analysis? Should there be standards for physical distribution performance, and, if so, what should they be? What standards exist for measuring comparative channel performance when viewed on the basis of multi-firm involvement? Finally, do current concepts of regulation and corporate taxation restrict realization of potential benefits available to cooperative vertical channel marketing systems?

During the years ahead a renewed interest can be expected in the financial affairs of physical distribution. Accounting will take a back seat in favor of the development of managerial decision models. For example, a problem common to industry, but not solved in reported research, is the question of measuring buyer performance. How can the traditional viewpoint of the open-to-buy be reconciled to the overall cost trade-offs acknowledged from physical distribution systems analysis?

The questions could go on, since they flow far easier than answers. The fact of the matter seems to support the conclusion that the state of the art in applied

[20]For an expanded development of costs related to distribution see: L. Gayle Rayburn, "Setting Standards for Distribution Costs," *Management Services,* Vol. 4 (March-April, 1967), pp. 42-52.

distribution costing has not significantly improved despite wide acclaim for the theory of total cost analysis.

The Channel—A Research Media

The time now seems right for the distribution channel to be subjected to comprehensive research.

The dichotomy between textbook descriptions and real-world experience regarding channels has often been noted. The research questions which evolve from channel issues extend beyond the exclusive domains of physical distribution. However, penetrating answers to the following questions will require research steeped in a physical distribution orientation.

Does ample opportunity for specialization exist to justify separation of physical distribution and marketing activities in terms of channel structure? What techniques of leadership or other persuasive forces can and should be applied to encourage greater channel efficiency? To what degree are alternative methods of channel integration preferable from a social viewpoint? Have middlemen, in fact, been decreasing in numbers and importance? If so, what type or classification has been eliminated? Is there a disproportionate degree of change between those intermediaries engaged in physical distribution as contrasted to those who perform traditional marketing functions? What opportunities exist for experimental analysis of channel design prior to resource commitment?

The channel appears to have been one of the most elusive of marketing subjects. Therefore, channel subjects offer rich research opportunities. The functions of physical distribution extend far into channel domains. In the years ahead, we can expect significant returns from channel-oriented physical distribution research.

The International Arena

Perhaps the most significant thing that can be said about international physical distribution is that it is currently nonexistent in terms of the literature. Beyond some elaborate statements regarding documentation and some attention to container standards, little has been written about international product flow.

Little doubt exists that industrialized economies are now moving toward worldwide markets. Accordingly, individual firms are now becoming multinational in scope of operations. With few exceptions, international efforts have concentrated upon marketing and manufacturing competence with lesser attention to logistical operations. While traditional notions of comparative economic advantage have diminished and restrictive trade barriers can be anticipated to lower with the passing of time, little can be done to alter the natural geo-reference arrangement of international markets. What countries will emerge as vital new commercial forces as a result of superior geographical proximity in time and distance to international mass markets? Will free ports be a major concern to the formulation of new world commercial powers? Does Hawaii, for example, possess an inherent competitive advantage from a logistical viewpoint that will render the islands the commercial center of the Pacific?

While many hold that marketing is properly a feature of highly developed economies, physical distribution may be a major factor toward helping emerging nations become tomorrow's mass markets. Extensive research into international physical distribution capability and opportunities may well constitute a profitable national as well as individual firm investment.

Issues of Time in Physical Distribution System Design

As noted earlier, the impact of interfirm information flows upon physical distribution channel performance has received increased attention during recent years. However, in reviewing available material one gets the feeling that a great deal remains to be discovered concerning the many ramifications of time relationships upon physical distribution performance and system design.[21] For the most part to date, inventory models have been temporal in orientation, whereas location models have been spatial in perspective.[22] A realistic view of a physical distribution system is that the network consists of one or more storage points interconnected by a series of transportation linkages. Thus, integration of the temporal aspects of inventory must be accomplished in terms of the geography of location. A major deficiency of existing quantitative models available to guide physical distribution system design is the inability to accomplish spatial and temporal integration.

To elaborate, consider alternative treatment of transportation capability in location and inventory models. Most locational models seek a solution to the number and geographic arrangement of network facilities by minimizing the transportation expenditure in relation to facility operating costs. Inventory is normally assumed at a specified level (average inventory) in order to estimate possession costs. In locational models transportation costs are normally assumed linear or near linear as a function of distance. Accordingly, alternative transport methods are evaluated on a total cost basis using cost-per-ton mile. This is a spatial measure of transport capability.

The relevant concept in inventory models that embraces transportation is the order cycle. The order cycle is defined as the total elapsed time from initial

[21] For expanded elaboration of this deficiency see: J. L. Heskett, "Spatial and Temporal Aspects of Physical Distribution," in Peter D. Bennett, editor, *Marketing and Economic Development*, Proceedings American Marketing Association (Chicago, Ill.: American Marketing Association, 1965), pp. 679-687.

[22] For two exceptions see: Donald J. Bowersox, *Food Distribution Center Location: Technique and Procedure* (East Lansing, Michigan: Bureau of Business and Economic Research, Michigan State University, 1962), and Ronald H. Ballou, "Dynamic Warehouse Location Analysis," *Journal of Marketing Research*, Vol. 5 (August, 1968), pp. 271-276.

purchase commitment until the arrival of goods or materials. One significant aspect of order cycle is transit time between two specific locations (buyer and seller). Transportation is now considered in terms of elapsed time to transverse a specified geographical distance with at best passing attention to the question of cost-per-ton mile.

At the extremes, one could conclude that the fastest mode of transport would always be favorable to inventory solutions while the lowest total cost movement would always be favored in location solutions. Such extremes do not materialize as a result of common sense applications. Average inventory in transit is evaluated and costed in the selection among alternatives in location solutions, thereby reducing some element of error. Conversely, the fixed location network assumed for inventory models normally specifies the transportation method to be employed as a function of size of shipment. However, complete integration of time and space is lacking.

The research questions which unfold from an integration of temporal and spatial factors may well lead to a new level of understanding regarding the dynamics of physical flow. At this junction, it appears likely that the entire field may well move toward more dynamic modeling in an effort to integrate inventory and locational considerations.

Some Final Issues

The list of potential research questions could continue far beyond the intent of this article. However, a few additional areas which appear worthy of consideration are listed in these final paragraphs.

As with any emerging field, physical distribution currently suffers from a lack of standardized definitions and vocabulary. The overall field would gain significantly from a clear definition of subject matter and issues.

The question of organization must be treated in a more comprehensive manner than thus far accomplished. Initially, it appeared physical distribution should be part of a firm's marketing operation. However, it is hard to justify the contribution marketing can make to the logistical support of manufacturing operations. Likewise, wouldn't the overall strength of marketing be improved if it could contract for a specified level of customer service without the accompanying problems of operational performance?

The impact of total information systems is currently being felt in all dimensions of traditional corporate structure. Mass information systems need data coding systems to perform accurate and relevant analysis of operation. This overall subject appears so important to future corporate vitality that considerable study from the viewpoint of the physical distribution operation appears justifiable. Of course, once again, this subject extends beyond the strict domains of physical distribution.

A final subject worthy of concern is the relationship between current business practice and the theoretical development of physical distribution subject matter.

Initially, business seemed to lead the way for increased attention to the general field of physical distribution. However, this gap was soon closed by research in academic circles. The situation now seems to support the generalization that practical applications have not fully capitalized upon academic contributions. The burden of responsibility to disseminate research findings rests with the academic community.

Conclusion

The purpose of this article was to review the where been, where now, and where going of physical distribution. While a few short years ago physical distribution was relegated a rather passive role in the study and practice of business administration, forces of the past decade have caused a marked reversal. The long-range contribution of physical distribution to a better understanding of business and toward an improvement in the quality of commercial performance remains to be judged with the passing of time. It appears certain the course of future events will be significantly altered by the quality and comprehensiveness of physical distribution research efforts. It is difficult to draw an analogy to any previous area of inquiry that held forth the opportunity for improvement in current business operations offered by physical distribution. At this juncture in time, the future of this new and vital dimension of business study appears bright indeed.